AMERICAN DIALECT RESEARCH

AMERICAN DIALECT RESEARCH

Edited by

DENNIS R. PRESTON, Chair
American Dialect Society Centennial Research Committee

with the assistance of the members of the committee
John G. Fought, Frank P. Parker, Herbert Penzl,
John R. Rickford, Arnold M. Zwicky

and the distinguished honorary members of the committee
Dwight Bolinger and Charles F. Hocket

This books is a publication in the
Centennial Series
of the
American Dialect Society
in celebration of the beginning of its
second century of research in
language variation in America

JOHN BENJAMINS PUBLISHING COMPANY
AMSTERDAM/PHILADELPHIA

1993

Library of Congress Cataloging-in-Publication Data

American dialect research / ed. by Dennis R. Preston : with the assistance of the members of the committee, John G. Fought ... [et al.] and the distinguished honorary members of the committee, Dwight Bolinger and Charles F. Hockett.
p. cm. (Centennial series of the American Dialect Society)
Includes bibliographical references (p.) and index.
1. English language--Dialects--United States. 2. Americanisms. I. Preston, Dennis Richard. II. Fought, John G. III. Series.
PE2841.A74 1993
427'.973--dc20 93-18385
ISBN 90 272 2132 4 (Eur.)/1-55619-488-9 (US) (Hb.: alk. paper) CIP
ISBN 90272 2133 2 (Eur.)/1-55619-489-7 (US) (Pb.: alk. paper)

John Benjamins Publishing Co. · P.O. Box 75577 · 1070 AN Amsterdam · The Netherlands
John Benjamins North America · 821 Bethlehem Pike · Philadelphia, PA 19118 · USA

Acknowledgments

It goes without saying, although it will be said, that the editor is especially grateful to the members of the committee in conceiving, aiding, and abetting this enterprise. The authors of the individual chapters were patient and cooperative. Paul Peranteau and Yola de Lusenet of John Benjamins Publishing Company saw merit in the project and recommended it. Bob Ferrett and Sudhakara Rao Gunturu of the Center for Instructional Computing at Eastern Michigan University helped bring DOS and Mac together in producing the final camera-ready version. Cheryllee Finney of the Publication Office of the College of Arts and Letters at Michigan State University helped schedule the use of the laser printer which actually did the trick. Most importantly, George F. Peters, Chairperson of the Department of Linguistics and Germanic, Slavic, Asian, and African Languages at Michigan State University saw to it that my home base duties in the Winter Quarter of the 1991-92 academic year were such as would permit the final work on this project.

We note with great sadness the death of our friend and colleague Professor Dwight Bolinger, one of the honorary members of our committee. Dialectologists, no less than linguists of every other persuasion, will miss his insight and patience, qualities not so often yoked together in the same scholar.

As usual, Carol G. Preston has been enormously supportive. In this particular case, she has caught not only my usual infelicity and obfuscation but has even been able to detect minor blips in the prose of my learned colleagues, the contributors to this volume. Whatever remains wrong with it is not her fault.

Finally, such volumes as these do not provide a convenient space for the individual authors to thank the countless cooperative and patient respondents whose words (and reactions) are the very stuff of our entire enterprise. As we dedicate this volume to the one hundred years of accomplishment of the American Dialect Society, let us acknowledge that foundation on which those years of accomplishment are built.

This volume is one of the official publications celebrating the centennial year of the American Dialect Society (1889-1989), and the proceeds from its sales benefit the Society exclusively.

We gratefully acknowledge the following permissions (all *gratis*) to reprint material from previously published work:

Belknap Press, Harvard University, for DARE entries for 'about' and 'bank (n.)' [partial], Frederic G. Cassidy (ed.), *Dictionary of American Regional English* (Vol. 1), 1986.

Brown University Press, for Maps 550 and 415, Hans Kurath (ed.), *Linguistic Atlas of New England*, 1938.

Cambridge University Press, for Figure 1, p. 190, Barbara Horvath & David Sankoff, Delimiting the Sydney speech community, *Language in Society* 16:179-204, 1987 and for Figure 11-6, p. 191, J. K. Chambers and Peter Trudgill, *Dialectology*, 1980.

Center for Applied Linguistics, for Figure 11, p. 160, William Labov, *The social stratification of English in New York City*, 1966.

Chicago Linguistic Society, for Figure 4, J. K. Chambers, The Americanization of Canadian raising. In M. F. Miller, C. S. Masek, & R. S. Hendrick (eds), *Parasession on Language and Behavior*, 1981, 20-35.

Croom Helm, for map, p. 184, R. K. S. Macaulay, Linguistic maps. In J. M. Kirk, S. Sanderson & J. D. A. Widdowson (eds), *Studies in linguistic geography*, 1985, 172-6.

Department of Linguistics, University of Victoria, for Tables 3 & 5, 217 & 219, Donald Larmouth, Gravity models, wave theory, and low structure regions. In Henry Warkentyne (ed.), *Methods IV*, 1981, 199-219.

Mouton de Gruyter, for Table 1, p. 179, Richard Tucker & Wallace E. Lambert, White and Negro listeners' reactions to various American-English dialects. In Joshua Fishman (ed.), *Advances in the sociology of language*, 1972, 175-84.

Multilingual Matters, for Figures 1 & 4, J. K. Chambers, Acquisition of phonological variants. In Alan Thomas (ed.), *Methods in dialectology*, 1988, 650-665.

University of Alabama Press, for Map 2, p. 248, William A. Kretzschmar, Jr., (ed.), *Essays in general dialectology by Raven I. McDavid, Jr.*, 1979 and for Tables 1, 2, & 3 (pp. 14, 15, & 16), Guy Bailey and Natalie Maynor, The divergence controversy, *American Speech* 64:12-39, 1989.

University of Michigan Press, for Figures 5a and 18, Hans Kurath, *A word geography of the Eastern United States*, 1949.

Contents

III. Group Studies

IV. Special Topics

Appendix

Index

Figures and Tables

I. AREA STUDIES

Chapter 1:

Chapter 2:

Chapter 3:

Chapter 4:

Chapter 5:

II. COMMUNITY STUDIES

Chapter 6:

Chapter 8:

III. GROUP STUDIES

Chapter 9:

Chapter 10:

IV. SPECIAL TOPICS

Chapter 11:

Preface

Dennis R. Preston
Michigan State University

This volume displays how questions are formulated and how data is collected, stored, and interpreted in various traditions of research of the American Dialect Society (ADS). The volume serves as a how to text for scholars and at the same time shows how current techniques have emerged from older ones, urging no rediscoveries of the wheel but not failing to condemn or praise the old or new where appropriate. Most generally, it is a trip to the scholar's laboratory. How is this work done? What pitfalls in fieldwork, processing, and interpretation lurk for the unwary? What rewarding techniques and devices have been used to get at the mysteries of language variation? What lies over the horizon?

The need for this volume rests not only in its being a publication appropriate for the ADS centennial celebration, although it is meant to contribute to that jubilee. It brings together in one place, as no previously published work has, current approaches to the general problems of language distribution and variation. In summary, it focuses on the construction of hypotheses, the elicitation of variable and restricted data, the interpretation of regional data (from both historical and structural or systematic points of view), the use of statistical models to ascertain the strength of social and linguistic factors on the probability of occurrence of variables, the discovery and use of archival and other resources, the methods employed in obtaining and analyzing nonlinguists' reactions to and perceptions of language variety, the discovery of variation beyond the sentence, and the special techniques employed in the study of language varieties in the Americas.

Although some excellent recent collections exist (e.g., Allen and Linn 1986, Baugh and Sherzer, 1984), they have provided exemplary surveys of the field by selecting largely from previously published materials. *American Dialect Research (ADR)* contains only material specifically written for it. Although some of the data and studies cited are modern classics, the combination of the speculation, methodological remarks, and suggestions for continuing research and consideration is unique.

Each chapter deals with a large subarea and contains ample illustrative material, and each contributor is an experienced gatherer and interpreter of socially and regionally variable linguistic data; moreover, each has made specific contributions to the ways in which such data are studied. The chapters are often reflective and personal, but they allow others to model research on the best current advice, yielding not only models for research on new topics and in new areas but also bases for experimentation with new means of eliciting, archiving, presenting, and interpreting dialect data.

Before introducing the individual chapters, a word about *dialect*. This anthology treats dialect in a way consistent with the ADS's scope of concerns: language variation and varieties in the Americas. *Dialect* refers here, therefore, not only to the regional distribution of language (and such attendant matters as responses to and uses of such distribution) but also to the varieties of language which are constrained by and are appropriate to such variables as setting, purpose, role, gender, ethnicity, art, and others. Those who find absolute meanings of words lurking in their roots will be unhappy with this distortion of *dia-*, but the variability which interests the scholars represented here is that of much more than space. Such catholicity has been a hallmark of the ADS throughout its history. *Dialect Notes* (*DN*), Part IX, 1896 contains 'The English of the lower classes of New York City and vicinity' by E. H. Babbitt, and although modern social scientists would be happy with neither Babbitt's methods for determining class nor his comments on ethnic diversity, here is very early evidence indeed of concern for variables other than geographical location. In the Society's *Publication of the American Dialect Society* (*PADS*), regard for the variety of concerns suggested above was evident in the early years. Number 3, 1945 contained Lorenzo D. Turner's 'Notes on the sounds and vocabulary of Gullah'; Number 4 was exclusively devoted to Margaret M. Bryant's 'Proverbs and how to collect them'; Frederic G. Cassidy's

'The place-names of Dane County, Wisconsin' was Number 7; Number 8 contained the contribution 'Maple sugar language in Vermont,' also by Margaret M. Bryant; Alfred P. Kehlenbeck's 'An Iowa Low German dialect' was Number 10; Number 16 was David W. Maurer's 'The argot of the race track'; Sumner Ives' 'The phonology of the Uncle Remus stories' was Number 22, and Number 26 (1956) was Einer Haugen's 'Bilingualism in the Americas: A bibliography and research guide.' In addition to numerous regional speech articles, then, the years 1895 to 1956 provided examples of concern for social status, creoles, onomastics, bilingualism, folk and belletristic literature, and professional and other restricted varieties. Contributions to later *PADS* and to the more recently acquired *American Speech* (*AS*) display a continuing and increasing range of concerns in ADS-sponsored publications. This collection reflects and celebrates that diversity of concern.

I. Area Studies

It is fitting to begin an anthology of dialect study with reference to area, but it will become immediately apparent on reading the chapters in this section that even area studies are very much influenced by new theoretical perspectives and by new procedural and mechanical techniques.

What dialect patterning means and suggestions for dealing with interpretations of it are the general concerns of Chapter 1. After a warning about the quality of data from previous studies, Francis goes on to apply various techniques to data from the *Linguistic Atlas of New England* (*LANE*), noting that earlier scholars often believed their atlases and lists were ends in themselves. The use of the data was left up to later scholarship, and Francis first provides a general taxonomy of the varieties of interpretive approaches now open to scholars who deal with these archived data, including comparisons of similar items from different efforts (e.g., *LANE* and *DARE*).

In his illustrations, Francis uses both historically sensitive, nonlinguistic considerations and the mathematical treatment of linguistic variety distance known as *dialectometry* to address such perennial questions as that of origin and spread on the one hand and of degree of dialect differentiation on the other. Francis' contribution brings together a consideration of existing and emerging data, a variety of techniques for looking at such data, and a re-evaluation of some of the oldest questions in the field.

One great tradition is atlas-making, and Chapter 2 provides the details of how a modern linguistic atlas is constructed. It is, of course, a computer-sensitive undertaking, and Pederson offers a full account of the details. A reading of this chapter for no more than the solution to the problem of intelligible recovery of phonetic detail from an alphabetic computer system is rewarding, but there is much more here, and the great promise of the *Linguistic Atlas of the Gulf States* (*LAGS*) is already being delivered in derived studies, illustrating the importance of dialect materials as retrievable archives. That retrievability allows Pederson to illustrate not only traditional dialect boundaries but also differences in apparent time diachrony, sex, age, ethnicity, and social status within the Gulf States, one indication that regional dialectology is answering the sociolinguistic challenge laid down by Chambers in Chapter 5. The computer generation of maps in the *LAGS* project makes for comprehensible, visual confirmation of patterns and is, perhaps, the impetus for recent gatherings of dialectologists to discuss the possibilities of new technologies (Kretzschmar, et al., 1989).

Another great tradition is dialect lexicography, and Cassidy's parenting of the *Dictionary of American Regional English* (*DARE*) is one of its great successes. Chapter 3 provides an insight into the collection procedures involved in sampling the regional vocabulary of the United States, combining fieldwork with an extensive program of reading and consultation. The decision to load these data on computer tapes, allowing for retrieval in a map format (distorted to reflect respondent density) permits the use of a very large lexical data base (with morphological and phonological capacities) sensitive to concerns which engage sociolinguist and dialectologist alike (see Chapter 5). Those who intend to collect vocabulary which is restricted or distributed in any way will want to consult Cassidy's procedures.

In Chapter 4 Girard and Larmouth apply the techniques of other statistical models, some especially adapted to geographical dispersion, in their look at even more regionally circumscribed data. Most importantly, however, they show how multivariate analyses of dialect data (again, demographically subdivided) allow for a parsimonious representation of influential factors, even if such factors are not independent, a possibility not carefully worked out in earlier sociolinguistic treatments (e.g., VARBRUL).

Although already mentioned as a sub-theme in all the preceding chapters, Chambers outlines in Chapter 5 the reasoning behind the necessary rapprochement between dialectology and sociolinguistics, what he calls *sociolinguistic dialectology*. He emphasizes the age-old concern of dialectology with language change, but points out the need for the study of the low-level mechanisms and forces involved in such change and different approaches to the spread of features in geographical space. In addition to the classic demographic subdivisions of sociolinguistics, Chambers opens up other fronts. He offers, for example, an introductory program and hypotheses for the study of dialects in the post-modern age, an attempt to determine the impersonal linguistic influence of literacy, television, and the like. From a more sociologically oriented foundation, he cites the changing pattern of heteronomy in the Canadian-United States English interface as an explanatory factor in the apparent reversal of the phenomenon known as Canadian raising. Finally, like Girard and Larmouth, he is concerned with new approaches to patterning, although his concern, as suggested above, is with the character of strategies at transition points, within the isogloss boundary itself, leading to dynamic interpretations (and mappings) of variable data. Appropriately enough, Chamber's contribution ends with a discussion of the formal characterization of variability, a topic elaborated on in Part II.

II. Community Studies

Of course all the studies in Part I were done in communities, but their emphasis is often on the larger geographical patterning of forms, long-term historical change, and inventories of distribution. Their newer concern for demographic subdivision and explanatory social forces, however, makes them much less distinguishable from their sibling studies in Part II than older strictly dialectological contributions would have been, another indication that the sociolinguistic dialectology Chambers calls for in Chapter 5 is well on the way to realization.

Part II focuses on the conduct of investigations which highlight the dynamism of the interaction of social and linguistic factors in a variety of settings. The principal concerns are those of acquiring, extracting, and processing variable data.

Since the variability of performance according to the setting itself is one of the areas of interest, Baugh examines in Chapter 6 the importance of elicitation sensitivity in the acquisition of dialect data. Although his contribution is set in the personal context of his experiences as an African-American fieldworker concerned with African-American linguistic data, it is not at all restricted to those cultural identities. A major theme in this chapter, and one Baugh would apparently recommend for any linguistic survey, is the importance to the investigator of ethnographic knowledge of the speech community. That stance leads him to emphasize the importance of nonperformance characteristics of variety, especially language attitudes. Moving beyond attitude, however, Baugh hopes to establish native respondent intuitions and judgments in variety study, a program which, among any group except perhaps professional linguists, requires techniques rather different from the familiar 'Can you say this in your dialect [sic]?' strategy. Baugh's review of the demographic variables involved in variety studies and of the variationists' methodological preferences emphasizes the social and cultural nature of dialectology.

In Chapter 7, Wolfram is concerned with the problem of variety data once they are acquired and with the deeper question of the relationship between linguistic and social concerns. First, he struggles with what one might call the psycholinguistic or cognitive grammatical foundations of dialect study; he has interesting reservations about variable rules and their integration into general linguistic theory. On the other hand, he does not doubt the patterning of linguistic material along social as well as linguistic lines. Second, he echoes Labov's now famous remark that '... what to count is actually the final solution to the problem in hand' (1969:728). Indeed, most of this chapter is spent in a careful detailing of how to identify the likely constraining contexts of what is to be counted in dialect study and how those constraints are a clue to the identity of the object of study itself. Finally, he offers practical guidelines for the extraction of data from fieldwork samples, readying them for the statistical manipulation which is the subject matter of Chapter 8.

Guy's contribution is a thorough review of the sorts of statistical concerns a modern dialectology must reflect. Although he reviews some of the concerns for collection and reliability of extraction already discussed by Baugh and Wolfram, his principal concern is with the readying of data for mathematical display and interpretation. Guy provides a full account of the benefits of variable rule analysis, emphasizing the importance of a multivariate analysis for the predictably uneven data obtained in most fieldwork, but he offers, as well, both a review of general statistical concerns and a sample of post-statistical reasoning or interpretation, a reminder as strong as Wolfram's that dialectology is a branch of general linguistics: that data, difficult enough to collect and extract in the first place, are not mechanically interpreted by statistical processes.

III. Group Studies

Part III illustrates some special areas of dialect study to which the procedures of Part II have been applied and from which the need for new procedures and evaluative strategies have emerged. Other subgroups which might have been chosen (e.g., gender, pidgin-creole, medicine, the underworld) have figured and continue to figure prominently in dialect studies. These chapters only represent the scope of demographic subdivisions which engage students of dialect.

Perhaps most problematic of the areas of variety study is language contact and multilingualism. Poplack, in Chapter 9, shows how the variationist techniques outlined in Part II apply to questions of code-switching, mixing, borrowing, incorporation, and the like. She also provides a full account of the gathering, segmenting, processing, and interpreting of data from this field, touching especially on problems of coding in a large corpus and on contact between typologically similar as well as dissimilar varieties. Her characterization of contact types is especially appropriate in a centennial volume for a society which published Haugen's *Bilingualism in the Americas* nearly thirty-five years ago in its *PADS* series (Number 26), a part of which (especially Chapter 3, 'Language Contact') outlined many of the same issues.

No volume on dialect study could appear without reference to the work which has been done and is being done on African-American English. Bailey outlines the history of concerns: the so-called deficit issue, the degree of difference issue, the pidgin-creole origins hypothesis, and the divergence-convergence controversy.

Like Poplack, Bailey shows how special techniques have developed in reference to special demographics and concerns. His chapter is especially useful in illustrating how an array of data-gathering techniques (reaching from respondent interviews to historical texts) may be brought to bear in dialect study. Additionally, Bailey provides controversial and up-to-date interpretations of, at least, the pidgin-creole and divergence-convergence issues.

In Chapter 11 O'Barr elaborates on the first discourse-oriented approach of this volume. Although few would deny the importance of variation at the highest levels, studies in dialectological and sociolinguistic traditions alike have, at least in the past, focused on smaller (phonological, morphological, lexical) units. One of the ways in which conversation and discourse analysis has been brought to our attention has been through its application in specialized language use settings, particularly medicine, education, and law.

O'Barr outlines a variety of ethnographic approaches to language in courtroom settings, emphasizing that variation in performance not only results from setting but also contributes to the identity of outcomes of settings themselves. Although he suggests that no uniform methodology will emerge for the study of language in restricted settings, the results of his work and others will show that the study of variation at this level leads to important understandings of how lay and professional people alike expose and create their understandings of the law and legal processes in interaction.

IV. Special Topics

Like Part III this section might be larger. Social psychologists may be unhappy to find no chapter devoted to attitude studies, particularly since their early work focused on varieties in the Americas (Lambert, et al. 1960). A number of chapters, however, touch on such matters (e.g., Baugh); others comment on some of the most productive and general notions to emerge from that tradition (e.g., the section of Chambers' chapter which discusses *accommodation*), and Chapter 12 elaborates techniques seen as a necessary supplement to attitude studies.

Other readers, perhaps at the other end of the arts and science scale, will be unhappy to see no consideration of the role of dialect in literature, a long-standing interest in ADS. Perhaps the most elaborate excuse for that exclusion will emerge in the last chapter in which Briggs attempts to show that much of what goes for variation is art. Perhaps the only really good excuse for the exclusion of any favorite topic is simply finiteness.

Chapter 12 outlines a variety of quantitative and ethnographic methods for understanding the perception of language variety by non-linguists. Preston argues that it is one thing to know the limits (social and geographical) of performance data, another to know nonlinguists' responses to variation data, but still another matter to understand the perceptual slots into which varieties are put by ordinary speakers. In the cognitive map of folk speakers, for example, what dialect areas are there for the varieties of performance data to be classified in? Where are the biggest mismatches between a *production dialectology* and a *perceptual (folk) dialectology*? Preston also provides methods for studying distinctly nonlinguistic evaluative responses to language variety and offers, in conclusion, an attempt to develop generalizations in this area drawn from respondent conversations.

Finally, in Chapter 13, Briggs details the patterned variety of performance genres. His conclusions suggest that more highly-marked and presumably more delimitable artistic genres parallel the sensitivity of performance adjustment to the needs of context in every level of speech activity. This anthropological and folkloristic emergence in variation studies is a realization at least in part of a call for interdisciplinary cooperation made by Hymes nearly twenty years ago (1972). Again, the special techniques of collection and analysis are provided in considerable detail.

In the Appendix, Linn provides a practical guide to some large collections of dialect data. He avoids duplicating lists easily available elsewhere, except for the prominent items in the field, and offers detailed descriptions of the sorts of data already collected which are available to investigators and, most importantly, specific instructions about their accessibility.

ADR does not intend to close the book on one hundred years of ADS activity or on the study of language variation in the Americas. Although the Centennial Research Committee hopes this volume will honor ADS, it hopes as well that it will be at least a small part of the greatest contribution that could be made: an indication of the scope, scholarship, vividness, involvement, and concerns of the field which drew scholars to it in the past and will draw them for at least the next one hundred years. If that attraction is sufficiently strong, perhaps all the questions of dialectology will be answered in the bicentennial research volume and the society may safely disband, but we suspect there will always be more to learn about the complex and creative interaction between language and the environment.

References

Allen, Harold B. and Michael D. Linn (eds). 1986. *Dialect and language variation.* New York: Academic Press.

Baugh, John and Joel Sherzer (eds). 1984. *Language in use: Readings in sociolinguistics.* Englewood Cliffs NJ: Prentice-Hall.

Hymes, Dell. 1972. The contribution of folklore to sociolinguistics research. In Américo Paredes and Richard Bauman (eds), *Toward new perspectives in folklore* (Publication of the American Folklore Society. Bibliographical and Special Series, Vol. 23). Austin: University of Texas Press, 42-50.

Kretzschmar, William A., Jr., Edgar Schneider, and Ellen Johnson (eds). 1990. *Computer methods in dialectology.* Special issue of *Journal of English Linguistics* 22,1.

Labov, William. 1969. Contraction, deletion, and inherent variability of the English copula. *Language* 45:715-62.

Lambert, Wallace E., R. Hodgson, R. C. Gardner, and S. Fillenbaum. 1960. Evaluational reactions to spoken language. *Journal of Abnormal Social Psychology* 60:44-51.

I. Area Studies

The Historical and Cultural Interpretation of Dialect

W. Nelson Francis
Brown University

The product of a dialect survey of the more traditional kind is a large body or corpus of material purporting to be a sample of the language used over a specified area -- usually a country or recognized section of one. The *Linguistic Atlas of New England* (*LANE*) is a characteristic example. I shall draw illustrations from it, not so much because it was produced at my own university but more because it was a well planned and executed work, and remained for a long time the only published part of the ambitious Linguistic Atlas of the United States and Canada, a project still incomplete. The fact that it was based on materials collected nearly fifty years ago does not invalidate the illustrations used, since we are not here concerned with the current relevance of the material but rather with the mode of its collection and presentation and the kind of information which may emerge from its interpretation.

I said above that such a survey *purports* to be a representative sample. This was not intended as a derogatory statement; rather it is a reminder of the particular nature of the dialect corpus and the special circumstances under which it is accumulated. The accuracy and dependability of such a corpus depends on three main factors. The first of these is the preliminary planning, principally the provisions for sampling the speech community to be investigated and the type of language to be described. The former involves the type of localities to be visited and their geographical distribution, and the type and selection of informants; the latter is specified normally in the form of a questionnaire or worksheet giving instructions to the collectors (commonly called fieldworkers) as to what linguistic items they are to look for and in some degree how they are to go about it.

The second factor is the fieldworker or fieldworkers themselves. They must have not only linguistic training, especially in phonetics and phonology, but also patience, congeniality, and the capacity to capture the interest and enthusiasm of the persons interviewed (commonly called informants, though some do not like the term because of its derogatory connotations in police movies and television shows. An alternative form is respondent).

The third factor is the informants themselves. Since normally a single speaker or two or three at most are to be considered representative of a given locality, they must be carefully chosen. Hopefully, they will come to understand what is wanted of them and will avoid the temptation to show off either by attempting to speak more 'correctly' than is their norm, or conversely to produce an exaggerated caricature of the local dialect.

A corpus of dialect produced with these factors under good control is still subject to inherent qualities which may skew or hinder interpretation. At least until the tape recorder made possible the procurement of samples of connected discourse, the corpus consists of isolated words or short phrases (*citation forms*) spoken in the special style or register characteristic of such utterance. Many of the features which characterize normal speech are not present, including intonation contours, sandhi phenomena, syntax generally, slurring, vowel reduction, consonant loss and other phenomena that occur in fast normal speech. Informants often give more than one response to a question, even a string of more or less synonymous terms. Since many forms of analysis require a single form to be considered representative of each locality, how are these to be chosen? The doctrine, which goes back to Gilliéron, that the first response is the correct one is often followed, but it is often not true. Particularly in the early stages of an interview, an informant may first produce the standard form even though it has not been used in the question, and then, remembering that the local term is sought, will supply that in self-correction. One of my own English informants, in response to a question eliciting *forehead*, first said [ˈfɔ·əˌhɛd] and immediately followed with [ˈfʊrəd]. There may also be considerable variability within a community or even in the speech of a single speaker. This may indicate a change of register: an informant may use *isn't* and *doesn't* in answer to the questionnaire but *ain't* and *don't* in natural speech in the same interview.

Finally there will probably be variability among the fieldworkers when more than one are used in a survey. *LANE* is to be commended in this regard: a section of the Handbook (pp. 123-42) describes in detail differences in recording practice among the nine fieldworkers, which persisted even after they had undergone rather rigorous training before going into the field. For example, in two of six communities in Connecticut to be described below, the final unstressed vowel in words like *city* and *habit* was recorded as [i], while in the other four it was almost always [ɨ]. This looked very much like an isogloss, especially since the two communities with [i] were close together. But reference to the Handbook revealed that these two communities were recorded by a fieldworker who regularly recorded [i] where others used [ɨ]. The isogloss turned out to be non-existent.

All these phenomena and others beside warn us that a dialect corpus is not a body of rigorously reliable scientific data. Anyone attempting to use it for interpretative purposes must carefully study all the information available about its structure and collection and be on the alert for contrasts and variables that may be artifacts of the way these matters are handled and presented.

The above discussion deals with the kind of corpus produced by a broad general dialect survey. The reason for accumulating such a corpus is seldom clearly stated; it is taken for granted that such an enterprise is worthwhile. The Preface to the *LANE* Handbook alludes vaguely to the 'critical evaluation and historical interpretation' of the *LANE* materials (p. ix). A more recent handbook, that for the *Linguistic Atlas of the Gulf States* (*LAGS*), states that 'the atlas relates linguistic usage to other social facts in a description of regional speech' in the seven states covered, and claims that 'these relationships suggest a sociolinguistic pattern of American English in the Gulf States and offer a reference for further investigation' (Pederson 1986, p.1). These collections are considered ends in themselves, whose use is left to future scholars to determine. One distinguished dialectologist, Jean Séguy, editor of the regional atlas of Gascony, goes so far as to state that the survey must abjure any form of interpretation, which is to be left to the users. Jules Gilliéron, one of the founding fathers of our discipline, valued his fieldworker Edmond Edmont precisely because he was not a linguist, but an efficient recording machine. The editor of the *Survey of English Dialects*, Harold Orton, states that 'the ultimate aim of the compilation of the Dialect Survey ... is the compilation of a linguistic atlas of England' (Orton 1962, p. 14). No suggestion is made as to why or how the material is to be further used. An exception to this is the *Linguistic Atlas of Scotland*, whose editors claim that 'for the linguistic geographer, whose business is commonly held to be collection of material (and sometimes little else) it is necessary to assert that he will not first collect and then interpret. He will approach his problem with a declared intention and as a single creative act' (Mather and Speitel 1975, p. 2).

There are, of course, other corpora whose intent is clear and controls the collection. This is particularly true of sociolinguistic materials, the collection of which often follows the pattern originated by Labov (1966). But since several chapters of this book are devoted to these, we will not deal with them here.

So the question arises: what can we do with this large and often questionably accurate sample of regional variety in a language? My topic is 'the historical and cultural interpretation of dialect.' I should like to expand that mission a bit and make it somewhat more explicit. To begin with, I should like to point out that the interpretation of dialect corpora can be divided another way: into linguistic analysis and cultural in the broad sense. We thus arrive at four categories:

1. Synchronic linguistic variation: where it is found and how it affects the functional aspects of language use.

2. Linguistic history: what regional diversity can tell us about the inner history of the language.

3. Non-linguistic variation: what kinds of social variation are found in the region and how they are linked to linguistic phenomena. Since this is the domain of sociolinguistics, I shall leave it to others to deal with.

4. Non-linguistic history, demography, and ethnography: who are the speakers and where did they come from? What kinds of contacts are there among them?

Depending on the aims of the planners and the structure of the questionnaire, the most obvious synchronic linguistic information in the corpus is regional variation. This usually deals primarily with lexicon, but other linguistic aspects are represented, especially phonetic and phonological, morphological, and to some degree semantic. Syntax is generally not included, except for what can be elicited in short phrases, such as use of pronouns, negation, and the structure of verbal phrases. Since the lexical items are usually elicited orally and recorded in phonetic transcription, a good deal of phonetic and phonological material is incidentally derived. There may also be, as we shall see, special questions intended to elicit phonological material directly. Morphology is usually limited to such matters as irregular verbs, noun plurals and pronoun case.

A general survey aiming at collecting a wide variety of linguistic material must use different types of questions depending on what kind of information is sought. Specifically, phonological and lexical questions are in complete opposition. To illustrate phonological contrast, the responses must be items identical in all but pronunciation, in order to assure comparability. Lexical items, on the other hand, are chosen to illustrate as much variety as possible. The two maps from LANE included herewith admirably illustrate this contrast.

Figure 1, which is *LANE*'s Map 415, shows the responses to item 82.8 in the worksheets in Connecticut, Rhode Island, and part of southern Massachusetts. The worksheet item is 'the whole crowd [depreciative terms]'. As was the practice in this survey, it was left to the fieldworker to find the best way to elicit the responses. Study of the map reveals some interesting facts. The responses preceded by s. were suggested by the fieldworkers; clearly they were interested in the expression *kit and caboodle* and variants thereof. But the informants seldom produced this as the first response; usually they first gave a single word, usually a monosyllable. In Connecticut alone the following appeared:*band*, *bunch*, *clique*, *crew*, *crowd* (which may have been used by the interviewer), *gang*, *lot*, *mob*, *outfit*, *parcel*, *rabble*, *riff-raff*, *shebang*, and *tribe*, as well as the phrases *kit and crew*, *rag tag and bobtail*, and *shootin' match*. Usually some variant of *kit and caboodle* appeared as a second response, often at the suggestion of the field-worker. It is hard to know just what to make of this prolific variety: eighteen or more expressions from thirty-four localities. There is no obvious geographical distribution, though *gang* seems to be more common in the Connecticut Valley, *rabble* in the east toward Rhode Island, and *shebang* (probably an Irishism) in the west bordering New York. But this may well be accidental. One feels that each informant had his or her own favorite expression and that *kit and caboodle*, though known to most of the informants, was somehow considered an inferior or vulgar expression. It is interesting to see what a later survey, that of *DARE*, has to say about *caboodle*. The earliest quote is from Bartlett's *Americanisms* (1848) stating that the term was 'used in all the Northern States and New England.' But the *DARE* questionnaire of 1965-70 cites examples from 16 states, ranging from Maine to Texas and Hawaii.

Figure 2, which is *LANE* Map 550, gives the responses to work-sheet item 86.2, listed simply as *law and order*. It is obvious that this cliche was chosen expressly for phonetic and phonological information, since the same response appears from every informant in the area, with only a handful (eight in Connecticut) marked as suggested by the fieldworker. The expression was an excellent one to illustrate several points of diversity in the phonology. The most obvious is the treatment of /r/ in three contexts: post-vocalic pre-consonantal in *order*, final syllabic also in *order* and intrusive linking between *law* and *and*. The Connecticut River, which runs down the center of the state, marks a sharp division of usage in all these, constituting one of the most notorious isoglosses in the United States. Kurath uses it as part of the boundary between two dialect regions: Eastern and Western New England. To the east of the river, the postvocalic and final syllabic /r/ are almost completely missing, the former being commonly represented by lengthening of the stem vowel [ɔ] or [ɒ], and the latter by [ə]. With almost no exceptions these are both represented by [r] to the west of the river. On the other hand, the intrusive [r] appears in the east, espe-

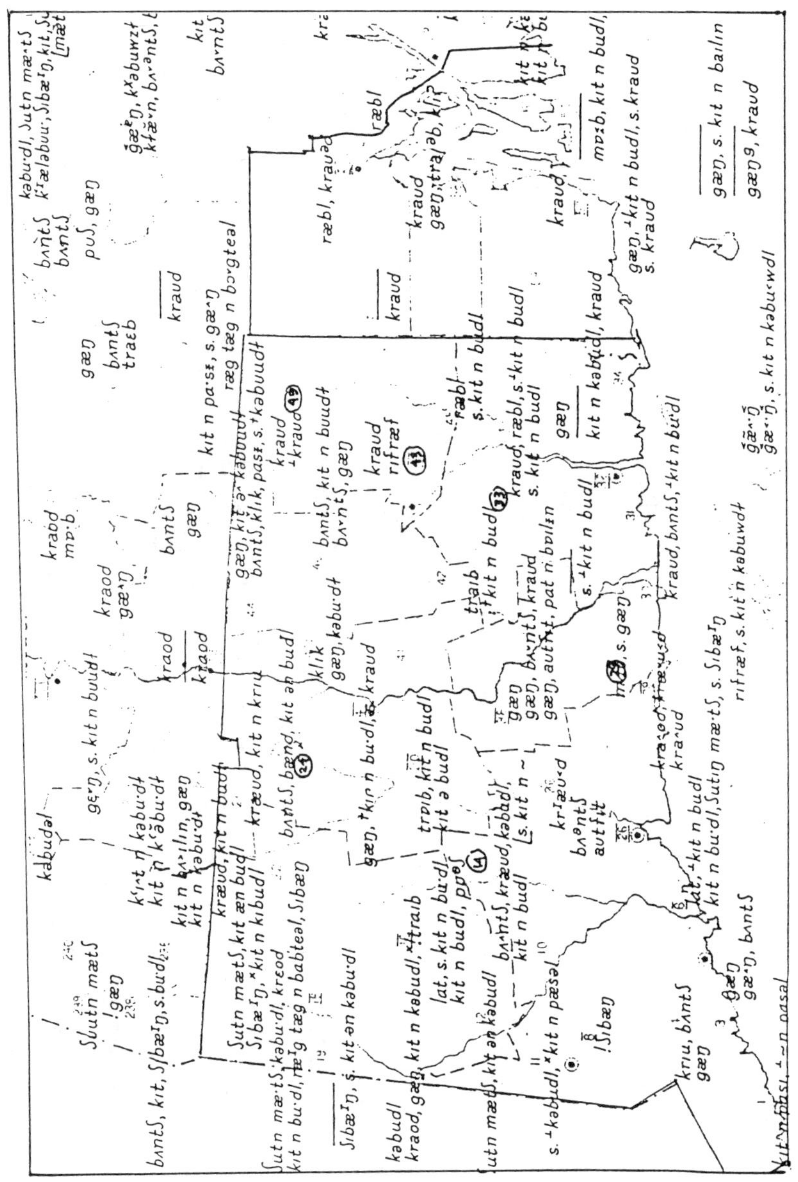

Figure 1. From *LANE* Map 415

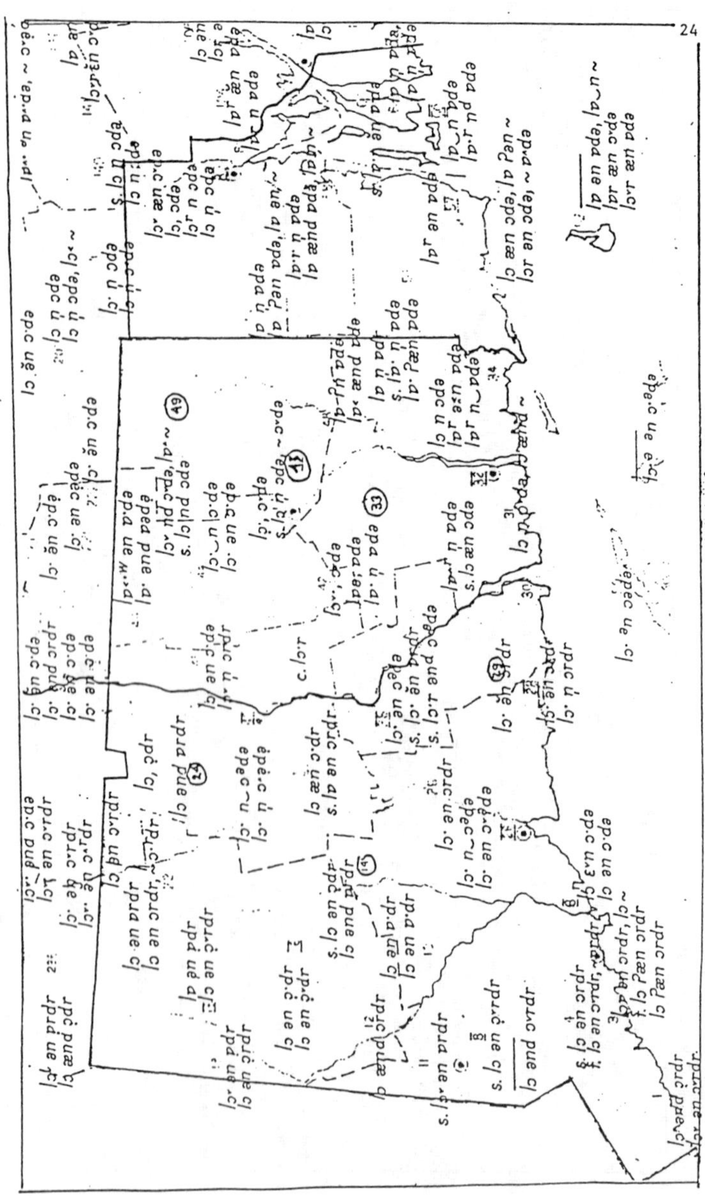

Figure 2. From *LANE* Map 550

cially in Rhode Island, rather frequently, but only twice in the west. In other words, it appears only in those areas which lack both postvocalic and final unstressed syllabic /r/.

This markedly contrastive distribution challenges historical explanation, both linguistic and extra-linguistic. Let us suppose that we have no other data beyond those on Figure 2. What kind of linguistic conjectures would we make? There are three possibilities:

1. The situation has always existed and goes back to a contrast in the 17th century English of the earliest settlers.

2. The whole area was at first rhotic; the 'loss of r' originating in the Massachusetts Bay area and spreading westward until stopped by the strong natural boundary of the Connecticut River.

3. The whole area at first lacked /r/ in all of these positions, an epenthetic and final /r/ developing in western Connecticut between New York City and New Haven and spreading eastward until blocked by the river.

Of these choices, 3. seems the least likely on linguistic grounds. Both the development of an epenthetic /r/ in [ɔ·də] and the changing of [ə] to [r] are much less likely phonological changes than the reverse.

As for 1. and 2., linguistically there is little to choose. If we allow the spelling to influence us, this is an argument for 2., but not a very strong one, considering the archaic nature of the spelling system. If we allow knowledge of contemporary dialects in England, we could argue for 1. that settlers east of the river came from the northern and eastern non-rhotic areas in England and the western settlers from the rhotic west and southwest. But if this were the case, we would expect other features of the English southwest to show up, notably the voicing of initial fricatives.

It is clear that to reach a decision we must turn to non-linguistic history, specifically that dealing with the settlement of the area, which is described in detail by Marcus Hansen in the Handbook (pp. 81-85). Simplified, this tells us that the eastern area was settled after the Pequot War by emigrants from the Massachusetts Bay area, and the western region by emigrants from the coastal area west of the river. This is similar to 2. above, except that what moved was not so much linguistic features as the speakers who used them. In either case, the Connecticut River was a significant obstacle to ready diffusion. How and why the Bay area became non-rhotic is another story; it is usually attributed to closer contacts between Boston and the old country, where the postvocalic and final /r/ was lost after the original settlements. The persistence of rhotic enclaves on Cape Anne and Martha's Vineyard is evidence that the post-settlement British influence did not extend over the whole area.

These two cases -- terms for a gang of ruffians and the pronunciation of *law and order* -- are single items. By themselves they cannot supply the answers to two related questions: are the areas east and west of the river distinct dialect areas? and if so, can the river be considered a dialect boundary? To attempt to answer these questions we must involve the whole survey, or at least a good-sized representative sample thereof.

Underlying these two questions are two broader and more general ones, which go back virtually to the beginning of dialectological study. These are: are there in fact such things as dialect areas, and can they be seen to be sharply delineated by dialect boundaries? The first of these was raised a century ago by Gaston Paris, the distinguished medievalist and philologian. He wrote, 'Actually there are no dialects ... . Varieties of common speech blend into one another by imperceptible gradations.' (quoted by Gauchat, 1903). Paris goes on to point out that a dialect speaker traveling in a straight line across country will ultimately reach a point where he has great difficulty understanding the speech, although at no time did he pass through an area where neighbors failed to communicate. This conclusion was taken up by the Swiss dialectologist Gauchat in a famous article, 'Gibt es Mundartgrenzen?' ('Are there dialect boundaries?'). While admitting that in a given area there may be considerable variation among speakers, he claims that they all will share some kind of Sprachgefühl which will cause them to recognize one another as people who speak the same language. So even though there is no sharp boundary around an area, there is a common core of language usage which the speakers themselves are aware of and which allows the linguist to call it a dialect area.

Over the years there have been many attempts to put a more precise definition to the concept of dialect area. A century ago, Alexander J. Ellis, on the basis of rather meager evidence collected by mail from local vicars, felt able to divide England and eastern Wales into thirty-two dialect districts, bounded by sharp black lines. Each of these was characterized by a relatively small group of features, many of them deriving from a common short anecdote as spoken by a native and recorded more or less impressionistically by the local vicar.

The next step was the invention of the *isogloss*. This term, rather unfortunately created by analogy with the meteorological terms *isobar* and *isotherm*, has been used in various senses. Whereas an isobar *connects* points having the *same* barometric pressure, an isogloss *separates* points having *different* responses to the same question. It was this that led Kurath (1972) to prefer *heterogloss*, but that term has never caught on. Practice varies as to how an isogloss is drawn: it may represent the farthest extent of a regional term, or the limit up to which such a term is universal, or something between these. In the first case, it may reach out a long loop to include a single stray form; in the second case it will fail to include instances which are mixed with contrasting forms; in the third case it will pass more or less smoothly through a transition area, leaving exceptions on both sides. Very rarely will it clearly separate one usage from another completely, though our example of rhotic vs. non-rhotic on either side of the Connecticut River approaches that ideal. Normally we must realize that the isogloss is already an act of interpretation by the dialectologist.

The next stage is the identification of bundles of isoglosses and raising them to the status of dialect boundaries. A bundle is defined as a group (presumably three or more) of isoglosses that run more or less closely together across a stretch of territory. Almost never do they coincide for more than one or more short stretches between areas where they separate. As we have seen, individual isoglosses may be determined in several ways, the choice among which will certainly determine the degree of their coincidence. Figure 3 illustrates a well known bundle, used by Kurath to establish the boundary between the Northern and Midland dialect areas in the eastern United States (Kurath 1949, Fig. 5a). Except in northeastern Pennsylvania and central New Jersey, these run rather close together, though at one point *pail* and *darning needle* are separated by about 100 miles. If three more isoglosses used by Kurath to mark the same line (Fig. 18) are superposed (see Figure 4) the distances grow greater: up to 150 miles between *pail* and *worm fence*. It is clear that though this is a transition area, it is far from a clear-cut dialect boundary in the normal sense of the word. In fact, if all six isoglosses are considered, it can be seen that there are dozens of small areas, contrasting with one another in one or more features. The best that can be done is to select one to represent the bundle. The favorite in this case is usually *pail*, which happens to be the southernmost. If *run* were chosen, the Midland region would extend considerably farther north in the western part of the area.

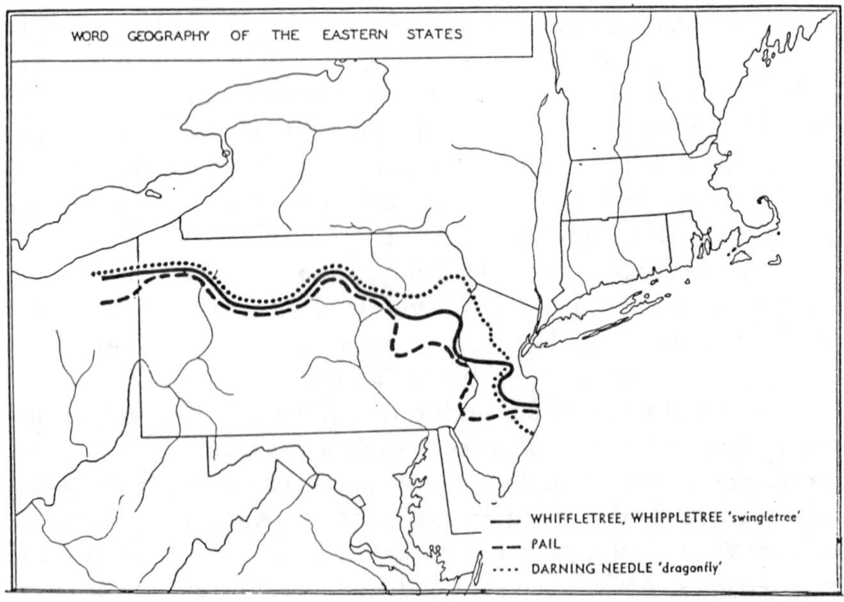

Figure 3. From *A Word Geography of the Eastern United States*

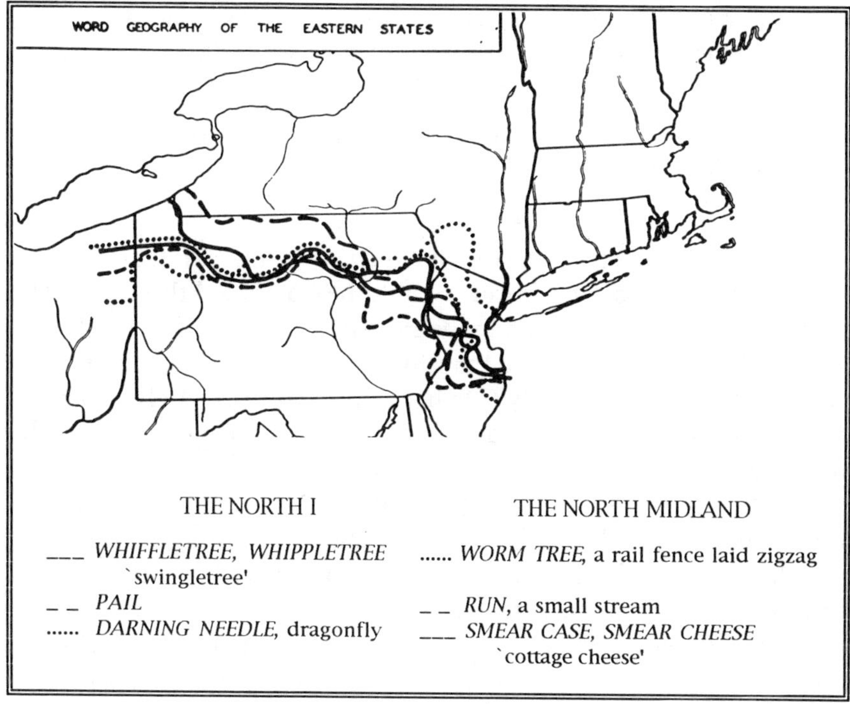

Figure 4. From *A Word Geography of the Eastern United States*

Isogloss bundles, then, are not very satisfactory as dialect boundaries. What they can do is establish that in some transitional areas the contrasts are closer together than in others. What we should be looking for is not a boundary between dialect areas but some method of locating focal areas and measuring the degree of contrast between them. Gauchat realized this fact eighty-five years ago. He picked up Schuchardt's analogy to the colors of the rainbow, which are individually distinct although there are no sharp boundaries between them. Gauchat goes on to say:

> But the contrasting proportion of dialects is much too complicated for it to be represented by such a simple example as the colors of the rainbow. If colors are to illustrate the bounding of dialect I would rather think of a layering of water-colors. Supposing we paint the region where one speech-feature appears with one shade, the other distributional areas with other shades, then in the center a characteristic mixed color would appear and reveal the extent of the dialect center. Many transitions will lead from one center to another. (Gauchat 1903, p. 397)

This analogy is interesting but it has a serious limitation: only a very limited number of features could be portrayed this way. The cross-hatching method used in the *Linguistic Atlas of Scotland* had a similar limitation: no more than three layers could be superposed without destroying legibility (Mather and Speitel, p. 21). How then to represent a large number of potentially contrasting features, even to the total accumulated in the corpus?

Various statistical and mathematical methods of doing this are treated by Larmouth and Gerard in Chapter 4 of this volume. But I should like to include here a brief description and illustration of a method involving no mathematics beyond simple addition and percentage: the method of dialectometry, originated by Jean Séguy and illustrated in volume VI of the *Linguistic Atlas of Gascony*. It consisted of identifying a large number of contrasting features and comparing one locality with another to determine the number of these features in which they contrast. This number, reduced to a percentage, Séguy called the *linguistic distance* between them. Theoretically this would amount to plotting the isoglosses for every feature and counting the number one would cross in going from one locality to another. But obviously this is technically impossible. If Séguy had plotted the isoglosses of the 426 features he used, his map would be an impossible tangle of overlapping lines. Instead, he put his data into a matrix, with the rows representing localities and the columns features. With numbers representing the versions of each feature, one could match one row against another and count the number of disagreements. Reduced to a percentage, this would be the linguistic distance between the localities. Séguy limited his comparisons to contiguous localities; to have compared all pairs of his 75 localities would have been a monumental task for a human, though easy enough for a computer. His results, when plotted on a map, revealed that in some areas the linguistic distances between contiguous localities were small, in others large. The former could be interpreted as dialect centers, the latter as areas of greater dialect difference, hence potential boundaries.

This method has been developed and illustrated by various European scholars, notably Hans Goebl of Salzburg and Wolfgang Viereck of Bamberg. Some of their writings on the subject are included in my bibliography. As a kind of mini-experiment in the Séguy technique, I used the *LANE* data from six localities in central Connecticut to test the validity of the often stated claim that the Connecticut River is a dialect boundary in that state. The localities I used are shown on Figure 5; they are 14 Wolcott, 24 Simsbury, 29 Killingworth, 33 Norwichtown, 43 Windham, and 49 Woodstock. It will be seen that the first three are to the west of the river and the other three to the east.

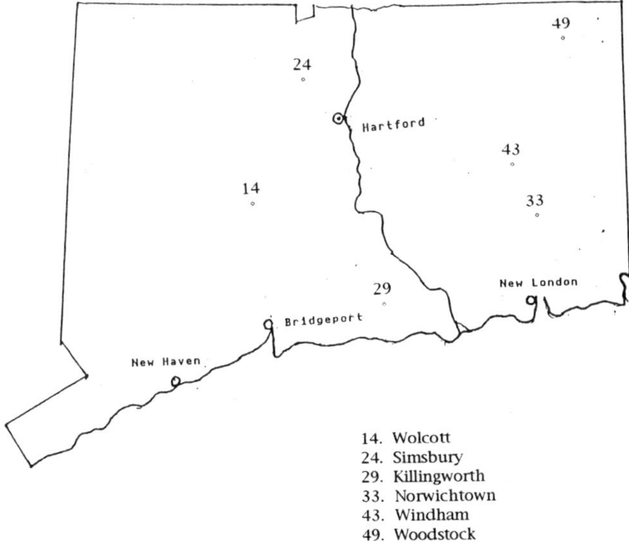

Figure 5. Six localities in Connecticut

I used forty-nine items from the *LANE* data, chosen at random from the total of 700-odd. In every case I used the first reported response of a Type I or Type II informant, yielding 141 potentially contrastive phonological features. The results of these calculations of linguistic distances are shown in Tables 1 and 2.

In the lexical chart, it will be seen that locality 49, the farthest east, is linguistically closer to the three western sites (33.6) than it is to the other two eastern ones (42.5). On the other hand, locality 29 in the west is about equally distant from each group (33.3 from the other two western localities and 35.5 from the three eastern ones). It is clear that, at least so far as this sample is concerned, there is no lexical boundary between east and west of the river.

	14	0.0					
W	24	50.0	0.0				
	29	37.0	29.5	0.0			
	33	42.6	38.3	34.0	0.0		
E	43	34.7	43.5	37.0	57.4	0.0	
	49	32.3	32.9	35.6	39.1	45.8	0.0

Table 1. Lexical linguistic distance by percentage

	14	0.0					
W	24	43.7	0.0				
	29	25.3	45.1	0.0			
	33	73.7	74.5	61.6	0.0		
E	43	74.3	81.6	59.2	30.8	0.0	
	49	73.3	78.4	61.1	27.0	16.8	0.0

Table 2. Phonological linguistic distance by percentage

The phonology figures in Table 2 tell quite a different story. It appears that the three eastern localities make up a fairly close-knit cluster (average phonological linguistic distance 24.9) in sharp contrast to their distance from the three western localities (average 70.8). The three western localities are also close together, but not so close-knit as the eastern ones (average 38.0) We can conclude that the river is indeed a phonological boundary (again within the limitations of this small sample). This is undoubtedly owing to a considerable extent to the /r/ situation described above. There are, however, some other features which show an east-west contrast. The low-back vowels show great variety, some of which is undoubtedly due to fieldworker variation (see pp. 126-7 of the Handbook). But there are some east-west contrasts. The west regularly has [ɑ] in *frog*, *hod*, *on*, where the east has a rounded vowel recorded as [ɔ] or [ɒ]. The western localities have [u] in *roof*, where the eastern ones have [ʊ]. Locality 49, in the northeast corner of the state nearest to Massachusetts and Rhode Island is the only one of the six localities that has a broad [a] not only in *father* and *palm* but also in *afternoon*, *half*, and *laughing*, where the other five have [æ]. So the phonological contrast is not simply a matter of rhotic west against non-rhotic east.

This rather amateurish mini-experiment comes to conclusions of interest. Above all it reveals that data collected with a quite different motivation and orientation can be exploited in new ways to good effect. It also shows that future methods of analysis and interpretation of large dialect corpora will have to be done by computer.

References

Cassidy, Frederic G. (ed.). 1985. *Dictionary of American regional English, Vol. I.* Cambridge MA: Belknap Press of Harvard University Press.

Ellis, Alexander J. 1889. *The existing phonology of English dialects.* London: Trubner.

Gauchat, Louis. 1903. Gibt es Mundartgrenzen? *Archiv für das Studium der neueren Sprache* 111:365-403.

Goebl, Hans. 1982. Atlas, matrices, et similarités: petit aperçu dialectométrique. *Computers and the Humanities* 16:69-84.

Goebl, Hans (ed.). 1984. *Dialectology.* Bochum: Brockmeier.

Kurath, Hans (ed.). 1938. *Linguistic atlas of New England,* 3 vols. Providence: Brown University.

Kurath, Hans. 1939. *Handbook of the linguistic geography of New England.* Washington, D. C.: American Council of Learned Societies.

Kurath, Hans. 1949. *Word geography of the Eastern United States.* Ann Arbor: University of Michigan Press.

Kurath. Hans. 1972. *Studies in area linguistics.* Ann Arbor: University of Michigan Press.

Labov, William. 1966. *The social stratification of English in New York City.* Arlington VA: Center for Applied Linguistics.

Mather, J. Y. & H. H. Speitel 1975. *The linguistic atlas of Scotland.* Scots Section, vol. 1. London: Croom Helm.

Orton, Harold 1962. *Survey of English dialects.* Introduction. Leeds: E. J. Arnold & Son.

Pederson, Lee (ed.). 1986. *Handbook for the linguistic atlas of the Gulf States.* Athens GA: University of Georgia Press.

Séguy, Jean (ed.). 1973. *Atlas linguistique de la Gascogne,* vol. VI. Paris: CNRS.

Séguy, Jean. 1973. La dialectométrie dans l'*Atlas linguistique de la Gascogne. Revue de linguistique Romane* 37:1-24.

Viereck, Wolfgang. 1984. The presentation and interpretation of English dialects: Computer assisted projects. *Proceedings of the XIIIth International Congress of Linguists,* Tokyo 1982.

An Approach to Linguistic Geography

Lee Pederson
Emory University

The Linguistic Atlas of the Gulf States (LAGS) reports findings of a general dialect survey.* LAGS begins a regional and social description of spoken words in eight Southern states. LAGS texts record usage as a phonographic outline that seeks the explicitness of photographic communication. Here, textual composition recapitulates traditional method in an expression of Hjelmslev's empirical principle (1961, 11) -- complete, consistent, and simple description of observed facts.

LAGS texts pursue the ideal of scientific description, specialized with the requisite transparency of a reference work. But the texts also demonstrate the impossibility of the task:

> All science is makeshift, a means to an end which is never attained. After all, the truest description, and that by which another living man can most readily recognize a flower, is the unmeasured and eloquent one which the sight of it inspires. No scientific description will supply the want of this, though you should count and measure and analyze every atom that seems to compose it. (Thoreau, *Journal* XIV, 117)

Only tape recordings preserve the unmeasured eloquence of the spoken word. LAGS maps and legends bear no resemblance whatsoever to the sounds and rhythms of Southern speech. Instead, they offer a convenient index. LAGS texts form a student's guide to 5300 hours of tape-recorded speech, specimens of Southern American English (1968-1983).

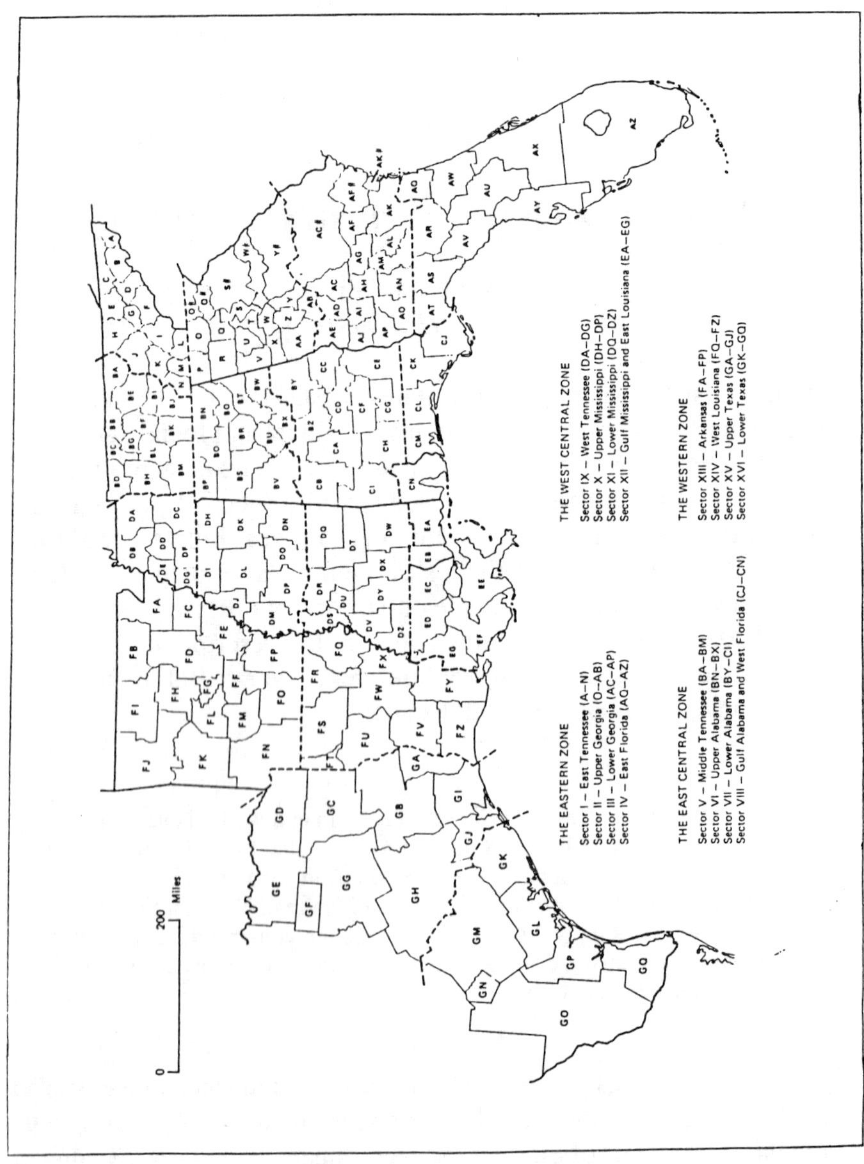

Figure 1. The Gulf States

Through the composition of graphic analogues in fiche, disk, and book collections, the work aims to match the resources of a conventional linguistic atlas. The maps and legends of this atlas initiate a description of dialects in the Gulf States. Such comprehensive interpretation, however, extends beyond the domain of inventorial reference work. A linguistic atlas maps basic materials and carries its results to the threshold of phonological word geography.

The texts transmit information about the behavior of words across the Lower South (Figure 1), recording evidence and laying a foundation for descriptive statements. In the process, the texts establish a baseline for dialect study and form a conduit between field observation and dictionary entry. Texts reduce speech to writing, through the transmission of phonetic strings, orthographic words, and matrix maps. Maps record the last words of an atlas project. But linguistic maps, like road maps, are not ends in themselves. They are guides that offer direction, identify hazards, suggest alternative routes.

As a research tool, a linguistic atlas works best in the hands of a craftsman. The writings of Raven I. McDavid, Jr., (Kretzschmar and Merman, 1986) offer an extended example. They form a rich collection of American regional speech study. They report the kinds of information ADS founders discussed in their earliest meetings (Shelton, 1889a, 1889b), and they answer the earliest call for the mapping of American speech (Hempl, 1894). As a matter of fact, McDavid's writings extend beyond all of that to offer interpretive scholarship of a kind unknown in this country before Hans Kurath and his associates undertook the *Linguistic Atlas of New England* (LANE). Virtually all of those major essays project regional, historical, and cultural explanations of American atlas data. Had no one else written a word on the implications of American linguistic geography, McDavid's writings alone justify the New England effort and codify other works in progress. For example, his essays have established the atlases of the Atlantic and North Central states as basic texts for students of American speech.

As Bach (1950) demonstrates, students of German dialects produced similarly extraordinary results from Wenker's *Sprachatlas des deutsches Reichs* (SDR). One of the rarest editions in the history of Western civilization, SDR existed in two copies, one in Berlin and the other in Marburg. In that form it endured as the German linguistic atlas of record until 1926, when Ferdinand Wrede initiated the *Deutscher Sprachatlas*, the heart of which was Wenker's data base.

These German and American linguistic geographers recognized an atlas as a file of files, not necessarily published volumes of maps or even word lists. From SDR through LANE, atlases formed master files of linguistic data entered on maps. Without the resources of inexpensive printing, microphotography, and computers, the pioneers built their files by hand. The centerpiece was Gilliéron and Edmont's *Atlas linguistique de la France.*

During the years between those atlases, the magnificent cartography of Jaberg and Jud raised the work to an art form. Their calligraphy, woodcuts, and multicolored overlays suggest fine art, rather than linguistic inventory. And, perhaps, the beauty of the *Sprach- und Sachatlas Italiens und der Südschweiz* carried readers away from the purpose of the work. But the title of the handbook allows no room for misunderstanding: *Der Sprachatlas als Forschunginstrument* (1928).

Beginning with Orton's *Survey of English Dialects* (SED), linguistic atlases concentrated on the publication of basic materials in tabular forms, giving more attention to legends than to the maps themselves. The Orton model stands directly behind McDavid, O'Cain, and Dorrill (1979), the first two volumes of the *Linguistic Atlas of the Middle and South Atlantic States* (LAMSAS); it underlies the sensible presentation of Allen's *Linguistic Atlas of the Upper Midwest* (LAUM). Orton's work makes explicit the concept of a linguistic atlas as a file of files. SED reflects the orderly mind of a classical philologist, as Orton's work unites the resources of linguistic and literary study. Its composition ignored the fashions of criticism and theory, producing a text of inestimable value. Even without immediate cartography, SED recapitulates method through an elegant data base.

The LAGS Project had the advantage of all that experience. From a tactical standpoint, when preliminary discussions began in 1966, the study of American speech had already been revitalized by the example of the Dictionary of American Regional English (DARE) Project (See Chapter 3, this volume). Cassidy and his associates opened the way for all kinds of North American dialect research through the support of regional universities, federal agencies, and the active membership of ADS itself.

When LAGS fieldwork began in 1968, the portable tape recorder had already proven itself as an essential field instrument in the study of colloquial speech. As scribal work neared completion in 1978, University Microfilms International and the University of Georgia Press agreed to publish basic and descriptive materials after the convincing examples of Kurath, Allen, and Cassidy. When editorial work began in 1981, the computer had become a conventional tool in the manipulation of linguistic data. The project developed in the shadows of these historical accidents that offered precedence, programs, and electronic equipment to study native speech in the American South.

Those resources produced the components of the atlas, the LAGS tape/text (T), fiche/text (F), disk/text (D), and book/text (B). Together, they form a textual chain within which a reader moves from speech to writing, from analysis to synthesis (>), or back again (<): T >< F >< D >< B. The chain identifies the tape/text as the basic file, the others as analogues and indexes of that data base. Of the four links in the chain, the substance of only the tape/text is inviolate. All others can be revised, rewritten, or reinforced with additional description.

The Tape/Text

The LAGS tape/text includes 1121 interviews in 5300 hours. These are field records, recordings of every form discussed in the atlas. This base form provides a working text more complicated than LANE and LAUM records, but its composition follows their standards.

The tape recorder produces a field record that must be reconciled with traditional aims and methods. The tape/text not only reflects modified field procedures but also determines the form and substance of the atlas itself. As data base, it determines the ultimate content and quality of its analogues, whether typescripts, maps, or ASCII files. Today, magnetic tapes, not field notes, are the texts of dialect study.

Pederson (1974) abstracted six minutes of an interview recorded in Wear Valley, Tennessee, in the summer of 1973. It identified segmental phonemes based on phonetic transcription and offered sample texts in phonetics, phonemics, and conventional orthography. The latter text, repeated here in part, identifies informant responses in quotation marks, a few pronunciations in conventional dialect spellings, deleted units in square brackets, and work-sheet items in italics.

'The shotgun's loaded. *One* a-sittin' agin one *door* and one the other. Well, [if] burglars *come* in on you, if you're fixed for it, you can protect yourself. I keep *two* or *three* shotguns. *Wife's* good with a shotgun. She *can't* use a pistol much, but she *can* use a shotgun. I *got* two pistols in there that I keep loaded, but I never had to use them for anything like that.'

. . . .

Yesterday when we were talking about hogs, I forgot to ask you what you call a hog that's been fixed or castrated.

'*Barry.*' [barrow]

Would you say that again, please?

'Barry. I don't know how that's spelled; b-a-r-r-y, *I guess*. He's a *boar* till he's *trimmed*, I mean, and you'd call it *caster-rated*. Anyway, it *takes* his seed out. Then he's a *barry*. Well, that's the kind you fatten. You *can't eat boar* meat. I don't know how they *do* it. I've been to the stockyards and *see* them fellers buy 'em by the truckloads, but I don't know how they do it. You kill a *boar*, and you can't eat it. Or you kill a sow that's in season, you know, a-boarin' -- you can't *eat* that. Used to, when we killed sows, we had to watch that awfully close. You get one in there. You *can't eat* it. They're just *strong*. You can *smell* it!'

'Fella up here *'bove me*, I used to *take* my sows up there. He had a great big *boar*. I *guess* he'd weigh *six* or *seven hundred pounds*. He's mean! And they got to they couldn't do *nothin'* with him, and this fella let his renter have the *boar*. He had a big family. And he let him have that, and they kill it, and they couldn't *eat* it. And he sold it to *one* of his sister's boys, and he took it out there to Fred Atchley: it was a big supermarket he had there then. And he sold it -- they didn't know it, you know -- and said they cut *them* hams and meat, and they'd sell 'em; and said the folks would *bring* 'em back just about as fast as they *took* 'em. They was about to get in a lawsuit about it. I don't know what they *done*, what they ever *did do* about it. But they probably was all innocent. I mean this boy *didn't know no* better; and Fred -- or the man that bought it for Fred -- they didn't know no better. But, boy, when they went to fryin' it, they *knowed* better. Why, you could *smell* that stuff for a long ways!'

'You *can't eat* it. Nor if an old sow is in heat. You *can't eat* that *neither*. You got to watch that. But now how they do that at the stockyard, I don't know. These boars, I don't know what they *do*. I've *asked* fellers, and they said they *give* shots or *somethin'* another. And *I've been* there. I *used to* sell a lot of *hogs* there in [the] East *Tennessee* Packin' *House*. And you'd be in there, and you'd *see* them *come* in there unloadin' them old sows, you know, and them all *swelled* up. And I don't know what they *do*.'

'There's some kind of processes. Just like people that *runs dairies*. There's a wild *onion*, *smells* like ramps, you know. Well, a *cow eats* them; you *can't drink* her *milk*. *Woman* lives right *down below* us here, and she *used to* work for a *dairy*. She said they had some kind of powder they'd *put in* that *milk* to kill that scent, you know.'

'But there's something funny about that. You milk a cow *of a morning*, it *wasn't* in it, but *milk* her *of a night*, it *was* in it. We *used to have* a lot [a plot?] of 'em. They *grow* along in the *creeks*, you know, the *bottoms*.'

You mean ramp, or something like ramp?

'Well, they're a wild *onion*; they're between a wild *onion* and a ramp. *Cow eats* 'em. They like 'em. And they make a bloom on top of 'em, of a seed, you know, on top. And I don't know, you *just can't drink* it.'

'*One* time I got the stuff *down* here at this drugstore, somewhere, to *put in* it. It *helped* a little, but it didn't *help* it too much. But this *woman* said that they had some way of *doin'* that. And *cows'll* take what they call mastitis, and their bags will *swell* up, you know, and crud, *can't hardly* get the *milk* out. Well, country people wouldn't use that. Well, she said if they could *milk* them with -- *'cause* they *milked* 'em with *milkers* -- she said they *didn't pay no attention* to that.'

'So there you are. You don't know what you're *eatin'* when you get meat, and you don't know what you're *a-drinkin'* when you get *milk*.'

A complete typescript of the LAGS tape/text will yield, perhaps, 100 million words. That outlines the probable resources of the data base, materials of inquiry for the future. In 1973, the plan anticipated an atlas of 600 records and looked forward to computer processing through punch cards. Despite this revised understanding, no effort was made to change directions, to limit the number of interviews or to control their duration. As a result, an exhaustive index of the tape/text awaits the technology of another generation and its automatic linguistic geography. Today, that seems a certainty. A voice-operated terminal, for example, makes much more sense today than would a description, 17 years ago, of the machine on which this report is written.

The tape/text yields more free-conversational information than the ablest field worker could possibly gather. The short passage from the Wear Valley record includes some of the most difficult forms to elicit through direct interrogation. It also reveals lexical, morphological and syntactic structures that the planners could not anticipate when the work sheets were organized. Who would anticipate a sow in heat described as 'a-boaring,' in search of a boar? But other records in East Tennessee identified a cow in the same state to be 'a-bulling.' Word study might also conjecture on that vegetable occupying some uncharted semantic territory between a wild onion and a ramp. References to 'wife' imply several underlying strings: 'my wife,' 'the wife,' or the nickname 'Wife,' a problem that might be solved through prosodic analysis. The text also records function word deletion -- conjunctions, determiners, and prepositions. These interesting grammatical forms can be easily evaluated in a tape/text, but field workers with pencils had no time to record the necessary contexts to frame the features in syntax. Similarly, aberrant inflections of pronouns, nouns, and verbs appear with clarity in context.

After that, the tape/text carries investigation beyond the eminent domain of linguistic geography. It offers materials for discourse analysis, (structural) narrative study, and oral literary interpretation. The text suggests possibilities that extend beyond the primary targets of linguistic geography, the work-sheet items. It points toward interdisciplinary research that offers unedited materials to study language as action, structure, and art.

Consider the introductory commentary of the informant, still suspicious of the interviewer. 'The shotgun's loaded' and right near-by. Elsewhere there are two loaded pistols. Is the message an inventory of personal property, a warning to an outlander, or both? His wife is good with a shotgun, and she might be right around the corner.

Consider the compositional form of the narrative that begins with 'Barry.' The boar's revenge comes down to a highly stylized Ciceronian tricolon: 'I mean this boy didn't know no better; and Fred -- or the man that bought it for Fred -- they didn't know no better. But, boy when they went to fryin' it, they knowed better.' The section closes in a metrical line approximating iambic pentameter, with a spondaic terminal foot: 'Why you could smell that stuff for a long ways!'

The next two transitional paragraphs move toward the discussion of food processing, pork and milk. And the passage closes with a contrast of country people and commercial dairymen. The final paragraph unites the two parts in a perfectly balanced construction: 'So there you are. You don't know what you're eatin' when you get meat, and you don't know what you're a-drinkin' when you get milk.' Recorded in a tape/text, spontaneous oral composition of this kind offers more to students of language, culture, and literature than any list of words or gathering of isoglosses.

But the tape/text serves first as data base for a linguistic atlas. It stores the materials that may be someday indexed as a file of files. For the time being, the tape/text offers three immediate resources. It provides contexts for all LAGS transcriptions. It provides evidence for closer study of linguistic behavior within a field record, across a dialect area, or over the full expanse of the eight-state zone. And, finally, it provides verification of every observation made in the atlas with every graphic form documented in tape-recorded spoken word.

To preserve this text, a duplicate set of the 2700 reels will be archived in William Kretzschmar's office at the University of Georgia. With a third set on 3500 cassettes, the tape/text will be more accessible than SDR, and that served German linguistic geographers for nearly a half century.

As suggested when the editorial work began (Pederson 1981), the tape/text will serve American English studies best when it is reduced to writing. Current research in Wyoming begins with abbreviated interviews fully recorded as ASCII files (Pederson and Madsen, 1989). This experiment aims to develop a method that combines the resources of the LAGS fiche/text and disk/text in a unified analogue -- a complete orthographic text of the field record. A concordance program by John Nitti indexes the Wyoming data base and provides an example for transcribing the LAGS tape/text.

The Fiche/Text

Two microfiche publications record LAGS basic materials. The protocol collection, the core of *The Basic Materials* (1981) includes more than two million phonetic strings abstracted from the tape/text in 1121 field interviews. *The Concordance of Basic Materials* (1986) rewrites those strings as orthographic words, indexing each entry according to work-sheet page and line in an exhaustive and fully permuted list. Together, they identify every linguistic form described in the atlas. The concordance provides the orthographic forms for both lexical word geography and phonological description -- whether lexical, morphemic, phonemic, or phonetic. The protocol collection provides impressionistic phonetic notation for all linguistic forms in the basic materials.

In editing the protocols for publication, editors identified 914 of them as analogues to primary field records, with the remaining 207 designated as secondary field records. The *Handbook* (1986, 34-40) explains criteria for that classification, as well as the social classification of informants. All those decisions were made before work began on the concordance in 1980. Although the concordance indexes the contents of all 1121 units, LAGS analysis confines itself to the 914 primary records, as reported in the protocols.

As a sample of the one hundred million words in the tape/text, the fiche/text is selective, scarcely two per cent of the complete record. To organize the evidence in an orderly way, LAGS scribes composed protocols that outline, sample, and index the tape/text.

The term *protocol* suggests three aspects of the form previously identified by American linguistic geographers as the field record.

These notes are (1) the first written draft of an event or transaction, the tape-recorded interview, (2) a preliminary memorandum prepared to assist auditors of the tapes, and (3) the formal account of the information included in the tapes. The first of these aspects indicates that the entire corpus is limited to that which is on tape and that the entire process of transcription is limited to that which the transcriber can perceive on the tape -- nothing is transcribed in the field. The second aspect indicates that the transcriptions are aimed at further, more nearly comprehensive or exhaustive, analysis and that the transcriptions are subject to correction. The third aspect indicates that the LAGS method remains squarely in the tradition of conventional linguistic geography and that all departures from that tradition are accretive and supplemental -- accretive in that additional information is provided and supplemental in that a self-corrective capacity is recognized within the project.

The concordance illustrates an application of the second aspect of that definition. It aims to improve analysis with a systematic conversion of phonetic strings as orthographic words. And it lays the foundation for deductive study in the establishment of the orthographic word -- the simplest and most easily understood linguistic unit -- as a sensible starting point for descriptive work.

Even with the concordance available to locate forms in the protocols, the notations also needed a phonological index and idiolect summary. Published with the protocols in 1981, the idiolect synopses offer a preliminary guide to the contents of each tape-recorded interview. Idiolect synopsis #25 (Figure 2) abstracts the Wear Valley protocol. It outlines pronunciation, grammar, and regional vocabulary in 120 slots organized to illustrate usage of 136 words and phrases.

The descriptor MMY identifies a male, middle-class, Caucasian informant, age 76, with an elementary-school education, and an insular perspective. ET identifies the East Tennessee sector of the LAGS grid (Figure 1); WEAR VALLEY, the community. LP/73:LP/73 identifies field worker/interview year: scribe/transcription year. The code F 015.01 identifies the LAGS grid unit, F (Sevier and Blount counties), 015 (Sevier County), and .01 (first interview recorded in Sevier County).

MMY 76 1A
LP/73:LP/73

ET WEAR VALLEY
F 015.01

/ɪ/	* hwɪ ᵊps	k'rɪ˄ ᵊb	t'ɪ˄ ᵊn	hɪ˄ ᵊlz	* jɪ˄ɚz (= ears)
/ɛ/	t'ɛ˃ksɛ̈s	lɛːᵻg	* t'ɛ̃˅n	nɛ́˅ʃɛ̈˄	mɚ̀˂i˅
/æ/	græ̂ᵻs hɑ̀·pəz	bæᵋgz	hæ̃ːᵋmɚz	* væ̃ᵋʃɛ̈	* mæː·ɚɛ̈d
/ʊ/	bʊ́˂ʃɛ̈l (pl.)	wʊ˂d	wʊ̃ːmn̩	* p'ʊ˂l	ʃɔ˅ɚ
/ʌ/	* ʃʌ˂t	gʌ́˂vɚmn̩t	sʌ́˂n ɛ̀p	bʌːᵚb	
/ɑ/	* krɑ˃·p	* fɑ́˃ðɚ	dʒɑ́˃nɨ	k'ɑ́˃lɛ̈ʒ	k'ɑ˂·ɚ
/i/	i˅·ist	* θɾɪ˃i˃	* bɪːinz	fɛːᵊld	stɪ˄ɚz
/e/	eɛ̈t	meɛ̈	streːᵊn	ɾeːɛ̈l	mɛ́˃ɚɛ̈
/u/	tɛ̈ʉθ	* tɛ̈ʉ	wɛ̈ːʉ˄nd	mjʉlz	p'ʊː·ɚ
/o/	k'o˂ʊ˂t	jɪ́˄ɚ əgò˂ʊ˂	hò˂ʉmz	o˂ʉld	ho˅·ɚs
/ɔ/	* dɒ̀˄ɔ˄tɚ	* dɒ˄ɔ˄g	* gɔ̃ːn	wɒ́ɯnəts	* hɔ˄·ɚs
/ɜ/	tʃɚ́˃tʃəz	θɚ́zdɨ	* wɚmz	* gɚ˂l	wɚ̂i˅d
/aɪ/	rɑ˃·ᵋt	rɑ·ᵋd	nɑ·ᵋn	* mɑ·ᵋl (pl.)	* wɑ˃·ɚ
/aʊ/	* hæo˂s	* k'æo˄z	dæoːn	* æəl	flæ·ɚ (= flour)
/ɔɪ/	ɔ˜ɛ̈stɚz	* p'ɔ́ɛ̈˅zn̩	—	ɔ˄ə˄t	lɒ̂˄ɛ̈jɚz
PL	p'o˂ʊ˂st	* p'æo˂n	—	* wɒ˄·s·	—
FW	kwɑ̀ɚtɚ tə	—	—	ɛ̈tʃɚ stʌ́˂mɛ̈k	—

rɑ·ᵊz / — / —	drɑ·ᵋv / dro˂ʊ˂v / dro˂ʊ˂v
dɾæᵻg / — / —	ɪ˄it ~ i˅it / e˃ɛ̈t / i˅·t
drɪːŋk / dɾʌ˄ŋk / —	hɛ˅ᵊp / hɛ˅ᵊpt / —
— / dɑ·ᵊvd / —	—

dɒ˄ɔ́˄g ɑ˃·ɚnz	* fɑ́·ɚ bo˅·ɚd	* gʲæᵋp	rɑ˃k fɛ̈ːntsɛ̈z
* p'o˂ʊ˂ks	* t'ó˂ʊ˂ sæᵋks	frɛ́˅ntʃ hɑ̀˂ɚp	sɪ˃i˃ sɒɔ̃˅z
læᵋmp	* kənʊ́ʉz	—	—
sɑ́˄os mɪ˄it	k'ɑ̂˃tɛ̈dʒ ʃí˅iz	mʌ˂·ʃ	kl̥ɪ́˄ŋ p'ɪ˄itʃ
* ɔ́˅ʊ˂pn̩ sto˂ʊ˂n	p'í˅nəts	t'ɑ́˃mi˅to˅z	* gɾí˅·n bi˅inz
* wʊ́ːd tʃʌ́˂ks	rɛ́dwɚ̀mz	* t'ɑ́˃ɚpn̩	* krɔ́˄·dædz
snɛ́ɛ̈k fɪ˄idɚz	tʃɪ́ːgɚz	sɚ́ɛ̈neɛ̈d (v.)	—

Figure 2. LAGS idiolect synopsis #25

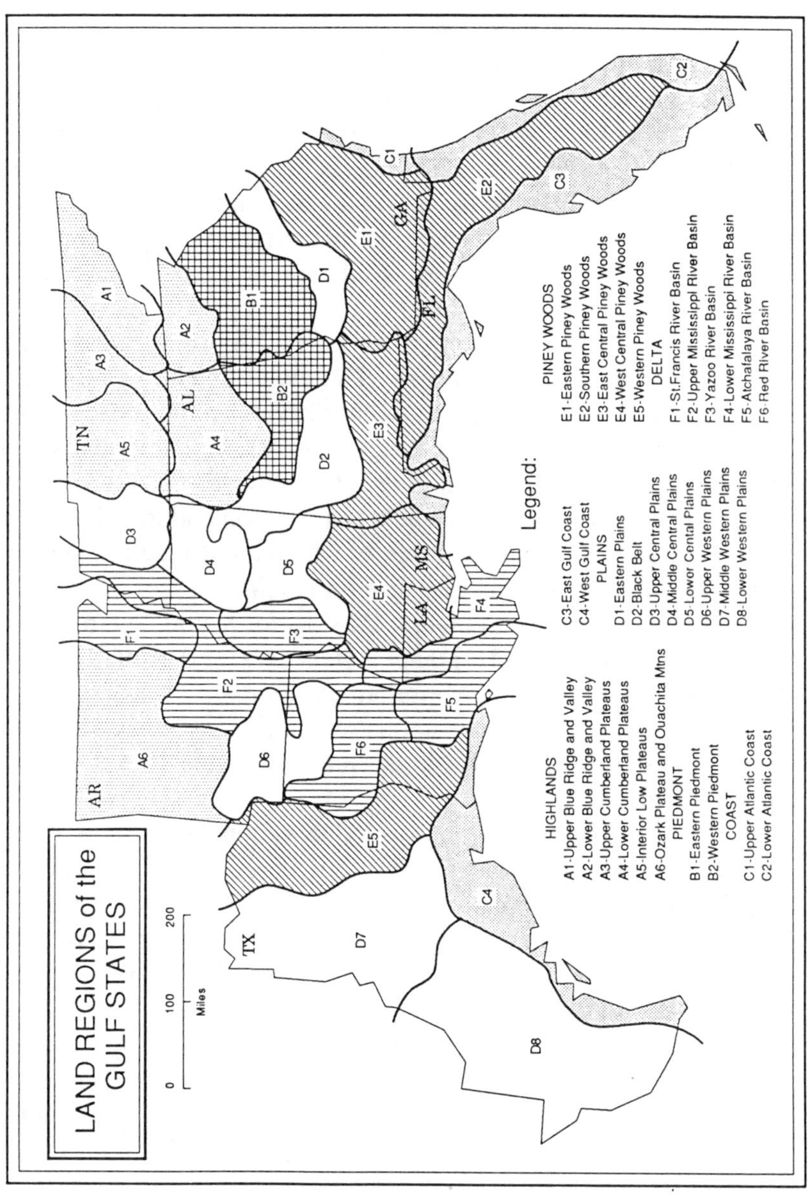

Figure 3. LAGS regions

In the first 15 lines, Synopsis #25 lists 73 of the 74 phonetic targets, excluding only the vowel /oi/ before nasals, as in *joints*. The empty slot in line five reflects a peculiarity of unitary phonemic analysis: the mid-central vowel before postvocalic /r/ becomes a member of the /ɜ/ phoneme of line 12. Elsewhere, the phonetic substance of each phoneme is exemplified in five positions (columns): (1) before a voiceless obstruent, (2) before open juncture or a voiced consonant, (3) before a nasal consonant, (4) before a lateral liquid consonant, and (5) before a retroflex liquid consonant.

The second section has three parts, including noun plurals, function words, and verb forms. The example shows uninflected plurals for *post*, *pound*, and *wasp*, but provides no text for *shrimp* or *desk*. The next line illustrates function words, in this case *quarter to* (the hour) and (sick) *at your stomach*, but provides no text for *toward*, *ran into*, or (wait) *for you*. The next four lines intend to exhibit principal parts of eight verb forms, seven of which are realized in part in the Wear Valley record, with no evidence for *climb*.

The final seven lines include 28 slots for regional words. Missing here are synonyms for *wishbone*, *pancakes*, and a small gift (such as *countra* among Florida Minorcans, *lagniappe* in Louisiana, and *pilón* in Texas). The 25 texts in this section, nevertheless, share many features of American English in the East Tennessee Blue Ridge division (A1, Figure 3).

Figures 4-6 are three more LAGS synopses of male, middle-class, white informants, who are age 76 with elementary-school education. These summarize features in three other land regions of the Gulf States -- the Piney Woods of Alabama (#444) and Mississippi (#582), as well as the Red River Basin of Louisiana (#800). All three might be called 'Deep South' communities -- near or below the Thirty-Second Parallel, south of Montgomery, Jackson, and Vicksburg.

The four synopses include many linguistic correspondences.

Beyond the general currency words -- *cottage cheese*, *crawfish*, *gruel*, *milk pen*, *pancakes*, *peanuts*, and *string beans* -- the forms show recurrent incidence of *firedogs*, *flambeau (deal)*, *souse*, *clear seed (peach)*, *(mo)squito hawk*, *mantelboard*, *crocus sack*, *pirogue*, *red-worm*, *red bug*, *French harp*, *harp*, *pulley bone*, *mush*, *tommyto*,

MMY 76 1A
GB/76:LP/76

LA GANTT
CG 283.01

/ɪ/	* hwɪ˃ ᵊp	* kr̥ɪ˃bz	* t̟ʻɪ˄ᵊn	hɪ˄.ᵊl̩	* ɪ:ə
/ɛ/	nɛ˄k	* le˅·ɪg	tʻɛ˃n	nɛ́˄·ʎɪ̆	mɛ̂˄r̮ɪ krɪ́˄sməs
/æ/	* glæᵉs	* bæ·ᵉgz	* hǽᵋmmə̆	vǽ·ʎɪ̆˄	* mɛ́˄·r̮ɪ̆d
/ʊ/	* pʻʊ˂·ʃ	* wʊ˂ᵊd	wʊ́:·mn̩̆	* pʻʊ˂l̩	ʃʊ˂ᵊ
/ʌ/	* bʌ́:kɪ̆t	* hʌ́˂ᵊzbn̩̆	s̬ʌ́˂nʌ̀˂·p	* bʌ̯ᵊɯb	fʌ́˂·ʳə̆
/ɑ/	* kr̥ɑ˃·p	fɑ́·ðə̆	pʻɑ˃ᵊm	k̟ʻɑ́˂ʎɪ̆dʒ	* kʻɑ˃ᵊ˞
/i/	ji˃·st	* ˢθr̥i˃	bi˃·nz	* fi˃ᵊld	bɪʲəd
/e/	e˅ɪt	me˃ɪ	* stre˃ɪn	re˃ɪl	mé˅·r̮ɪ̆
/u/	tʻʊ˂ʉθ	bǽ·tˀn̩̆ rʉ̀ʉdʒ	wʊ˂͡ʉ˂:nᵈ	* mjʉ·lz	* pʻʊ˂ə̣
/o/	kʻo˂ɵt	əgó˂ɵ	* ho˂ɵm	kʻo˂ɵɫd	hɔ˄·əs
/ɔ/	dɔ́˅·ɔ˄t̬ə̆	dɔ˅·o˄g	gɔ˅on	sɒˀɫt	* hɔ˅·ᵊs
/ɜ/	* tʃɜ̮·ᶦtʃ	θə̣d	* wɜ̮·mz	* gɜ̮·ɫ	stɜ́·ə̆˄ps
/aɪ/	ra˃·ᶦt	ra:ᶦd	na:ᵋn	* ma·ᶦlz	* wá·ᶦə̆
/aʊ/	* ha˄ʊ˂s	* kʻa˄o˂z	* da˄o˂n	* a˃·əlz	fla˃·wə̆z
/ɔɪ/	ɔ́ɪ˅·stə̮̆z	pʻɔ́˄ɪ˅zn̩̆	dʒɔ˄ə˄nts	ɔ˅·ᵊl	—
PL	pʻo˂ɵst	* pa˄onᵈ	ˢʃrɪ͂:mp	wɒ˄ᵊsts	—
FW	* kwɔ̂·t̬ə̣ df̆	kʻʌ̂˂mn̩ tɵʉ mì˃	rǽᵋn ʌ́˂p ɔ̀:n	ɪ̆t ðə̆ stʌ́˂·mɪ̆k	—

— / r̮o˂ʉ̯˅z / r̮ɪ́˃·ᵊzn̩̆	dra·ᶦv ~ dra·ᵋv / dro˂ɵv / –
dræ·ᵉg / — / —	i˃·t / e:t / i˃·t ~ í:·tˀn̩̆
drɪ͂:ŋk / dræ:ᵋŋk / dræ͂ᵋŋk	hɛ˃ᵊp / hɛ˃ᵊpt / hɛ˃ᵊp
da˃ᶦv / do˂ɵv / dɪ́˃ᵊvn̩̆	kla·ᶦm / — / kl̥ʌ˂m ~ kla·ᶦmd

fá:ə dɔ̀˅·o˄gz	mǽ·nɪ̆l̮ bò:·ɔ˃d	kʻá˄ʊ˂ p̀ɛ͂:n	—
* pʻé:ɪpə̆ bæ̀ᵉgz	* kró˂ɵkə̆ sæ̀ᵋk	* ha˃·˞p	* rá·ᶦdɪ̆˄ hɔ̀˄·ɚs
ə̆ flǽᵋmbò˂ dî˃·ᵊl	* r̮ó˂ɵ bò˂ɵt	pʻʊ́˂ʎɪ̆ bò͂˂ʊ˂n	* pʻǽᵋn kè·ɪks
* sa˃·ʊ˂s	kʻá˃·tᶠɪ̆dʒ tʃì˃·z	* mʌ́˂·ᵊʃ	ə̆ prɛ́˃ᵊs (art.+n.)
kl̥ɪ́:ə sì˃·dz	* pʻɪ́:ndə̆z	* tʻá˃mɪ̆˅tò˂	strɪ́:ŋ bì˃·nz
pʻɛ́˃kə̆wʊ̀˂ᵊdz	* ɪ̂˄ŋlɪ̆ʃ wɜ̮·mz	* gó˂·ɵfə̆	* kŕɔ˅ɔ˄ fɪ̀˄ʃ
* mə̆skí˃·t̬ə̆ hɒ̀˄ˀks	* rɛ́˃·d bʌ̀ˠgz	—	—

Figure 4. LAGS idiolect synopsis #444

MMY 76 1A
MB/80:LP/80

LM QUITMAN
DT 375.01

/ɪ/	* hwɪ>·ᵊp	krɪ^·ᵊb	tʻɪ^n	* hɪ·ᵊtz	* ɪ꞉ɚ
/ɛ/	nɛ̨꞉k	lɛ·ᵻgz	* tʻɛ^n	nɛ̃^ʒɨ	mɛ^ɾɨ
/æ/	græ^·ᵋs ha>ᵊpəz	bæ^ᵋgz	hæ·ᵋmə	væ·ᵋʒɨ	* mɛ꞉rɨd
/ʊ/	* pʻʊ꞉·ᵊʃ	* wʊ<ᵊd	* wʊ̃<ᵊmn̩	* pʻʊ<t	* ʃʊ<ᵊ
/ʌ/	ʃʌ<t	hʌ꞉ᵊzbn̩	sʌ<n ʌ<p	bʌ<ᵊb	
/ɑ/	kra>ᵊp	fa>ᵊtə	* dʒɑ<꞉ᵊn	kʻa·lɨdʒ	* kʻa>·ɚ
/i/	ʲi>·st	* θr̥i>·	bi>·nz	fi>·ᵊtd	bɪ^·ɚd
/e/	* e>ɨt	* me>ɨ	stre꞉ɨnd	* re>ɨt	me꞉ɾɨ
/u/	tʻʉʉθ	bæ·ᵋtʔn̩ rʉʉdʒ	wʉ̃ʉ·n	mjɨʉlz	pʻʉ^ɚ
/o/	kʻo<ʉt	jɪ>ɚz əgo<·ʉ	* ho<·ʉm	kʻo<ʉtd	ho^·ɚs
/ɔ/	dɑ<·ɔ^tɚz	dɔ^o^g	* gɔ^o^n	wɒᵊtnəts	* hɔ^ɚs
/ɜ/	* tʃɚtʃ	θɚd	* wɚmz	* gɚ·ᵊtz	wɜ꞉ɾɨ
/aɪ/	* ra>·ᵋt	ra>ᵋd	na>ᵋn	* ma>·ᵋt (pl.)	wa>·ᵋɚ
/aʊ/	* ha꞉ʉs	* kʻa꞉ʉ	* da꞉ʉn	* æ꞉ʉt	* fl̥a꞉·wəz
/ɔɪ/	ɔ^ɨ·stəz	pʻɔ^·əzn̩	dʒɔ̃^ə^nts	* ɔ^·ᵊt	—
PL	* pʻo<ʉst	* pʻa^ʉn	§ ʃrɪ̃^ᵊmp	wɑ<ᵊsp	dɛ>ᵊsk
FW	kwɔ̂ɔ^tɚtt	* təwo^·ɚdz	ɪ^n tʉʉ	ɨt ɨz stʌ<·ᵊmɨk	—

ra>·ᵋz / ro<ʉz / ɾɪ>ᵊzn̩	dra>·ᵋv / dro<ʉv ~ dro<·ʉv / drɪ>ᵊvn̩
dræ^ᵋg / drʌ꞉ᵊg / drʌ꞉ᵊg	i>·t / e>ɨt ~ i>·t / i>·tʔn̩
drɪ̃^ŋk / dræ̃^ᵋŋk ~ drɪ꞉ŋk / drʌ̃^ŋk	hɛ>ᵊp / hɛ>ᵊtpt ~ hɛ>ᵊtptʔ / hɛ>ᵊt ptʔ
da·ᵋv / dɪ>ᵊv / dɪ>ᵊvd	kla>·ᵋm / klʌ<ᵊm / kla·ᵋmd

fa>·ᵋə a>·ᵻənz	mæ^ᵋnʃt bo^·əd	kʻa꞉ʉ pʻɛ̃꞉n	sto<ʉn fɛ^ntsɨz
* pʻe·ɨpə sæᵋk	* kro<ʉk ə sæᵋk	* frɛ̃^ntʃ hɑ·ɚp	si꞉i>sɔ^ɔ^
* flæ^ᵋm bo<ʉz	* pʻi>·ro<ʉz	pʻʊ<·ʃɨ bo<ʉn	* pʻæ̃·ᵋn ke>ɨks
* sa꞉ᵘs	kʻa>ᵊtɨdʒ / tʃi·z	* grɨʉ ət	pr̥ɛ>ᵊs
klɪ꞉ɚ si>d	pʻi>·nəts	lɪ·ᵊtt təme>ɨtəz	* ŋʲæᵋp bi>·nz (=snap)
* wʊ<ᵊd tʃʌ꞉ᵊk	* rɛ>ᵊd wɚ<m	* hɪ·ᵊt tʻæ·ɚspn̩	krɔ^ɔ^ fɪ·ʃ
* ski>·tə hɒᵊk	* rɛ꞉ᵊd bʌ<ᵊg	* sɛ>·rɨne>ɨd	* læ̃ᵋnj æᵋp

Figure 5. LAGS idiolect synopsis #582

MMY 76 1B
BR/75:SL/76

WL ENTERPRISE
FX 536.02

/ɪ/	* hwɪ˃p	kr̥ɪ˃b	* tʻɪ˃ᵊn	hɪ˃ᵊɨz	* ɪːɚ
/ɛ/	nɛːk	lɛ·ɪg	* tʻɪ˃n	* dʒɛᵊʃɪz	mɛ̀ɚ<ɪ kr̥ɪ˃s mə́s
/æ/	gl̥æ^ᵋs	bæ^ᵋg	* hæᵋmmɚ	* væ^ᵋʃɪ	mæ^ɚɪd
/ʊ/	pʻʊːᵊʃ	* wʊːd	—	* pʻʊ<ᵊɨ	* ʃʊ<ɚ
/ʌ/	ʃɜt	hʌ<ʳz bɚ	sʌ<nra^·ɪz	* bɤːb	
/ɑ/	kr̥a˄p	fa^·ɪɚ	* dʒa˃·ᵊn	kʻa^·lɪ˃dʒɪz	* kʻa^ɚ
/i/	ʔi˃·st	* θr̥i˃·	* bi˃·nz	fi˃·ᵊɨ	bʲɪːɚd
/e/	e˃ɪt	me˅ɪ	str̥e˃ɪn	re˃·ᵊɨ	mɛ^·ɚɪ
/u/	* tʻʉ˅ʉ·θ	bæ^tʔn̩ rʉʉʃ	wʉʉnd	mɪʉ·ɨz	pʻʊ<ɚ
/o/	kʻo<·ʉt	* jɪ˃ɚ əgo<ʉ	ho<·ʉm	kʻo<ʉl̩	ho<ɚs
/ɔ/	dɔ<tɚ	* dɔ˅ɔ^gz	* gɔ˅ɔ^n	* sɔ˅ɔ^ɨt	* hɔː·ɚs
/ɜ/	* tʃɚ<tʃ	θɚd	wɚmz	* gɚɨ	* wɚ<ɪ
/aɪ/	ra^·ɪt	raː·ɪd	* na^·ɪn	ma^·ɪlz	wa<ɚ
/aʊ/	* hæ˅o<s	* kʻæ˅o<	* dæ˅o<n	æ˅o<ɨ	fl̥æ˅o<wɚz
/ɔɪ/	ɔ<ᵋ stɚ	* pʻɔ<ɪzn̩	dʒɔːɪ^nts	ɔ<ᵋl	—
PL	pʻo<ʉst	—	ʃrɪ˃mp	* wa^·s	dɛːskɪz
FW	fɪ˃ftin tʻɪ˃ᵊl	tʻɪwɔ<dz	* rʌ<n ʌ<p ɔ<n	ɪ˃n ðɪ stʌ<mək	we˃ɪtɪŋ fɜɚ

ra^·ɪz / ro<ʉz / rɪː·zn̩	dra^·ɪv / dro<ʉv / ədro<ʉv
dʒɪæ^ᵋg / drʌ<ʳg / drʌ<ʳg	i˃·t / i˃t / ɛ·t
dʒɪɪːŋk ~ drɛ˃ŋk / — / —	hɛ˃p ~ hɛᵊp / * hɛᵊpt ~ hɛ˃p / * hɛᵊpt
da^ɪv / do<·ʉv / dɪ˃v	kl̥a^·ɪm / kl̥ʌ<m / kl̥a^·ɪmd

* fa^ɚ dɔ˅ɔ^gz	mæ^ᵋnnɨ bo<ɚd	kʻæ˅o< pʻɪːᵊn	ra^k fɪ˃nts
* pʻe˃ᵋpɚ bæ^ᵋgz	* græ·ᵋs sæᵋks	ha·ɚp	ra^·ɪdɪ hɔːɚs
—	* pʻi·iro<ʉz	pʻʊ<lɪ bo<ʉnz	* fl̥ɪ˃ʃɚz
sæ˅·o<s	—	grʉʉ·ɛ˃l	pr̥ɛ·s
kl̥ɜ<ɚ si˃·d	pʻi˃·nʌ<ts	* tʻa^mɪto<ʉz	* str̥ɛːŋ bi˃·nz
* ɪ˃ndɪən hɪ˃nz	* rɛːd wɚm	tʻæ^ɚpɪn	kr̥ɔ˅ɔ^ fɪ˃ʃ
məski˃·tə haːɔ^ks	* rɛːd bɚgz	ʃɪ˃vɚɪ (v.)	—

Figure 6. LAGS idiolect synopsis #800

terrapin, *serenade*, *rock fence*, *ridy-horse*, *seesaw*, and *press (peach)*. All of these enter regional patterns in Gulf States speech. They also record single instances of these critical units in regional word geography: *dog irons*, *poke*, *souse meat*, *snake feeder*, *tow sack*, *chigger*, *gap*, and *crawdad* in #25; *pinders* and *gopher* (plains tortoise) in #444; *stone fence*, *snap beans*, and *lagniappe* in #582; *Indian hen*, *grass sack*, *shivaree*, and *flitters* in #800.

Recurrent grammatical features include function words, as well as inflections of nouns and verbs. Among the function words are (quarter/fifteen) *till* (the hour), (sick) *at* (his/the/your stomach), and (ran) *up on* ['encountered']. Distinctive preterits occur among the principal parts of *climb* (*clum*), *dive* (*div*), *drag* (*drug*), and *eat* (*eat*) [unmarked]. Uninflected noun plurals of *pound*, *post*, and *wasp* also reflect the morphophonemics of folk speech.

In pronunciation the four synopses report the most striking correspondences. All four include substantial incidence of post-vocalic /r/ in tautosyllabic environments, vocalization, or total assimilation of /l/ in *bulb*, contrasting vowels in *hoarse* and *horse*, voiceless fricative onset /h/ in *whip*, intervocalic 'clear' /l/ in *Nelly*, *jelly*, and *valley*, upgliding low back / ɔ / before voiced obstruents (as in *dog*), raised onsets of /au/ before obstruents and nasals, ingliding offsets of /oi/, and several other features recurrent in two or more synopses.

Such information outlines no dialect area with authority, but it gives a reader a hint at protocol content. As indexed in the concordance, protocol notation points toward the tape/text. Thus, the fiche/text explicitly identifies the work completed and makes the atlas vulnerable to proofs. The protocols identify all forms that scribes recorded from the tape/text, and those preliminary documents also invite observers to evaluate the thoroughness and accuracy of the phonetic notations. In the process, auditors can assess the quality of the field work, as well as the contexts in which the recorded strings are heard.

The concordance also offers links to further synthesis and analysis. In reducing phonetic texts to orthographics, the index identifies the product of every phonographic conversion in the data base. It follows simple rules without exception and tries to show exactly what is going on. The word analysis of the disk/text proceeds directly from the fiche/text. In that way, the protocols, the idiolect synopses, and the concordance combine to make LAGS an open book.

The Disk/Text

This analogue of the tape/text rewrites LAGS data in ASCII files. These combine with mapping programs to form an automatic atlas in microform. The term *automatic* means more than automated, but less than magic. It uses mechanics, intuition, and a common-sense progression from simple to complicated problems in the data base. It depends upon microcomputer resources which point the most casual observer to the next step in the analytical chain. The process illustrates itself in the course of the work, particularly in the application of phonographic codes and in the mapping of data from files.

Disk/text files include four graphic analogues, indexed in three writing systems and coded in ASCII. The alphabet provides abbreviations for all lexical and some grammatical files. These include entries found in traditional word geographies. All graphophonemic files appear in the orthography of the Automatic Book Code (ABC), a system that records unitary phonemes (consonants, vowels, and stress), deleted units, and as many phonetic differences as are needed to characterize the contents of a file. All phonetic files record distinctive features as orthographic strings in the code of Systematic Phonetics (SP). So far, these apply only to stressed vowels because the work has not yet recommended analysis of consonant features. Neither code requires special software or keyboard characters beyond those of an ordinary IBM PC. Susan Leas McDaniel and William H. McDaniel, Jr. wrote all LAGS programs in BASIC, and each sorting and mapping program is a self-explanatory and independent tool (McDaniel, 1989).

With such tools, anyone can run LAGS programs and create new files without special equipment. This resource gives the atlas its recursive attribute. Because maps, files, and indexes are given as preliminary analogues to the data base, readers can follow the chain back to the tape/text, creating new files from the field records and producing as many maps as may be needed to solve a problem.

Lexical Files

Lexical files include 591 sets of contrastive data. Of these, 390 report responses to regular work-sheet items; the remaining 201 files cover the urban supplement. The disk/text orders each lexical target as a file and list. The file records the information to be mapped by the program. The list first indicates the number of informants who offered no response, then the incidence of appropriate forms, the inappropriate responses rejected by the editors, and, finally, all recorded combinations (multiple responses). Numbered according to work-sheet page and line, the file and its list directs the reader back to the LAGS work sheet for the context.

For example, *open stone* (peach) in Synopsis #25 responds to page 54, line 4, in the work sheets:

> freestone peach *clear seed peach, *soft peach, *clear stone, *free seed, *slip seed
>
> L: The other kind where it is not [i.e., not tight against the stone]?
> M: The kind of peach you break open and take the seed out of?

The entry shows what the field worker had to work with -- a target, several synonyms (if suggestions are needed) and the ways in which Guy Lowman ([L]) and Raven I. McDavid, Jr., ([M]) approached the item in other atlas projects.

The list (Figure 7) includes 54 appropriate responses, coded *A-bb*. Charted by the LAGSMAP program, three recurrent and apparently related synonyms (*ag open peach*, *ah open seed*, and *ai open stone*) cluster in East and Middle Tennessee, as well as Upper Georgia (Figure 8). The same program maps the term *J clear seed* that appears in the other three synopses, as well as *K clear seed peach* (Figure 9). These maps offer a contrast of usage in northern (Highlands and Piedmont) and southern (Piney Woods and Plains) divisions of the Gulf States. On the maps, the four LAGS informants are identified at these grid coordinates #25 (D/57), #444 (O/43), #582 (N/39), and #800 (O/28).

No Response (233)

A break peach (1)
B breaking-open peach (1)
C busting-open peach (1)
D canning peach (1)
E clay stone peach (1)
F clear (2)
G clear cut (1)
H clear one (1)
I clear peach (3)
J clear seed (180)
K clear seed peach (43)
L clear seeded (1)
M clear seeded peach (2)
N clear sing peach (1)
O clear stone (35)
P clear stone peach (4)
Q clears peach (1)
R cling free (3)
S cling peach (1)
T eating peach (2)
U Firestone peach (1)
V free (5)
W free cling (2)
X free seed (6)
Y free seed peach (1)
Z freestone (290)
aa freestone Indian peach (1)
ab freestone peach (35)
ac juice peach (1)
ad loose peach (1)
ae mellow peach (2)
af open heart (1)
ag open peach (4)
ah open seed (3)
ai open stone (29)
aj peach (4)
ak peche a jus [F] (1)
al peche au jus [F] (1)
am (pe)tit noyau [F] (1)
an plum (1)
ao press peach (2)
ap regular peach (1)
aq ripe peach (1)
ar seedless (1)
as slip seed (1)
at smooth stone (1)
au soft (2)
av soft cling peach (1)
aw soft peach (9)
ax stone free (2)
ay stone peach (1)
az white clear seed (1)
ba white English peach (1)
bb yellow clear seed (1)

Inappropriate/Substitute Responses

Belle of Georgia peach
Elberta
Elberta peach
Fair Beauty
Georgia Belle
Georgia Belle peach
Georgia Boy
Georgia peach
nectarine

Figure 7. LAGS lexical list {054.4} ('freestone peach')

A *open peach* (4)
B *open seed* (3)
C *open stone* (29)
\+ *open peach* + *open stone*
\# *open seed* + *open stone*
. another response or no response

Figure 8. Open (seed/stone) peach {054.4}

A *clear seed* (180)
B *clear seed peach* (43)
. another response or no response

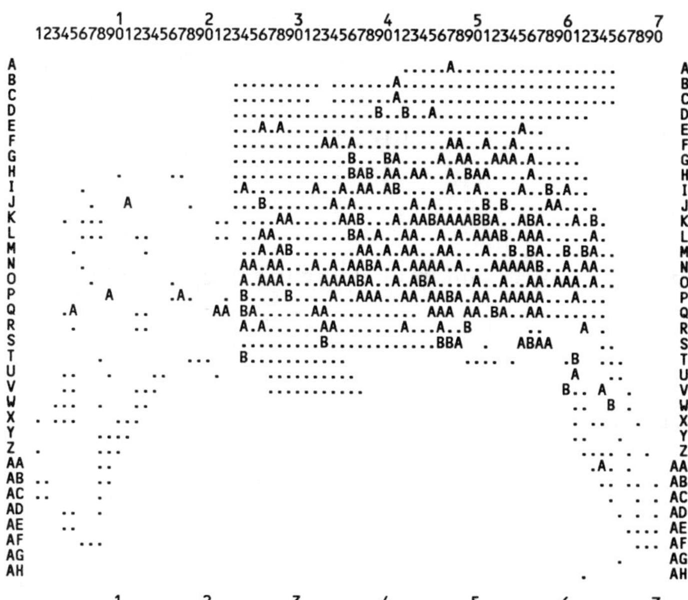

Figure 9. Clear seed (peach) {054.4}

The SECTOTAL program tabulates responses according to the 16 sectors of the LAGS grid (Figure 1): Arkansas (AR), West Tennessee (WT), Middle Tennessee (MT), East Tennessee (ET), West Louisiana (WL), Upper Mississippi (UM), Upper Alabama (UA), Upper Georgia (UG), Upper Texas (UT), Lower Mississippi (LM), Lower Alabama (LA), Lower Georgia (LG), Lower Texas (LT), West Gulf, including East Louisiana and Gulf Mississippi (WG), East Gulf, including Gulf Alabama and West Florida (EG), and East Florida (EF). The matrix has this configuration:

```
AR WT MT ET
WL UM UA UG
UT LM LA LG
LT WG EG EF
```

This matrix is illustrated in mapping the five synonyms of 'freestone peach':

```
open peach        open seed         open stone
{054.4} 4         {054.4} 3         {054.4} 29

0  1  0  1        0  0  1  1        0  1  5 18
1  0  0  1        0  0  0  0        0  0  0  4
0  0  0  0        0  0  0  0        0  0  0  0
0  0  0  0        0  1  0  0        1  0  0  0

      clear seed        clear seed peach
      {054.4} 180          {054.4} 43

       3  2  2  1         1  2  0  0
      17 12 17 22         5  4  3  8
       6 18 31 32         0  3  4  5
       0  4  7  6         0  1  3  4
```

open peach {054.4} 4/914 0%

A	2/207	1%	B	0/84	0%	C	0/109	0%	D	0/176	0%	E	0/181	0%	F	2/157	1%
A1	1/52	2%	B1	0/59	0%	C1	0/12	0%	D1	0/19	0%	E1	0/55	0%	F1	0/15	0%
A2	1/20	5%	B2	0/25	0%	C2	0/23	0%	D2	0/30	0%	E2	0/29	0%	F2	1/49	2%
A3	0/18	0%				C3	0/48	0%	D3	0/17	0%	E3	0/33	0%	F3	0/15	0%
A4	0/37	0%				C4	0/26	0%	D4	0/22	0%	E4	0/37	0%	F4	0/31	0%
A5	0/39	0%							D5	0/19	0%	E5	0/27	0%	F5	0/24	0%
A6	0/41	0%							D6	0/17	0%				F6	1/23	4%
									D7	0/23	0%						
									D8	0/29	0%						

open seed {054.4} 3/914 0%

A	2/207	1%	B	0/84	0%	C	0/109	0%	D	0/176	0%	E	1/181	1%	F	0/157	0%
A1	1/52	2%	B1	0/59	0%	C1	0/12	0%	D1	0/19	0%	E1	0/55	0%	F1	0/15	0%
A2	0/20	0%	B2	0/25	0%	C2	0/23	0%	D2	0/30	0%	E2	0/29	0%	F2	0/49	0%
A3	0/18	0%				C3	0/48	0%	D3	0/17	0%	E3	0/33	0%	F3	0/15	0%
A4	0/37	0%				C4	0/26	0%	D4	0/22	0%	E4	1/37	3%	F4	0/31	0%
A5	1/39	3%							D5	0/19	0%	E5	0/27	0%	F5	0/24	0%
A6	0/41	0%							D6	0/17	0%				F6	0/23	0%
									D7	0/23	0%						
									D8	0/29	0%						

open stone {054.4} 29/914 3%

A	27/207	13%	B	0/84	0%	C	1/109	1%	D	1/176	1%	E	0/181	0%	F	0/157	0%
A1	17/52	33%	B1	0/59	0%	C1	0/12	0%	D1	0/19	0%	E1	0/55	0%	F1	0/15	0%
A2	4/20	20%	B2	0/25	0%	C2	0/23	0%	D2	0/30	0%	E2	0/29	0%	F2	0/49	0%
A3	4/18	22%				C3	0/48	0%	D3	1/17	6%	E3	0/33	0%	F3	0/15	0%
A4	0/37	0%				C4	1/26	4%	D4	0/22	0%	E4	0/37	0%	F4	0/31	0%
A5	2/39	5%							D5	0/19	0%	E5	0/27	0%	F5	0/24	0%
A6	0/41	0%							D6	0/17	0%				F6	0/23	0%
									D7	0/23	0%						
									D8	0/29	0%						

clear seed (peach) {054.4} 223/914 24%

A	26/207	13%	B	35/84	42%	C	9/109	8%	D	51/176	29%	E	86/181	48%	F	16/157	10%
A1	1/52	2%	B1	23/59	39%	C1	1/12	8%	D1	8/19	42%	E1	29/55	53%	F1	0/15	0%
A2	6/20	30%	B2	12/25	48%	C2	0/23	0%	D2	13/30	43%	E2	12/29	41%	F2	4/49	8%
A3	0/18	0%				C3	7/48	15%	D3	4/17	24%	E3	18/33	55%	F3	2/15	13%
A4	15/37	41%				C4	1/26	4%	D4	7/22	32%	E4	20/37	54%	F4	0/31	0%
A5	2/39	5%							D5	9/19	47%	E5	7/27	26%	F5	1/24	4%
A6	2/41	5%							D6	7/17	41%				F6	9/23	39%
									D7	3/23	13%						
									D8	0/29	0%						

Figure 10. Area totals {054.4} ('freestone peach')

The AREATOT program reports information according to the six land regions and 31 subdivisions (Figure 3). Each matrix includes total incidence for the region and for each subdivision, as well as simple percentage statements after each sum. Figure 10 summarizes the five synonyms for 'freestone peach.' Editors evaluate incidence here according to the regional mean. In a land area or its subdivisions, significant incidence of a form means its total at least equals the regional average and includes at least three occurrences of the form. This arbitrary standard is useful in interpreting LAGS data, where forms are rarely confined to one subdivision or even a single region.

This interpretation automatically excludes *open peach* and *open seed*. It shows the *open stone* variant as significant only in the Highlands (A), concentrated in the East Tennessee Blue Ridge (A1) with numbers worth noting also in the Georgia Blue Ridge (A2) and the East and Middle Tennessee Cumberland Plateaus. In contrast, *clear seed* recurs significantly in five of six land regions, with the steadiest concentration in the Piedmont (B1-2) and the Piney Woods (E1-5). The full form *clear seed peach* adds the East Gulf Coast to the pattern.

A fourth matrix program, SOCTOTAL, identifies incidence of a form according to nine sets of social characteristics: (1) racial caste, (2) gender, (3) perspective, (4) narrow age grouping, (5) broad age grouping, (6) formal education, (7) Warner's social class, (8) O'Cain's speech type, and (9) Kurath's informant type. The classification of *perspective* reports designations A/B after Kurath *et al.* (1939), *social class* after Warner *et al.* (1960) -- reducing eleven social groups to three, *speech type* after O'Cain (1972) -- based on observations of field worker and scribe, and *informant type* after Kurath *et al.* (1939). The program reports information in this configuration:

```
1)  Black    4) 14-30  31-60   61-99    197 108 224 582
1)  White    5) 14-45  46-70   71-99    717 197 317 400
2)  Female   6) Elem.  High    College  422 350 333 231
2)  Male     7) Lower  Middle  Upper    492 295 513 106
3)  Insular  8) Folk   Common  Cultured 529 344 352 218
3)  Worldly  9) I      II      III      385 349 348 217
```

It summarizes social incidence for the three principal synonyms in these matrix maps:

open stone {054.4} 29				*clear seed* {054.4} 180				*clear seed peach* {054.4} 43			
1	0	5	24	32	3	30	147	17	0	9	34
28	2	6	21	148	9	60	111	26	5	17	21
13	19	7	3	87	92	62	26	19	22	16	5
16	14	14	1	93	61	107	12	24	22	19	2
26	17	11	1	131	86	71	23	34	26	14	3
3	17	11	1	49	87	69	24	9	25	15	3

A fifth program, CODEMAP, combines the basic graphic plotter grid of the LAGSMAP format with the social characteristics of the SOCTOTAL program. Figure 11 maps incidence according to the 'Code 1' CODEMAP configuration (race, class, and age) -- the SOCTOTAL codes 1, 7, and 4, respectively.

Grammatical Files

Grammatical files cover work-sheet items that produce structural, rather than lexical, contrasts. These include 209 sets of function words, verbs, animal calls, and other nonlexical forms. The simplest of these files reports deletion of six function words -- verb copula, conjunction, article, preposition, relative pronoun, and verb auxiliary. Figure 12 maps preposition deletion. Like all files written in conventional orthography, this set takes its information from the concordance. Here, the map identifies the 627 informants whose protocols include at least one instance of preposition deletion.

Code 1: Race/Class/Age

1	=	W/L/13-30	0/5	A	=	B/L/13-30	3/13
2	=	W/M/13-30	6/67	B	=	B/M/13-30	2/13
3	=	W/U/13-30	1/10	C	=	B/U/13-30	0/1
4	=	W/L/31-60	6/25	D	=	B/L/31-60	5/19
5	=	W/M/31-60	31/118	E	=	B/M/31-60	2/25
6	=	W/U/31-60	7/33	F	=	B/U/31-60	1/4
7	=	W/L/61-99	64/149	G	=	B/L/61-99	39/84
8	=	W/M/61-99	86/256	H	=	B/M/61-99	19/35
9	=	W/U/61-99	10/54	J	=	B/U/61-99	1/3

Figure 11. *Dog irons* {008.3} 283

Code 2: Race/Class/Age

1	=	W/L/13-45	7/12	A	=	B/L/13-45	14/21
2	=	W/M/13-45	54/110	B	=	B/M/13-45	18/29
3	=	W/U/13-45	7/23	C	=	B/U/13-45	1/3
4	=	W/L/46-70	44/63	D	=	B/L/46-70	37/41
5	=	W/M/46-70	105/155	E	=	B/M/46-70	13/17
6	=	W/U/46-70	19/38	F	=	B/U/46-70	2/3
7	=	W/L/71-99	83/104	G	=	B/L/71-99	50/54
8	=	W/M/71-99	122/176	H	=	B/M/71-99	23/27
9	=	W/U/71-99	27/36	J	=	B/U/71-99	1/2

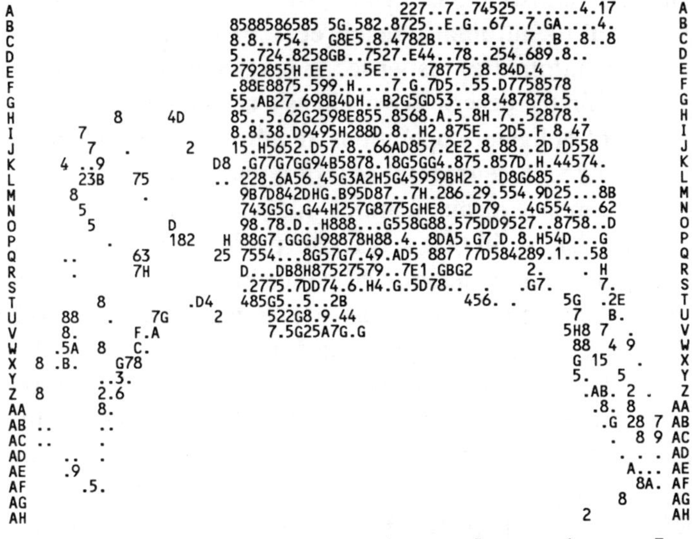

Figure 12. Deleted prepositions 627

ABC notation records verb forms and graphophonemic targets. This graphophonemic code (G) unites the synthetic systems of ordinary orthographics (O) and concordance orthographics (C), on the one hand, and analytic systems of phonetic notation (P) and Systematic Phonetics (S) on the other. The five components are links in a chain that extends from the terminal synthesis of ordinary writing to the terminal analysis of Systematic Phonetics: O>< C >< G >< P >< S.

ABC Files

Basically a keyboard-compatible unitary phonemic code, the ABC system has five distinctive characteristics. All reflect the design of the disk/text and its automatic resources. First, ABC records intuitive (cognitively automatic) responses to language signals. Second, ABC operates within the descriptive chain as a self-regulating mechanism. It forms a set of obligatory operations, requiring a scribe to make a graphic decision at each segmental unit of a phonetic string -- segmenting contrastive units as formal features, like an automatic lathe in machine metal work. Third, in that way, ABC performs tasks of phonological word geography at predetermined points in an operation (at the boundaries of a phonological word), like an automatic feeder in modern printing. Fourth, ABC provides automated (machine readable) phonographics for atlas texts, whether disks or hardcopy books. Finally, ABC depends primarily on the resources of the English alphabet, the primary book code of Western civilization. All five considerations turn on the final point: they are inseparable from the classical form and traditional applications of the alphabet. In that code, intuitive conversions reduce speech to writing with greater ease and authority than is possible with any other phonographic system. The Roman/English alphabet transmits collective intelligence, experience, and learning, sharpened by several thousand years of cultural interaction.

Figure 13 identifies ABC letters and numbers, the primary graphic code for LAGS phonological description. Recorded in carets, the code follows the example of concordance orthographics. It notes deleted letters in parens, as, for example, in the three plural forms in

Synopsis #25: <poest(s)>, <pown(dz)>, and <waws(ps)>. It also records the phonotactic sequences in conventional form, for example, as <whips> not <*hwips>, as <gurl> not <*grl>, and <drink> not <*dringk>.

ABC records vocalized consonants in square brackets, as, for example, the pronunciations in Synopsis #25 of vocalized <l> in *bulb* <bu[l]b]>, *walnuts* <waw[l]nAts=14>, *help* <he[l]p>, and <he[l]pt> and in #444 of vocalized <r> in *sure* <shoo[r]>, *beard* <bee[r]d>, *hoarse* <hoe[r]s>, and other words. Phonemic vowel nasality replacing nasal segments also recurs in other LAGS records, yielding *ham* <ha[m]>, *tin* <ti[n]>, and *thing* <thi[ng]>.

Finally, braces identify subphonemic contrasts within files. For example, weakly retroflex <r> recurs in #444. In *horse*, ABC notation might include braces to mark that phonetic feature in the file: <haw{r}s>. In that file, braced <{r}> means only weakly retroflex, but in another file the notation could signal a devoiced <r>, as in *tree*, a flapped <r> as in *three*, or a labialized <r> as in *pretty*.

Figure 14 lists the contents of ABC file {071.5B}, *right ear*. It includes 88 different strings, five multiple responses, and six subphonemic distinctions. The list illustrates five features recorded in the four idiolect synopses: (1) a palatal onset <y> (#25), (2) a long glide <ie> (#444, #800), and (3) a monophthong or short glide <{ie}> (#25, 582), (4) a postvocalic retroflex consonant <r> (#25, #444 [in *car*], #582, 800), (5) a weakly retroflex postvocalic consonant <{r}> (#444 [in *poor*], #582 [in *fire irons*]) and (6) a vocalized postvocalic consonant <[r]> (#444, #582 [in *sure*]). Among other features in the file, these five suggest patterns of regional and social variation.

Figure 15 shows <y> in *ears* recurrent in the Highlands (A-E/23-62), the Delta (K-U/26-36), and the Coast (Eastern Gulf) (Q-V/42-60). Here, the age factor is clearly operative with 39 of 41 instances recorded among informants age 46 and over in four subregions, with a slightly higher proportion among whites than blacks. In both racial groups, the consonantal onset in *ear* is most common among members of the lowest social class.

1. Consonants

<p>	*pill*	<f>	*feel*	<h>	*hill*
<b>	*bill*	<v>	*veal*	<m>	*mill*
<t>	*till*	<th>	*ether*	<n>	*sin*
<d>	*dill*	<dh>	*either*	<ng>	*sing*
<k>	*kill*	<s>	*sue*	<r>	*race*
<g>	*gill*	<z>	*zoo*	<l>	*lace*
<ch>	*chill*	<sh>	*shoe*	<y>	*you*
<j>	*pledger*	<zh>	*pleasure*	<w>	*will*

2. Syllabic Consonants (weakly stressed)

<M>	*bottom*	<L>	*bottle*
<N>	*button*	<R>	*batter*
<NG>	*butting*		

3. Vowels

<a>	*bat*	<ai>	*pail*	<aw>	*paw*
<e>	*bet*	<ee>	*feet*	<oy>	*boy*
<i>	*bit*	<ie>	*pie*	<ui>	*buoy*
<o>	*pot*	<oo>	*foot*	<oe>	*foe*
<u>	*putt*	<ue>	*moot*	<ow>	*fowl*
		<ew>	*mute*		

4. Weakly Stressed Vowels

<A>	*comma*	<komA=14>
<I>	*comic*	<komIk=14>

5. Syllable Stress

<1>	primary	<bat=1>	<3>	tertiary	<batboy=13>
<2>	secondary	<newbat=21>	<4>	weak	<batR=14>

6. Modifications

[C]	Vocalized Consonant
(C/V)	Deleted Consonant or Vowel
{C/V}	Diaphonic Consonant or Vowel

Figure 13. Automatic book code (ABC)

Subphonemic Units

{ai} lax onset
{ie} monophthong/short upglide
{r} weakly retroflex
{t} flap
{z} devoiced

No Response (106)

Strings

1. <a[r]z> (1)
2. <ai{r}> (1)
3. <e[r]> (2)
4. <e[r]z> (5)
5. <eer> (1)
6. <er> (5)
7. <erz> (1)
8. <e{r}> (1)
9. <e{r}z> (2)
10. <i[r]> (16)
11. <i[r]z> (3)
12. <i[r]{z}> (2)
13. <ir> (17)
14. <irz> (11)
15. <ir{z}> (1)
16. <i{r}> (6)
17. <i{r}z> (3)
18. <riechee[r]=13> (1)
19. <riet> (66)
20. <rietair=13> (1)
21. <riete[r]=11> (1)
22. <riete[r]=13> (14)
23. <rietee[r]=13> (5)
24. <rieteer=11> (1)
25. <rieteer=13> (8)
26. <rieteer=31> (1)
27. <rieter=13> (8)
28. <rieter=21> (1)
29. <riete{r}=31> (1)
30. <rieti[r]=11> (4)
31. <rieti[r]=13> (108)
32. <rieti[r]=21> (6)
33. <rieti[r]=31> (2)
34. <rietir=11> (10)
35. <rietir=13> (200)
36. <rietir=21> (9)
37. <rietir=31> (4)
38. <rieti{r}=11> (1)
39. <rieti{r}=13> (42)
40. <rieti{r}=21> (1)
41. <rieti{r}=31> (1)
42. <rietyer=13> (1)
43. <rietyi[r]=11> (1)
44. <rietyi[r]=13> (3)
45. <rietyi[r]=21> (1)
46. <rietyi[r]=31> (1)
47. <rietyi[r]z=13> (1)
48. <rietyir=13> (3)
49. <rietyi{r}=13> (5)
50. <rie{?}> (1)
51. <rie{?}yi(r)=13> (1)
52. <rie{t}ee[r]=13> (5)
53. <rie{t}eer=13> (8)
54. <rie{t}i[r]=13> (1)
55. <rie{t}i[r]=31> (1)
56. <rie{t}ir=13> (2)
57. <rie{t}i{r}=13> (1)
58. <r{ie}t> (32)
59. <r{ie}tai[r]=21> (1)
60. <r{ie}te[r]=13> (3)
61. <r{ie}teer=13> (1)
62. <r{ie}tee{r}=13> (1)
63. <r{ie}ter=13> (13)
64. <r{ie}te{r}=11> (1)
65. <r{ie}te{r}=13> (3)
66. <r{ie}ti(r)=13> (1)
67. <r{ie}ti[r]=13> (14)
68. <r{ie}tir=11> (7)
69. <r{ie}tir=13> (77)
70. <r{ie}tir=21> (7)
71. <r{ie}tir=31> (1)
72. <r{ie}ti{r}=11> (1)
73. <r{ie}ti{r}=13> (14)
74. <r{ie}ti{r}=21> (1)
75. <r{ie}tur=13> (1)
76. <r{ie}tye[r]=13> (1)
77. <r{ie}tyi[r]=13> (1)
78. <r{ie}tyi[r]=21> (1)
79. <r{ie}tyir=13> (6)
80. <r{ie}tyir=21> (2)
81. <r{ie}tyi{r}=13> (2)
82. <r{ie}t{ai}r=13> (1)
83. <r{ie}{t}ee[r]=13> (1)
84. <r{ie}{t}ir=13> (1)
85. <yi[r]> (4)
86. <yi[r]z> (1)
87. <yir> (5)
88. <yirz> (1)

Combinations (Multiple Responses)

A. <e[r]+i[r]> (1)
B. <e{r}+i[r]{z}> (1)
C. <e{r}z+irz> (1)
D. <ir+i{r}> (1)
E. <irz+i{r}z> (1)

Figure 14. ABC strings: {071.5B} *right ear*

Code 2: Race/Class/Age

1	=	W/L/13-45	0/12	A	=	B/L/13-45	0/21
2	=	W/M/13-45	1/110	B	=	B/M/13-45	1/29
3	=	W/U/13-45	0/23	C	=	B/U/13-45	0/3
4	=	W/L/46-70	7/63	D	=	B/L/46-70	2/41
5	=	W/M/46-70	1/155	E	=	B/M/46-70	0/17
6	=	W/U/46-70	0/38	F	=	B/U/46-70	0/3
7	=	W/L/71-99	13/104	G	=	B/L/71-99	6/54
8	=	W/M/71-99	4/176	H	=	B/M/71-99	4/27
9	=	W/U/71-99	2/36	J	=	B/U/71-99	0/2

Figure 15. <y> in *ear* {071.5B} 41

Code 2: Race/Class/Age

1	=	W/L/13-45	4/12		A	=	B/L/13-45	17/21
2	=	W/M/13-45	80/110		B	=	B/M/13-45	23/29
3	=	W/U/13-45	17/23		C	=	B/U/13-45	3/3
4	=	W/L/46-70	33/63		D	=	B/L/46-70	29/41
5	=	W/M/46-70	89/155		E	=	B/M/46-70	12/17
6	=	W/U/46-70	19/38		F	=	B/U/46-70	2/3
7	=	W/L/71-99	41/104		G	=	B/L/71-99	32/54
8	=	W/M/71-99	93/176		H	=	B/M/71-99	17/27
9	=	W/U/71-99	19/36		J	=	B/U/71-99	2/2

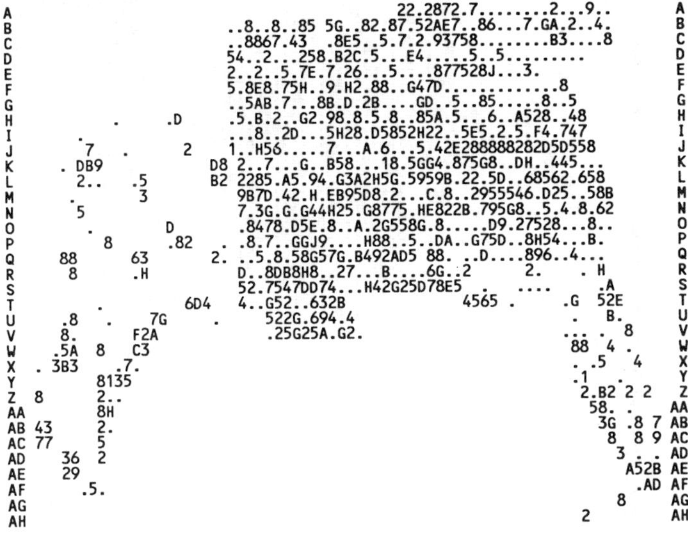

Figure 16. <ie> in *right* {071.5B} 532

Code 2: Race/Class/Age

1	=	W/L/13-45	7/12	A	=	B/L/13-45	2/21
2	=	W/M/13-45	19/110	B	=	B/M/13-45	5/29
3	=	W/U/13-45	5/23	C	=	B/U/13-45	0/3
4	=	W/L/46-70	19/63	D	=	B/L/46-70	0/41
5	=	W/M/46-70	36/155	E	=	B/M/46-70	0/17
6	=	W/U/46-70	7/38	F	=	B/U/46-70	0/3
7	=	W/L/71-99	35/104	G	=	B/L/71-99	6/54
8	=	W/M/71-99	42/176	H	=	B/M/71-99	3/27
9	=	W/U/71-99	6/36	J	=	B/U/71-99	0/2

Figure 17. <{ie}> in *right* {071.5B} 192

Figure 16 maps incidence of the stressed vowel in *right* as a long glide. The vowel in this context recurs across the territory as a dominant feature, everywhere except in the Highland subdivisions of Arkansas, Tennessee, Alabama, and Georgia and in the Piney Woods subdivisions of Alabama, Georgia, and Florida. The form prevails in all nine varieties of black speech and in white speech among the middle and upper classes.

Figure 17 maps <{ie}> as a monophthong or short glide. It recurs most frequently in the Highlands and Piney Woods, where the long glide was rare, and extends across the interior plains and western Piney Woods of Mississippi, Louisiana, and Texas. The feature is recorded among neither the middle group of black speakers (ages 46-70) nor the eight upper-class black informants. Conversely, the vowels reported as <{ie}> recur frequently in all nine varieties of white speech.

SP Files

Basically a keyboard-compatible distinctive features code, the SP system identifies phonological components of speech sounds. It reports primary (positional), secondary (conditional), and tertiary (modificational) features in alphabetic strings, as recognized by Raven I. McDavid, Jr., and the eight regular LAGS scribes, who composed the protocols.

These features are the ultimate descriptive variants of the atlas. Their configurations represent the final analysis. Their distribution -- as discrete units or bundled features -- represents the operations of deductive phonetics. This analysis begins with the graphophonemic unit, the ABC letter (or phoneme), and ends at the door of acoustic phonetics and descriptive statistics.

SP serves as a tool for the inventory of segmental units in the atlas and the terminal link in its descriptive chain. Limited here to the 74 stressed vowels recorded in the first 15 lines of the idiolect synopses, the code reports syllabic nuclei as triads of positional, conditional, and modificational features. It provides a descriptive summary of each feature in every syllabic construction -- whether monophthong, diphthong, triphthong, or tetraphthong. And it yields an index for summary interpretation and mapping. Figure 18 identifies the abbreviations of the SP code. Its notation appears between vertical bars. Primary features mark positions on the vowel quadrant. These appear in the initial position in SP triads.

For example, the string |A..| reports a vowel with its nucleus in the higher high front position, as in the monophthongs of *yeast*, *three*, and *beans* in Synopsis #444 (Figure 4). Secondary features identify another set of contrastive signals: Unmarked (A), Tense (B), Long (C), Nasal (D), Retroflex (E), and Round (F), singularly (A-F) or in combinations (G-6). Thus, in #444, the second character in the vowel of *yeast* and *beans* is |.G.| (B + C: tense and long) and |.B.| in *three* (tense), or |AG.| and |AB.|, respectively. Tertiary features record noncontrastive signals, regularly noted by LAGS scribes: Unmarked (A), Raised (B), Lowered (C), Advanced (D), and Retracted (E) in combinations (F-I); Weakly realized (J) in combinations (K-R), and Glottalized (S) in combinations (T-0). In #444, all three texts show the same tertiary marking, retraction recorded as |..E|, or fully as |AGE| and |ACE|, respectively.

The code reports the same non-nuclear features in onglides and offgildes with lowercase letters. Thus, the diphthong of *field* in #444 yields the string |ABC-maj| and the phonetic triphthong of *beard* |BAA-abc-maa|. Although ABC segmentation reports that string as <-i[r]->, SP includes postvocalic units as immediate constituents of the nucleus. Thus in the line of the four synopses marked by the unitary phoneme /i/, these SP strings appear:

	yeast	*three*	*beans*	*field*	*steers/beard*
#25	AGC-aba	bae-ABE	bag-ABA	KAG-maj	BAB-mae
#444	AGC	ABE	AGC	ABE-maj	BAA-abj-maa
#582	AGC	AGC	AGC	AGC-maj	BAB-maj
#800	AGW	AGC	AGC	AGC-maj	BAG-mae

1. Primary Features (Positional)

Vowel Quadrant Position	ABC Range	
A Higher High Front	<ee>	
B Higher High Central	<{ee}>	retracted
C Higher High Back	<ue>	
D Lower High Front	<i>	
E Lower High Central	<I>	
F Lower High Back	<oo>	
G Higher Mid Front	<ai>	
H Higher Mid Central	<{ai}>	retracted
I Higher Mid Back/Advanced	<{oe}>	advanced
J Higher Mid Back	<oe>	
K Lower Mid Front	<e>	
L Lower Mid Central/Advanced	<{u}>	advanced
M Lower Mid Central	<A>	
N Lower Mid Back	<u>	
O Higher Low Front	<a>	
P Higher Low Central	<o>	raised
Q Higher Low Back	<aw>	
R Lower Low Front	<ie>	onset
S Lower Low Central	<o>	
T Lower Low Back	<o>	retracted

2. Secondary Features (Conditional)

A Unmarked	I B+E	Q B+C+D	Y C+E+F
B Tense	J B+F	R B+C+F	Z D+E+F
C Long	K C+D	S B+C+F	1 B+C+D+E
D Nasal	L C+E	T B+D+E	2 B+C+D+F
E Retroflex	M C+F	U B+D+F	3 B+C+E+F
F Round	N D+E	V B+E+F	4 B+D+E+F
G B+C	O D+F	W C+D+E	5 C+D+E+F
H B+D	P E+F	X C+D+F	6 B+C+D+E+F

3. Tertiary Features (Modificational)

A Unmarked	J Weak	S Glottal	2 S+J
B Raised	K J+B	T S+B	3 S+K
C Lowered	L J+C	U S+C	4 S+L
D Advanced	M J+D	V S+D	5 S+M
E Retracted	N J+E	W S+E	6 S+N
F B+D	O J+F	X S+F	7 S+O
G B+E	P J+G	Y S+G	8 S+P
H C+D	Q J+H	Z S+H	9 S+Q
I C+E	R J+I	1 S+I	0 S+R

Figure 18. Systematic Phonetics Code

Such notation amplifies ABC description in the identification of monophthongs and diphthongs and positional variants. As sets, SP entries also form paradigms that outline patterns of complementary distribution, as well as regional and social incidence. SP strings also provide materials for an evaluation procedure that identifies scribal habits. They help a LAGS reader understand the contents of the phonic data base. Most important, the system gives a reader a consistent system for narrow phonetic notation, comparison, and description that can be used without special equipment. Sophisticated software now can produce phonetic characters in a microcomputer, but these require special graphics cards and editorial programs. SP serves LAGS editors as an editorial code of index and analysis. When such programs can isolate, sort, and map distinctive features, the SP code will become obsolete.

Figure 19 lists 94 SP strings that identify the stressed vowels of *write/right* in the idiolect synopses. These include monophthongs and diphthongs that begin in the mid-central (P), low-front (R), and low-central (S) ranges, texts 1-3, 4-88, and 89-94, respectively. Synopses #25 (Figure 2) and #582 (Figure 5) illustrate Text 76 (|RCE-kaj|); #444 (Figure 4), Text 73 (|RCE-eaj|); #880 (Figure 6), Text 64 (|RCB-eaal).

Figures 20-22 map three sets of allophones, gathered under the ABC designation <{ie}> in *right* in Figure 17. That classification interpreted monophthongs and two short-gliding diphthongs in a set. Analyzed in SP notation, the three sets show related, but distinctively different, patterns of regional and social distribution.

Figure 20 maps the 70 monophthongs |R..|, Texts 4, 11, 19, 37, 47, 63, and 81. Sixty-four of these occur in white speech in a regional pattern that extends westward to Texas from the north out of the Tennessee Highlands and from the south out of the Georgia and Florida Piney Woods. The vowel is recorded only twice in middle-class black speech with no instances among the eight upper-class representatives in the sample. Only four of 97 upper-class white speakers offered the vowel.

1.	|PAHeaa|	[e˯ɨ]	(1)
2.	|PCAeaa|	[e.ɨ]	(2)
3.	|PCAeaj|	[e.ᶤ]	(2)
4.	|RAA|	[a]	(2)
5.	|RAAeaa|	[aɨ]	(16)
6.	|RAAeab|	[aɨ˄]	(1)
7.	|RAAead|	[aɨ˂]	(2)
8.	|RAAeaj|	[aᶤ]	(24)
9.	|RAAeak|	[aᶤ˄]	(1)
10.	|RAAkaj|	[aᵋ]	(5)
11.	|RAB|	[a˄]	(7)
12.	|RABdaa|	[a˄ɪ]	(1)
13.	|RABdab|	[a˄ɪ˄]	(1)
14.	|RABeaa|	[a˄ɨ]	(6)
15.	|RABeaj|	[a˄ᶤ]	(66)
16.	|RABkaj|	[a˄ᵋ]	(11)
17.	|RACeaj|	[a˅ᶤ]	(1)
18.	|RADeaa|	[a˂ɨ]	(1)
19.	|RAE|	[a˃]	(3)
20.	|RAEdaa|	[a˃ɪ]	(2)
21.	|RAEeaa|	[a˃ɨ]	(36)
22.	|RAEeab|	[a˃ɨ˄]	(4)
23.	|RAEeac|	[a˃ɨ˅]	(1)
24.	|RAEead|	[a˃ɨ˂]	(1)
25.	|RAEeaj|	[a˃ᶤ]	(178)
26.	|RAEeak|	[a˃ᶤ˄]	(5)
27.	|RAEeal|	[a˃ᶤ˅]	(5)
28.	|RAEeaq|	[a˃ᶤ˂˅]	(1)
29.	|RAEkab|	[a˃ɛ˄]	(1)
30.	|RAEkaj|	[a˃ᵋ]	(30)
31.	|RAEkak|	[a˃ᵋ˄]	(7)
32.	|RAEkal|	[a˃ᵋ˅]	(1)
33.	|RAEkan|	[a˃ᵋ˃]	(1)
34.	|RAEmaj|	[a˃ᵊ]	(4)
35.	|RAEmak|	[a˃ᵊ˄]	(1)
36.	|RAFeaj|	[a˂˄ᶤ]	(1)
37.	|RAG|	[a˃˄]	(23)
38.	|RAGbbj|	[a˃˄ɨ]	(1)
39.	|RAGeaa|	[a˃˄ɨ]	(14)
40.	|RAGeaj|	[a˃˄ᶤ]	(78)
41.	|RAGeak|	[a˃˄ᶤ˄]	(9)
42.	|RAGeal|	[a˃˄ᶤ˅]	(1)
43.	|RAGkaj|	[a˃˄ᵋ]	(1)
44.	|RAGkak|	[a˃˄ᵋ˄]	(1)
45.	|RAGmaj|	[a˃˄ᵊ]	(1)
46.	|RAGmam|	[a˃˄ᵊ˂]	(1)
47.	|RCA|	[a.]	(17)
48.	|RCAbbj|	[a.ᶤ]	(1)
49.	|RCAdaj|	[a.ᴵ]	(2)
50.	|RCAeaa|	[a.ɨ]	(21)
51.	|RCAeab|	[a.ɨ˄]	(2)
52.	|RCAeaf|	[a.ɨ˂˄]	(1)
53.	|RCAeaj|	[a.ᶤ]	(63)
54.	|RCAeal|	[a.ᶤ˅]	(1)
55.	|RCAeam|	[a.ᶤ˂]	(1)
56.	|RCAeas|	[a.ᶤˀ]	(1)
57.	|RCAkaj|	[a.ᵋ]	(16)
58.	|RCAkak|	[a.ᵋ˄]	(1)
59.	|RCAkan|	[a.ᵋ˃]	(1)
60.	|RCAkap|	[a.ᵋ˃˄]	(1)
61.	|RCAmaj|	[a.ᵊ]	(8)
62.	|RCAmak|	[a.ᵊ˄]	(1)
63.	|RCB|	[a˄.]	(3)
64.	|RCBeaa|	[a˄.ɨ]	(5)
65.	|RCBeaj|	[a˄.ᶤ]	(17)
66.	|RCBkaj|	[a˄.ᵋ]	(1)
67.	|RCBmak|	[a˄.ᵊ˄]	(1)
68.	|RCE|	[a˃.]	(14)
69.	|RCEeaa|	[a˃.ɨ]	(23)
70.	|RCEeab|	[a˃.ɨ˄]	(2)
71.	|RCEeac|	[a˃.ɨ˅]	(1)
72.	|RCEead|	[a˃.ɨ˂]	(1)
73.	|RCEeaj|	[a˃.ᶤ]	(50)
74.	|RCEeak|	[a˃.ᶤ˄]	(1)
75.	|RCEeal|	[a˃.ᶤ˅]	(2)
76.	|RCEkaj|	[a˃.ᵋ]	(39)
77.	|RCEkak|	[a˃.ᵋ˄]	(2)
78.	|RCEkan|	[a˃.ᵋ˂]	(1)
79.	|RCEmaj|	[a˃.ᵊ]	(1)
80.	|RCEmak|	[a˃.ᵊ˄]	(1)
81.	|RCG|	[a˃˄.]	(1)
82.	|RCGdaj|	[a˃˄.ᴵ]	(2)
83.	|RCGeaa|	[a˃˄.ɨ]	(6)
84.	|RCGeaj|	[a˃˄.ᶤ]	(23)
85.	|RCGmaj|	[a˃˄.ᵊ]	(1)
86.	|RGAeaa|	[a˃.ɨ]	(1)
87.	|RKAmdj|	[ã.ᵊ̃]	(1)
88.	|RKEedj|	[ã˃.ᶤ̃]	(1)
89.	|SABeaj|	[ɑ˄ᶤ]	(1)
90.	|SCAdaj|	[ɑ.ᴵ]	(1)
91.	|SCDeaj|	[ɑ˂.ᶤ]	(8)
92.	|SCEeaa|	[ɑ˃.ɨ]	(1)
93.	|SKAedj|	[ɑ̃.ᶤ̃]	(1)
94.	|SKDmdj|	[ɑ̃˂.ᵊ̃]	(1)

Figure 19. Systematic Phonetics Strings: File {100.5S}
Stressed Vowel <ie> in *write/right*

Code 2: Race/Class/Age

1	= W/L/13-45	5/12		A	= B/L/13-45	0/21
2	= W/M/13-45	7/110		B	= B/M/13-45	1/29
3	= W/U/13-45	2/23		C	= B/U/13-45	0/3
4	= W/L/46-70	7/63		D	= B/L/46-70	3/41
5	= W/M/46-70	16/155		E	= B/M/46-70	0/17
6	= W/U/46-70	1/38		F	= B/U/46-70	0/3
7	= W/L/71-99	12/104		G	= B/L/71-99	1/54
8	= W/M/71-99	13/176		H	= B/M/71-99	1/27
9	= W/U/71-99	1/36		J	= B/U/71-99	0/2

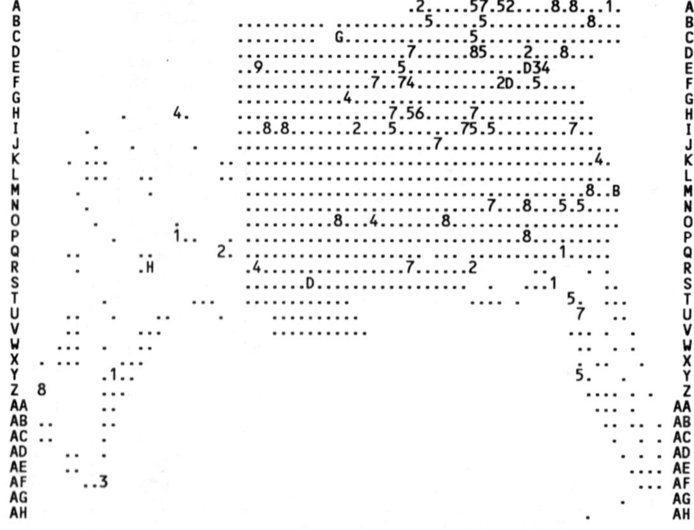

Figure 20. |R..| in *right/write* 70

Code 2: Race/Class/Age

1	=	W/L/13-45	1/12	A	=	B/L/13-45	0/21
2	=	W/M/13-45	13/110	B	=	B/M/13-45	2/29
3	=	W/U/13-45	1/23	C	=	B/U/13-45	0/3
4	=	W/L/46-70	8/63	D	=	B/L/46-70	3/41
5	=	W/M/46-70	30/155	E	=	B/M/46-70	3/17
6	=	W/U/46-70	5/38	F	=	B/U/46-70	0/3
7	=	W/L/71-99	14/104	G	=	B/L/71-99	6/54
8	=	W/M/71-99	29/176	H	=	B/M/71-99	1/27
9	=	W/U/71-99	4/36	J	=	B/U/71-99	0/2

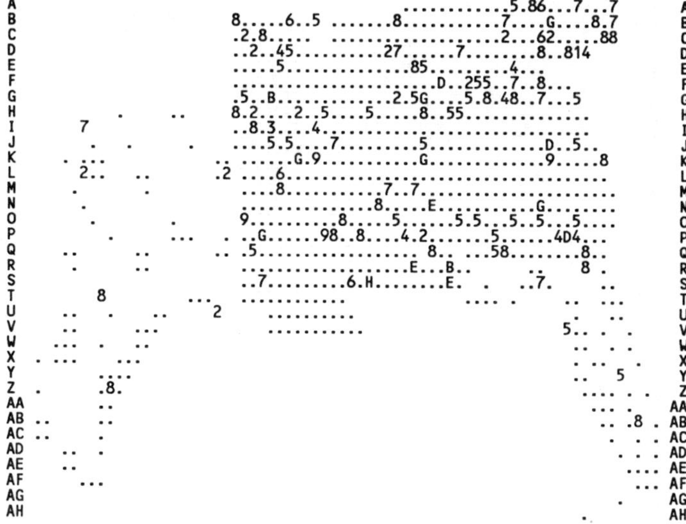

Figure 21. |..k..| in *right/write* 120

Code 2: Race/Class/Age

1	=	W/L/13-45	0/12	A	=	B/L/13-45	1/21
2	=	W/M/13-45	0/110	B	=	B/M/13-45	1/29
3	=	W/U/13-45	0/23	C	=	B/U/13-45	0/3
4	=	W/L/46-70	1/63	D	=	B/L/46-70	1/41
5	=	W/M/46-70	2/155	E	=	B/M/46-70	0/17
6	=	W/U/46-70	1/38	F	=	B/U/46-70	0/3
7	=	W/L/71-99	4/104	G	=	B/L/71-99	1/54
8	=	W/M/71-99	9/176	H	=	B/M/71-99	0/27
9	=	W/U/71-99	1/36	J	=	B/U/71-99	0/2

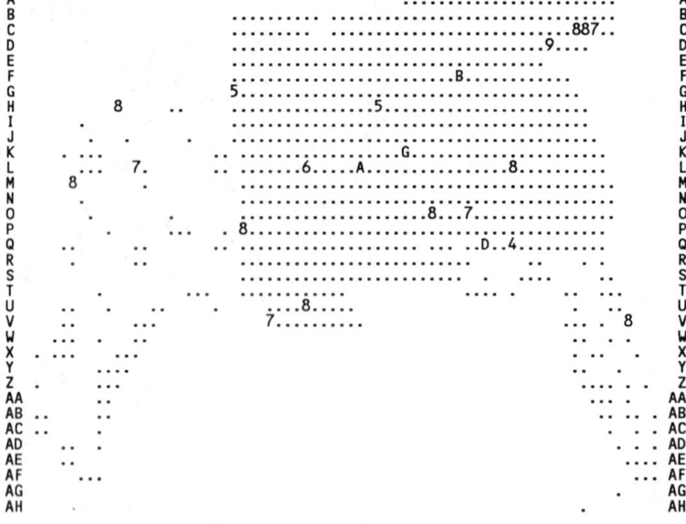

Figure 22. |...-m...| in *right/write* 22

Figure 21 maps 120 occurrences of short upglides lR..-k..l, Texts 10, 16, 29-33, 43-44, 57-60, 66, and 76-78. Distribution here shows essentially the same social pattern among blacks and whites as did the monophthong. Regional incidence, however, is significantly different in the west. The short upglide is common in both the Arkansas Highlands and the Ouachita Plains below them.

Figure 22 maps 22 occurrences of short ingliding diphthongs, lR..-m..l, Texts 34-35, 45-46, 61-62, 67, 79-80, 85, and 87. This recessive form shares the same geographic region with the monophthong. But its social incidence is more narrowly restricted. Fifteen of 22 instances occur among people over age 70, with none in the speech of whites under age 46.

With these maps, the disk/text transmits evidence to outline regional and social patterns of Gulf States speech. The files illustrate the resources and limitations of the work as an explicit statement, an inventory of the data base as a research tool. A reader can observe the strengths and weaknesses of field, scribal, and editorial work through this analogue. For that reason, the disk/text offers the best LAGS materials for evaluation of the effort as systematic study -- complete, consistent, economical, and transparent linguistic geography.

The Book/Text

The LAGS book/text remains a work in progress. Current plans project seven volumes. Four of these are published, two more are in advanced stages of composition, but the final texts must await completion of the other books. Taken together, the book/text volumes report a synthesis of the project. The text transmits LAGS data in the simplest way and reflects the underlying assumptions of the work.

The *Handbook*, Volume 1, (1986) summarizes the information gathered through field work. The *General Index*, Volume 2, (1988) summarizes the contents of the concordance. The *Technical Index*, Volume 3, (1989) lists the contents of LAGS files in the disk/text. The *Regional Matrix*, Volume 4, (1990) outlines the regional dialects with 7,422 matrix maps that report linguistic evidence from the files in

A Eastern Piney Woods: Georgia and Florida (84)
B Central Piney Woods: Alabama, Mississippi and East Louisiana (70)
C Western Piney Woods: West Louisiana and Texas (27)

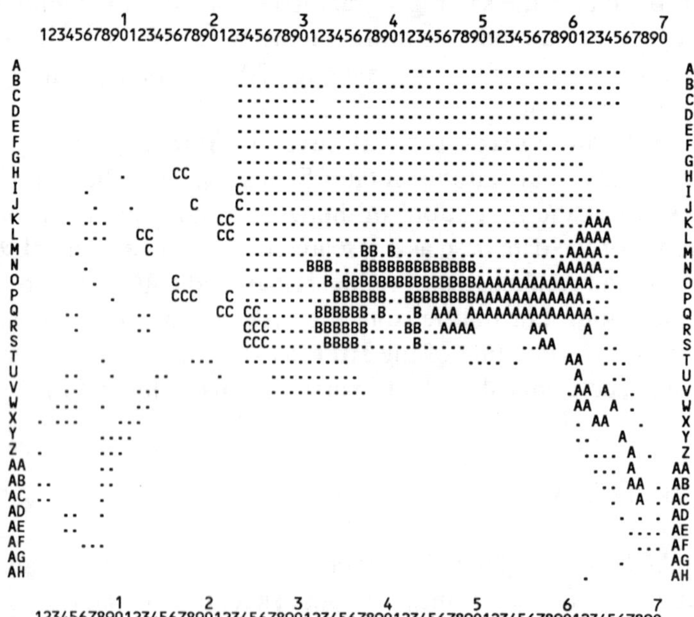

Figure 23. Piney Woods Informants

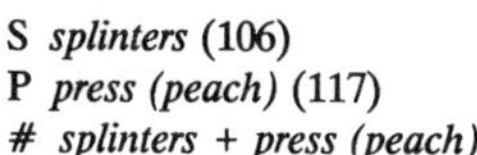

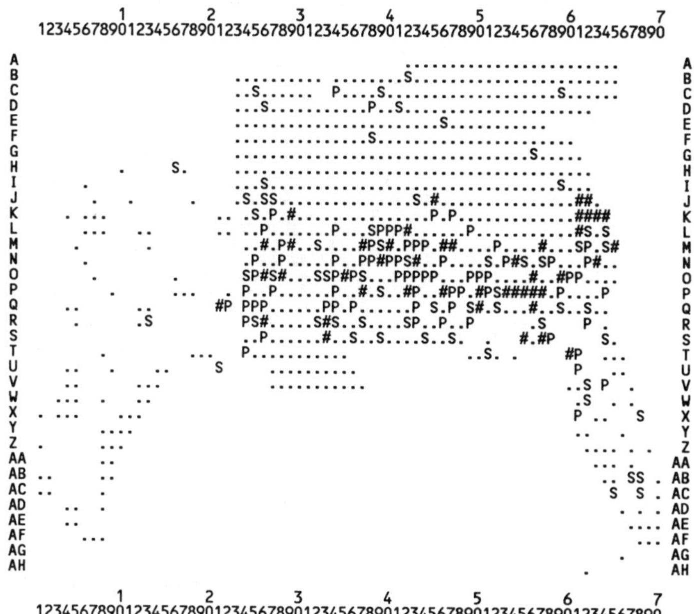

Figure 24. *Splinters* {008.6}/*Press (Peach)* {054.3}

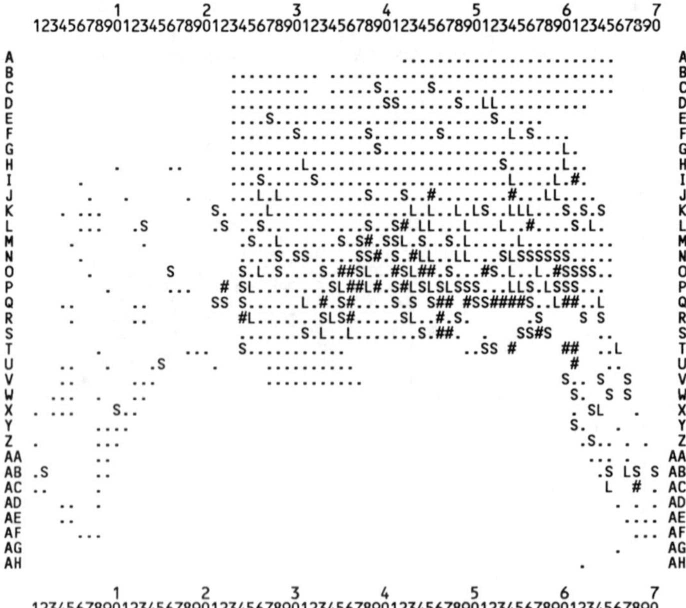

Figure 25. *Lighterd* {008.6}/*Smut* {008.7A}

SECTOTAL and LAGSMAP formats. These 7,422 maps include 6,578 SECTOTAL forms, charting all basic work-sheet items and contrastive lexical features from the urban supplement. Selected from 10,000 preliminary maps, these forms index all features (lexical, grammatical, and phonological) mapped in the book/text. The second part of the volume records 844 LAGSMAP graphic plotter grids that suggest regional patterns.

Figures 23-25 are LAGSMAP grids that identify the Piney Woods domain and the incidence of two lexical features of the several dozen that distinguish that region. Figure 23 identifies the positions of all LAGS informants in the domain of the Piney Woods land region (Figure 3). Figure 24 records the incidence of *splinters* ('kindling') and *press (peach)* ('cling peach'); Figure 25, *lighterd* ('rich-pine kindling') and *smut* ('soot').

The Regional Pattern, Volume 5, (forthcoming) reports 844 features in AREATOTAL summaries and pattern maps based on the land regions of Figure 3. Each summary records the incidence of four dialect features in simple and composite patterns. Each pattern map records the regional distribution of the features in simple and composite patterns. Figure 26 identifies the 15 possible graphic designations that might appear in pattern maps, prepared by Borden D. Dent.

The following examples are limited to lexical distribution because that is where deductive word geography begins. As the analysis proceeds, pattern maps will combine lexical, formal (morphological and grammatical), and phonological features in the identification of dialect areas. The examples included here illustrate the inseparable relationship of AREATOTAL summaries and pattern maps.

The maps interpret the summary statistics in a mechanical way. Each summary item records the incidence of a feature identified in a file that is recorded in the *Technical Index* according to the page and line of a work-sheet entry. In Figure 27, Item 1, for example, the entry *tow sack* {019.7} (work-sheet page and line) reports 315 instances among 914 informants. The regional mean (here, 34%) provides a basis for interpreting distribution in the 31 subregions, A1-F6. If a subregional mean equals or exceeds the regional mean, the territory is marked on the pattern map. Thus, A1-6, C4, D3-4, D6-8, E5, F1-2, and

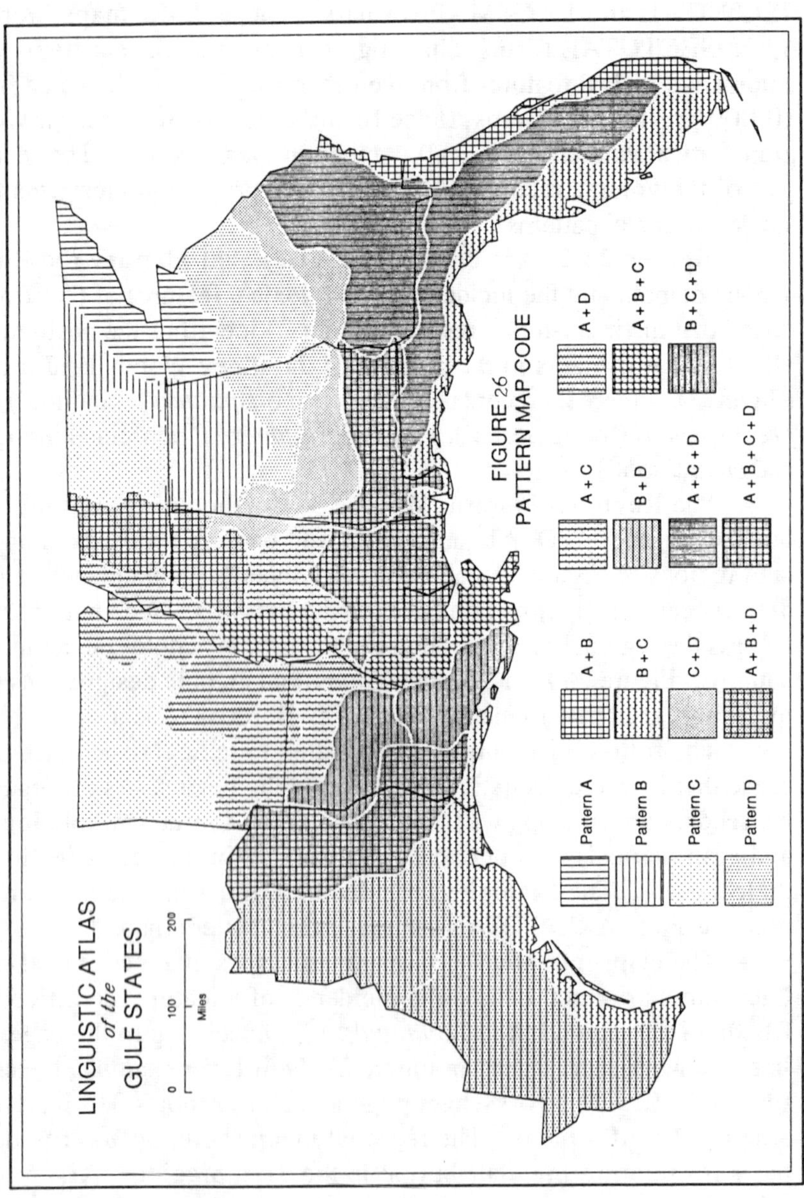

Figure 26. Pattern Map Code

1. *tow sack* {019.7} 315/914 34%

A 136/207 66%	B 13/84 15%	C 14/109 13%	D 69/176 39%	E 31/181 17%	F 52/157 33%
A1 35/52 67%	B1 8/59 14%	C1 0/12 0%	D1 0/19 0%	E1 1/55 2%	F1 9/15 60%
A2 7/20 35%	B2 5/25 20%	C2 0/23 0%	D2 3/30 10%	E2 2/29 7%	F2 24/49 49%
A3 13/18 72%		C3 2/48 4%	D3 14/17 82%	E3 1/33 3%	F3 2/15 13%
A4 17/37 46%		C4 12/26 46%	D4 13/22 59%	E4 8/37 22%	F4 2/31 6%
A5 29/39 74%			D5 2/19 11%	E5 19/27 70%	F5 3/24 13%
A6 35/41 85%			D6 13/17 76%		F6 12/23 52%
			D7 13/23 57%		
			D8 11/29 38%		

2. *French harp* ("harmonica") {020.5} 292/914 32%

A 131/207 63%	B 14/84 17%	C 7/109 6%	D 61/176 35%	E 35/181 19%	F 44/157 28%
A1 36/52 69%	B1 7/59 12%	C1 0/12 0%	D1 0/19 0%	E1 0/55 0%	F1 6/15 40%
A2 10/20 50%	B2 7/25 28%	C2 0/23 0%	D2 3/30 10%	E2 0/29 0%	F2 18/49 37%
A3 14/18 78%		C3 0/48 0%	D3 7/17 41%	E3 1/33 3%	F3 4/15 27%
A4 17/37 46%		C4 7/26 27%	D4 8/22 36%	E4 19/37 51%	F4 2/31 6%
A5 24/39 62%			D5 10/19 53%	E5 15/27 56%	F5 2/24 8%
A6 30/41 73%			D6 9/17 53%		F6 12/23 52%
			D7 13/23 57%		
			D8 11/29 38%		

3. *green beans* {055A.4} 328/914 36%

A 131/207 63%	B 21/84 25%	C 36/109 33%	D 51/176 29%	E 42/181 23%	F 47/157 30%
A1 37/52 71%	B1 18/59 31%	C1 1/12 8%	D1 1/19 5%	E1 7/55 13%	F1 7/15 47%
A2 12/20 60%	B2 3/25 12%	C2 4/23 17%	D2 6/30 20%	E2 7/29 24%	F2 14/49 29%
A3 9/18 50%		C3 14/48 29%	D3 6/17 35%	E3 8/33 24%	F3 1/15 7%
A4 19/37 51%		C4 17/26 65%	D4 5/22 23%	E4 7/37 19%	F4 12/31 39%
A5 28/39 72%			D5 1/19 5%	E5 13/27 48%	F5 6/24 25%
A6 26/41 63%			D6 6/17 35%		F6 7/23 30%
			D7 11/23 48%		
			D8 15/29 52%		

4. *chigger* {060A.9} 407/914 45%

A 159/207 77%	B 46/84 55%	C 31/109 28%	D 79/176 45%	E 34/181 19%	F 58/157 37%
A1 40/52 77%	B1 34/59 58%	C1 1/12 8%	D1 3/19 16%	E1 3/55 5%	F1 9/15 60%
A2 10/20 50%	B2 12/25 48%	C2 6/23 26%	D2 10/30 33%	E2 4/29 14%	F2 33/49 67%
A3 18/18 100%		C3 14/48 29%	D3 12/17 71%	E3 8/33 24%	F3 4/15 27%
A4 25/37 68%		C4 10/26 38%	D4 10/22 45%	E4 6/37 16%	F4 3/31 10%
A5 33/39 85%			D5 7/19 37%	E5 13/27 48%	F5 1/24 4%
A6 33/41 80%			D6 7/17 41%		F6 8/23 35%
			D7 14/23 61%		
			D8 16/29 55%		

Figure 27. Area Totals, North Carolina Patterns

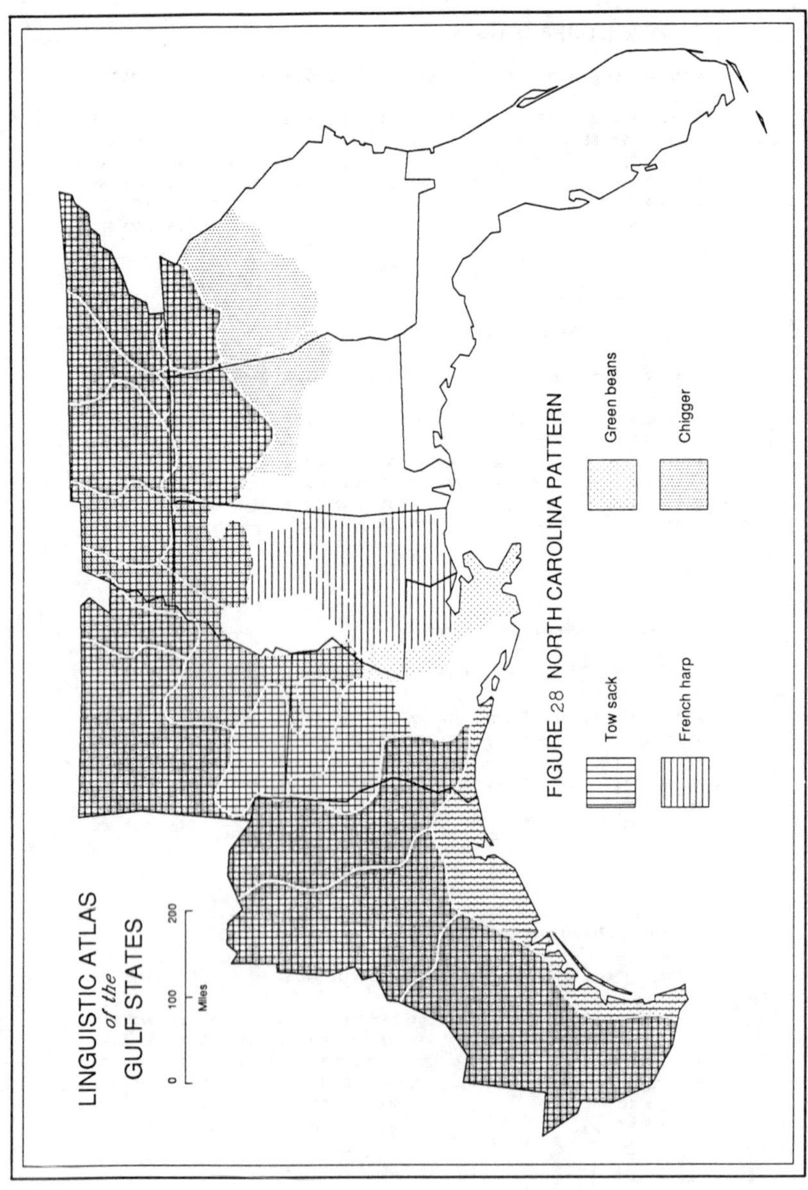

Figure 28. North Carolina Pattern

F6 form the *tow sack* pattern in Figure 28. Elsewhere, to avoid misrepresentation among items of low incidence, the interpretation requires a minimum of three occurrences in any subregion for inclusion in a mapped pattern.

Figures 27-28, a North Carolina source pattern, record the incidence of *tow sack*, *French harp*, *green beans*, and *chiggers*. The configuration includes the six Highland divisions (A1-6 in Figure 3) and extends in a southwesterly direction, reaching the Mexican border through the South Texas plains (D8). In contrast, figures 29-30, a Highlands pattern, record the incidence of *fireboard*, *barn lot*, *(paper) poke*, and *snake feeder* across the six subdivisions of the Highlands. Figures 31-32, a Lower Delta and Gulf Coast pattern, include *armoire*, *gallery*, *pirogue*, *cream cheese* ('cottage cheese') and outline the probable domain of the New Orleans focal area.

Figure 32 illustrates the referential function of the pattern map. With its regional explicitness, the map draws attention to its limitations. All four summaries in Figure 31, for example, signal marked incidence in the Eastern Gulf subdivision (C3). LAGSMAP grids of the same features show such terms as *armoire* and *gallery* (Figure 33) rarely reaching eastward beyond the Mobile focal area -- grid coordinates P-S/40-42. The Gulf Coast subdivision will therefore be revised to include Mobile in the western unit (C4) or to identify a pair of eastern subdivisions, divided at the eastern boundary of New Orleans influence. Because a parallel distinction occurs along the Texas coast, where features tend to divide as they do across the interior plains (D7-8), the Gulf Coast will need four subdivisions. Similarly, the expansive Black Belt subregion -- from the Thirty-Second Parallel in Lower Alabama to the Thirty-Fourth in Upper Mississippi -- may also require analysis into upper and lower subdivisions. All such modifications reflect the deductive method applied in the identification of areas in the Gulf States. Even in the process of synthesis, the recursive power of the method allows one to return to the data and revise interpretation. This self-corrective capacity will make possible further refinements as the work progresses toward publication. More important, readers of LAGS texts will be able to make similar adjustments through closer study of information, whether recorded on tape, fiche, disk, or in print.

1. *fireboard* ("mantel") {008.4} 69/914 8%

A	45/207 22%	B	8/84 10%	C	0/109 0%	D	4/176 2%	E	9/181 5%	F	3/157 2%
A1	16/52 31%	B1	6/59 10%	C1	0/12 0%	D1	0/19 0%	E1	3/55 5%	F1	2/15 13%
A2	6/20 30%	B2	2/25 8%	C2	0/23 0%	D2	1/30 3%	E2	1/29 3%	F2	0/49 0%
A3	4/18 22%			C3	0/48 0%	D3	0/17 0%	E3	3/33 9%	F3	0/15 0%
A4	6/37 16%			C4	0/26 0%	D4	2/22 9%	E4	1/37 3%	F4	0/31 0%
A5	4/39 10%					D5	0/19 0%	E5	1/27 4%	F5	0/24 0%
A6	9/41 22%					D6	0/17 0%			F6	1/23 4%
						D7	1/23 4%				
						D8	0/29 0%				

2. *barn lot* {015.6} 73/914 8%

A	45/207 22%	B	2/84 2%	C	4/109 4%	D	8/176 5%	E	9/181 5%	F	5/157 3%
A1	20/52 38%	B1	2/59 3%	C1	1/12 8%	D1	0/19 0%	E1	3/55 5%	F1	1/15 7%
A2	3/20 15%	B2	0/25 0%	C2	1/23 4%	D2	2/30 7%	E2	2/29 7%	F2	2/49 4%
A3	4/18 22%			C3	0/48 0%	D3	1/17 6%	E3	2/33 6%	F3	0/15 0%
A4	5/37 14%			C4	2/26 8%	D4	2/22 9%	E4	1/37 3%	F4	2/31 6%
A5	8/39 21%					D5	1/19 5%	E5	1/27 4%	F5	0/24 0%
A6	5/41 12%					D6	1/17 6%			F6	0/23 0%
						D7	1/23 4%				
						D8	0/29 0%				

3. *(paper) poke* ("paper bag") {019.5} 109/914 12%

A	86/207 42%	B	9/84 11%	C	5/109 5%	D	3/176 2%	E	4/181 2%	F	2/157 1%
A1	39/52 75%	B1	8/59 14%	C1	1/12 8%	D1	0/19 0%	E1	1/55 2%	F1	1/15 7%
A2	7/20 35%	B2	1/25 4%	C2	3/23 13%	D2	0/30 0%	E2	1/29 3%	F2	1/49 2%
A3	10/18 56%			C3	1/48 2%	D3	1/17 6%	E3	1/33 3%	F3	0/15 0%
A4	6/37 16%			C4	0/26 0%	D4	1/22 5%	E4	0/37 0%	F4	0/31 0%
A5	6/39 15%					D5	0/19 0%	E5	1/27 4%	F5	0/24 0%
A6	18/41 44%					D6	1/17 6%			F6	0/23 0%
						D7	0/23 0%				
						D8	0/29 0%				

4. *snake feeder* ("dragonfly") {060A.4} 55/914 6%

A	53/207 26%	B	1/84 1%	C	0/109 0%	D	1/176 1%	E	0/181 0%	F	0/157 0%
A1	34/52 65%	B1	1/59 2%	C1	0/12 0%	D1	0/19 0%	E1	0/55 0%	F1	0/15 0%
A2	4/20 20%	B2	0/25 0%	C2	0/23 0%	D2	0/30 0%	E2	0/29 0%	F2	0/49 0%
A3	13/18 72%			C3	0/48 0%	D3	1/17 6%	E3	0/33 0%	F3	0/15 0%
A4	0/37 0%			C4	0/26 0%	D4	0/22 0%	E4	0/37 0%	F4	0/31 0%
A5	0/39 0%					D5	0/19 0%	E5	0/27 0%	F5	0/24 0%
A6	2/41 5%					D6	0/17 0%			F6	0/23 0%
						D7	0/23 0%				
						D8	0/29 0%				

Figure 29. Area Totals, Highlands Pattern

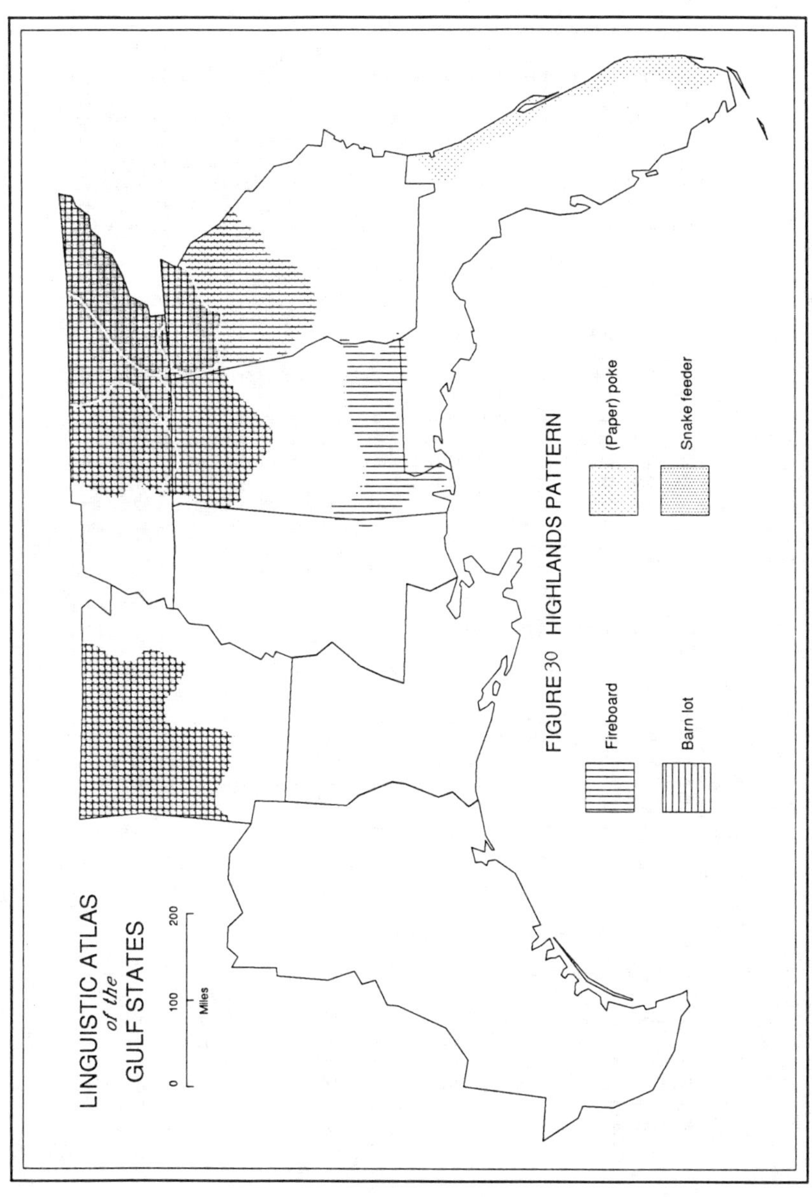

Figure 30. Highlands Pattern

1. *armoire* {009.7} 100/914 11%

A	B	C	D	E	F
A 3/207 1%	B 2/84 2%	C 13/109 12%	D 15/176 9%	E 18/181 10%	F 49/157 31%
A1 0/52 0%	B1 1/59 2%	C1 0/12 0%	D1 0/19 0%	E1 3/55 5%	F1 0/15 0%
A2 0/20 0%	B2 1/25 4%	C2 1/23 4%	D2 1/30 3%	E2 0/29 0%	F2 1/49 2%
A3 1/18 6%		C3 7/48 15%	D3 1/17 6%	E3 2/33 6%	F3 1/15 7%
A4 1/37 3%		C4 5/26 19%	D4 0/22 0%	E4 12/37 32%	F4 23/31 74%
A5 1/39 3%			D5 4/19 21%	E5 1/27 4%	F5 15/24 63%
A6 0/41 0%			D6 4/17 24%		F6 9/23 39%
			D7 4/23 17%		
			D8 1/29 3%		

2. *gallery* {010.8} 180/914 20%

A	B	C	D	E	F
A 7/207 3%	B 1/84 1%	C 26/109 24%	D 36/176 20%	E 50/181 28%	F 60/157 38%
A1 0/52 0%	B1 1/59 2%	C1 0/12 0%	D1 0/19 0%	E1 1/55 2%	F1 0/15 0%
A2 0/20 0%	B2 0/25 0%	C2 0/23 0%	D2 5/30 17%	E2 4/29 14%	F2 11/49 22%
A3 0/18 0%		C3 10/48 21%	D3 1/17 6%	E3 13/33 39%	F3 9/15 60%
A4 3/37 8%		C4 16/26 62%	D4 1/22 5%	E4 19/37 51%	F4 17/31 55%
A5 1/39 3%			D5 7/19 37%	E5 13/27 48%	F5 12/24 50%
A6 3/41 7%			D6 8/17 47%		F6 11/23 48%
			D7 5/23 22%		
			D8 9/29 31%		

3. *pirogue* {024.6} 80/914 9%

A	B	C	D	E	F
A 0/207 0%	B 0/84 0%	C 11/109 10%	D 3/176 2%	E 16/181 9%	F 50/157 32%
A1 0/52 0%	B1 0/59 0%	C1 0/12 0%	D1 0/19 0%	E1 0/55 0%	F1 0/15 0%
A2 0/20 0%	B2 0/25 0%	C2 0/23 0%	D2 0/30 0%	E2 0/29 0%	F2 3/49 6%
A3 0/18 0%		C3 5/48 10%	D3 0/17 0%	E3 0/33 0%	F3 3/15 20%
A4 0/37 0%		C4 6/26 23%	D4 1/22 5%	E4 9/37 24%	F4 17/31 55%
A5 0/39 0%			D5 0/19 0%	E5 7/27 26%	F5 20/24 83%
A6 0/41 0%			D6 2/17 12%		F6 7/23 30%
			D7 0/23 0%		
			D8 0/29 0%		

4. *cream cheese* ("cottage cheese") {048.1} 62/914 7%

A	B	C	D	E	F
A 3/207 1%	B 2/84 2%	C 14/109 13%	D 6/176 3%	E 7/181 4%	F 30/157 19%
A1 0/52 0%	B1 2/59 3%	C1 0/12 0%	D1 0/19 0%	E1 0/55 0%	F1 0/15 0%
A2 1/20 5%	B2 0/25 0%	C2 0/23 0%	D2 2/30 7%	E2 0/29 0%	F2 0/49 0%
A3 0/18 0%		C3 7/48 15%	D3 0/17 0%	E3 0/33 0%	F3 1/15 7%
A4 2/37 5%		C4 7/26 27%	D4 0/22 0%	E4 6/37 16%	F4 13/31 42%
A5 0/39 0%			D5 0/19 0%	E5 1/27 4%	F5 13/24 54%
A6 0/41 0%			D6 1/17 6%		F6 3/23 13%
			D7 1/23 4%		
			D8 2/29 7%		

Figure 31. Area Totals, Lower Delta/Gulf Coast Pattern

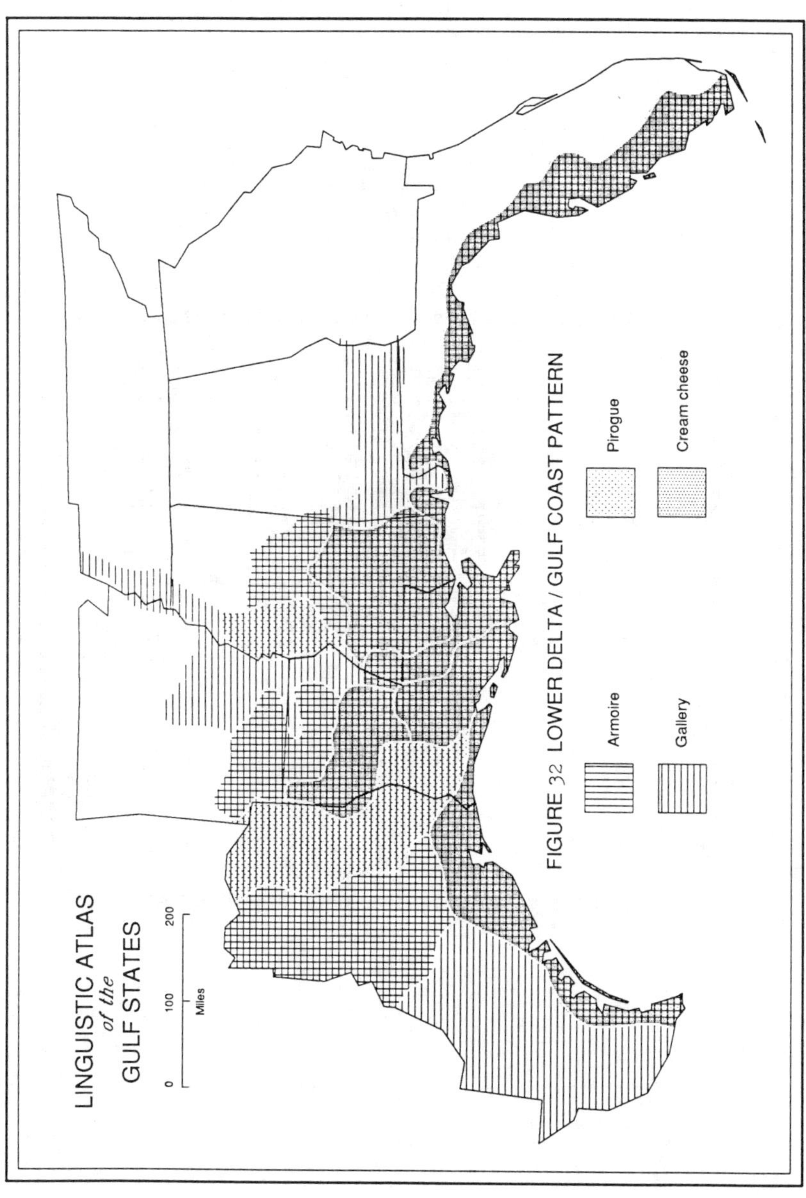

Figure 32. Lower Delta/Gulf Coast Pattern

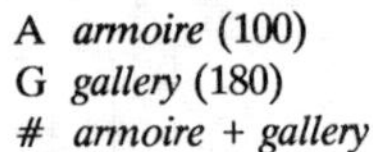

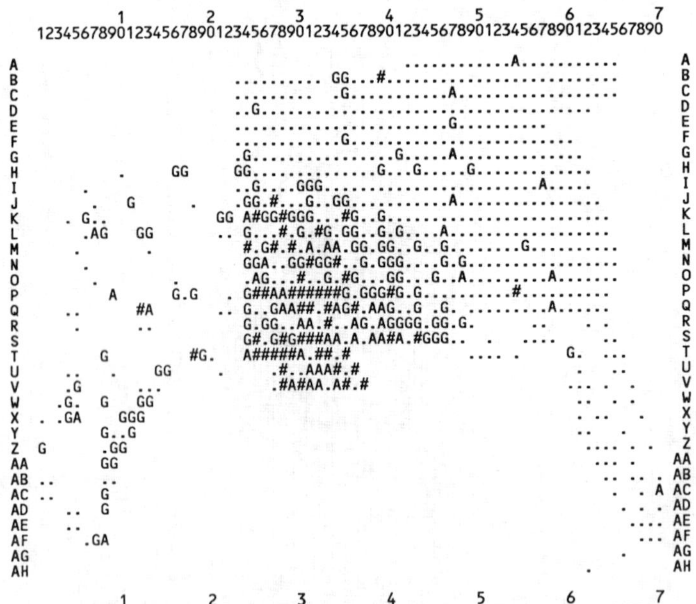

Figure 33. *Armoire* {009.7}/*Gallery* {010.8}

The Social Matrix, Volume 6, (forthcoming) will outline social dialects with more than 5000 maps. These will report linguistic evidence from the files in SOCTOTAL and CODEMAP formats. As a summary of social incidence in general (SOCTOTAL) and specific (CODEMAP) perspectives, this matrix follows the deductive approach established in Volume 4 with SECTOTAL and LAGSMAP presentations.

The Social Pattern, Volume 7, (forthcoming) will identify configurations suggested in the maps of the Social Matrix. The Pattern Map Code (Figure 26) makes possible the mapping of four social factors on a single plane. AREATOTAL summaries will identify significant incidence according to the nine sets of social characteristics used in the SOCTOTAL and CODEMAP formats. Social pattern maps, then, will illustrate findings according to the code illustrated in Figure 26. For example, in that map, the patterns might identify white (A), female (B), college-educated (C) and upper-class (D) informants. Figure 26, then, would indicate socially significant incidence (the regional mean) of a linguistic form in the Blue Ridge Divisions (A1-2) only among whites and in the western Piney Woods (E3-5) among white, female, college-educated upper-class informants.

As the contents of the book/text outline the atlas as a research tool, the atlas itself recapitulates the discipline itself, from Wenker and Gilliéron forward. The tape/text illustrates the magnificent specimens of spoken language observed by field workers over the past century. The tape recorder makes it possible for other auditors to appreciate the experience that draws a linguist into the field. The fiche/text orders a small part of that record, showing a reader just how much spoken language the scribes were able to control. The disk/text makes cartography a simple task, reducing a day's work to a few seconds, while conducting business as usual and doing good old-fashioned mapmaking with improved office equipment. The book/text outlines the domain of the research with comprehensive indexes, maps, and legends.

Finally, as a procedural statement, LAGS texts summarize the methods and materials of the research project. Files inventory evidence in hand; maps outline implications of the evidence. As current revisions suggest, the atlas aims to report facts as found. Its recursive capacity makes it possible to reconsider findings, to rewrite generalizations, and to recast maps at any juncture. At any point in the study of a problem, at any link in the descriptive chain, one can carry the investigation forward -- toward closer analysis or broader synthesis. Taken together, the texts lay a foundation for descriptive dialect study in the context of phonological words. And those are first and last words in this approach to linguistic geography.

Note

* This report reflects the work of many people and the generous support of Emory University and the Research Tools Program of the National Endowment for the Humanities. To list them all would carry me beyond my allotted space. Instead, I extend broad thanks to LAGS informants, field workers, scribes, and editors and special appreciation to Carol M. Adams, Borden D. Dent, and Susan L. McDaniel, who helped me organize this report.

References

Allen, Harold B. 1973-6. *The linguistic atlas of the Upper Midwest.* 3 vols. Minneapolis: University of Minnesota Press.

Bach, Adolph. 1950. *Deutsche Mundartforschung.* 2nd. ed. Heidelburg: Carl Winter.

Cassidy, Frederic G. (ed.). 1985. *Dictionary of American regional English.* Vol. 1. Cambridge: Belknap/Harvard University Press.

Gilliéron, Jules & Edmund Edmont. 1902-10. *Atlas linguistique de la France.* Paris: E. Champion.

Hempl, George. 1894. American speech maps. *Dialect Notes* 1:315-18.

Hjelmslev, Louis. 1961. *Prolegomena to a theory of language.* Translated by Francis J. Whitfield. Madison: University of Wisconsin Press.

Jaberg, Karl & Jakob Jud. 1928. *Der Sprachatlas als Forschunginstrument.* Halle: Max Niemeyer.

Jaberg, Karl & Jakob Jud. 1928-40. *Sprach- und Sachatlas Italiens und der Südschweiz.* 8 vols. Zofingen: Ringier.

Kretzschmar, William A., Jr. & P. W. Merman. 1987. Bibliography of the writings of Raven I. McDavid, Jr. *Journal of English Linguistics* 20:13-37.

Kurath, Hans, Marcus L. Hansen, Julia Bloch, & Bernard Bloch. 1939. *Handbook of the linguistic geography of New England.* Providence: Brown University and American Council of Learned Societies. 2nd ed., with additional materials by Raven I. McDavid, Jr. and Audrey R. Duckert, AMS Press, 1972.

Kurath, Hans, Marcus L. Hansen, Miles L. Hanley, Guy S. Lowman, & Bernard Bloch. 1939-43. *Linguistic atlas of New England.* 3 vols in 6 parts. Providence: Brown University and American Council of Learned Societies.

McDaniel, Susan L. 1989. Databases of the LAGS automatic atlas. *Journal of English Linguistics* 22:63-68.

McDavid, Raven I., Jr., Raymond K. O'Cain, & George T. Dorrill (eds). 1979. *Linguistic Atlas of the Middle and South Atlantic States.* 2 fascicles. Chicago: University of Chicago Press.

O'Cain, Raymond K. 1972. A social dialect study of Charleston, South Carolina. Ph.D. dissertation, University of Chicago.

Orton, Harold, *et al.* 1962-71. *Survey of English dialects.* Introduction and 4 vols in 12 parts. Leeds: E. J. Arnold & Sons Limited for the University of Leeds.

Pederson, Lee. 1974. Tape/text and analogues. *American Speech* 49:5-23.

Pederson, Lee, Guy H. Bailey, Marvin W. Bassett, Charles E. Billiard, & Susan E. Leas (eds). 1981. *LAGS: The basic materials.* Ann Arbor: University Microfilms International.

Pederson, Lee & Susan L. McDaniel (eds). Forthcoming. *The social pattern. Linguistic atlas of the Gulf States.* Vol. 7.

Pederson, Lee, Susan L. McDaniel, and Carol M. Adams (eds). 1988. *The general index. Linguistic Atlas of the Gulf States.* Vol. 2. Athens: University of Georgia Press.

Pederson, Lee, Susan L. McDaniel, & Carol M. Adams (eds). Forthcoming. *The regional pattern. Linguistic atlas of the Gulf States.* Vol. 5.

Pederson, Lee, Susan L. McDaniel, Carol M. Adams, & Caisheng Liao (eds). 1989. *The technical index. Linguistic atlas of the Gulf States.* Vol. 3. Athens: University of Georgia Press.

Pederson, Lee, Susan L. McDaniel, Carol M. Adams, & Michael Montgomery (eds). 1990. *The regional matrix. Linguistic atlas of the Gulf States.* Vol. 4. Athens: University of Georgia Press.

Pederson, Lee, Susan L. McDaniel, Carol M. Adams, & Michael Montgomery (eds). Forthcoming. *The social matrix. Linguistic atlas of the Gulf States.* Vol. 6.

Pederson, Lee, Susan L. McDaniel, Guy H. Bailey, & Marvin W. Bassett (eds). 1986. *The handbook. Linguistic atlas of the Gulf States.* Vol. 1. Athens: University of Georgia Press.

Pederson, Lee, Susan L. McDaniel, & Marvin Bassett (eds). 1986. *A concordance to the basic materials of the Linguistic atlas of the Gulf States.* Ann Arbor: University Microfilms International.

Pederson, Lee & Michael W. Madsen. 1989. Linguistic geography in Wyoming. *Journal of English Linguistics* 22:18-24.

Shelton, E. S. 1889a. The first year of the American Dialect Society. *Dialect Notes* 1:1-12.

Shelton, E. S. 1889b. The American Dialect Society: Plan of work. *Dialect Notes* 1:25-29.

Thoreau, Henry David. 1906. *The journals of Henry D. Thoreau.* 14 vols. Bradford Torrey and Francis H. Allen (eds). Boston: Houghton Mifflin.

Warner, W. Lloyd, *et al.* 1960. *Social class in America.* New York: Harper and Row.

Wenker, Georg & Ferdinand Wrede. 1895. *Der Sprachatlas des deutschen Reichs, Dichtung und Wahrheit.* 2 vols. Marburg: Elwert.

Wrede, Ferdinand. 1926. *Deutscher Sprachatlas.* Marburg: Elwert.

Area Lexicon: The Making of *DARE*

Frederic G. Cassidy
University of Wisconsin -- Madison

Dialectal variation runs through all languages at all times. The first task of the investigator is to set limits to what can be accomplished in the time and with the resources at hand. Sometimes a job cannot wait, as in the famous case when Morris Swadesh was interviewing the two last surviving speakers of an Indian language of Mexico, an elderly husband and wife, whose own idiolects differed within their dialect. When they died, Swadesh became the only living speaker.[1] He came just in time; many investigators have come too late. It is a perennial complaint of dialectologists that the best informants are always dying. Most fieldworkers must have met this situation, as I have myself in trying to question local people: 'Oh yes, Nellie Jones, she passed away last winter. If you had only come a year ago....' So, evidence is constantly being lost. We cannot step into the same river even once. Compromise is inevitable. The ideal, total, instant picture of the object in all its detail is unattainable. But we can get something like a fair facsimile by effective planning. How is this to be achieved for American English, and what is the best way to present our discoveries?

The two approaches favored at present, linguistic geography and lexicography, are both valid and are not in competition. The same evidence, or some of it, can be gathered and displayed with advantages and disadvantages both ways. The plan for a 'Linguistic Atlas of the U.S. and Canada' made in the 30's will probably never be carried out as such; it was simply too huge a project to be accomplished within one or two lifetimes. To undertake it at all, and to carry it on, require a kind of heroism. Yet the part that has been accomplished, with the *Linguistic Atlas of New England* (1939-1943) and the *Linguistic Atlas of the Upper Midwest* (1973-1976) are excellent and have added greatly to our knowledge, of American English. Several other atlases approaching completion will cover most of the Eastern and Southern states, with good progress in other parts of the country.[2] They pattern the phonological and some of the lexical variations. Unfortunately, because of the lapse of time, they cannot give a synchronic picture of the country as a whole.

The other method of presenting the variations within American English is with a dictionary, and both word lists and mapping were envisioned in the first place when the American Dialect Society was founded a hundred years ago. It is true that the founders thought in these terms partly because Joseph Wright was just then beginning to edit his *English Dialect Dictionary*, based on data largely gathered by members of the English Dialect Society. It was felt that a similar society on this side of the Atlantic could do as much for American dialects. Another reason was that in 1889 linguistic geography was a relatively new discipline. To make word lists and special studies and publish them in *Dialect Notes* (*DN*) seemed the way to go about it.

While a dictionary was not specifically mentioned by the founders of the Society, it appears definitely to have been in their thinking. The Secretary, E. H. Babbitt, in his report of 1894, wrote,

> The ideal result [of collecting]...would be a *complete record of American speech forms in our day*, say in 1900. This would form, when published, an authoritative dictionary of American usage, which would supersede all other work in that line, and remain the standard reference book till usage changes so far as to require a revision. (*DN* I, 7, 360)

The title 'American Dialect Dictionary,' though not specifically mentioned till later, was a natural parallel to Wright's title.[3]

However, dictionaries have their disadvantages too. They are subject to the tyranny of the alphabet, whose sequence is irrational and arbitrary, a product of historical accidents. Alphabetic presentation of dialect data fragments the geographic picture and forces heavy use of cross-reference. Its great advantage is that of familiarity: everybody knows the alphabet, it simplifies look-up of individual items, and it accommodates the largest part of the lexicon. Further, it can utilize maps, the chief feature of an atlas.

For many years the Society published word lists and special studies made by the members in various parts of the country (as Raven McDavid used to say, from those parts where English professors spent their summer vacations). One can sympathize with the frustration of an early Editor, William E. Mead, for criticizing what he called the 'drifting policy' of the Society's first seventeen years. He estimated that if anything comparable to Wright's *English Dialect Dictionary* was to be produced, the collecting must be increased twentyfold. He called for a 'systematic investigation' (*DN* III, 2, 168-69), but for various reasons, chiefly lack of money, the years went by and none was forthcoming. It was not until the late forties that the idea of the Dictionary surfaced again and two special meetings were held for actual planning. At the second, having proposed a plan of my own[4] and pressed for concrete action I found myself appointed Editor and encouraged to get on with the job. That was 1963 -- sixty years after William Mead had made his complaint. It was high time to attempt the 'systematic investigation' he had called for. The first volume of *DARE*, published in 1985, can serve to illustrate the systems and procedures used to produce it.

The *DARE* project dated officially from July 1, 1965, when it was assured five years' support by the U.S. Office of Education, and the University of Wisconsin had furnished office space.[5] Since the title 'American Dialect Dictionary' had been pre-empted by Harold Wentworth in 1944 for his dictionary [6] (which, however, was not accepted by ADS) a new title had to be found. Prof. Audrey Duckert, then my research assistant, and I had in anticipation worked out the new title. Our use of 'regional' rather than 'dialect' followed Hans Kurath's lead. The acronym 'DARE' was no accident; it expressed the hope that the long time goal of the Society could at last be reached. We toasted the new title and the project on the University's Union Terrace in good Wisconsin beer.

The plan was simply to gather all the data possible for the entire country: everything relevant from existing written sources and previous studies, but especially to make a fresh lexical survey, in linguistic atlas fashion, by direct interview of speakers in every state. The problem was to ensure that our results would be orderly and representative, not a patchwork of random bits and pieces. Appropriate communities must be chosen for investigation and a maximally efficient questionnaire be prepared for use in the field collecting.

With only five years' support assured, we felt we must limit ourselves to one thousand communities. Counting fifty weeks to the year and one week per community, our fieldworkers would have to cover four communities per week to get the whole way round the fifty states. The choice of communities could not be random. To get a numerically accurate representation of speakers we went to the most recent U.S. Census report (1960) and proportioned the number of communities and questionnaires per state to the population, making allowance for the rapid postwar rush to Florida and California. Allowance was also made for the types of communities to be investigated according to the make-up of each state. Five types were recognized on a scale from rural to metropolitan. Then the actual communities were chosen state by state after a study of the composition of each. Settlement history was taken into account as well as activities for which each state was known, such as tobacco growing, fishing, mining, and various industries. The fieldworkers sent to the chosen communities had to find appropriate informants: representative natives of all ages from eighteen years up, with emphasis on the oldest generations who, presumably, would know a wider range of usages, especially those that might be dying out. Race also would, as nearly as possible, be proportioned to population and similarly all ranges of education from the barest to some college training. In a word, *DARE* informants constitute in the aggregate a good spectrum of native speakers of American English.

The realities of population led to another innovation: the more than 500 *DARE* maps which appear in the columns alongside the words they illustrate. At first sight these seem distorted, as geographically they are: they are not areal but populational. On these maps the states are kept in proper relation to each other but each is enlarged or diminished according to density of population, not to square miles. This evens out the distribution of speakers in the nation as a whole and shows the language patterns more clearly. *DARE* maps are computer drawn; they help the reader to visualize 'word geography.'

For the field collecting we recruited mostly graduate students, some well-trained undergraduates, and a few faculty -- eighty in all over the five years. The first few were sent out in campers that we called 'Word Wagons,' though one classically inclined colleague dubbed them 'Logomobiles.' But these proved too comfortable; production was slow; we had to go to a 'piece-work' system, paying a fixed sum for each questionnaire satisfactorily completed. By the skin of our teeth, and with good management by Prof. James Hartman, 1002 questionnaires were completed in the five years.

One question of practice arose: was it better for fieldworkers to know their territory already, or to go to it as total strangers? In which case would they be better alert to the local speech and its differences and be more able to record it accurately? We were never able to decide the question: it was put aside by practical considerations of time and convenience. The other question we asked ourselves was, would Black fieldworkers do better than White ones in getting unguarded responses from Black informants? We tried it both ways but found no provable difference either way.

A few words may be said about the perils of dialect collecting. The *DARE* fieldworkers varied in training experience, interest, and what might be called 'scholarly conscience.' The questionnaire includes, to aid the fieldworker, lists of responses already collected but often unfamiliar to the inexperienced or untraveled. One man expressed his disbelief that anyone would respond to an unheard question, 'What say?' I told him to ask the question without warning of our bibliographer, an elderly lady from southern Indiana, and to ask it in a low voice. He did. She answered 'What say?' and he was convinced. Fieldworkers were instructed to ask the questions in the exact phrasing of the questionnaire, not to suggest possible responses except in unusual cases, and to mark such responses clearly. Informants were not to be questioned on a subject unfamiliar to them, therefore several informants were sometimes needed to complete a questionnaire in a single community. Each, of course, was coded separately, and all are accounted for in the Informant list. Under field conditions, there are bound to be interruptions and background noises. Though the best informants spoke clearly and were easy to question and record, not all were 'best.' And what I called 'scholarly conscience' did not always win over weariness. Some errors in hearing and in recording inevitably creep in. But a sharp fieldworker will catch these questionable things and note them marginally. Such notes are ultimately a great aid to the Editors. Despite much care taken in constructing and, after first use, revising the Questionnaire, it is not perfect. In Jules Gilliéron's classic statement, 'The questionnaire, to have been notably better, should have had to be made after the fieldwork.' Ironic but true. In the end one has to settle for the doable.

The fieldwork for *DARE* was accomplished without serious troubles. One man did 'roll' his Wagon when forced off the road by a snow plow. Oil leaked in and spoiled some of his questionnaires. But, not daunted, while the wagon was being repaired he rented a bicycle and continued his work. One recalls the devotion of Edmond Edmont, the field collector for Gilliéron's *Atlas Linguistique de la France*, riding his bicycle from village to village throughout France long before the era of Word Wagons.[7] Our completed questionnaires were sent back by bus. The only one lost had been put, against instructions, into the Christmas mail and disappeared. But in the end our quota was achieved. As the questionnaires returned to the office, they were computer-entered and form our 'Data Summary.' But the number of responses was far higher than expected -- close to two and a half million -- a rich haul which required a much longer time to process than anyone had estimated.

The *DARE* questionnaire, specially developed for the job, requires some description. It began with the Linguistic Atlas 'work sheets' used in New England and the Midwest, but these were enlarged to emphasize the lexical evidence. A pilot project had been tested in anticipation and published as *PADS* 20 'A Method for Collecting Dialect.' There were two innovations here, later worked into the *DARE* questionnaire. Obviously, a complete set of questions to cover the entire range of subjects and catch all the dialect vocabulary would have been impracticably long. How was the number of questions to be held within workable limits without omitting something essential? We analyzed all the material published up to that time in *Dialect Notes* and *PADS* -- some 40,000 items -- sorting them by senses -- all the weather terms together, all the food terms, all the farming terms, and so on. In this way we had a clear indication of the subjects which elicited the greatest number of terms and variations. These subjects could logically be expected to be the most fruitful. In this way, collecting already done over a sixty-year period became the means of maximizing the questionnaire. Forty- one categories of subject matter emerged and were put into a sequence to facilitate direct interview by fieldworkers. The sequence starts with perfectly neutral subjects -- time, weather, furniture -- to allay any possible suspicion on the part of informants, that we had clandestine motives. Once the neutral questions had been answered and confidence established, one could go on to more personal or sensitive subjects. This *PADS* 20 questionnaire was sent by mail to fifty Wisconsinites in twenty-five communities. Later on, for *DARE*, it was recast for use in person-to-person interviews. The other innovation was that each question was stated in a fixed form: the fieldworkers were to ask them exactly as stated, to ensure comparability in the responses, and ultimately computer handling. On the whole, the fieldworkers followed the system faithfully.

By 1965 it had become obvious that computers were to be the tool of the future, though then primitive by modern standards. Every informant was therefore tagged by state and personal number -- for example MD16, OH55. Each question and each response was similarly coded, as well as each informant's age, sex, race, degree of education, and type of community. Thus with present computers we can furnish such sociolinguistic information as the percentage of speakers of one type or another who gave a certain response. This permits a degree of exactness in labeling that has not been possible hitherto. Following the *OED* method, *DARE* set up a reading program, which, however, proved less successful than we had hoped. Volunteers, eager at first, showed little staying power. But mostly they did not have a feel for what might be dialectal: in the books we furnished they tended to underline anything that did not seem familiar, including even literary words. Reading is now done by the DARE staff under supervision. The present bibliography lists more than 7000 items, with others added every day.

They include past and present regional literature of every kind, diaries, letters, biographies, historical accounts, newspapers, and even the humble advertising sheet if it records palpably local usage. The field records of *LANE* and several regional collections were given outright for the *DARE* files.

This 'Main File' gives the diachronic dimension to match the 'Data Summary' compiled from the questionnaires. Together they furnish a base of more than five million items. Only the Data Summary is computer stored; we have never had the time or money to store the rest, though it would certainly have been desirable. With two volumes of five finished and the other three begun, it is now probably too late to be worth doing. However, everything we can do with computers is done. They save much of the drudgery of alphabetization, proofreading, and general putting-in-order. *DARE* maps are now made 'in house' rather than at the cartography laboratory and can be flashed on the Editors' screens upon command. Calculations of frequency, percentages, response lists, and many other annoying matters are now dealt with quickly and more accurately. Library search for books we want to quote from can be done directly by Modem. Other time-saving procedures are added whenever possible. But the main point is that *DARE* went early to computer processing: it was a pioneer in the field of lexicography, which is now computerizing everything at top speed. The *New Oxford English Dictionary* is already demonstrating advanced computing techniques which will make possible many language studies that no one even considered before because they would have taken lifetimes to accomplish.

To summarize what has been learned from the *DARE* project, it may be said, first, that when it is finished in ten or a dozen years, it should furnish a very full though not exhaustive collection of that part of American English which varies regionally or dialectally. It will be based on a century of collecting done by many scholars including latterly the *DARE* Editors. It will give dated quotations from all sources, oral and written, with definitions drawn from them. The information from fieldwork with facts geographical and social about the informants should greatly aid in interpretation of the American English lexicon, including the morpho-syntactic part that involves lexical forms. It will help to distinguish and classify the non-standard components of the lexicon which so frequently merge or overlap, too often being vaguely labeled as cant, jargon, slang, colloquialism, or -- what else? -- dialect. Seen historically, and even in the process of change, such components can be better understood and more accurately labeled.

The first volume of *DARE* contains a fresh outline of American regional pronunciation, its present state and tendencies toward future change; a fresh mapping of the regional divisions; a sketch of the chief grammatical and formal alterations that characterize dialect speech; a list of the communities in which the field collecting was done and of the native local people who answered the questionnaires, with pertinent facts about them: age, sex, race, degree of education, type of community they represent, and type of work they do or have done. *DARE* did not attempt to tape-record the interviews,[8] but each informant was asked to record the story of 'Arthur the Rat,' for reading style, and to speak freely for about half an hour on any familiar subject, for everyday speech, both pronunciation and vocabulary. These 1843 tapes from all over the United States form a unique collection; they are the basis of the section on pronunciation and are quoted often in the treatments of entries. They bring us as close to the genuine speech of the people as one can hope to come, at least in this century. A selection from these tapes will accompany the last volume. The tapes form part of the *DARE* collections which will remain as an archive for further studies since they will by no means have been exhausted in making the Dictionary.

As an example of the kinds of information that can be found in *DARE* Volume I, we may look at the entry for *about*. The head word or lemma is followed by part of speech labels: preposition and adverb. Pronunciations, given in phonemic characters follow: the usual forms, then the specifically regional variants heard chiefly in the South and Midland, and in the coastal area of Maryland, Virginia, and South Carolina; also one rare but sufficiently supported variant. Reference is made to the Introduction: the pertinent section on pronunciation (pages xli-lxi). Five pronunciation-spellings follow, in which writers have tried to spell the word the way they heard it pronounced. Next comes a section A on recorded forms, with quotations from thirteen

about prep, adv Usu |(ə)'baʊt, (ə)'bɑʊt|; also, **chiefly Sth, Midl** |ə'bæʊt|; in **MD, eVA, eSC,** often |ə'bo:ʊt, ə'b(ə)ʊt, ɑ'but|; rarely |ə'bɑt|. See Pronc Intro 3.II.14 Pronc-spp *abaout, abeout, abowoot, 'bout, erbout*

A Forms.

1861 Holmes *Venner* 152 **wMA,** What'y' been dreamin' abaout? **1895** *DN* 1.372 **wNC, eTN, seKY,** *Let go* . . . "The road is back yander, let go abeout a mile." **1901** *DN* 2.181 **KY** [Black], 'Bout. **1903** *DN* 2.291 **Cape Cod MA** (as of 1850s), *Ou, ow* were always *au,* never *æu:* how, . . about. **1917** Torrence *Granny Maumee* 51 [Black], I got er-bout—fifty er so. **1919** *DN* 5.40 **VA,** *Out,* . . pronounced *ow-oot.* Similarly, "a-bowoot." **1927** Shewmake *Engl. Pronc. VA* 24, In typical Eastern Virginia speech, diphthongal ou or ow is given the dialectal sound represented by (uh–oo) . . . Examples of words in which dialectal *ou* is heard are *about, couch, doubt,* [etc.]. **1930** *AmSp* 5.347 **cSC,** [æʊ] in *scouts, out, about.* **1930** *AmSp* 6.94 **VA,** In the Tidewater . . *about* . . [əbəut] or [əbut]. **1934** *AmSp* 9.213 **eVA, eSC,** Along the coast . . the diphthong in *about* and *out* tends to become . . [u] or [ʊ]. **1937** *AmSp* 12.290 **wVA,** [əbæʊt feɪs]. **1938** *AmSp* 13.369 **nePA,** *About* [ə'bɑt]. **1941** *AmSp* 16.7 **eTX** [Black], In Negro speech this diphthong is not often flattened to [æʊ] as in 'hill type' speech, but retains its standard form, with lengthening of the first element . . . *about* . . [ba:ʊt]. **1967–68** *DARE* FW Addits **MD,** About [ə'bʊt]; **cnNY,** About [ə'bot].

B As prep.

Foll by a vbl n (where an infin is now common): on the point of. [*OED about* A13, →1865] *?obs*

1802 (1941) Tucker *Diary* 313 **MA,** With the air of one about conferring a great favor. **1831** (1927) Rodman *Diary* 89 **MA,** Engaged part of the forenoon relative to a cottage which I am about building on the south side . . of School St. **1837** in 1926 *AmSp* 2.31 **IL,** An effort is about being made. **a1853** (1890) Cutler *Life & Times* 86 (as of 1806) **CT,** My brother . . was here on his first visit to Ohio, and was about returning on horseback to Massachusetts.

C As adv.

Alternately, in turns: see quots. [*OED about* B5b→1851] *arch*

1834 in 1956 Eliason *Tarheel Talk* 257 **NC,** I give . . unto my son Rezin . . his own choice of horse beast him and my son Henry chooseing one about. **1953** Randolph *Down in Holler* 166 **swMO,** A man in Forsyth . . said: "Maw used to call me an' Fred up *a morning about* to make the fire." That is, she called the two boys on alternate mornings, so that the task was evenly divided. Which reminds me of the two men in Christian County . . . "By God, I'll chop the damn' thing to pieces!" one yelled. "Good idea, Tom," cried the other. "Fetch the ax, an' we'll *take a lick about!*" He meant that they would take turns a-chopping.

Figure 1. *DARE* entry for *about*

bank n[1]

1 A heap of potatoes or other vegetables covered with mulch and earth, and over this sometimes a shed, to preserve them during winter. **chiefly Sth** See Map See also **bank v 2, cave n 1**

1837 Wheeler *Practical Treatise* 202 **SC**, It appeared the slave was stealing potatoes from a bank near the defendant's house. **1856** Davis *Farm Bk.* 12 **AL** *(DA)*, The Bank of cut potatoes was first used up but the cook failed to get all a few were left covered up in dirt. **1965–70** *DARE* (Qu. M19, *A place for keeping carrots, turnips, potatoes and so on over the winter*) 44 Infs, **chiefly Sth**, Potato bank; 10 Infs, **chiefly Sth**, Bank; **MS**46, **SC**32, **TX**40, Turnip bank; **AL**52, Cabbage bank; **NC**10, Sweet potato bank; (Qu. M22, . . *Other kinds of buildings . . on farms*) Inf **AR**52, Potato shed or potato bank—potatoes were banked in dirt, covered with hay and then the shed over that; **TX**32, Tool shed, potato bank, cotton house; **GA**16, Tater bank. **1969** *DARE* FW Addit **GA**51, Bank—a construction of mulch and earth for preserving sweet potatoes over winter. Pyramidal heap in back yard.

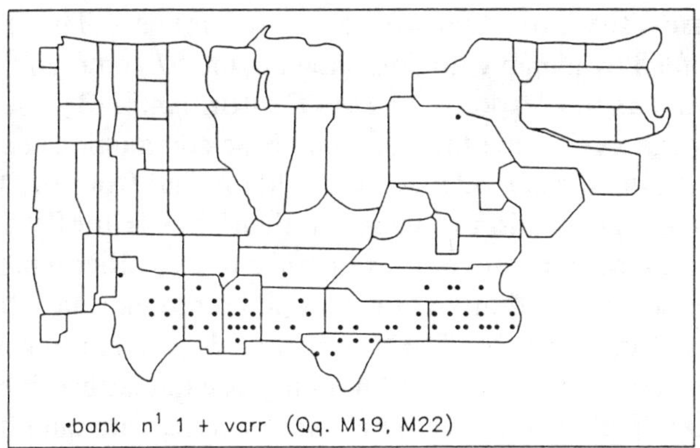

•bank n[1] 1 + varr (Qq. M19, M22)

2 also attrib, also *coal bank:* A coal mine and its immediate surroundings; the surface of a mine.

1804 (1904) Clark *Orig. Jrls. Lewis & Clark Exped.* 1.58, At 3 Miles [we] passed a Coal-Mine, or Bank of stone Coal, . . this bank appears to Contain great quantity of fine Coal. **1946** Stuart *Tales Plum Grove* 122 **seKY**, "You didn't have any business goin' in that coal mine on Bill Sexton," Grandma answered. "You went in that coal bank to whop him." **1968** Adams *Western Words, Bank* . . . In mining, the surface of the mouth of a mine pit. **1969** *DARE* Tape **KY**28, He loaded coal in the cars, in the bank cars what brought the coal outside. **1973** *PADS* 59.42 **WV, wVA**, All the buildings, grounds, and underground passages associated with a particular coal mining operation . . . bank. *Ibid* **WV, wVA**, Coal haulage vehicle . . . bank car.

3 See **banking ground(s).**

4 See **tree bank.**

Figure 2. *DARE* entry for *bank* (noun, partial)

sources dated 1861 to 1967-68. Nine of these give the sounds in International Phonetic Alphabet notation. Section B follows with definition and examples of the word as a preposition, four quotations from 1802 to 1853. Finally in section C, the word is shown as an adverb with quotations from 1834 to 1953, a definition, and a cross-reference to the Oxford Dictionary. The treatment takes up a little more than half a column. Note that none of the examples given represents standard usage: they are regional and can be 'placed' socially by their language context and by other facts, such as those given in the list of *DARE* informants in the introductory section (pages xxxvi-cli).

Another sample treatment showing additional features might be that of *bank*, with three entries: noun[1], noun[2], and verb. Noun[1] lists four senses, the latter two with cross-references. The first sense is accompanied by a map with dots showing the 57 communities in which this word was the response of *DARE* informants. By use of the key map on page xxxi of the Introduction, these communities can be identified. Individual respondents can be identified from the list already mentioned. The region of use is indicated as 'Chiefly South' with reference to the map and cross-reference to two other words pertinent to this sense. The definition of the second sense indicates that the word is also used attributively. The treatment of *bank* noun[1] takes about two thirds of a column. *Bank* noun[2] has only one quotation: it explains the use in marble play. *Bank* verb has three senses, with quotations dating from 1720 to 1972. Sense 1 notes that the verb is sometimes used with the adverb *up*; sense 3 similarly is sometimes used with *out*; sense 2 notes that there is a related verbal noun *banking*. In short, pronunciation, spellings, meanings, and phrase-formation are all historically illustrated, with examples of use from the eighteenth century to the present time, labeling for type of usage, division into senses, and cross references to related or semantically comparable words.

It should be obvious that the model for *DARE* was the *Oxford English Dictionary*, with some innovations, chiefly the use of maps and of oral data specially gathered throughout the country in a single five-year period. Our field collecting was done just in time before the enormously powerful penetration of television to every corner of the nation began. Thus a great body of data was saved from oblivion.

Nevertheless, *DARE* gives no more than an overall picture. For the study of American English, regional or not, a great many special studies remain to be made. The American Dialect Society may begin its second century with a full agenda.

Notes

1 This is from memory but, in essence, I think correct.

2 Reference is to the *Linguistic Atlas of the Middle and South Atlantic States*, the *Linguistic Atlas of the North Central States*, the *Linguistic Atlas of the Gulf States*, the *Linguistic Atlas of Oklahoma*. They are at present in the editorial charge respectively of William Kretzschmar, Jr., Virginia McDavid, Lee Pederson, and Bruce Southard.

3 The title 'American Dialect Dictionary' is first used in *DN* II,1:72, by the Secretary, E.H. Babbitt, in connection with contributions by ADS members to Wright's *EDD*.

4 These meetings were held in New York City, 1947, and Stanford, California, 1949. I was present at the first and sent a paper which was read for me by Allen Walker Read at the second. The latter outlines the plan later used for *DARE*. See also *PADS* 39, The ADS Dictionary--How Soon?, 1963.

5 Support also has come from the National Endowment for the Humanities and the National Science Foundation, a number of private foundations and individuals, and especially the Andrew W. Mellon Foundation.

6 *American Dialect Dictionary*, Thomas Y. Crowell, N.Y.

7 See Jules Gilliéron, *Atlas Linguistique de la France, Notice Servant a L'intelligence des Cartes*, Paris, 1902.

8 Interviews for the *Linguistic Atlas of the Gulf States* were recorded in their entirety and later transcribed. *DARE* had not the time or the resources to do this, though it is certainly preferable.

Some Applications of Mathematical and Statistical Models in Dialect Geography

Dennis Girard and Donald Larmouth
University of Wisconsin -- Green Bay

Introduction

Whether the purpose of dialect geography is to establish a record for historical comparison, as in early atlas work, or to characterize the distribution of variant forms, as in *DARE*, dialectologists have recognized for a long time that an assortment of geographical and social variables could influence the occurrence and distribution of linguistic features. As a result of this tradition and more recent work in social dialectology, a data set in dialect geography is very likely to include not only the variant features observed in a region, but also their distribution in different speech registers, along with the age, gender, and socioeconomic status of the informants, the social networks in which they participate, and further background information about the region's topography, political structure, settlement history, and population centers.

Not content merely to catalogue the linguistic variables in a data set, some dialectologists have sought to describe their geographical distribution and thereby define dialect areas. Others have tried to characterize the inherent variability observed in individual informants and relate it to different social variables, while others have tried to infer the regional and social dynamics which underlie the diffusion of dialect features from one population to another. In some instances, these problems have been approached with a mathematical or statistical model chosen *a priori*, such as Sankoff (1978) or Trudgill (1974); more often, dialectologists have begun with a data set and sought out models after the fact, such as Linn (1981) and Miller (1984). Many different mathematical and statistical techniques are available for such applications -- so many that it can be difficult to choose among them. It would seem that the choice ought to be made in terms of the nature of the data set and the interpretive goals of the study; hence, the basic purpose of this chapter is to explore a variety of mathematical and statistical models through which efforts to interpret regional dialect data might be supported.

Defining Dialect Areas as 'Fuzzy Sets'

Traditional methodology in dialect geography has focused upon the demarcation of isoglosses as a way of characterizing dialect areas. If the isoglosses appeared to bundle together, they defined a dialect boundary. Although the technique seems straightforward enough, in practice it has produced many disputes about just where the dialect boundary ought to be drawn, because the isoglosses usually form very loose 'bundles,' and often they don't seem to bunch together at all. Indeed, the technique perpetuates a fiction in much the same way that weather maps do, implying that people on one side of an arbitrary line behave one way, while their neighbors on the other side behave another way. In real life, of course, dialectologists have remarked that the area of the dialect 'boundary' is actually an area of heterogeneity and mixture, but such remarks are really a way of excusing an inherent deficiency in their representation of a dialect area.

From the perspective of set theory or geometry, dialect areas are only planar sets, and the problem of determining dialect boundaries is a problem of determining set membership. However, the realization that the boundary between two dialect areas is actually an area of heterogeneity or mixture naturally suggests interpreting dialect areas as 'fuzzy sets,' that is, sets whose boundaries are nebulous.

In ordinary set theory, a subset A of a set U is a collection of elements of U. If we designate an element of U by the symbol x, then we represent the fact that x is in subset A by writing $x \in A$. If x is not in subset A, this is indicated as $x \notin A$. An alternative and particularly useful manner of expressing membership in a subset is to apply the notion of a characteristic function. Thus, we define a function $\mu A(x)$ by the following:

$$\mu A(x) = 1 \text{ if } x \in A$$

$$\mu A(x) = 0 \text{ if } x \notin A$$

This is simply a function of the elements of subset A which takes on the value 1 when an element belongs to A and takes on the value 0 when the element does not belong to A. As an example, suppose that U = {a, b, c, d, e} and that A = {a, c, d}. Then $\mu A(a) = 1$, $\mu A(b) = 0$, $\mu A(c) = 1$, $\mu A(d) = 1$, and $\mu A(e) = 0$. It is common in this context to list the subset A as a collection of ordered pairs (Kaufmann 1975)

$$A = \{(a,1), (b,0), (c,1), (d,1), (e,0)\}$$

where each element is followed by the value of the characteristic function for the subset.

Using this convention, the concept 'fuzzy set' is easy to define. The notion of the characteristic function is simply extended to that of a 'membership' function, $\mu A(x)$, which can take on any value between 0 and 1, not just 0 or 1. The value of the membership function then indicates the degree or level of membership in a set or perhaps even represents a measure of the probability that a particular element lies within the set. The subset A in the above example might take the form

$$A = \{(a,0.3), (b,0.2), (c,1.0), (d,0.5), (e,0.0)\}$$

where the pair (b,0.2) indicates that the element b belongs to the subset A with a 'level of certainty' equal to 0.2. Similarly, in (c,1.0), the figure 1.0 indicates that it is 100% certain that element c belongs to A.

This idea of a membership function makes it possible to characterize the set of boundary points between two dialect areas by specifying any one of a variety of possible membership functions. For example, suppose that dialect areas A and B are separated by a bundle of isoglosses as illustrated in Figure 1.

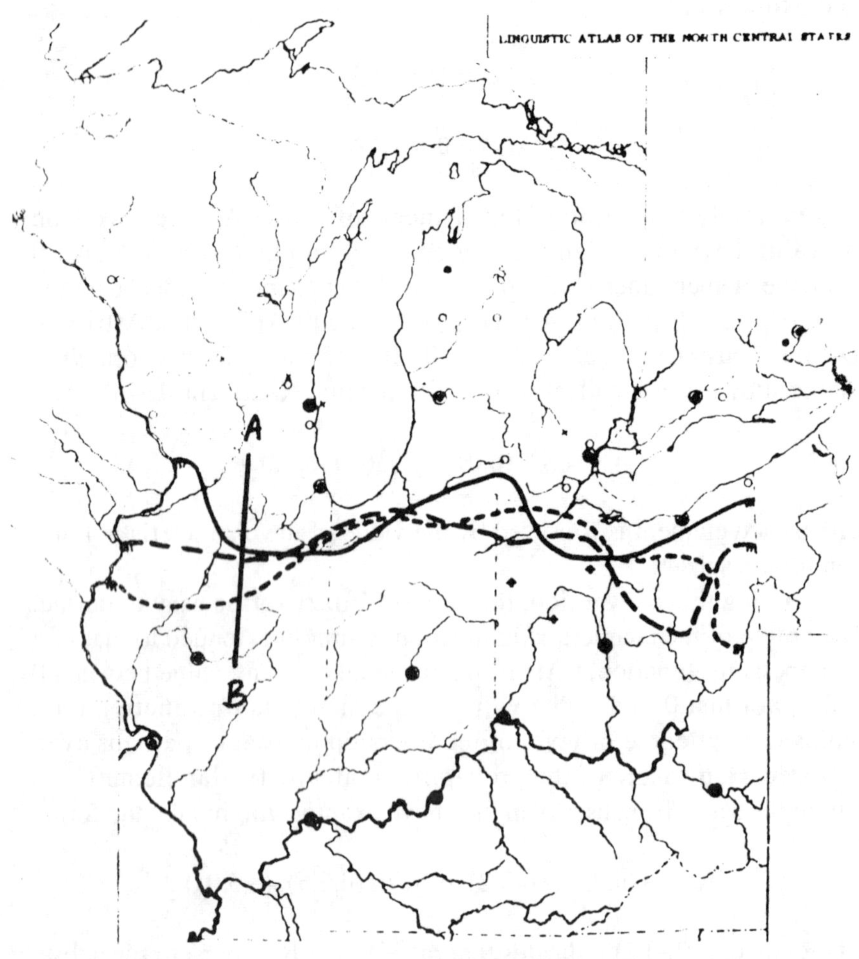

Figure 1. Fuzzy set transect superimposed on dialect area map (McDavid 1979:248)

The mixture of dialect features could be described by a suitable membership function. For simplicity, consider the dialect variation along the transect from A to B in Figure 1 above. The nature of the mixture of any two features could be characterized by the structure of such a function. For instance, in Figure 2 the membership function describes a sharp boundary between the two dialect features with no mixture at all, while in Figure 3 the membership function indicates a more gradual change from one feature to another, with a narrow region in which the feature changes quite rapidly. In contrast, Figure 4 suggests a very gradual transition from one feature to the other, indicating that there is perhaps no dialect boundary but rather a transition zone. In practice one would define the membership function as a bivariate function of the location of a point along that transect, be it a city, a village, or a crossroads hamlet. The form of such functions could be conjectured *a priori* and field data then used to test the goodness of fit of the model. Although in general no further constraints need to be imposed on the membership function, in practice there seems to be little reason not to insist that the function be some sort of univariate or bivariate probability density function. This immediately makes available a full array of statistical techniques, both for estimation and inference, which is essentially the approach currently being taken by Davis and Houck (1989) in a recent paper on the North Midland/South Midland dialect boundary which shows that what had previously been represented as a boundary is better characterized as a transition zone.

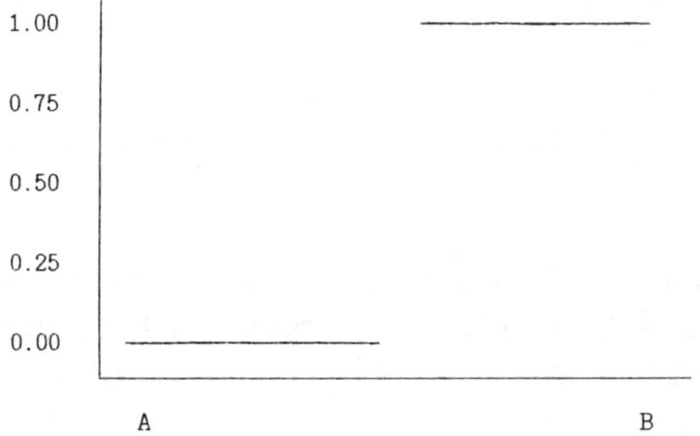

Figure 2. Fuzzy set calculation: sharp boundary

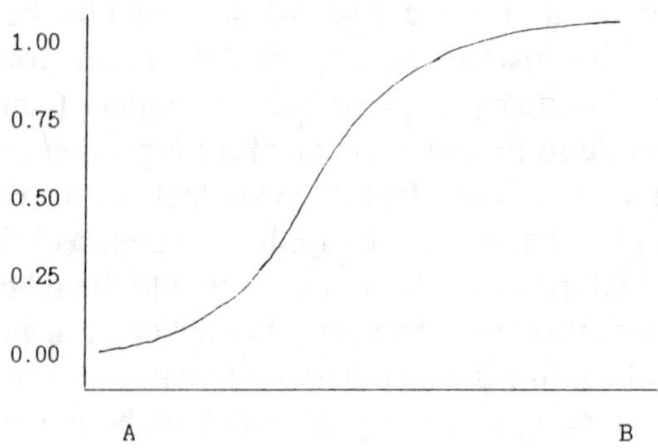

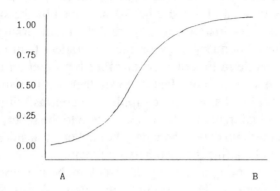

Figure 3. Fuzzy set calculation: gradual boundary

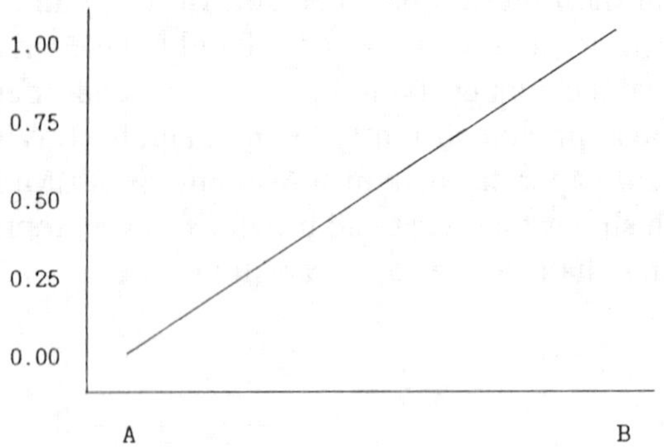

Figure 4. Fuzzy set calculation: transition zone

If we wish to relax the notion of a membership function somewhat, it is possible to see a connection between a fuzzy set characterization of a dialect area and the use of break-point gravity models. In such models, as discussed below, 'influence' functions are constructed which vary from one value to another for communities at different distances from a population center. The boundary between two dialect areas would then be defined as the point where the functions take on equal values. Given two influence functions, it is a straightforward task to construct a corresponding membership function where the break-point corresponds to a value of 0.5 for the membership function.

This similarity between existing approaches to the definition of dialect areas and models which would arise from the specialization of fuzzy set membership functions suggests that perhaps the most appropriate use of the fuzzy set model is simply to draw out the intrinsic similarities of the various models which can be used to define dialect areas.

Characterizing Regional Interaction with Gravity Models

While the characterization of a dialect area may be more satisfying if it is defined as a fuzzy set, it would seem to be even more satisfying if it were also possible to reflect the underlying regional dynamics which have produced it. There are clearly cases in which physical topography and political boundaries have figured significantly in the distribution of dialect features in a region, at least in historical terms. But in many regions, modern transportation systems have greatly reduced the significance of physical topography, and there are also many 'low-structure' regions which seem not to have obvious barriers to social interaction. In such instances, the significant variables are frequently the sizes of the populations of different communities and the distances which separate them, and their interplay can be discovered and expressed through gravity models, which establish relationships between population and distance.

Gravity models emerged from a tradition of 'social physics,' in which the behavior of human populations was assumed to be analogous to the laws of physics, specifically in this instance Newton's law of gravitation, in which the force of attraction between two bodies is directly proportional to their mass and inversely proportional to the square of the intervening distance (Exline, Peters & Larkin 1982). Gravity models have a long and successful history in economic geography, beginning with Ravenstein (1885), who demonstrated a relationship between population and distance in human migration. Over the years, many different gravity models have been proposed, all of which postulate that interaction between two communities varies directly with some function of their population and inversely with some function of the distance between them. The various forms of the gravity model are summarized in the following expression (Yeates & Garner 1976):

$$I_{ij} = \frac{(W_i \; P_i) \qquad (W_j \; P_j)}{D^b_{ij}}$$

In this expression,

I_{ij}	=	the volume of interaction between places i and j
W_i and W_j	=	empirically determined weights
P_i and P_j	=	population sizes of places i and j
D_{ij}	=	the distance betweeen places i and j
b	=	an exponent expressing the 'friction of distance'

The above formulation is an 'attraction' model which expresses the volume of interaction between two communities. Trudgill (1974) used this kind of model, incorporating a factor of dialect similarity which was analogous to the notion of 'friction of distance,' arguing that diffusion of a dialect feature from one community to another was partly a function of the degree of similarity between the two dialects. He used this attraction or 'influence' model to explain why the dialect of Norwich incorporated features from London speech while the dialects of smaller nearby communities did not, even though they were closer to London.

A basically similar formulation of the gravity model which had its earliest and most successful application in the study of retail market areas became known as 'Reilly's Law of Retail Gravitation':

> All things being equal, two cities attract retail trade away from any intermediate town or city approximately in direct proportion to the population of the two cities and in inverse proportion to the square of the distances from the two cities to the intermediate town.

However, this formulation evolved into a 'break-point' gravity model which projected the point at which the attraction or influence generated by competing communities would be exactly equal:

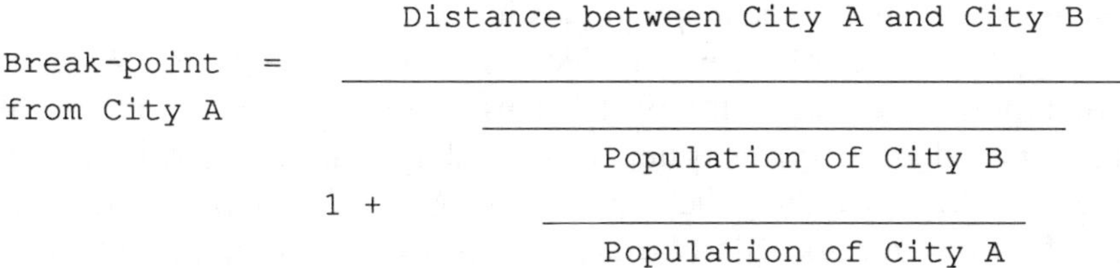

$$\text{Break-point from City A} = \frac{\text{Distance between City A and City B}}{1 + \sqrt{\dfrac{\text{Population of City B}}{\text{Population of City A}}}}$$

This formulation predicts the geographical boundaries or the spheres of influence generated by communities of various sizes as they compete with each other. Larger communities have larger influence areas and compete directly with each other as well as with smaller intervening communities which generate more localized influence. Constructing the influence areas with a break-point gravity model ultimately yields a hierarchy of interaction -- a mosaic of small, localized influence areas generated by smaller communities over which are superimposed the large influence areas of major cities in the region. As might be expected, behavior is most heterogeneous near the break-points, where the homogenizing influence of the population centers is the weakest and where local influence can compete more effectively.

It is important to emphasize that the influence area of a large population center is not bounded by immediately adjacent smaller communities, and this is borne out not only by many studies of economic interaction, but also by observations of the ways in which dialect features diffuse. While it is useful to think of the directionality of linguistic variation as vectors through time and space (Bailey 1973), such that features more distant from their origins will be statistically weaker or will alternate with features from a competing point of origin, the actual pattern of diffusion seems to reflect the hierarchy of interaction revealed by the gravity model. Rather than simply spreading across a landscape in oil-spot fashion, linguistic features seem to move from one regional center to another before spreading into the hinterland communities, reflecting the hierarchical patterns of social and economic interaction and hence the linguistic and cultural orientation of the inhabitants in the region (cf. Trudgill 1986). Not surprisingly, therefore, dialect mixture appears to be greatest in those areas along the break-point between the major population centers.

These principles were applied to data from east central Wisconsin, reported by Larmouth (1981). This region has few topographical barriers and an excellent system of secondary roads along with a main highway directly linking the regional centers, the Green Bay metropolitan area (population 145,000) and Manitowoc (population 32,547). Between Green Bay and Manitowoc lie two smaller towns (Denmark and Mishicot) and several villages (Maribel, Whitelaw, and Francis Creek). Smaller unincorporated villages and hamlets also exist in the region, such as Kellnersville, Langes Corners, Grimms, Larrabee, and Bellevue, but their populations are not separately counted in the census; hence, for purposes of the gravity model, they have 'disappeared' and are absorbed into the population data for larger communities. Figure 5 displays the interactive structure of this region as it was calculated with the break-point gravity model by Richard Hoffman, a former student at the University of Wisconsin-Green Bay.

In this area, the features of the dominant dialect compete with local features which typically reflect a residue from earlier times when immigrant languages were in wider use. In such conditions, the effect of the immigrant language upon the dominant language is typically greatest at the phonological level, while the dominant language exerts its greatest effect at the lexical level (Thomason 1981). Hence, several phonological features from immigrant languages remain in the speech of the hinterland, alternating with higher-status features from the centers of population. A classical instance is the alternation between interdental [ð] and apico-dental [d̪], as displayed in Table 1, where the

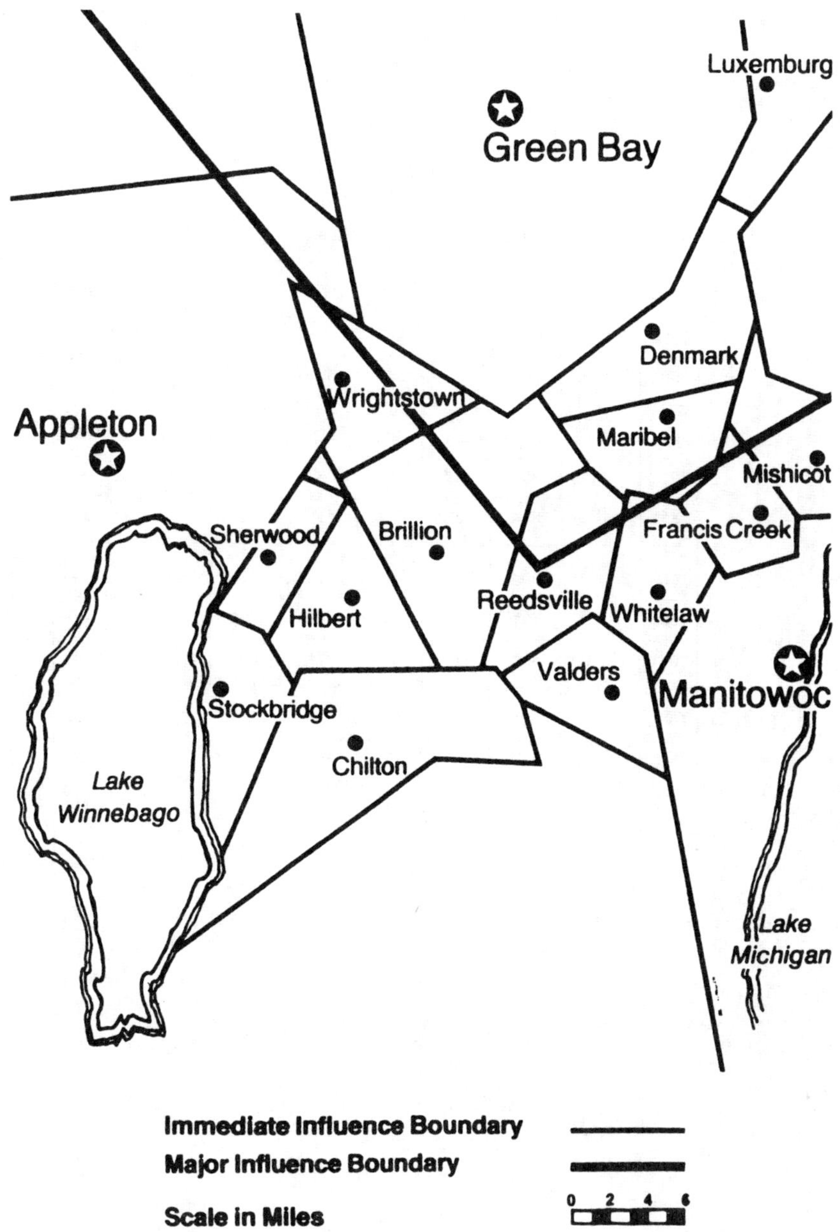

Figure 5. Break-point gravity model map: East-Central Wisconsin

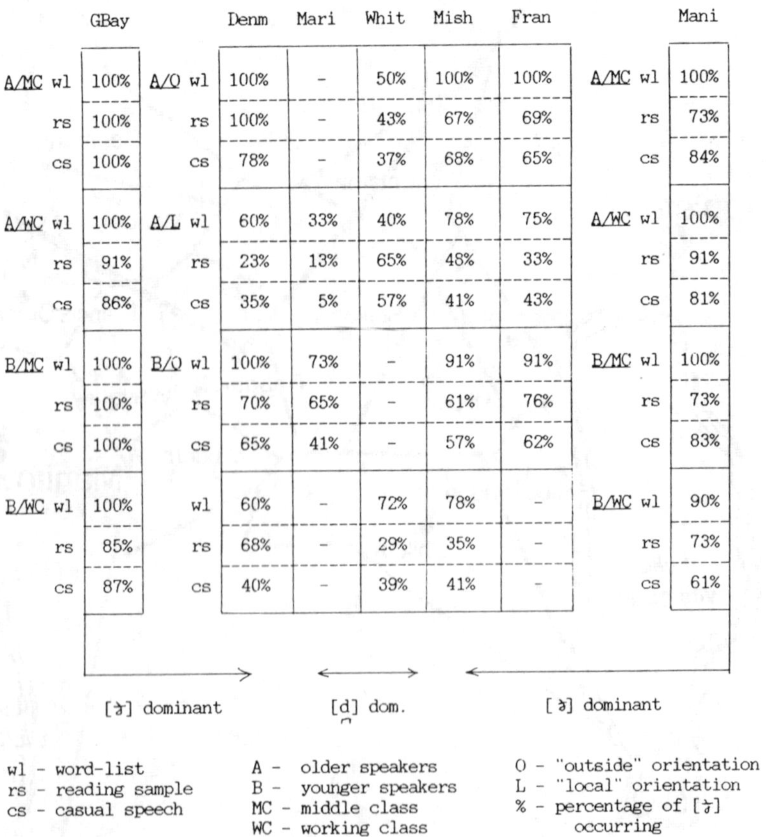

		GBay
A/MC	wl	100%
	rs	100%
	cs	100%
A/WC	wl	100%
	rs	91%
	cs	86%
B/MC	wl	100%
	rs	100%
	cs	100%
B/WC	wl	100%
	rs	85%
	cs	87%

		Denm	Mari	Whit	Mish	Fran
A/O	wl	100%	-	50%	100%	100%
	rs	100%	-	43%	67%	69%
	cs	78%	-	37%	68%	65%
A/L	wl	60%	33%	40%	78%	75%
	rs	23%	13%	65%	48%	33%
	cs	35%	5%	57%	41%	43%
B/O	wl	100%	73%	-	91%	91%
	rs	70%	65%	-	61%	76%
	cs	65%	41%	-	57%	62%
	wl	60%	-	72%	78%	-
	rs	68%	-	29%	35%	-
	cs	40%	-	39%	41%	-

		Mani
A/MC	wl	100%
	rs	73%
	cs	84%
A/WC	wl	100%
	rs	91%
	cs	81%
B/MC	wl	100%
	rs	73%
	cs	83%
B/WC	wl	90%
	rs	73%
	cs	61%

[ð̆] dominant — [d̪] dom. — [ð̆] dominant

wl - word-list
rs - reading sample
cs - casual speech

A - older speakers
B - younger speakers
MC - middle class
WC - working class

O - "outside" orientation
L - "local" orientation
% - percentage of [ð̆] occurring

Table 1: Distribution of [ð̆]/[d̪] variants (Larmouth 1981:217)

		GBay			Denm	Mari	Whit	Mish	Fran			Mani
A/MC	wl	100%	A/O	wl	75%	-	81%	30%	30%	A/MC	wl	76%
	rs	100%		rs	85%	-	71%	60%	30%		rs	41%
	cs	100%		cs	68%	-	83%	25%	22%		cs	26%
A/WC	wl	100%	A/L	wl	83%	79%	74%	41%	36%	A/WC	wl	29%
	rs	100%		rs	80%	90%	80%	65%	63%		rs	40%
	cs	100%		cs	83%	80%	80%	28%	40%		cs	33%
B/MC	wl	100%	B/O	wl	100%	81%	-	43%	40%	B/MC	wl	81%
	rs	100%		rs	100%	71%	-	69%	74%		rs	83%
	cs	100%		cs	84%	74%	-	29%	34%		cs	40%
B/WC	wl	100%		wl	71%	-	74%	45%	-	B/WC	wl	38%
	rs	100%		rs	80%	-	82%	65%	-		rs	83%
	cs	100%		cs	81%	-	81%	34%	-		cs	36%

[tr-] dominant → ← [čr-] dominant

wl - word-list
rs - reading sample
cs - casual speech

A - older speakers
B - younger speakers
MC - middle class
WC - working class

O - "outside" orientation
L - "local" orientation
% - percentage of [tr-] occurring

Table 2: Distribution of [tr]/[čr] variants (Larmouth 1981:219)

interdental variant dominates in the most guarded speech (elicited through circumlocution questions) but loses ground to the local apico-dental variant in a reading sample and in casual speech. The speakers with the greatest likelihood of using the apico-dental variant are locally-oriented residents of smaller communities near the break-point between Green Bay and Manitowoc. Not surprisingly, residents of the same communities who are culturally oriented toward the larger population centers are more likely to use the interdental variant. For them, the 'friction of distance' is apparently less than it is for the locally-oriented residents. A similar distribution appears for some other phonological variants in the region.

Another instance reflects more clearly the direct competition between the population centers, as shown in Table 2. These data show that initial [tr] predominates in the Green Bay area of influence in such words as *train, truck*, etc., while a [č] variant with an initial affricate predominates in Manitowoc and the communities within its influence area. It's not as clear-cut as all that (if it were, a simple isogloss would do), because there is a lot of mixture of the two variants in the smaller communities near the break-point. At the same time, the distribution within the Manitowoc samples indicates that the Green Bay [tr] predominates in careful speech among the older and the younger middle-class informants, suggesting that the diffusion pattern reflects the hierarchy of interaction projected by the gravity model.

Thus, while there are different formulations for gravity models, their basic application in dialect geography is to develop a sense of the interactive dynamics of the communities in a region, which will in turn enable further explication of the ways in which dialect features diffuse from one community to another--a process which will often result in dialect mixture.

Relating Linguistic and Social Variables through Multivariate Analysis

The foregoing discussion of inherent variability amongst the speakers in larger population centers and in hinterland communities suggests that some understanding of the interactive dynamics of the communities in a region can be developed through gravity models which relate population and distance. At the same time, there are several social variables within these regional data that are not fully incorporated into the explanation of the diffusion process -- factors such as age, gender, socioeconomic class, social network, etc. Much recent work in dialectology has made use of chi-square statistics to demonstrate two-way relationships between linguistic and social variables (see Davis 1982, Davis 1988), e. g., correlating gender with the relative frequency of linguistic forms which are sanctioned in the schoolroom (McDavid 1988), or correlating age with variant plurals for *hoof* (Miller 1984). But in this kind of procedure, the results are 'significant' only if there is a large discrepancy between observed and expected values, indicating that there is an association between the two variables used for classifying the observations. Thus, even though the researcher recognizes that several different social variables may be important and has taken pains to collect the necessary background information, a two-way table can only examine the relationship between the response and one social variable at a time. Since it seems likely that more than one social variable may be important and that they may interact in some fashion, that is, the nature of the relationship between the response and one social variable may change as the *level* of a second social variable changes, a statistical procedure which could express multivariate effects of different social variables would seem to hold more promise for a richer interpretation of the data.

In conventional chi-square analysis of data arranged in a two-way table, expected values are computed by multiplying row total by column total and dividing by table total. These are then compared with the observed values in the table by using Pearson's statistic. This mode of analysis assumes that the classification of observations into row categories is independent of their classification into column categories. If this model of independence is correct, with high probability that the observed values will be close to the expected values, then Pearson's statistic will be a small number. In contrast, if the model of independence is not correct, there will (again with high probability) be significant discrepancies between some of the observed and expected values, resulting in a relatively large value of Pearson's statistic. Thus, for a two-way table there are only two possibilities, or models -- independence or no independence.

As an aside, Pearson's chi-square statistic is sensitive to the size of the table total and this has stimulated the development and use of several measures of association based on chi-square which reduce this sensitivity. There are four measures of association based directly on chi-square: the co-efficient of contingency, the root mean square contingency, Cramer's V, and Tscheprow's T. Each is an attempt to adjust the value of chi-square for sample size and all vary between 0 and 1. Because of this it is possible to use them to compare the relative significance of individual variables in separate two-way tables, as Miller (1988) does in showing that residence in Chicago is more important than gender in predicting the pronunciation of a particular item, but this technique still does not reflect the possible interactions among these or other social variables.

In this discussion, the notion of a 'model' now becomes crucial. In the case of a two-way table, the 'choice' of the model of independence leads directly to the formula for the calculation of the expected values: row total times column total divided by table total. Although it is not usual to think in these terms for a typical chi-square analysis, a common statistical paradigm is to construct a model of the responses measured in an experiment or obtained from a survey. The 'goodness' of the model is then tested in one fashion or another by comparing the observations with the expected values calculated under the assumptions of the model. Thus, the choice of the model determines the expected values.

In a multidimensional contingency table, many more choices for a model are available. For example, using all the variables in a three-way table, there are eight hierarchical models which could explain the relationship among them, and there are 113 such models in a four-way table. In such an analysis, the objective is to find which of potentially many different models produces the smallest discrepancy between observed and expected values and best represents the interactions between social and linguistic variables, including possible n-way (multivariate) interactions as well as two-way interactions (see Fienberg 1980 or Upton 1978 for an introductory treatment of log-linear methods; see Goodman 1978 or Bishop *et al.* 1975 for more detailed discussion).

Other investigators have employed multivariate statistical techniques for a variety of purposes. For example, Cichocki (1988) uses dual scaling to quantify sociolinguistic variation where the phonetic data involve more than two variants and are not amenable to ordering along a continuum, while Linn (1981) investigates the use of discriminant analysis to classify dialect speakers. Linn and Regal (1988) give a detailed introduction to the use of multivariate methods for verb analysis in data from the *Linguistic Atlas of the North Central States*, illustrating the use of graphical techniques and the analysis of variance-covariance matrices. A somewhat earlier approach to the use of multivariate data involves the use of the so-called 'variable rule' models. Based on initial work of Labov (1969) and others which postulated linguistic performance as a stochastic function of competence, Cedergren and Sankoff (1974) extended and refined the notion of a grammar rule varying as a function of environmental features. More precisely, for example, in their case of a multiplicative non-application rule they assumed that

$$1 - p = (1 - p_0)\ (1 - p_1)\ (1 - p_2)\ .\ .\ .\ .\ (1 - p_k)$$

where p is the probability that a particular rule will obtain in the presence of a combination of specific features of the linguistic environment, each occurring with a probability of p_k. Once the form of a model has been selected and data collected on the incidence of combinations of features and the number of applications (or non-applications) of a specific rule, the probabilities are estimated using maximum likelihood techniques. More recently, others have suggested different models for the variable rule paradigm. For instance, a class of logistic models has been defined where

$$\frac{p}{1 - p} = \frac{p_0}{1 - p_0} \times \frac{p_1}{1 - p_1} \times\ .\ .\ .\ \times \frac{p_k}{1 - p_k}$$

(see Rousseau & Sankoff 1978). It is important to note that in both of these models there is an assumption of independence, that is, a lack of conditioning among the environmental features as they relate to the expression of the grammatical rule. Although discussed in detail by Cedergren and Sankoff, this lack of interaction appears to place an inherent limitation on the models: it is not possible to postulate the interaction of any of the 'explanatory' features. In contrast, the class of log-linear models discussed below place no *a priori* constraints on the possible interactions of environmental features or social variables present in the model.

Log-linear statistical analysis is employed to discover the best explanation of the data, given a set of underlying categorical variables (gender, age, socioeconomic status, etc.), including the relative importance of each of these variables in any multivariate interactions. The process is analogous to regression analysis, where the logarithms of the expected values are written as a function of the categorical variables:

$$\log e = \theta + \lambda^{A} + \lambda^{B} + \lambda^{C} + \lambda^{AB} + \lambda^{AC} + \lambda^{BC} + \lambda^{ABC}$$

In this expression, where there are three categorical variables, e is the expected value, θ is a constant (the mean of the logs of all expected values), and λ is the component of the log of the expected values due to factor A. The letters A, B, and C indicate that the model contains the main effects due to these categorical variables. The letter pairs AB, AC, and BC indicate that two-way interactions among the categorical variables are also in the model, and the term ABC indicates a three-way interaction among all three of the variables. In such a model, a three-way interaction ABC also entails any simpler interactions, such as AB, AC, and BC as well as the individual categorical variables A, B, and C. This is the hierarchy principle (see Fienberg 1980, p. 43, or Girard & Larmouth 1988, p. 254).

Using the same regional data set as for the gravity model analysis above, the informants are classified according to gender, age (younger/older), socioeconomic status (middle class/working class), size of home community (big city/smaller city/town/village), and social network ('local'/'outside' cultural orientation). The informants are also classified as 'modern' vs. 'archaic' in terms of the relative frequence of occurrence of interdental [ð] and [θ] vs. apico-dental [d̪] and [t̪], using Bailey's concept of variable vs. categorical rules (Bailey 1973), because the apico-dental form most likely represents older immigrant speech. The data set includes three registers: word-list, reading sample, and casual speech. Taken together, the social variables and the speech registers would produce a table with 128 cells, but since the sample includes only 63 informants, there are many zero cells. Accordingly, following Goodman (1978), a value of 0.5 was added to each cell to make up for the sparseness of the table.

For most log-linear models there are no simple formulas for calculating expected values, as there are in a simple chi-square analysis. The expected values are calculated using an iterative process, and the only practical way to proceed is to use a statistical analysis program. In this instance, the P4F program in BMDP was used; other systems such as SAS are also suitable. (The BMDP package produces observed values, expected values, standardized deviates, components of chi-square, the log-linear paramaters, etc., including G-square, which is similar to chi-square but has a purely additive property from model to model.) Given so many variables, the first step is to attempt to reduce the complexity of the problem by searching for any variables which are independent of the others (Fienberg 1980). In this instance, age and gender were independent of the other variables, which allows collapsing the table for each register to four dimensions. It would be possible to fit the data perfectly in the table using the model with a four-way interaction WPNC, where W is the word-list register, P is community population, N is social network, and C is social class, but such a model is extremely complex and difficult to interpret, and the goal is to produce a parsimonious model.

As noted above, a saturated model (with the four-way interaction WPNC) also contains all possible three-way and all possible two-way interactions. In a fashion analogous to stepwise regression procedures, stepwise log-linear analysis proceeds to search among all the possible three-way interactions to discover which one can be eliminated with the least increase (suitably measured) in the discrepancy between observed and expected values. As the tree diagram in Figure 6 shows, elimination of the WPC interaction creates the least discrepancy, so the next simplest model contains three three-way interactions PNC, WNC, and WPN with a chi-square value of 1.37 and six degrees of freedom.

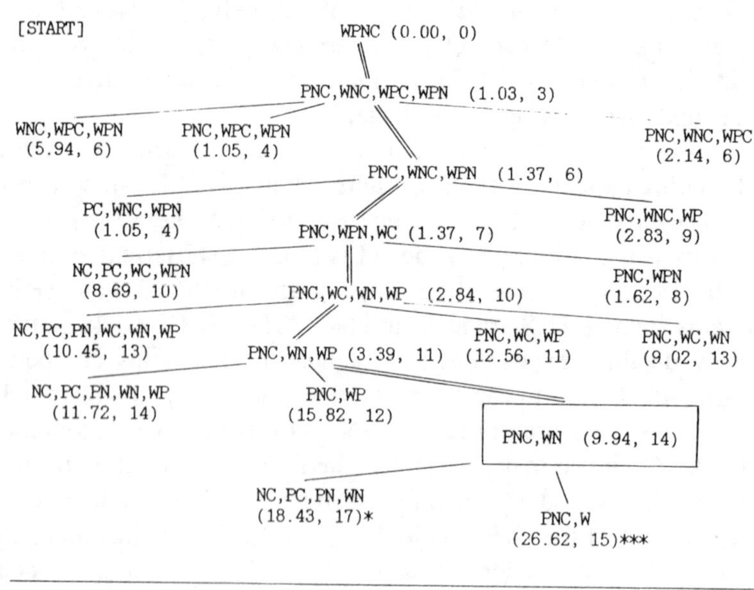

KEY: First number in parentheses is the added G-square value

Second number in parentheses specifies degrees of freedom

"Most Promising Model" appears in a box

Double line marks pathway through best-fit models

W - word-list register N - social network

P - community population size C - socioeconomic class

* - significant discrepancy created between observed and expected values (*** - very significant discrepancy)

Figure 6: Diagram of BMDP evaluation of word-list register models

In similar fashion, the program searches through all the two-way interactions contained in the model PNC,WNC,WPN and finds that the next simplest model is PNC,WC,WPN, eliminating one three-way interaction WNC and maintaining the two-way interaction WC (which was contained within WNC--WN, WC, NC). This step is also represented in Figure 6.

Following the same strategy again, as represented in the tree diagram in Figure 6, the process eventually discovers that the 'best fit' model is PNC,WN, which includes a three-way interaction among community population, social network, and socioeconomic class. The standardized deviates of observed and expected values are very small for this model, as indicated in Table 3, and any effort to simplify the model beyond this point results in a big increase in the G-square value; if either PNC or WN is eliminated from the model, it loses significant explanatory power, again as shown in Figure 6 above.

However, continuing beyond the point of 'best fit' does reveal the relative importance of the categorical variables in the PNC,WN model. The next simplest model NC,PN,WN eliminates the PNC three-way interaction, and the next simplest after that eliminates the two-way interaction PC (community population and socioeconomic class), and so on, as shown in Figure 6 above. The ultimate outcome of this analysis is that social class (C) is less important than the remaining two-way interactions PN (community population and social network) and WN (wordlist register and social network). In practice it is also common to examine the estimates of the lambdas to explore how each factor affects the size of the expected values, but this has not been done here.

A similar analysis of data from reading register and casual speech register shows that each requires the same three-way interaction amongst community population, social network, and socioeconomic class (PNC) in the best-fit model (Girard and Larmouth 1988); in other words, the models which fit the data best must involve a multivariate interaction among these three social variables to explain the observed variability between archaic and modern phonological variants. Since both community population and social network have regional implications, as suggested in the earlier discussion of gravity models, this multivariate analysis offers an enriched understanding of how the interactive dynamics of the region relate to the linguistic variables -- in this case the alternation between an archaic immigrant feature and a 'modern' feature.

Social Class	Social Network	Community Population	Word-List Register Archaic	Modern
Working	Local	Village	1.2	-1.2
		Town	-0.8	0.8
		City	0.0	-0.0
		BigCity	0.0	-0.0
	Outside	Village	1.5	-0.4
		Town	0.1	-0.0
		City	-0.1	0.0
		BigCity	-0.3	0.1
Middle	Local	Village	0.5	-0.5
		Town	-1.2	1.2
		City	0.0	-0.0
		BigCity	0.0	-0.0
	Outside	Village	-0.1	0.0
		Town	0.2	-0.1
		City	0.2	-0.1
		BigCity	-0.3	0.1

Table 3: Standardized deviates for the PNC,WN model

Conclusion

This discussion has shown that there can be two fundamentally different strategies involved in the analysis of regional linguistic variation. In one case the exact form of a model is conjectured *a priori* and computations involving external factors are used to derive linguistic measures. In the second case there are linguistic data as well as data on external factors from which a model to account for them can be extracted or inferred. Both of these strategies have been explored here. The idea of a fuzzy set has been introduced to show that both kinds of models can be derived from slightly different perspectives on the notion of the membership function. The membership function can act as a tool to characterize the nature of a dialect boundary without insisting that it be a density function; it is demonstrated that it could reflect the nature of the interaction between two dialect areas by examining the data along a transect to discover whether there is a sharp boundary, a gradual change with a sharper transition, or just a smooth transition from one region to the other. In gravity models, the underlying interactive dynamics of the region are established *a priori* through formal computations of external factors (population, distance, 'friction of distance,' etc.) and used to interpret the resulting mixture of dialect features or to discover the transition zones in the region. However, the form of this relationship is not presently supported by *independent* information on linguistic interaction. Even Trudgill's use of a 'linguistic similarity' factor is conjectural. But if independent measures of interaction were available, the linguistic similarity or friction of distance exponent in the gravity model formulations could be estimated using regression techniques, and this would shed more light on the nature of the relationship among population sizes, distances, and interaction which in turn, by comparing observation and prediction, would provide a basis for further exploration of the relationship.

This second form of modelling, involving random processes, is the more standard technique in statistical analysis. Chi-square statistical methods implicitly presuppose a model of independence, where row values (linguistic features) are independent of column values (social variables). Multivariate techniques, including regresson, discriminant analysis, principal component analysis, or log-linear analysis also postulate models for the data. In particular, log-linear analysis, where the 'best fit' model is chosen from a large number of possible models, opens the way to discovering multivariate interactions among social, geographic, and linguistic variables and their relative priority or significance in explaining the linguistic variation observed in the region. For example, showing that a three-way interaction amongst population, social network, and socioeconomic class is required in the best-fit model for a particular data set affords a richer interpretation of the data than a series of two-way chi-square analyses which relate one linguistic variable and one social variable at a time. It is also a very credible interpretation, since it emerges from the data set itself rather than being assumed in advance of any analysis, and satisfying because it explicitly reveals the interrelationship of social, geographic, and linguistic variables which otherwise could only be presumed to be related in some general fashion to the variation observed in the data set. Thus, in this modelling process, the nature of the underlying variables may have contributed substantially to the choice of analytical technique, and the model accounts for random variation in the observed data and allows for the expression of a degree of confidence in the conclusions, using the language of probability -- something which cannot be done with other, non-statistical models.

References

Bailey, Charles-James N. 1973. *Variation and linguistic theory.* Washington DC: Center for Applied Linguistics.

Bishop, Y., Fienberg S., & P. Holland. 1975. *Discrete multivariate analysis.* Boston: MIT Press.

Cedergren, Henrietta & David Sankoff. 1974. Variable rules: Performance as a statistical reflection of competence. *Language* 50:333-355.

Cichocki, Walter. 1988. Uses of dual scaling in social dialectology: Multi-dimensional analysis of vowel variation. In Thomas, 187-199.

Davis, Lawrence M. 1982. American social dialectology: A statistical appraisal. *American Speech*, 57:83-94.

Davis, Lawrence M. 1988. The limits of chi square. In Thomas, 225-240.

Davis, Lawrence M. & Charles Houck. 1989. Kurath's Midland: Fact or fiction? Paper presented at the Midwest Regional meeting of the American Dialect Society.

Exline, C., G. Peters & R. Larkin. 1982. *The city: patterns and processes in the urban ecosystem.* Boulder, CO: Westview.

Fienberg, S. 1980. *The analysis of cross-classified categorical data*, 2nd ed. Boston: MIT Press.

Girard, Dennis & Donald Larmouth. 1988. Log-linear statistical models: Explaining the dynamics of dialect diffusion. In Thomas, 251-277.

Goodman, L. 1978. *Analyzing qualitative/categorical data.* Cambridge MA: Abt Books.

Kaufmann, A. 1975. *Introduction to the theory of fuzzy sets: fundamental theoretical concepts I.* New York: Academic Press.

Labov, William. 1969. Contraction, deletion, and inherent variability of the English copula. *Language*, 45:715-762.

Larmouth, Donald. 1981. Gravity models, wave theory, and low-structure regions. In Warkentyne, 199-219.

Linn, Michael. 1981. A statistical model for classifying dialect speakers. In Warkentyne, 244-253.

Linn, Michael. and R. Regal. 1988. Verb analysis of the Linguistic Atlas of the North Central States: A case study in preliminary analysis of a large data set. In Thomas, 138-154.

McDavid, Raven I., Jr. 1979 [1960]. Grammatical differences in the north central states. In William Kretzschmar, Jr. (ed.), *Dialects in culture: Essays in general dialectology by Raven I. McDavid.* University, AL: University of Alabama Press, 245-253.

McDavid, Virginia. 1988. Sex-linked differences among Atlas informants: Irregular verbs. In Thomas, 333-361.

Miller, Michael. 1984. The city as cause of morphophonemic change. *The SECOL Review*, 8:28-59.

Miller, Michael. 1988. Ransacking linguistic survey data with a number-cruncher. In Thomas, 464-473.

Ravenstein, E. 1885. *The laws of migration.* London: Trubners.

Reilly, W. 1931. *The law of retail gravitation.* New York: Knickerbocker.

Rousseau, Pascal & David Sankoff. 1978. Advances in variable rule methodology. In Sankoff, 57-69.

Sankoff, David (ed.). 1978. *Linguistic variation: Models and methods.* New York: Academic Press.

Thomas, Alan (ed.). 1987. *Methods in dialectology: Proceedings of the Sixth International Conference.* Philadelphia: Multilingual Matters Ltd.

Thomason, S. 1981. Are there linguistic prerequisites for contact-induced language change? Paper presented at Language Contact Symposium, University of Wisconsin-Milwaukee.

Trudgill, Peter. 1974. Linguistic change and diffusion: Description and explanation in sociolinguistic dialect geography. *Language in Society* 3:215-246.

Trudgill, Peter. 1986. *Dialects in contact.* London: Blackwell.

Upton, G. 1978. *The analysis of cross-classified data.* New York: John Wiley & Sons.

Warkentyne, Henry (ed.). 1981. *Methods IV: Papers from the Fourth International Conference on Methods in Dialectology.* Victoria, BC: University of Victoria, Department of Linguistics.

Yeates, M. & B. Garner. 1976. *The North American city*, 2nd ed. New York: Harper & Row.

Sociolinguistic Dialectology

J. K. Chambers
University of Toronto

Both sociolinguistics and dialectology investigate varieties of language. Both disciplines are, of course, complex and multi-faceted.[1] They overlap to some extent but prototypically they are distinctly different. Dialectology concentrates on regional varieties of accent and dialect as elicited in the speech of predominantly non-mobile, older, rural males (NORMs). Sociolinguistics concentrates on urban varieties of language as used in interactions among and within groups determined by such factors as class, age, gender, ethnicity, or network.

Sociolinguistic dialectology applies the methods of sociolinguistics to the study of accent and dialect. Although the twelve-syllable moniker is awkward, it is unavoidable as long as 'dialectology' (without an attributive) remains in the minds of some scholars a synonym for dialect geography.

1. Emphases

Sociolinguistic dialectology may be relatively new but it is by no means revolutionary. It is merely, in one perspective, dialectology reformed as a social science. Traditional dialectology, or dialect geography, has been largely idiosyncratic in its methods and goals. The extent of the divergence of dialectology from social-scientific methods and goals became clear when Pickford (1956), in an influential critique, rebuked dialect geographers for the lack of representativeness in their sampling procedures and the narrowness of their data-gathering techniques. The dialectologists, in what became a standard defense, argued that their aim was neither representativeness nor breadth in Pickford's terms, which were those of a sociologist.[2] Instead, their goal, according to the dialectologists, was the recovery of older speech forms. McDavid (1981, 71) stated the standard defense this way:

> There is a deliberate bias in the choice of communities -- in the direction of smaller and often isolated places; there is a deliberate bias in the selection of informants, insistence on local roots and a statistically disproportionate sample of the older and less educated; there is a deliberate bias in the choice of items for the questionnaire, in the direction of the old fashioned rural society, the horsedrawn vehicle, the mule-powered plow and homemade bread. All of these biases are essential to the purpose of the investigation, to push the historical records as far back in time as possible. Whether this is interesting or worthy of investigation is a matter of taste and purpose.

Hence the sampling of predominantly NORMs, notwithstanding the fact that the majority of our population is mobile, younger, urban and female. Hence the elicitation format characterized by Labov (1971, 113), in a trenchant discussion of methodology, as 'a long question from the interviewer and a short answer from the subject.'

By such means, dialectologists compiled atlases showing broad patterns of lexical choices and pronunciation variants. Among their more significant findings were distributions of linguistic elements that apparently perpetuated ancient alliances -- the Papal States in central Italy (Hall 1943), the Danelaw in Britain (Orton & Wright 1974) -- centuries after their dissolution.

Sociolinguistic dialectology necessarily abandons the antiquarian impetus of dialect geography. Its preoccupation with social and regional uses of the vernacular precludes it. Numerous differences follow from that one. In the end, the only incontrovertible points of similarity between the two may be their subject matter, dialect, and accent.

One of the more striking differences is the role of issues in the disciplines. In sociolinguistics, the seminal works and the formative investigations have been impelled by specific issues, that is, by the need to develop or refine or refute a particular hypothesis. Many of those issues became by-words at the height of their currency: the Creolist vs. Dialectologist theory of Black English, the 'logic' of variable rules, the Divergence hypothesis, and so on.

Clearly, dialect geography has not been driven by issues in the same way. In more than a century, it developed no body of critical literature examining the concept of the isogloss, or issues in linguistic cartography, or other substantive notions. The questions that stimulated debate in the heyday of dialect geography, according to Francis (1983), were whether dialectologists and philologists had any common interests (p. 148), whether women could serve adequately as fieldworkers (p. 84), and whether fieldworkers should be trained in anything beyond phonetic transcription (pp. 82-83, 92-94).

The value of issues as a driving force in a discipline cannot be measured by the intrinsic merits of any of the particular issues. Even relatively ephemeral issues can exercise an organizing and energizing force. Specific formulations or statements of issues come and go, rendered moribund by an impasse as to how the data bears on the issue, or, in the best case, supplanted by a more productive reformulation in the light of the evidence it provided. In retrospect, particular formulations of issues may appear to be naïve or even addled. Even that can represent an advance in the discipline if the new perception follows from the testing of the old one.

As long as the issues arise from -- or are instances of -- attempts to elucidate the open-ended questions about language in its social context, they are likely -- however naïve and addled -- to be productive.

2. Questions

Here I pose some of the questions that imbue sociolinguistic dialectology. In the next section, I look at some of the studies that have attempted to shed light on some aspect, however minor, of those questions.

2.1. Language change.

How do the changes we observe in progress reflect the changes we find in the history of languages? Linguistic variation more often than not characterizes a transition from one structural state to another. Are the stages in the transition instances of comparable stages in language changes not observed in progress, such as the First Slavic Palatalization or the Great Vowel Shift? To some extent, we must accept the similarity axiomatically, and we have done so, at least tacitly, by allowing Labov's 'Uniformitarian Principle' to go unchallenged: 'the forces operating to produce linguistic change today are of the same kind and order of magnitude as those which operated in the past five or ten thousand years' (1972a, 275).[3] But the linguistic conditions, as Labov also points out, include some distinctly post-modern factors such as widespread literacy, mass media, global language spread, and instantaneous international transmission devices for both speech and writing. What effects, if any, do these have on language change?

2.2. Social correlates.

The most conspicuous advance in two decades of sociolinguistic research has come in the correlation of independent social variables with linguistic variants, reifying the age-old impression that people's speech is emblematic of their class, age, gender, ethnicity, and region. Further advances will not come by proliferating results uncritically on the model of Labov's New York survey. How well-defined is our notion of class? Can it possibly have the same meaning in Old-World communities as in New-World communities? How do social networks, in the sense of Milroy (1980), cut across social variables, especially class? Do sociopolitical factors correlate with dialectal variation? How, if at all, do the grand concepts of the sociologists of language -- concepts such as diglossia, language shift, heteronomy, linguistic legislation and planning -- affect individual and small-group interaction? Are they encoded emblematically in sociolinguistic variants?

2.3. Geolinguistic patterns

How do dialect features spread throughout a region? What linguistic patterns recur in zones where dialectal varieties come together? Can such zones be represented accurately on maps? Are such zones ever really isoglossic? How 'real' is such a boundary? How does it affect the linguistic behavior of people in the speech community?

2.4. Function

What is the adaptive function of dialect and accent? Variation across communities and groups appears to be irrepressible, yet that same variation constitutes at least a barrier and at worst a cause of conflict. Why does linguistic variability exist? What, if anything, is its biological function?

3. Issues

Such large, open-ended questions cannot be solved by equally large answers -- what Bertrand Russell once called 'heroic answers.' Instead, they break down into smaller, more mundane issues. In what follows, I review some of these smaller issues with a view to sketching some results that seem to me to be interesting or at least promising. In keeping with the editor's scheme for this volume, the issues are mainly those in which I have a professional interest and to which I have made some contribution. They are, needless to say, a small subset among the possible issues that might have been discussed here, which are (fortunately) unbounded.

3.1. Post-modern factors in language change.

Two centuries ago, the ordinary citizens of Norfolk or Newfoundland or New Hampshire might have gone six months or more without hearing an accent that was very different from their own. And neither their speech nor their neighbors' included any 'spelling pronunciations' or literary calques. They were, for the most part, semi-literate, and their movements were circumscribed by their townships or parishes.

In both respects, their lives seem exotic today, and not only by comparison with the lives of their descendants in Norfolk, Newfoundland and Nebraska but with virtually everyone in the world. The sociocultural milieu for which language is the medium has altered, and so has the individual 'experience' of language. It is altogether likely, in the terms of Labov's Uniformitarian Principle, that the conditions under which the historical record was produced, whether in the Golden Age or the Dark Ages, were more similar to the conditions of two centuries ago than to those of today.

If these altered conditions are dialectologically salient in any way, they should be detectable in close studies of language variation and change. That is to say, the effects of mass media and universal literacy-to take the two most obvious forces-should be discernible in our data.

So far, any effects have been far from obvious. Their discussion among dialectologists is rare. Few sociolinguistic studies address them directly, by, say, objectifying them (in some way) as independent variables. Few sociolinguistic results invoke them as mitigating factors. It may be, then, that their effects are simply nonexistent. At least as likely, however, their effects may simply be more subtle than our sociolinguistic methods have been able to discern.

Although the evidence is scant and far from compelling, it appears that inferences can be drawn about the effects of widespread literacy on linguistic change in at least one study to be described below. The effects of the mass media have, by contrast, resisted detection, and may indeed prove to be linguistically inconsequential. At any rate, the limited available evidence seems to me to allow two reasonable but opposed hypotheses-one that literacy impedes or promotes language change in specific and predictable ways, and the other that the mass media have no significant effect on language change.

This latter hypothesis runs contrary to the deep-seated popular conviction that the mass media influence language profoundly. It turns up, for instance, as a presupposition in this passage from a novel set in a Newfoundland outport (Horwood 1966):

> The people of Caplin Bight, when addressing a stranger from the mainland, could use almost accentless English, learned from listening to the radio, but in conversation among themselves there lingered the broad twang of ancient British dialects that the fishermen of Devon and Cornwall and the Isle of Guernsey had brought to the coast three or four centuries before.

The novelist's claim that the villagers mastered standard inland Canadian English -- what he calls 'almost accentless English' -- from the radio is pure fantasy, or linguistic science-fiction.

The only obvious effect of mass communication on dialect is the diffusion of catch-phrases. At the furthest reaches of the broadcast beam are heard echoes of Sylvester the Cat's 'Sufferin' succotash,' or Jack Paar's 'I kid you not,' or Mork's 'Nanoo nanoo.' Such phrases are more ephemeral than slang, and more self-conscious than etiquette. They belong for the moment of their currency to the most superficial linguistic level.

Another effect of the mass media which seems plausible though far from obvious is the diffusion of tolerance toward other accents and dialects. The fact that standard speech reaches dialect enclaves from the mouths of anchorpersons, sitcom protagonists, color commentators, and other admired people presumably adds a patina of acceptability to the way they speak, and thus, presumably, adds the same patina of respectability to any regional changes which are standardizing. This effect has not yet been measured in any study I know of, but it is surely not immeasurable.

The patina of acceptability, if it proves real, should not be confused with the stimulus for language change. There is no evidence whatever that the speech conveyed by the mass media motivates linguistic changes or (apart from catch-phrases) affects speech in any other significant way. Ervin-Tripp (1973) provides the best evidence to date: hearing children of deaf parents cannot acquire language from exposure to radio or television. Similarly, Labov (1984) shows that in the most segregated black communities in Philadelphia the 'dialect is drifting further away' from other dialects despite 4-8 hours daily exposure to standard English on television and in schools. Both of these studies deal in some sense with 'extreme' cases, but their conclusion apparently follows from a general principle, namely, that changes in phonology and grammar require face-to-face interactions among speakers. The speakers on our mass media, seeking no response and evoking none, make no impression on our dialects.

Literacy, by contrast, appears to influence the rate and, possibly, the very occurrence of phonological changes. In a developmental study of dialect acquisition by young Canadians transplanted to the south of England (Chambers 1988), I concluded that the orthographic representations of certain phonological variables affected the rate of change. That conclusion followed as an inference about the strikingly different sociolinguistic actuations of two linguistically similar processes.

The subjects were six Canadian youngsters who had moved with their families to Oxfordshire. One of the features of their native Canadian accents was t-Voicing, the rule that makes homophones of such pairs as *flutter:flooder*, *beetle:beadle* and *hearty:hardy*; an index of their acquisition of the southern England accents was the absence of t-Voicing in their speech. One of the features of the southern England accent was r-lessness, the deletion of postvocalic /r/ in such words as *north* and *nor*; another index of their acquisition of the accent was the presence of r-lessness in their speech.

The subjects' behavior with respect to these two phonological rules turned out to be almost diametric, as Figure 1 shows. All of the subjects have eliminated some 'voiced' alveolars, but none have made much headway in acquiring r-lessness; no one scores more than 30%, and the pattern shows no hint of age-grading or any other coherent social correlate.

The difference in these results does not seem to follow from any phonological (or structural) properties of t-Voicing and r-lessness. Both are categorical rules in the two dialects. In the terms explicated in the original article (1988, 661-2), both are non-complex rules, that is, they have only one conditioning factor and no variants or exceptions.

One dialectological difference between them is that t-Voicing is being eliminated from the subjects' accents and r-lessness is being acquired in them, a factor of some consequence although probably not considerable enough to account for the discrepancy illustrated in Figure 1. Besides this difference, the two rules are opposed in another respect. The elimination of t-Voicing gives rise to pronunciations that are not only heard in the new dialect area but are also reinforced by the orthographic representations of the data. Words such as *flutter*, *beetle* and *hearty* are orthographically transparent in the sense that they are spelled with <t>, not <d>, and in England pronounced with [t], not [d]. The acquisition of r-lessness gives rise to pronunciations that are heard in the new dialect area but are contradicted by the orthographical representations of the data. Words such as *north*, *nor* and *water* are orthographically opaque in the sense that they are spelled with <r>, pronounced [r] in Canada but deleted (or realized obliquely in vowel modifications) in England.

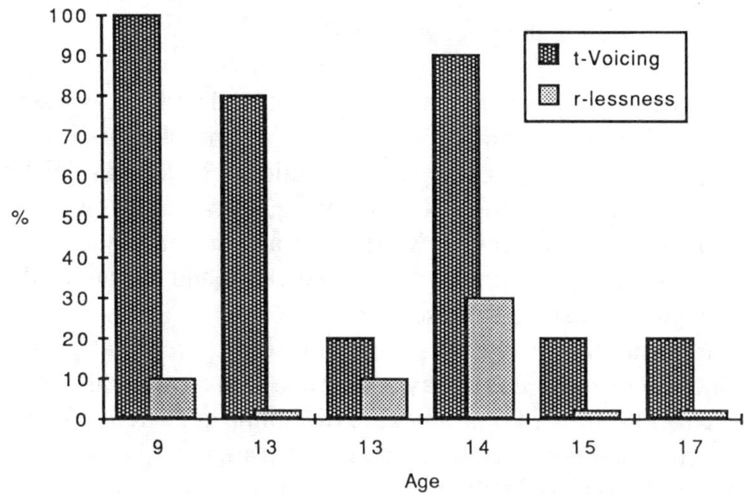

Figure 1. Absence of t-Voicing and presence of r-lessness in the speech of six Canadian emigrants in southern England (based on Chambers 1988, Figs. 1 and 4)

All the subjects are literate, as is typical in studies of dialect acquisition but not in first-language acquisition and usually not in second-language acquisition. At least in the early stage of dialect acquisition, features which are orthographically transparent apparently progress faster than features which are orthographically opaque.

It remains to be seen whether orthographically opaque features can ever be completely mastered by learners who are literate. Such features may exist in dialects (and languages) only because first-language learners are invariably illiterate. If so, the spread of literacy in the last two centuries could impose a mitigating effect on dialect variation where it has always been most diverse, in the rural areas and working-class neighborhoods. Perhaps it is no coincidence that accents have been most diverse among social groups in which illiteracy has been most common. If literacy does impede language variation and change, its effects must constitute a salient codicil on the Uniformitarian Principle.

3.2. Heteronomy as an independent variable

The correlation of linguistic variation with independent social variables provided the first demonstrable achievement of sociolinguistics. Labov's early correlations, especially the dramatic ones such as r-deletion in New York department stores (Labov 1972a, 49-53) and vowel variants among adolescents leaving Martha's Vineyard or staying home (1972a, 32), gained great currency in the late 1960s and had an incalculable effect on establishing the discipline.

The immediate result was corroboration by replication -- in effect, since no one saw it this way at the time -- in several other cities in America and Europe. For a time, the discipline appeared to consist mainly of corroborative exercises, that is, replications of Labov's New York survey. Necessary as the corroboration was, in many cases any further implications were overlooked.

To some extent, the further implications can still be developed. One of the major advances of sociolinguistic dialectology is the development of quantification in the analysis of data. The quantitative approach allows comparisons between different studies and different accents.

So far, comparative dialectology has been underexploited.[4] Best known is Guy's classic study (1980 [originally circulated 1974]) of morpheme-final cluster simplification based on surveys in New York, Detroit, Washington and Philadelphia. The comparison allowed the first comprehensive categorization of variable constraints, tested relative weightings in the VARBRUL program, and uncovered the 'Q-Factor' as a cause of interdialectal variation.

More comparisons are necessary for the discipline's development. They serve not only to generalize hypotheses beyond the communal settings of each survey, but also to test cross-cultural realizations of the independent variables, which appear to have frozen prematurely into a standard list -- class, age, gender, ethnicity, region -- of uncritical acceptance. Social class in particular, though it is at the core of most sociolinguistic studies, is a fuzzy notion. It is realized much more loosely in North America than in Europe, but, so far, none of our studies explicitly differentiates it in the two places or reports distinctions that follow from the difference. If the difference is real, it surely colors the results in ways that are detectable by comparative studies.

Perhaps the only independent variable to challenge for a space on the standard list is the network. Its principal advocate, of course, has been Lesley Milroy (1980), and its utility has been demonstrated largely through applications to working-class Belfast speech (in, for example, Milroy 1982). One of the more impressive results is a coherent view of the agents of linguistic innovation (Milroy & Milroy 1985). Whereas standard correlates have been able to identify innovators of a change only in the broadest terms, as, say, lower middle-class or young adults or women (or some combination thereof), an analysis of network structure -- at least potentially -- can make a finer distinction. The segment of the social group responsible for carrying innovations from one network to another will be those with 'weak intergroup ties' (p. 365) and the 'early adopters' in the network will be core members with strong ties (p. 367).

So far, sociolinguists have applied network structure exclusively to more or less closed social clusters -- the Milroys' Belfast parishes,

Harlem street gangs (Labov 1972b, 258-85), Detroit high-school cliques (Eckert 1988), and the like. In more mobile segments of society, the individual's networks proliferate to the point where analysis may quickly become cumbersome or even unmanageable. Nevertheless, the individual's relationship to the numerous informal groups with which he or she is associated probably reflects more accurately than any other system yet devised the complexity of our participation in society. It may be that further headway on sociolinguistic correlates requires finding the means to make that complexity manageable.

The networks in which we participate to some degree, as Milroy (1982) points out, include not only those which circumscribe our mundane activities but also more distant ones. We are, consciously or not, speakers of Torquay English or Toledo English or Toronto English, and, more remotely, speakers of (southern) English English or (northern) American English or (urban) Canadian English. Insofar as these language varieties are perceived as distinct entities, they are said to be 'focused' (Le Page & Tabouret-Keller 1985). Linguistic focusing arises as a by-product of the group solidarity and cohesiveness of social networks.

Focusing appears to be a sociological concept rather than a sociolinguistic one, since it is defined in terms of the social perception of an accent or dialect rather than of its structure or use. It is presumably a prerequisite for another useful concept from the sociology of language, heteronomy, characterized by Stewart (1962) as follows:

> A linguistic system will be *heteronomous* in terms of another, historically related one when the former functions in the linguistic community as a dependent variety of the latter, and is consequently subject to 'correction' in its direction, i.e., is subject to regular structural readjustment so that it will come to resemble the other more closely.

The histories of all languages can undoubtedly be interpreted in terms of focusing and heteronomy.

Dialectologists have observed that isogloss bundles often coincide with national boundaries. Speitel (1969), for instance, describes a staggering set of lexical isoglosses along the Scottish-English border. Such patterns find their natural explanations in the concept of heteronomy. Whether or not a national boundary is etched along a physical barrier, it usually demarcates an attitudinal barrier, and one of the attitudes that is likely to contrast on the two sides is linguistic heteronomy.

Focusing and heteronomy are not fixed ideas, but are, like virtually everything else in the social contract, subject to fluctuation and change. As sociolinguistic dialectologists, we might well ask how the speech of individuals and groups reflects the norms of focusing and heteronomy that form part of their sociocultural heritage. If the reflection of those norms is detectable at all, it should be so under conditions of change, where one might expect to find age-graded distinctions in attitudes about group solidarity and nationalism that correlate with linguistic changes in progress.

Changing heteronomy appears to correlate with a sound change in Canadian English. The change threatens to eradicate from the phonology of CE its most distinctive trait. The process known as Canadian Raising predicts, as one of its reflexes, the diphthong [ʌw] in the words *house*, *south*, and other words where the vowel is followed by a tautosyllabic voiceless segment, and the vowel [ɑw] in *houses*, *how*, and all similar words. Among CE adults over 40 in Toronto, Vancouver and Victoria, this feature remains relatively stable, but among younger speakers it has become a variable with fairly profuse phonetic possibilities. (The change in progress is summarized in more detail in Chambers 1989, 80-83.) Phonetically, younger people can have [ɑw], [aw] , or [æw] in the 'elsewhere' environment, and any of these as well as [ʌw] , [ɐw] or [ɛw] before voiceless consonants.

Sociolinguistically, certain facts are clear. In all cities, the age-grading holds, and the change is also gender-graded: in all age groups, females lead the males.

Much less clear is any motive for the change. The non-back onsets for this diphthong are in fact characteristic of most United States varieties, making plausible the idea (advanced first, I must say, by audiences hearing about the change in progress and greeted skeptically by me) that the change constitutes an 'Americanization' of Canadian Raising. The plausibility was not harmed by the fact that women were leading the change. One of the established results of sociolinguistic research is that women are more likely to be innovators of changes which are standardizing (Labov 1972a: 301-04, Trudgill 1972, Cameron & Coates 1988). The fronting of the onsets, if viewed narrowly in the Canadian context, appears to be a change *away* from the standard, but if the change is viewed more broadly, in terms of the North American context, it can be seen as a change *toward* the American standard, and the role of women in leading the innovation is the expected one.

Testing the Americanization hypothesis required attitudinal information that might be correlable -- positively or negatively -- with the linguistic results. Heteronomy, for the purposes of this study, was defined as 'the extent to which things American were in the heads, on the lips and in the hearts of the Canadian subjects.' The linguistic interviews fortuitously included three kinds of relevant information. First, the interviews began with mildly personal conversations about neighborhoods, parents, friends, sports and, inevitably, viewing and listening habits; these habits, as is typical across Canada, generally divide into preferences for either non-American or American programming. Secondly, the interviews included a short lexical questionnaire, which was added, originally, to increase the self-consciousness of the youngest group, who (in pilot studies) had shown no style shifting at all; as it happened, six of the 12 elicited items had American variants competing with the indigenous ones. Thirdly, the main conversational section of the interviews included discussions of American influence on Canada. For each of these topics, the responses of the subjects were reduced to a separate index, called, respectively, the HEAD index, the LIPS index, and the HEART index.

The calculation of the HEAD index will give the flavor. (The complete results, with caveats, are in Chambers 1981.) For most of the 12-year-olds in the survey, the questions about television watching elicited long lists of weekly American programs. For both the 12-year-olds and the 22-year-olds, the questions about radio often elicited a short list of 'top forty' stations, all of them dominated by rapid-fire announcers with vaguely southwestern American accents. The adults, who ranged in age from 46 to 52, sometimes named newscasts as their regular television fare, but usually could not name anything less frivolous.[5]

The scale for the HEAD index involved two interlocking classifications: (a) frequency of exposure to TV and radio, which can vary from almost none (0) to occasional (1) to frequent (2); and (b) exposure to American or American-style programming, including top-forty radio as well as TV serials, as opposed to Canadian or other (BBC imports, FM concerts, etc.) programming. The two classifications interlock by assigning negative values to frequent and occasional exposure to non-American programming and positive values to frequent and occasional exposure to American and American-style programming. The scale for the HEAD index is as follows:

frequent	occasional	nearly none	occasional	frequent
-2	-1	0	+1	+2
non-American				American

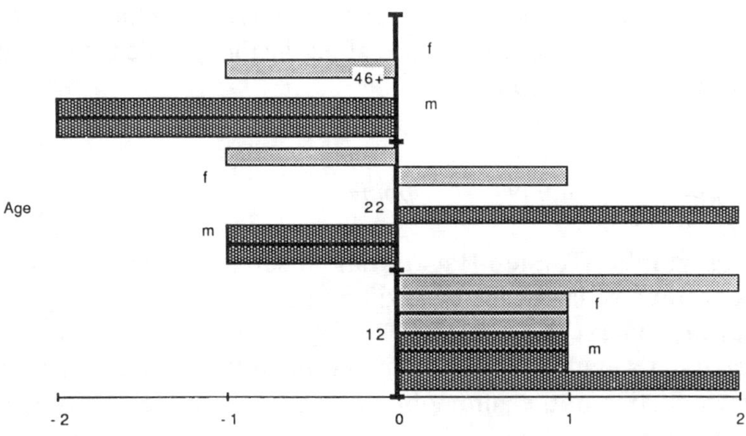

Figure 2. HEAD Index Scores for individual speakers (Chambers 1981, Fig. 4)

When the individual subjects are placed along the scale, the result, which is shown as Figure 2, indicates a sharp stratification of the age groups, with the 12-year-olds all showing positive values and the adults all showing negative values. The young adults occupy a kind of transitional space, with a much wider range and a mix of positives and negatives.

Similar stratification shows up in the LIPS index. There is, then, a gross correlation between two of the heteronomy scales and the linguistic indices for the change in progress. That is, age-grading characterizes both the linguistic change and the heteronomy scales. Although finer correlations cannot be made, the intuition that the change represents the Americanization of Canadian Raising is at least weakly supported by attempts to measure changing heteronomy. Subsequent research on middle-class CE in Vancouver shows the same linguistic change in progress; presumably, the changing heteronomy motivates the same change in those distant cities (Chambers & Hardwick 1986).

Although heteronomy is an inherently fuzzy notion, it is no fuzzier (in the technical sense) than some of the familiar independent variables of sociolinguistic research such as social class and contextual style. In the case of the change in progress in Canadian English, the altered heteronomy of the different age groups appears to be the most revealing correlate for their linguistic behavior. To that extent, the Canadian case provides an instance of the sociolinguistic manifestation of a sociological concept.

3.3. Language variation and mapping.

The geographer Torsten Hägerstrand discovered that innovations spread across the landscape by leaping, as it were, from one population center to the next (Hägerstrand 1967 [originally 1953]). Although Hägerstrand's evidence came from non-linguistic innovations such as the introduction of the automobile into Sweden and controls against bovine tuberculosis, there was no *a priori* reason to think that the regional diffusion of linguistic innovations would work differently. Indeed, some well-known innovations with hitherto puzzling distributions now become straightforward. The distribution of uvular /r/ in European vernaculars (that is, not restricted to educated and upper-class speech) includes a large continuous region encompassing Paris, Marseille, Stuttgart and Cologne, but also discontinuous occurrences in several other areas. As Figure 3 shows, the discontinuous regions are all dominated by large cultural centers: the Hague, Berlin, Copenhagen, and Bergen. The distribution, of course, makes perfect sense in the light of Hägerstrand's findings about the spatial process of diffusion.

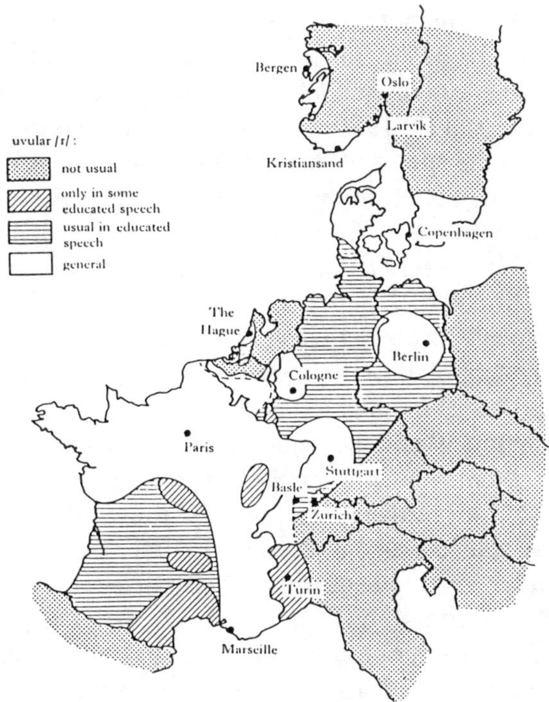

Figure 3. Uvular /r/ in Europe (Chambers and Trudgill 1980:191)

Until quite recently, such geographical findings have made little impression upon linguists. For the most part, dialectologists have assumed that innovations diffuse continuously along immigration routes or transportation lines. Although I know of no attempt at developing this 'continuous' model explicitly, the 'wave' model seems to me to be one version of it. The analogy of the wave visualizes diffusion as a pebble-in-a-pond effect, with a point of impact sending ripples in all directions. The notion of continuousness is still implied, but at least the analogy adds the idea of a center of influence.

A more accurate analogy, in the light of empirical studies, would be skipping a stone across a pond. Innovations diffuse from one center of influence to others -- the population clusters down the urban hierarchy --and from those into the intervening regions.

Some of the geolinguistic variables affecting diffusion have been integrated into a 'gravity model' similar to a type used by geographers (Chambers & Trudgill 1980, 196-204).[6] In attempting to provide an explanation for the spread of innovations from center A to center B, the formula encodes the basic hypothesis that influence is a function of population and distance. Empirical tests of this basic model indicate the need to weigh other factors in the model, such as terrestrial barriers and dialect-particular resistance.

The model has thus proven useful for isolating factors like interaction, distance, population, barriers (Gerritsen & Jansen 1980) and resistance as well as for attempting to make them explicit. The various aspects of the model and their interactions are by no means settled. If they appear complex now, when the model is undeniably a fairly gross approximation of geolinguistic reality, they will almost certainly become more complex as it is developed further.

A similar development is now, belatedly, underway with respect to the isogloss. Although the isogloss was the principal theoretical construct of dialect geography in the first half of this century, it was never subjected to empirical testing or critical scrutiny. Yet the isogloss, as any dialect geographer would surely agree, represents a very primitive conceptualization of the way in which dialect regions meet. In order for dialect regions to abut as abruptly as the isogloss implies, they would have to be separated by an unbridgeable abyss.

Only recently have dialectologists begun asking what really underlies the isoglossic boundary. Traditional dialectologists, as if to avoid encountering such questions, restricted their data to single tokens of single utterances: the isogloss, by definition, is the series of points at which one member of a sample population volunteers a different lexeme or pronunciation from the one volunteered by the geographically most proximate member in response to the same question. Maintaining the isoglossic abyss depended upon counting only one response to each question. Counting more than one answer or amalgamating answers for several questions inevitably revealed variability, causing the isogloss to vanish.

Now, several studies have appeared which deliberately amalgamate answers and count variants in order discover what form is taken by the variability that underlies the isogloss. For example, variable (u) indicates the distinction in British English vernaculars in which certain words with traditional [ʊ] in the North occur in the South with [ʌ] (Chambers & Trudgill 1980, 127-37). A traditional isogloss for a word like *some* or *duck* would trace a line through the English Midlands from the Potteries in the west to the Wash in the east. However, the Survey of English Dialects (Orton et al. 1962-71) includes 63 responses in addition to *some* and *duck*, among them *brother*, *cud*, *hundred*, *mongrel*, *puppies*, *shut*, *truss*, and *uncle*. By collating the responses to all 65 forms in the region of the putative isogloss, it is possible to identify speakers with 100% [ʊ] and other speakers with no [ʊ] at all -- i.e., speakers with 100% [ʌ]. While the former group are invariably to the north of the latter, as expected, the two groups are not contiguous to one another. Instead, in between the two is a transition zone comprised of speakers with less than 100% [ʊ] but more than zero.

By examining the responses of the speakers occupying the transition zone, certain differences appear in the transitional lects. Not surprisingly, the most common lectal type is a hybrid of the 'pure Northern' and 'pure Southern' types, with [ʊ] pronunciations in some words and [ʌ] in others. Many of these speakers, of course, have variable (u), pronouncing the same word sometimes with [ʊ] and sometimes with [ʌ]. These **mixed** lects correlate quantitatively with their location in the transition zone: that is, those closer to the Northern edge have higher percentages -- are 'more Northern' -- than those close to the Southern edge.

A second lectal type, less predictable perhaps than the mixed ones, is called **fudged**, because it includes tokens which are phonetically neither Northern nor Southern but are phonetic compromises. In the transition zone for (u), the fudge is [ɤ], the higher-mid central unrounded vowel. SED fieldworkers report instances of the fudge in the speech of six villagers in the piece of the transition zone studied carefully by Chambers & Trudgill (1980). The [ɤ] vowel shares certain properties with both [ʊ] and [ʌ], and thus provides speakers with a means of sounding both Northern and Southern simultaneously.[7]

Even though the change from [ʊ] to [ʌ] is centuries old -- it began as a split of Middle English 'short u' in seventeenth century London-- it is presumably still progressing. The transition zone determined from the SED data gathered two generations ago has presumably inched its way northward since then. The characteristics marking it as a transition zone -- mixed lects, fudged lects, and their distributional properties -- are presumably still intact, though not in the speech of the direct descendants of the villagers who spoke that way for the SED fieldworkers.

The general characteristics of dialects in transition zones have been corroborated in other studies. The variable (a), another well-known North-South difference in England contrasting pronunciations of words like *after*, *basket*, *path* and *shaft* with either Northern [a] (sometimes [æ]) or Southern [a:] (sometimes [ɑ]), shows the same essential properties (Chambers & Trudgill 1980, 137-42). Glauser's study (1988) of variable (ai) in the North of England, though couched in rather different terms of reference, is a thorough dissection of a transition zone with some indication that the mixed lects may resolve eventually into phonologically conditioned variants. Lathrop (1979), using data on occurrences of preconsonantal /r/ from the *Linguistic Atlas of New England* (Kurath 1939-43),[8] found that the transition zone in Vermont and New Hampshire resolved into a set of variable constraints on /r/-dropping: it is more probable after [ɜ] than [a], and successively more probable before voiced obstruents, voiceless obstruents, and sonorants.

In an interesting study, Macaulay (1985) applied the methods used in the study of transition zones to a body of SED data and discovered a kind of anti-transitional pattern. He collated words with final velar nasals in the West Midlands, where some speakers pronounce a velar stop after the nasal, that is [ŋg], in words like *among*, *string*, *tongue* and *wrong*. Instead of revealing a progression from 100% to 0 across the region of variability, Macaulay's results, as shown on Figure 4, reveal a kind of nesting of frequencies, with the categorical users (100%) surrounded by a region of relatively high frequency users (70%), who are in turn surrounded by a band of infrequent users (25-60%).

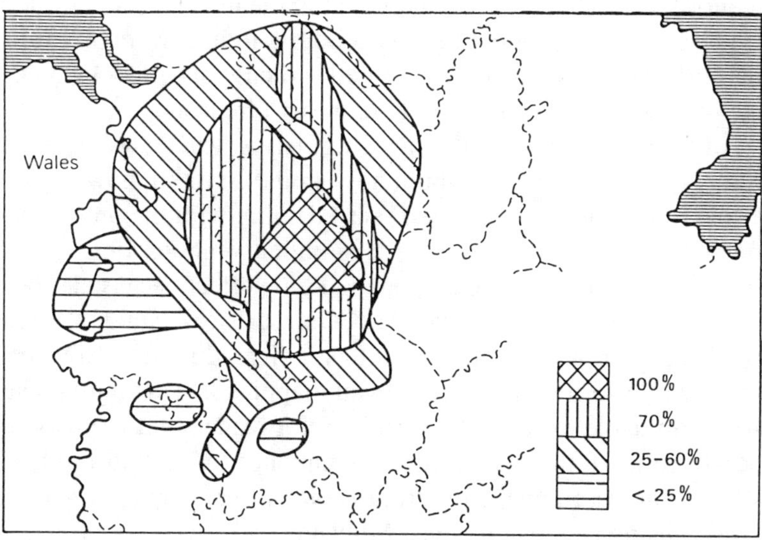

Figure 4. Occurrences of final velar stops in the West Midlands of England (Macaulay 1985:184)

The pattern appears to be the cartographic representation of a relic area, where a formerly widespread feature survives in isolation. Macaulay's map gives a variationist view of a recessive linguistic feature, which is quite familiar in static views from traditional dialectology (as discussed, for instance, in Chambers & Trudgill 1980, 109 and Map 7-5). The velar stop pronunciation is presumably not stable in the West Midlands but is receding, and the encroaching standard is made visible in the layers of diminishing frequency.

Macaulay's map thus implies the dynamism of the linguistic change taking place in the West Midlands. In a sense, capturing the dynamism of linguistic change and diffusion poses the primary challenge for sociolinguistic dialectology, and all of the studies mentioned above can be seen, in a sense, as attempts to represent some dynamism cartographically. It is not a purpose for which the map, as a graphic device, is intrinsically well suited. Subsequent research may require more radical revisions of cartographic resources, particularly the development of multi-dimensional and holographic techniques. For now, as all the examples above and the two below indicate, the mapping of variability can be satisfactorily implied -- though it cannot be made explicit -- by distinguishing areas of contrastive frequency.

The call for a reformed geolinguistics was stated by Glauser (1985, 113) this way: 'we should now stop discussing how to arrange reflexes [on linguistic maps, and] start dealing with the processes that underlie them.' A similar call was sounded years earlier by Keyser (1963), and sounded eloquently, but had little effect because at the time dialectology was relatively inactive.[9] Glauser's case study, the phonological rule of rounding adjustment as indicated in the SED data, requires 19 rule formulations and seven mappings. That may make it a rather formidable exposition, especially for readers not predisposed to generativism, but those who have the patience to work through it will surely be impressed by the orderliness of his final map (p. 126), detailing the transition zone in the East Midlands.

The complexity of Glauser's case study arises from the numerous versions of the rule of rounding adjustment he must posit in order to account for the SED data. In an earlier study with the same purpose -- the mapping of a linguistic process rather than its reflexes -- but slightly less complex rule schemata, I investigated the variable (CC), that is, morpheme-final consonant cluster simplification, in the North of England (Chambers 1982). As is well-known from several urban studies (esp. Guy 1980), variable (CC) is susceptible to numerous variable constraints. The constraints relevant to my study, which is to say the ones recoverable (with reasonable confidence) from the SED materials, were final stop deletion before a following consonant (as in *pos' card*, *han'ful* for *post card*, *handful*) or vowel (*pos' office*, *han' out* for *post office*, *hand out*), and final stop deletion following a sonorant (*han'*, *hand*) or an obstruent (*pos'*, *post*).

The SED data from 75 Northern England speakers conformed to the general findings for these constraints: deletion occurs more frequently before a following consonant than a following vowel, and more frequently after a preceding sonorant than a preceding obstruent. (In the following summary, I discuss only the following consonant/vowel environment in order to simplify the exposition.) Some speakers, it turns out, delete final consonants only in the more favored context: that is, deletion is possible before a following consonant, but not before a following vowel. If these speakers deleted the consonant invariably, their phonologies would include the categorical rule (R1):

(R1) C ------> null / C __ # C

While three of the speakers in the sample might be construed as having this categorical rule, they are grouped with 13 others for whom deletion occurs only before a following consonant but occurs variably there, that is, their phonologies include (R2):

(R2) C -------> (null) / C __ # C

For certain other speakers in the sample, cluster simplification occurs in the environment CC#V as well as CC#C, though of course it is less frequent in the former environment; the variable rule which describes the data is (R3):

(R3) C -------> (null) / C - # ^{a}C, ^{b}V (where a > b)

In variable rules, the more restricted rule (R2) is properly included in the more general one (R3). Figure 5 shows that this property has a geographical correlate: the lects with the less general rule are located within the area of the more general one, wherever both rules occur in the same region. (Where both do not occur in the same region, the one that occurs is the less general.) This geographical pattern is altogether natural if one considers that the linguistic situation which it reflects involves rule generalization. Presumably, R2 is the older rule and R3 represents the extension of cluster simplification into a new environment. It follows that the range of speakers with R2 and R3 will be contiguous, since one rule develops from the other. And it is not surprising to find that speakers with one rule or the other tend to cluster.

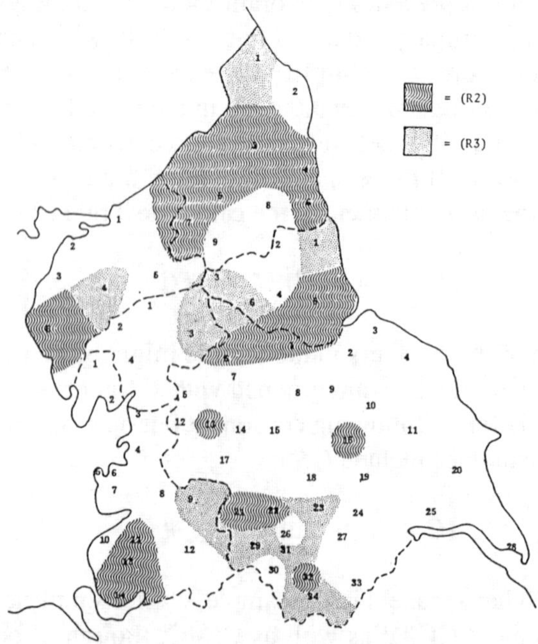

Figure 5. The geographical dispersion of R2 included in the range of R3, whenever both rules occur, in six northern counties of England (map drawn by H. A. Gleason, Jr. from Chambers 1982)

The geographical patterns for (R2) and (R3) recur in further extensions of the rule. Because this study is so far (to my knowledge) neither corroborated nor challenged by similar further studies, it would be imprudent to place much stock in the patterns that emerge. The orderliness is, however, promising. Only a few years ago, variable rules like (R2) and (R3) were held to be beyond the domain of linguistic theory. Once admitted, their utility was quickly recognized in describing the variability which is so commonplace in linguistic behavior. Their use in urban sociolinguistic studies reveals them to be interesting theoretical objects, with their own attributes and implications. It should not be surprising to discover that they also have geographical correlates.

3.4. The function of linguistic variability.[10]

Dialectologists have seldom inquired explicitly about the biological or social function of linguistic variety. To my knowledge, the only discussion couched in ontological terms is by Labov (1972a, 323-25), who briefly addresses this question: 'Is there an adaptive function to linguistic diversity?' Labov was inspired to ask the question by the biologists studying songbird dialects, for whom the question about adaptive function is commonplace. By way of an answer, Labov suggested that continuing research into bird-song dialects might eventually provide clues about the adaptive function of human dialects.

Current findings in bird song dialectology do not encourage optimism in this regard. Baker & Cunningham (1985), in a useful survey, show that the adaptive significance of bird songs is far from decided, and suggest that future clarifications are unlikely to narrow the range of possibilities even if they succeed in eliminating some of them. In any event, the functions postulated by biologists extrapolate unsatisfactorily to humans. Genetic functions such as gene flow and allele fixation can be ruled out, and the social functions of mating and territoriality appear to have little bearing. Mating is not determined linguistically for humans, although in communities with very dense networks some stigma is attached to a member who takes a spouse from 'outside.' Territoriality along dialectal lines seems more pervasive, with speech-based antagonisms detectable at several social levels, but it probably becomes a fighting matter only between the most insular groups, if at all.

As with humans, in bird populations, evidence for the genetic functions of dialect differences is not convincing, and may in all cases be explained as an accident of sociality. That is to say, the social clustering over several generations may be the cause of both dialectal and genetic specializations in the population. In birds no less than in humans, dialect appears to develop irrepressibly from the inevitable circumstance of growing up with regional bonds and community ties. If membership in tightly circumscribed social groups -- the family, the neighborhood, the parish -- is necessary for the physical and spiritual well-being of the individual from infancy to, perhaps, adolescence, then donning their stigmata -- their gestures, their costume, their accent -- appears to be an adaptive mechanism.

Unlike birds, humans are capable of reflecting on their circumstances, even apparently irrepressible ones, and evaluating them. Although dialectologists have spent little energy on discussing the purpose of linguistic diversity, others have been less reluctant. The first attempt, some three millennia old, is the myth of Babel, which postulates linguistic diversity as a punishment for humanity's hubris. In modern terms, we would say that the Babelian hypothesis maintains that linguistic diversity is counteradaptive. Consistent with that, Judaeo-Christian cultures have erected numerous institutions and policies with the primary or secondary purpose of curtailing diversity in favor of standardized speech: prescriptive dictionaries, school grammars, nationalized authorities such as the Académie française, Esperanto societies, school bussing, training in the dramatic arts, British 'public' schools, and media hiring practices, to name a few.

Perhaps it is because the Babelian hypothesis is so deeply ingrained in our culture that speech varieties become emblematic. By now, it is commonplace for subjective reaction experiments to reveal stereotypes based solely on accent and dialect. For example, in a matched guise experiment, New Yorkers reacted to a minuscule phonetic difference -- r-lessness of one word -- from one speaker by revaluating her occupation from 'television personality' to 'receptionist' (Labov 1972a, 147-48); and British teachers downgraded (hypothetical) students when the taped speech sample in their dossier was in a local accent, regardless of the quality of samples of schoolwork (Giles & Powesland 1975, 2-3). These and many similar results leave no doubt that dialect differences can impose a priori constraints on an individual's social acceptability and occupational mobility.

Against such evidence in support of the Babelian hypothesis stands the overwhelming fact that linguistic diversity not only endures but prevails. If linguistic diversity is counteradaptive, why has the most adaptable species of all failed to eliminate or curtail its effects? The answer may lie in the fact that it is not absolutely counteradaptive. In fact, it is adaptive as long as people remain within their 'natal population.' It is counteradaptive only when they move beyond it.

The antinomy between local adaptivity and global counteradaptivity is discernible sociolinguistically in the few extant studies of individual aberrations from well-defined local speech norms. Douglas-Cowie (1978) discovered that individuals in Articlave, Northern Ireland, whose speech was measurably less regional than that of their peers were also generally the most 'ambitious' members of the community, with aspirations to 'get on in the world' beyond Articlave. Milroy (1980) showed that people who kept 'dense network' ties by working, shopping, and pubbing exclusively within their Belfast working-class parishes exhibited more local (i.e., less standard) speech than their peers who occasionally ventured outside. Labov's classic study of Martha's Vineyard (1972a, 1-42) demonstrated that a highly localized dialect variant correlated with individuals' allegiance to their home territory: among teenagers, the variant occurred much less frequently in the speech of those who intended to leave the island for education or employment than in that of those who intended to stay.

In their social predilections, individuals and groups range along a continuum between the polar extremities of global mobility and local insularity. The rich sociolinguistic reflections of the antinomy between mobility and insularity have barely begun to come clear. The answer to Labov's question -- Is there an adaptive function to linguistic diversity? -- will differ depending upon where one looks on the continuum.

It ought to be posed as a kind of ultimate question in linguistics as it is in biology. Like many of the other questions posed here, this one will not have an easy answer. But if we keep asking the large, daunting questions, someday our fine-grained, minute researches should contribute something to their answer.

Notes

1 The breadth of the coverage of either discipline can be appreciated by reviewing the useful textbook surveys now available, such as Wardhaugh (1986) and Francis (1983).

2 Pickford's argument and the traditional defense are concisely stated by Petyt (1980, 110-16).

3 Earlier (1971, 101), Labov stated the Uniformitarian Principle slightly differently: 'the linguistic proccsses taking place around us are the same as those that have operated to produce the historical record.'

4 For a straightforward example of comparative dialectology, see the discussion of h-dropping in Bradford and Norwich, in Chambers & Trudgill (1980, 69-70). A more complex example can be found in the comparison of a sound change in progress in two Canadian cities 3500 kilometers apart (Chambers & Hardwick 1986).

5 The HEAD index is based, obviously, on the subjects' *reports* of their listening and viewing habits and does not necessarily reflect their behavior. It seems to me there are two social forces working in opposite directions to distort the answers given. Among MC adults there is a social stigma attached to television watching, and it seems quite likely that the adults might unconsciously have minimized the amount they do. Among the pre-teens, the stigma is just the opposite: it is un-hip to be ignorant about the most popular shows. (See Chambers 1981, 25-26.)

6 Gravity models are, of course, literally based on the Newtonian formula for measuring the force of attraction of one heavenly body on another. The geolinguistic gravity model was developed originally by Peter Trudgill (1974). The version presented in Chambers & Trudgill (1980, 196-202) silently amends the original in a couple of ways, most significantly by providing a formula for determining a rank order among population centers influenced by the center of diffusion.

7 The discovery of *fudged* lects has an interesting theoretical implication. The theory of lexical diffusion maintains that 'words change their pronunciations by discrete, perceptible increments (i.e. phonetically abrupt), but severally at a time (i.e., lexically gradual)' (Chen 1972, 472). The change

from Northern [ʊ] to Southern [ʌ] is progressing as a lexical diffusion, as I have shown elsewhere (Chambers & Trudgill 1980, 176-80). It is lexically gradual, but for some speakers -- those with the fudge [ɤ] -- the change is phonetically gradual, not abrupt.

8 Most variability studies that have been based on data from dialect geography surveys, including studies of transition zones, have used materials from the Survey of English Dialects (Orton et al. 1962-71). The reason for this is simply that the SED data were published in tables rather than on maps. While Orton regretted having to publish tables because maps were too expensive, that format has proved to be a happy accident so far as subsequent research is concerned. The tables are user-friendly. The maps of other projects, such as the *Linguistic Atlas of New England* (Kurath 1939-43), require the daunting preliminary step of extracting data from them and reassembling it in tabular form.

9 Keyser's review deserves the attention of the new generation of dialectologists. Davis (1983, 137-39) discusses Keyser's main example, but there are interesting theoretical implications that could also be profitably revived.

10 The discussion in this section is developed in more detail in Chambers (1985).

References

Baker, M.C. & M.A. Cunningham. 1985. The biology of bird-song dialects. *The Behavioral and Brain Sciences* 8:102-4.

Cameron, D. & J. Coates. 1988. Some problems in the sociolinguistic explanation of sex differences. In J. Coates & D. Cameron (eds), *Women in their speech communities*. London: Longman, 13-26.

Carver, Craig. 1986. The influence of the Mississippi River on Northern dialect boundaries. *American Speech* 61:245-61.

Chambers, J. K. 1981. The Americanization of Canadian raising. In M. F. Miller, C. S. Masek & R. S. Hendrick (eds), *Parasession on Language and Behavior*. Chicago Linguistic Society, 20-35.

Chambers, J. K. 1982. Geolinguistics of a variable rule. *Discussion Papers in Geolinguistics* 5. Stafford: North Staffordshire Polytechnic.

Chambers, J. K. 1985. Social adaptiveness in human and songbird dialects. *The Behavioral and Brain Sciences* 8:85-100.

Chambers, J. K. 1988. Acquisition of phonological variants. In Alan R. Thomas (ed.), *Methods in dialectology*. Clevedon: Multilingual Matters, 650-65.

Chambers, J. K. 1989. Canadian raising: fronting, blocking, etc. *American Speech* 64:75-88.

Chambers, J. K., & M. F. Hardwick. 1986. Comparative sociolinguistics of a sound change in Canadian English. *English World-Wide* 7:23-46.

Chambers, J. K., & Peter Trudgill 1980. *Dialectology*. Cambridge University Press.

Chen, M. 1972. The time dimension: contribution toward the theory of sound change. *Foundations of Language* 8:457-98.

Davis, Lawrence M. 1983. *English dialectology: an introduction*. University of Alabama Press.

Douglas-Cowie, E. 1978. Linguistic code-switching in a Northern Irish village. In Peter Trudgill (ed.), *Sociolinguistic patterns in British English*. London: Edward Arnold, 37-51.

Eckert, Penelope. 1988. Adolescent social structure and the spread of linguistic change. *Language in Society* 17:183-207.

Ervin-Tripp, Susan M. 1973. Some strategies for the first two years. In Timothy Moore (ed.), *Cognition and the acquisition of language*. New York: Academic Press, 261-86.

Francis, W. Nelson. 1983. *Dialectology: An Introduction*. London: Longman.

Gerritsen, M., & F. Jansen 1980. The interplay of dialectology and historical linguistics: some refinements of Trudgill's formula. In P. Maher (ed.), *Proceedings of the 3rd International Congress of Historical Linguistics*. Amsterdam: John Benjamins.

Giles, Howard & P. F. Powesland. 1975. *Speech style and social evaluation*. NY: Academic Press.

Glauser, Beat. 1985. Linguistic atlases and generative phonology. In J. M. Kirk, S. Sanderson & J. D. A. Widdowson (eds), *Studies in linguistic geography: The dialects of English in Britain and Ireland*. London: Croom Helm, 113-29.

Glauser, Beat 1988. Aitken's context in Northumberland, Cumberland and Durham: a computer-assisted analysis of material from the Survey of English Dialects. In Alan R. Thomas (ed.), *Methods in dialectology*. Clevedon: Multilingual Matters Ltd, 611-24.

Guy, Gregory R. 1980. Variation in the group and the individual: the case of final stop deletion. In W. Labov (ed.), *Locating language in time and space*. NY: Academic Press, 1-36.

Hall, Robert A., Jr. 1943. The Papal States in Italian linguistic history. *Language* 19:125-40.

Horwood, H. 1966. *Tomorrow will be Sunday*. Toronto: Paperjacks.

Hägerstrand, T. 1967. *Innovation diffusion as a spatial process*. Postscript and trans. by A. Pred. Chicago: University of Chicago Press.

Keyser, Samuel J. 1963. Review of *The Pronunciation of English in the Atlantic States*. *Language* 39:303-16.

Kirk, J. M., S. Sanderson, & J. D. A. Widdowson (eds). 1985. *Studies in linguistic geography: The dialects of English in Britain and Ireland*. London: Croom Helm.

Kurath, Hans. 1939-43. *Linguistic atlas of New England.* 3 Vols. Providence, R.I.: Brown University Press.

Labov, William. 1971. Some principles of linguistic methodology. *Language in Society* 1:97-120.

Labov, William. 1972a. *Sociolinguistic patterns*. Philadelphia: University of Pennsylvania Press.

Labov, William. 1972b. *Language in the inner city: studies in the Black English vernacular*. Philadelphia: University of Pennsylvania Press.

Labov, William. 1984. The transmission of linguistic traits across and within communities. Symposium on Language Transmission and Change. Center for Advanced Study in the Behavioral Sciences.

Lathrop, A. 1979. Tracking (r) in the *LANE*: an investigation of the variable preconsonantal R in New England. Ms.

Le Page, Robert & A. Tabouret-Keller. 1985. *Acts of identity*. London: Cambridge University Press.

Macaulay, R. K. S. 1985. Linguistic maps: visual aid or abstract art? In J. M. Kirk, S. Sanderson, & J. D. A. Widdowson (eds), *Studies in linguistic geography: The dialects of English in Britain and Ireland.* London: Croom Helm, 172-86.

McDavid, Raven I., Jr. 1981. On obtaining spontaneous responses. In H. J. Warkentyne (ed.), *Papers from the 4th International Conference in Methods in Dialectology*. British Columbia: University of Victoria, 66-84.

Milroy, James & Lesley Milroy. 1985. Linguistic change, social network and speaker innovation. *Journal of Linguistics* 21:339-84.

Milroy, Lesley. 1980. *Language and social networks*. Oxford: Basil Blackwell.

Milroy, Lesley. 1982. Social network and linguistic focusing. In Suzanne Romaine (ed.), *Sociolinguistic variation in speech communities*. London: Edward Arnold, 141-52.

Orton, Harold, et al. (eds). 1962-71. *Survey of English dialects, the basic material.* Vol. I (3 Parts) with W. Halliday, *The Six Northern Counties and the Isle of Man*; Vol. II (3 Parts) with M. Barry, *The West Midland Counties*; Vol. III (3 Parts) with P. M. Tilling, *The East Midland Counties and East Anglia*; Vol. IV (3 Parts) with M. F. Wakelin, *The Southern Counties*. Leeds: E.J. Arnold.

Orton, Harold & N. Wright. 1974. *A word geography of England.* London: Seminar Press.

Petyt, K. Malcolm. 1980. *The study of dialect: an introduction to dialectology.* London: Andre Deutsch.

Pickford, G. R. 1956. American linguistic geography: a sociological appraisal. *Word* 12:211-33.

Speitel, Hans. 1969. An areal typology of isoglosses near the Scottish-English border. *Zeitschrift für Dialektologie und Linguistik* 36:49-66.

Stewart, William. A. 1962. A sociolinguistic typology for describing national multilingualism. In Joshua A. Fishman (ed.), *Readings in the sociology of language*. The Hague: Mouton (1968), 531-45.

Trudgill, Peter. 1972. Sex, covert prestige, and linguistic change in the urban British English of Norwich. *Language in Society* 1:179-95.

Trudgill, Peter. 1974. Linguistic change and diffusion: description and explanation in sociolinguistic dialect geography. *Language in Society* 2:215-46.

Wardhaugh, Ronald. 1980. *An introduction to sociolinguistics*. Oxford: Basil Blackwell.

II. Community Studies

Adapting dialectology: The conduct of community language studies[1]

John Baugh
Stanford University

1.0. Introduction

> I do not hesitate to claim that it was actual fieldwork experience which made all the difference to me personally in linguistics (Shuy 1983:345).[2]

This is especially true in my case; as a black American I strive to maintain contact with the vernacular African American community. Dialectology and sociolinguistics have provided this opportunity in concert with my professional research objectives. It was also for this reason that I chose to study with Labov, Hymes, Fought, and Goffman; each scholar placed paramount importance on the interpersonal nature of linguistic behavior, as well as other forms of human communication. My opinions regarding the value of fieldwork draw on the diverse interdisciplinary methods that were advocated by my mentors, and their mentors before them.

This chapter celebrates the value of community language studies and pays tribute to the long-standing commitment of the American Dialect Society to the empirical foundations of rigorous linguistic inquiry. Several methods are surveyed in this paper, following an evolutionary theme. Older, established, methods are examined first. Other significant milestones are then introduced, including discussion of implications for future research.[3] These comments are written with students in mind, and seek to offer some practical suggestions.

The chronological tenor of the text proceeds from simple methods to more advanced analytic procedures, from field questionnaires to laboratory recordings, and from elicitation techniques to controlled experiments. Linguistic research is robust, highly diversified, and often overlaps with more than one topic. There are important reasons for procedural dissimilarities because different research problems require alternative methods. How, then, does the student of language choose the proper method? There is, of course, no single answer, and therein lies the peril and the promise of dialectology and sociolinguistics. (Chambers and Trudgill 1980, Petyt 1980, and Walters 1988).

Thomas (1988) observed that disciplinary boundaries between dialectology and sociolinguistics continue to blur. Wolfram and Fasold (1974:xiii) made similar observations: 'Studies which deal with language in society have commonly been subsumed under the title of sociolinguistics. The types of studies that are sometimes included under the rubric actually cover a rather broad spectrum of topics.' Since that time their remarks have been reaffirmed, as various specialists continue to strive for independent intellectual identities. For the sake of illustration I too will gloss over some, admittedly significant, conceptual differences among scholars who study language in social context. By doing so I can address common methodological concerns.

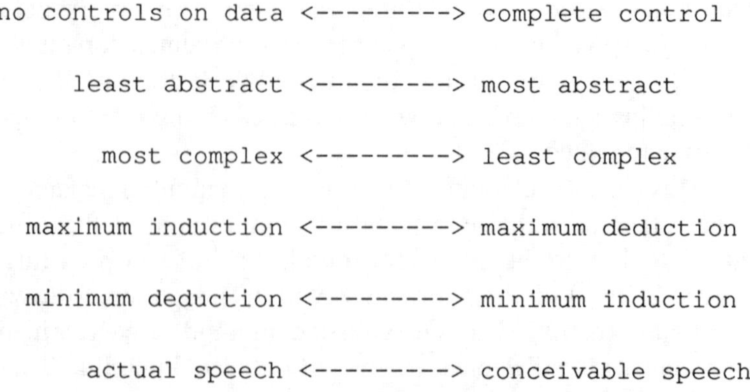

Figure 1. Alternative approaches to linguistics research

Figure 1 illustrates the range of linguistics methodology, based largely on data control. Some linguists are highly experimental, exerting maximum control over their evidence, while others place fewer controls on their data. Methodological diversity among linguists reflects the elastic nature of linguistic behavior and the fact that language can be examined in multifarious ways. Scholars rarely adhere to the extreme positions illustrated in Figure 1, although there are clear intellectual tendencies toward one pole or the other. Dialectologists do not have the luxury of engaging in too much linguistic abstraction, nor can we rely exclusively on personal linguistic intuitions as primary data -- that is, if we seek to delineate dialect boundaries beyond individual experiences. Dialects, pidgins, creoles, and other contact vernaculars are inherently social, regional, and political entities, and therefore beyond the intuitive power of any individual.

Community language studies are best represented by the left side of the continuum in Figure 1. Fieldwork and informant cooperation are essential to social studies of language because the most relevant data defy many experimental controls. It is precisely for this reason that linguistic performance is inherently more complex than linguistic competence (Chomsky 1957, 1965). The empirical foundations of community language studies have been at the core of dialectology since its European inception (cf. Gilliéron and Edmont 1902) and are mirrored in American contexts by Allen's (1964:214) methodological characterization:

> Essentially this evidence is gathered like this. Using a tested selective sampling technique, linguistically trained fieldworkers interview native residents representing three groups, older and uneducated speakers, middle-aged secondary school graduates, and younger college graduates. From each of these persons information is sought about more than 800 language items (in the first project there were 1200). Each response is recorded in a finely graded phonetic transcription, so that all responses have value as pronunciation evidence. Some items are included for that reason only; others are included for their lexical or grammatical or syntactic significance. The basic list of items in the questionnaire is usually modified slightly in each area through the dropping of some which are irrelevant there and the

> adding of others significant there. ... But this basic list is essentially the same countrywide, so that national comparative studies will be possible when the fieldwork is finished.

The methodological complexity embodied in Allen's remarks lays the foundation for the following discussion. We begin with questionnaires and worksheets, similar to those used for the preparation of linguistic atlases. The impact of tape recorders is then introduced, along with remarks about the 'observer's paradox.' Experimental procedures, and the advanced technology that has been developed to support them, are considered prior to the relevance of social demographics and concluding remarks.

2.0. Questionnaires and worksheets

American linguistic atlases are quite complex because of the pervasive multilingual history of the U.S., and this diversity was exposed through the tireless efforts of Kurath (1949), McDavid (1942), Allen (1973), Cassidy (1973), Ferguson and Heath (1981), and many others. Questionnaires and worksheets are staple tools for dialectologists. They are replicable and offer considerable flexibility due to their adaptability. Questionnaires can also be expanded to accommodate large teams of trained fieldworkers, as indicated in Allen's preceding remarks. Lone investigators can also develop pilot studies or independent research with the aide of questionnaires. The design of questionnaires must be tailored to the community under study. Comparable procedures must be used whenever possible, particularly if comparative analyses are desired.

This brings me to the value of portable recording equipment. Unlike the early pioneers in dialectology, we now have the advantage of using tape recorders for our fieldwork. Walters (1988) observed that the advent of tape recorders drastically changed dialectology; data collection and transcription were separated. Tapes provide excellent documentation and don't require on-the-spot transcription. Native fieldworkers can therefore be used to assist with data collection, even if they have no formal training in phonetics, etc. My situation, in African American speech communities, is special because many of the best black English informants are those who have been denied adequate educational opportunities. Their limited literacy skills prevented the use of written questionnaires (Baugh 1984), but with tape recordings I was able to introduce verbal questionnaires. As we shall see below, the use of recorded questionnaires maintains greater control over more linguistic variation than do written questionnaires (§2.2).

Scholars examining other groups and other linguistic topics will face different requirements. Nevertheless, some common methodological denominators can be identified. Fieldworkers must study the culture of their informants to ensure that questionnaires adequately reflect the significant inventory of dialect features that are relevant to the speech community under investigation. These are major presumptions that should never be taken lightly; the value of the final results depends primarily on informant cooperation, and thorough ethnographic knowledge of the vernacular speech community is essential to successful community language research.

Different segments of the speech community probably will require alternative strategies. For example, in advanced industrial societies we find that the highest and lowest classes tend to be closed, albeit for different reasons, and successful fieldworkers take social diversity into account. The upper classes protect their privacy through a combination of economic and social barriers, while poor people are keenly aware of their sociolinguistic stigma. Both groups distrust 'outsiders' and this is true regardless of political persuasion. In many European countries discrimination against Gypsies is rampant (Hancock 1987), just as non-white minorities in the U.S. have been the object of racial discrimination. Whether one seeks to study language among the Gypsies, or among blacks and Latinos in America, sensitivity to cultural, ethnic, and racial differences must be considered prior to effective fieldwork.

In addition to basic training in phonetics and questionnaire design, dialectology demands access to representative members of the speech community. Elderly informants who have not traveled extensively have been the main source of traditional dialectological records, as indicated in Allen's remarks above (§1.0). Such individuals are least likely to be tainted by external linguistic norms, and most likely to reflect local vernacular dialects. By comparing the speech of older speakers with that of younger members of the same speech community one can determine patterns of linguistic change within a particular region. Slight modifications allow examination with emphases on other demographic contrasts, such as class, race, religion, gender, etc.(§5). As comparable data are gathered in different geographic regions, various linguistic distinctions begin to emerge and often resemble traditional isoglosses.

The practice of having several fieldworkers employing identical procedures in alternative locations is essential to successful dialectology and cannot be overemphasized (cf. Pederson, 1971). As already mentioned, the advent of tape recorders has allowed dialectologists to separate the tasks of recording and transcription (Walters 1988), although some scholars argue that recordings inhibit informants, formalizing their speech through restricted vernacular usage (Wolfson 1976, §3.0).

Computers have also enhanced linguistic atlas methodology, as reflected by on-going research. The Texas dialect survey illustrates the computer's contribution. Each semester hundreds of students are provided with training and linguistic questionnaires that they take 'back home' during holidays. Traditional informants are located and interviewed, and students transfer their results to computer coded worksheets, similar to those used for most standardized tests. Results are then compiled and up-dated biannually, providing a vivid evolutionary portrait of dialect variation across the state. Computer aided dialectology represents the cutting-edge of linguistic atlas research, and other technological advances -- like the use of video recordings -- will serve to expand the scope and analytic potential of language research in social contexts.

2.1. Language attitude surveys

Dialect diversity is a linguistic universal, and the fact that some dialects are more highly valued than others is socially universal. Most citizens in advanced industrial societies have clear impressions of the dialects they cherish and those they abhor. The parameters that distinguish these categories constitute the domain of language attitude research. However, this mixture of social and linguistic data has created a methodological paradox for linguists, as illustrated in Figure 1. From a conceptual point of view, linguists of every theoretical persuasion consider all dialects to be equal, regardless of the social status of their speakers. This egalitarian philosophy has no basis in social reality, however, because of the strong, and deeply emotional, linguistic opinions that abound. Dialectologists, sociolinguists, social psychologists, creolists, ethnolinguists, and educators seek to learn more about differential attitudes toward various languages and dialects. Preston's (1988a, 1988b) research on dialect perceptions is very informative in this regard. He has documented the variable nature of American dialect perceptions; his work also illustrates the foundation of stereotyping that reinforces typical linguistic value judgments that ordinary citizens harbor toward different dialects. Recent educational research (see Kerr-Mattox 1989) has demonstrated benign and overt linguistic prejudice among white school teachers toward minority students, and this research is relevant to many social problems beyond the educational realm (e.g. linguistic prejudice within corporations or during business transactions, etc.).

In order to conduct a language attitude survey one must first collect some recorded samples of speech. Whatever languages or dialects that are the object of evaluation need to be gathered. Ethnographic evidence is useful, if not essential, to the selection of representative informants. Although elderly informants have traditionally served dialectology, language attitude studies may seek to evaluate larger segments of society. Labov's (1966, 1972) studies of linguistic change in 'apparent time' are based precisely on this principle; age differences among informants provide illustrations of generational linguistic variability within the same community.

Mean Ratings[a] *and Ranks of Mean Ratings*[b] *of Each Dialect Type by Northern White University Students*

Dialect Groups	Traits															Sum
	Upbringing	Intelligent	Friendly	Educated	Disposition	Speech	Trustworthy	Ambitious	Faith-God	Talented	Character	Determination	Honest	Personality	Considerate	
Network	6.8	6.7	5.8	7.2	6.0	6.7	6.3	5.8	5.3	6.1	6.4	5.9	6.2	6.1	6.3	
	[1]	[1]	[2]	[1]	[1]	[1]	[1]	[1]	[2]	[1]	[1]	[2]	[1]	[1]	[1]	[18]
Educated Negro Southern	5.4	5.5	5.7	5.1	5.4	4.7	5.8	5.6	5.8	5.2	6.0	6.0	5.9	5.3	5.7	
	[3]	[3]	[3]	[3]	[4]	[3]	[2]	[2]	[1]	[3]	[2]	[1]	[2]	[4]	[3]	[39]
Educated White Southern	6.0	5.8	5.6	5.7	5.5	5.5	5.6	5.2	5.2	5.3	5.7	5.5	5.6	5.5	5.6	
	[2]	[2]	[4]	[2]	[3]	[2]	[3]	[3]	[3]	[2]	[4]	[3]	[4]	[3]	[4]	[44]
Howard University	5.2	5.4	6.0	4.6	5.9	4.6	5.6	5.1	5.2	5.1	5.9	5.2	5.8	5.9	5.7	
	[4]	[4]	[1]	[4]	[2]	[4]	[3]	[4]	[4]	[4]	[3]	[4]	[3]	[2]	[2]	[48]
New York Alumni	4.6	4.5	5.3	3.5	5.0	3.1	5.2	4.5	5.1	3.9	5.2	4.9	5.5	5.0	5.3	
	[5]	[6]	[5]	[6]	[5]	[6]	[5]	[5]	[5]	[6]	[5]	[5]	[5]	[6]	[5]	[80]
Mississippi Peer	4.3	5.0	5.1	3.9	5.0	3.3	4.9	4.4	4.9	4.1	5.0	4.5	5.1	5.1	4.8	
	[6]	[5]	[6]	[5]	[6]	[5]	[6]	[6]	[6]	[5]	[6]	[6]	[6]	[5]	[6]	[85]
Dialect difference, *F* ratios: ($df = 5{,}175$)[c]	22.5	14.3	2.0	35.1	4.9	35.7	6.5	5.5	3.0	14.5	6.1	7.3	4.6	3.4	3.9	

[a] Mean ratings are rounded to one decimal place.
[b] Ranks of mean ratings are set in brackets.
[c] All *F* ratios except that for the trait "Friendly" are significant at or beyond the *.05* level of confidence.

Table 1. Dialect ratings (Tucker & Lambert 1972:179)

Assuming that an adequate sample of speech has been gathered, appropriate judges must be selected to evaluate these linguistic stimuli. Randomized samples are presented to the judges, who evaluate them on several criteria. Tucker and Lambert (1972) presented the 'traits' listed in Table 1 to northern white university students who evaluated several black and white speech varieties, differentiated primarily on regional and educational differences.

Similar discussion by Wolfram and Fasold (1974), Labov (1972, 1984), Halliday (1978), Giles and Powesland (1975), Haugen (1972), Lambert (1972), Bloomfield (1933), Brown and Levinson (1978), Kontra (1982), Heath (1983), Lavandera (1988), Romaine (1982), Trudgill (1983), Gal (1978), Paulston (1976), Fishman (1989), and others has led to diverse, and innovative, approaches to language attitude research. The preceding illustration is but one of many analytic tools for language attitude analyses.

A common theme resounds in these works; each scholar stresses the multidimensional nature of language attitudes. These issues come up again below regarding the potential significance of various demographic factors -- that is, the ecological factors that have influenced linguistic evolution. Most of these attitudinal data can be derived from the judicious use of questionnaires and discrete participant observation.

2.2. Grammaticality judgments

Questionnaires are well suited to examinations of grammaticality, which may be crucial to a variety of theoretical-to-practical issues. From a theoretical perspective Trudgill (1983) and Walters (1988) observe that formal linguistic theory often fails to account for significant dialectal variation. They cite the form 'Give it him,' which has been rejected in several formal linguistic studies as being ungrammatical, despite its acceptability in Great Britain. One can find other such examples with ease. Natives of Pittsburgh, Pennsylvania typically use expressions like 'It needs fixed' rather than 'It needs fixing' or 'It needs to be fixed.' Although these differences are minor, in grammatical terms, they illustrate regional variation in morphophonemic and syntactical categories. Another example is found in Black English, where speakers use auxiliary verbs quite differently than do speakers of standard English (Labov 1969, Bailey 1965, 1966, Baugh 1980, 1983, Wolfram 1969, Kasse 1983). Formal theories of such variation tend to ignore or minimize the theoretical relevance of black English or other nonstandard linguistic norms.

In each of the preceding examples we observe grammatical variability among diverse speakers of English, and contemporary theories of universal grammar strive, at least in principle, to account for all dialects that compose a language. Dialectology, with its emphasis on strict empiricism, has played a major role in identifying syntactic variation among dialects within English and other languages.

The solicitation of grammaticality judgments is a controversial subject, as it has been for over twenty-five years. With the current prominence of formal linguistic theory we often forget that Chomsky's early work met with considerable skepticism and resistance, particularly from structural linguists. The debate between Hill (1961) and Chomsky (1961) regarding grammaticality judgments is still with us today, so much so that nearly independent methods have evolved in support of inductive versus deductive linguistic inquiries. Formal grammarians are uncomfortable with the lack of control over data derived from social contexts, but it is just for this reason (i.e. to implement scientific controls) that questionnaires are so useful to studies of grammar in social context. At the time that Chomsky and Hill debated the merits of their respective experimental procedures, the issues of data control and literacy were primary, and the potential value of recordings for the purpose of grammatical evaluation was not discussed. I, perhaps more than many linguists, am sensitive to the value of recorded questionnaires because of the impoverished educational opportunities that have confronted the vast majority of informants that I have interviewed in minority communities across the U.S. Many were unable to use written questionnaires, and without recording equipment the verbal questionnaires that I devised to examine the grammatical status of 'steady' could not have been distributed with reliability or the same degree of linguistic control (Baugh 1984). For example, had I read questionnaires to each informant, there is no guarantee that I would have maintained identical intonation. In fact, it would be nearly impossible to repeat the same utterance without some degree of linguistic variation; tape recordings eliminate this problem. More specifically, one controls intonation, prosody, and the tone of oral questionnaires, whereas readers impose their own, uncontrolled, intonation, pitch, and rhythm to written stimuli. Many dialect differences hinge on slight phonetic variation, and written questionnaires cannot confine these variables in ways that are comparable to oral recordings. Since I have had extensive exposure to standard English, other black English speakers provided the recordings for my questionnaires, to ensure that representative members of the speech community were providing the most authentic linguistic stimuli. These modifications were made possible through advanced technology and are not inherently tied to linguistic issues per se; however, the impact of technology on social studies of language is undeniable.

Dialectologists have taken full advantage of advanced technology in the quest for complete linguistic descriptions; some dialectologists now use video recordings to capture both verbal and nonverbal behavior, as well as interactional norms, such as posture, spatial relations among speakers, etc. Recalling the diverse methods that are illustrated in Figure 1, video recordings of vernacular conversations are inherently more complex -- in behavioral terms -- than are oral recordings of the same event. Goffman (1959) illustrates that glances, stances, and group memberships play major roles during any conversation, and video recordings have the potential to capture this data; audio recordings do not.

Returning, then, to the specific problems associated with grammaticality judgments, recorded stimuli offer strict control over potentially significant variation that is superior to printed sentences. Oral, recorded, grammaticality judgments have universal applicability, in the sense that one can provide the exact same stimuli to diverse speakers within the community. The methodological consequences of developing questionnaires that can be distributed to all segments of the society, not just those who are literate, allow us to complement the search for universal grammar with methods that are more accessible to broader populations, regardless of their educational status.

Whereas Chomsky strives for maximum abstraction and idealization through characterizations of perfect speaker-hearers in completely homogeneous communities, Weinreich et.al. (1968) see no basis for such extreme idealism in the face of social reality; they strive to account for 'typical speaker-hearers' in 'ordinary speech communities' (i.e. where language reflects orderly heterogeneity). Dialectologists and students of language in social context must employ theoretical abstractions, but in seeking to identify typical (i.e. not ideal) speakers and hearers in ordinary speech communities we strive for linguistic accounts that have considerable social validity. The simple recognition that some dialects are valued more than others reaffirms the value of community language research. Here it is most important to appreciate the potential social stratification of grammaticality judgments and to recognize that tape recorders and other forms of advanced technology can help us overcome some of the inadvertent limitations of written grammatical evaluations.

3.0. The observer's paradox

Have I just contradicted myself? On one hand I suggest that certain segments of the society are more difficult to approach than others, yet I also indicate that advanced technology provides greater potential to examine some of these same groups. In addition to this potential contradiction lies Wolfson's (1976) observation that interviews are not ordinary speech events. She argues that when speakers know they are being recorded, seeing recording equipment around them and occasionally commenting on its presence, it is naive to think that their speech is natural (i.e. similar to the way that they would speak if fieldworkers were not present or recording). However, some interviews can approximate ordinary conversations, and good linguistic interviews reflect colloquial norms.

Labov (1972) has addressed Wolfson's concerns regarding the observer's paradox, which is the sociolinguistic equivalent of the experimenter effect. How does the fieldworker record speech without distorting the very data (s)he seeks to collect? Familiarity with the culture and acceptance by informants is essential to successful fieldwork. Unlike interviews by spies, the police, or news reporters, linguistic interviews can cover a wide range of topics that need not threaten informants. Indeed, Labov (1984) advocates the gradual introduction of topics, beginning with non-threatening childhood experiences and moving toward dangerous episodes, culminating with questions regarding deeply personal experiences. This procedure allows the fieldworkers to monitor interviews in progress and shift topics when necessary to maintain informant rapport.

Trust is an important element in overcoming the observer's paradox. If informants are suspicious of fieldworkers, then they are not likely to be cooperative. When informants understand their role in linguistic research and the motivation behind the fieldwork, they are more likely to support our efforts. This was my experience in the black community. Most of my informants recognized the value of oral traditions in African American culture, and it has always been a simple matter for me to explain my motives to prospective informants. They also come to understand the central role they play in linguistic research and the paramount importance of their data to the reconstruction of the oral historical record.

Wolfson (1976) mentions that her informants made repeated reference to the tape recorder. I too have encountered similar comments from informants, but it has been my experience that attention to recording equipment varies during interviews. At times, particularly when potentially embarrassing topics are discussed, informants may occasionally refer to the recording equipment; they recognize the documentary nature of our research, and periodically express concern regarding confidentiality. This strikes me as a very natural response, particularly when one conducts fieldwork among oppressed people. Nevertheless, there were far more occasions where it was obvious that speakers were ignoring the equipment altogether.

The extent to which informants tend to ignore recording equipment in favor of speaking freely is a direct reflection of the extent to which fieldworkers have successfully overcome the observer's paradox. It is for this very reason that ethnographic familiarity with subjects is essential to successful fieldwork. If fieldworkers are unfamiliar with the culture under analysis, they will not know those topics that are potential sources of aggravation. Knowing the acceptable norms within a speech community is essential to reducing or eliminating unwanted experimenter effects.

Many years ago I studied handshakes and their variability among African Americans (Baugh 1978). Solidarity among a close network of male friends was conveyed through their black power handshakes, while formal relationships were marked by traditional handshakes. Outsiders to the community, most of whom were white, would often initiate the black power handshake -- in a gesture of friendship -- only to encounter rejection or insistence on using the traditional handshake by black men. Knowledge of these handshake norms is just one of many examples that could be cited in support of the point at hand; a considerable amount of research about the community needs to be completed prior to fieldwork, otherwise the potential for informant alienation runs high.

The more you know about the community the more likely you will be able to diminish unnecessary reactions to your recording equipment. I will not address the ethical issue of surreptitious recordings, nor will I pursue discussion regarding secret recordings as a solution to the observer's paradox. I have always told informants about my work; there has been no need to hide my interest in language or culture, as well as in the people who preserve them. Honesty may lead to the kind of rapport that can overcome the observer's paradox.

4.0. Experimental development

Recordings have not only separated the tasks of data collection and linguistic transcription but have also provided permanent documentation that can be used to examine different facets of language (or nonverbal behavior, including sign language, in the case of video recordings). This potential has been most evident in studies of linguistic sound change in progress (Labov, Yeager and Steiner 1972), which develop the types of theoretical bridges that were advocated by Weinreich's (1954) call for structural dialectology. Outstanding field recordings were largely responsible for successful studies of linguistic change because the recordings could be analyzed under controlled laboratory conditions through advanced phonetic analyses.

The marriage of phonetics and sociolinguistics has been fruitful, and as we begin to learn more about the nature of language in society we come to raise new questions that are better suited to laboratory research. One such example has to do with standard and nonstandard phonetic variation among speakers of black English. Field data clearly demonstrate style shifts between standard and vernacular norms, although they are highly relative, based on individual sociolinguistic histories (Dillard 1972, Baugh 1983). This variation, observed and recorded in the field, raised specific questions regarding vocalic and consonantal variation. Of greater significance to the discussion at hand, the resolution of these questions required laboratory experiments.

Native speakers of black English from Austin, Texas and (under)graduate black and white students at the University of Texas served as subjects for a series of phonetic experiments. All were asked to provide demographic information, similar to that discussed below. They met with a staff member who asked some preliminary questions, and provided them with instructions. Subjects were asked if they could detect the racial background of typical Americans based on their speech alone. All said 'yes.' These affirmative responses allowed us to introduce our primary experimental objectives; namely, we wanted to record these same individuals producing standard English on one occasion and non-standard English on another. Under ideal circumstances one would prefer to use field evidence for this purpose, but some of the most salient phonetic properties occur infrequently in natural discourse.

I should re-emphasize that field evidence was responsible for the identification of potentially significant phonetic variation. The analytic problem with the field data, at least in this regard, lies in the haphazard occurrence of relevant examples in natural contexts. In this case we have sacrificed the benefit of recording in native contexts for the technological advantages of the phonetics laboratory. Unlike traditional fieldwork, the phonetic experiments required that subjects leave their community, or dormitory, and arrive at the phonetics laboratory. In an effort to compensate for these unnatural surroundings every informant was given an opportunity to rehearse, privately, prior to recording either their standard or nonstandard renditions.

Preliminary results from a bidialectal speaker are informative. The speaker illustrated in Figures 2 and 3 and in Table 5 was judged to be white when speaking standard English, but was judged to be black when producing nonstandard English. All bidialectal speakers were identified in this manner. Several other subjects, both black and white, were unable to style shift with the same degree of dexterity; judges correctly identified their racial background regardless of speech style.

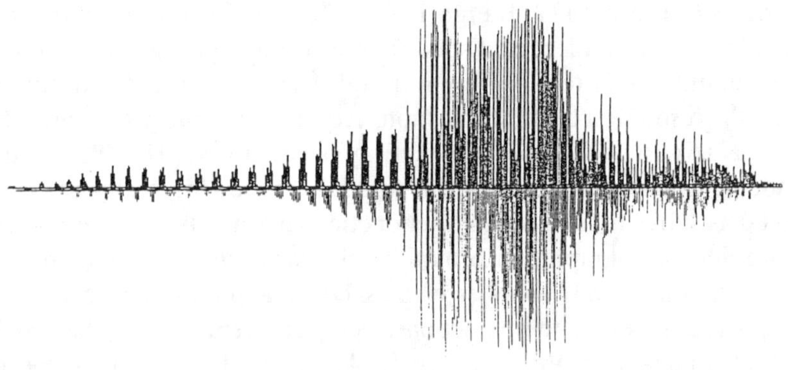

Figure 2. Nonstandard pronunciation of 'boot'

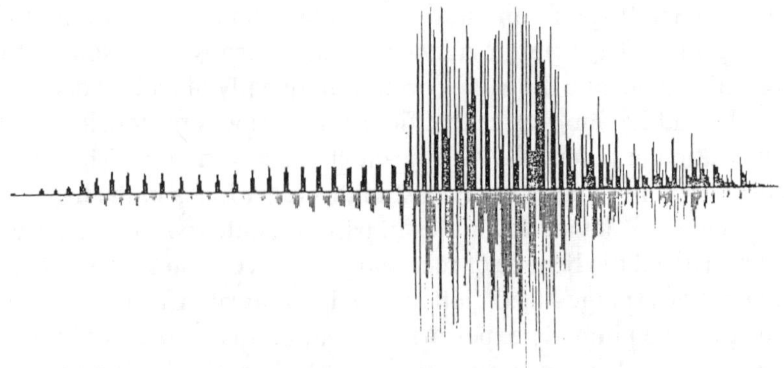

Figure 3: Standard pronunciation of 'boot'

		Word Lists		Sentential Contexts		
		Non-standard	Standard	Non-standard		Standard
be	1.	88.0	84.0	123	(58)	95
	2.	130.3	56.7	132	(52)	102
bit	1.	135.0	50.0	100		80
	2.	190.0	-11.1	105		78
bate	1.	128.7	-10.5	128		70
	2.	162.8	119.1	122		73
bet	1.	175.0	150.1	123	(67)	77
	2.	189.9	-9.7	113	(76)	89
bat	1.	167.0	-8.9	123		72
	2.	170.3	77.5	111		65
bite	1.	224.6	-17.4	107		83
	2.	174.4	-9.7	111		93
	(low energy)					
bought	1.	178.2	29.0	91		104
	2.	228.8	74.3	92		111
boat	1.	213.1	17.8	82		93
	2.	205.9	79.9	93		82
book	1.	223.7	98.1	133		106
	2.	167.2	-11.2	132		99
boot	1.	235.5	40.1	128		91
	2.	154.8	12.9	137		99
but	1.	186.8	105.0	98		108
	2.	142.7	97.6	101		109
above	1.	118.2	94.7	94		51
	2.	126.3	98.8	103		92
	(from offset of Hi Freq.)					

Pre-voicing of consonants measured by msec.; nonstandard sentences for 'be' and 'bet' were preceded by lexical items with /m/ in word final position.

Table 2. Relative duration of pre-voicing of initial /b/ consonants

The results clearly show a systematic pattern of prevoicing for the initial nonstandard /b/ consonant (Figure 2) and no such prevoicing of the standard phonemic equivalent (Figure 3). The linguistic significance of this observation is secondary in the present methodological context, although such findings re-emphasize the multifarious nature of linguistic variation. It is more important to recognize the relationship between field research, that is, our common concern with studies of language in communities, and their catalytic impact on the preceding phonetic experimentation. Had we not asked informants, both black and white, to participate in these experiments, the systematic prevoicing contrasts presented in Figures 2 and 3 and Table 2 would have gone undetected.

The linguistic results are quite interesting in their own right, but the sociolinguistic differences between those subjects who were judged to be linguistic chameleons (i.e. the balanced bidialectals), and those who were not, is illustrative of the significance of demographic data.

5.0. Social and demographic relevance

Another methodological paradox that confronts us lies between the obvious fact that language is a human sociological product and the need to measure social linguistic influence. Kroeber (1964) observed that linguistic science travels faster if one leaves all social baggage at the station. The intellectual separation of linguistic and social behavior has clear theoretical advantages, through the prospect of stricter data control, but those who seek to study language in society must grapple with the more complex integrated nature of social, cultural and linguistic behavior.

There are several productive ways to examine demographics. My personal preference leans toward replicability; that is, whenever possible I strive to identify extralinguistic factors that can be examined in different regions, or among different groups. However, there is a limitation to this approach, reflected by restrictions imposed through scientific controls. Although I have been able to quantify various social characteristics, such as those listed below, it may be wrong to assume cause-and-effect relationships between many social characteristics and corresponding linguistic behavior.

age
race
sex
genealogy
occupation
ethnicity
education
religion
number of languages spoken
political affiliations
residential history
etc.

Causal sociolinguistic relationships are important and quite welcome when they can be accurately identified. However there are many instances where some potentially significant social, ethnographic, or other demographic factors escape detection. Despite the inherent limitations of many interdisciplinary linguistic methods, community language studies strive to provide as much relevant extralinguistic data as possible.

As a general rule informants can be helpful in the selection and identification of significant sociolinguistic factors, such as wealth, race, or educational opportunities; however, a word of caution is in order. Walters (1989) demonstrates that western sociolinguistic methods are ill suited to Arab cultures, where the sex of the fieldworkers and informants has a profound effect on linguistic behavior, to say nothing of the special nature of the observer's paradox for linguists in foreign lands. The sex of fieldworkers is less significant in some speech communities than in others, and the selection of appropriate extralinguistic criteria requires extensive ethnographic knowledge, as advocated previously in association with data collection and overcoming the observer's paradox (§3.0).

One of the advantages of gathering substantial social information about informants and their speech communities grows from the increased flexibility and adaptability that it lends to research. Demographics may clearly demonstrate which social and cultural factors are (in)significant, and these results should also be confirmed by natives of the speech community whenever possible. If statistically relevant differences are observed, say, along ethnic lines, but informants claim that no ethnic divisions exist, then one can proceed to a more precise delineation of this apparent contradiction. The preceding example is illustrative of the tendency among many Americans to deny the existence of racial segregation, even when linguistic evidence and a host of other demographics emphatically contradict such an egalitarian view.

The list provided above is intended to be illustrative and not exhaustive. Some factors may need to be eliminated, and others could be added; the primary objective is to specify relevant demographics for the speech community under analysis. I intentionally avoid the long-standing debate between qualitative and quantitative approaches; both have value in their proper perspective. Kroch (1978) examines the theoretical significance of these tendencies in more thorough detail. I agree with most of his observations, and would add only that I believe all levels of language, including morphology, syntax, and semantics can -- and must -- be integrated into the development of a comprehensive sociolinguistic theory. The identification and measurement of relevant sociological and ethnographic factors will be an essential component of this enterprise.

6.0. Conclusion

Dialectologists already know what the world needs to know; linguistic diversity is the product of our evolution as a species. Some of us have had good fortune, while others have been the victims of oppression; the differential distribution of wealth and opportunity is also a product of human history; indeed, these social facts have served to shape the very languages and dialects that have survived or perished. Dialectologists consider all dialects or languages to be equally worthy of scholarly consideration, regardless of political, economic, or educational circumstances to the contrary.

This chapter celebrates the centennial of the American Dialect Society through a reaffirmation of these egalitarian principles, and strives to offer new suggestions -- including some technological advances -- that will allow us to pursue this quest through the next century and beyond. I have referred to the polemical tendencies that pervade the relevant literature, but there is no disagreement regarding the innate cognitive equality of linguistic behavior.

The fact that some dialects are considered to be 'standards' (whatever that means), while others are viewed as 'nonstandard' is merely an historical accident. The methods that I have advocated here can be applied to any living language, that is, regardless of its oral or written tradition. All too often linguistic methods have, quite inadvertently, artificially elevated the status of standard dialects through literary appeal (cf. Hill 1961, Chomsky 1961). Chomsky (1979) and Labov (1972) are equally outspoken regarding the equality of human linguistic behavior, as well as the psychological and social implications that linguistic parity implies. Here we have traced some of the basic methodological tenets that support community language studies. These methods are advocated in support of the rigorous linguistic research that is needed, and will continue to be needed, to thwart popular linguistic myths that perpetuate linguistic elitism and social divisiveness.

Notes

1 The writing and black English research has been supported by grants from the Center for Advanced Study in the Behavioral Sciences, the National Science Foundation(BNS87-00864), the University of Texas Research and Policy Institutes, the Ford Foundation, the American Council of Learned Societies, and the University of Texas Center for African and Afro-American Studies. All limitations are my own.

2 Shuy's discussion of the values of fieldwork deserves more attention than it receives in this paper. He points to a broader range of practical and applied linguistic functions that are instrumental to a complete survey of community language studies. Those who are unfamiliar with his remarks are encouraged to consult his text directly.

3 Fastidious readers seeking comprehensive methodological reviews should consult additional sources, including: Atwood 1963, McDavid 1942, Kurath 1949, Allen 1956, Walters 1988, Petyt 1980, Lavandera 1988, Labov 1984, Weinreich 1954, Chambers and Trudgill 1980.

References

Allen, Harold B. 1956. The linguistic atlases: our new resource. *The English Journal.* 45:188-94.

Allen, Harold B. (ed.). 1964. *Applied English linguistics.* New York: Appleton-Century Crofts.

Allen, Harold B. (ed.). 1973-6. *Linguistic atlas of the Upper Midwest,* 3 vols. Minneapolis: University of Minnesota Press.

Atwood, E. B. 1963. The methods of American dialectology. In Harold B. Allen and Gary Underwood (eds), *Readings in American dialectology,* New York: Appleton-Century-Crofts, 5-35.

Bailey, Beryl. 1965. Toward a new perspective in Negro English dialectology. *American Speech* 40:171-77.

Bailey, Beryl. 1966. *Jamaican Creole syntax.* London: Cambridge University Press.

Baugh, John. 1978. The politics of black power handshakes. *Natural History.* October.

Baugh, John. 1980. A reexamination of the black English copula. In William Labov (ed.), *Locating language in time and space,* New York: Academic Press, 83-106.

Baugh, John. 1983. *Black street speech: its history, structure, and survival.* Austin: University of Texas Press.

Baugh, John. 1984. *Steady*: progressive aspect in black English. *American Speech* 50:3-12.

Bloomfield, Leonard. 1933. *Language*. New York: Holt.

Brown, Penelope and Stephen Levinson. 1978. Universals in language use: politeness phenomena. In Esther Goody (ed.), *Questions and politeness: strategies in social interaction.* Cambridge: Cambridge University Press.

Cassidy, Frederic G. 1973. Dialect studies, regional and social. *Current trends in linguistics*, Vol. 10. The Hague: Mouton.

Chambers, J. K. & Peter Trudgill. 1980. *Dialectology*. Cambridge: Cambridge University Press.

Chomsky, Noam. 1957. *Syntactic structures*. The Hague: Mouton.

Chomsky, Noam. 1961. Some methodological remarks on generative grammar. *Word* 17:219-39.

Chomsky, Noam. 1965. *Aspects of a theory of syntax*. Cambridge, MA: MIT Press.

Chomsky, Noam. 1979. *Language and responsibility*. New York: Pantheon books.

Dillard, J. L. 1972. *Black English*. New York: Random House.

Ferguson, Charles & Shirley B. Heath, (eds). 1981. *Language in the U.S.A.* Cambridge: Cambridge University Press.

Fishman, Joshua. 1989. Linguistic diversity and social strife. ms.

Gal, Susan. 1978. Peasant men can't get wives: Language change and sex roles in a bilingual community. *Language in Society* 7:1-16.

Giles, Howard & P. E. Powesland. 1975. *Speech style and social evaluation*. London: Academic Press.

Gilliéron, J. & E. Edmont. 1902. *Atlas linguistique de la France*. Paris: Campion.

Goffman, Erving. 1959. *The presentation of self in everyday life*. New York, Anchor.

Halliday, M. A. K. 1978. *Language as social semiotic*. Baltimore: University Park Press.

Hancock, Ian. 1987. *The pariah syndrome*. Ann Arbor: Karoma Press.

Haugen, Einer. 1972. *The ecology of Language*. Stanford: Stanford University Press.

Heath, Shirley B. 1983. *Ways with words*. Cambridge: Cambridge University Press.

Hill, Archibald A. 1961. Grammaticality. *Word* 17:1-10.

Kasse, E. 1983. The syntax of auxiliary reduction in English. *Language* 59:93-122.

Kerr-Mattox, B. J. 1989. Language attitudes of teachers and prospective teachers toward black and white speakers. Unpublished M.A. thesis: Texas A&M University.

Kontra, Miklos. 1982. The relation of L1 vocabulary to L2: A study of Hungarian-Americans. In W. Gutwinski & G. Jolly (eds), *The eighth LACUS forum*, 1981. Columbia, S.C.: Hornbeam Press, 523-40.

Kroch, Anthony. 1978. Towards a theory of social dialect variation. *Language in Society* 7:17-36.

Kroeber, A. L. 1964. Foreword. In D. Hymes (ed.), *Language in culture and society*. New York: Harper and Row.

Kurath, Hans. 1949. *A word geography of the eastern United States*. Ann Arbor: University of Michigan Press.

Labov, William. 1966. *The social stratification of English in New York City*. Arlington, VA: Center for Applied Linguistics.

Labov, William. 1969. Contraction, deletion, and inherent variability of the English copula. *Language* 45:715-62.

Labov, William. 1972. *Sociolinguistic patterns*. Philadelphia: University of Pennsylvania Press.

Labov, William. 1984. Field methods of the project of linguistic change and variation. In John Baugh & Joel Sherzer (eds), *Language in use: readings in sociolinguistics*. Englewood Cliffs: Prentice-Hall, 28-53.

Labov, William, M. Yaeger, & R. Steiner. 1972. A quantitative study of sound change in progress. Report on National Science Foundation contract GS-3287. Philadelphia: U.S. Regional Survey.

Lambert, Wallace. 1972. *Language, psychology, and culture*. Stanford: Stanford University Press.

Lavandera, Beatriz. 1988. The study of language in its socio-cultural context: some observations. In F. Newmeyer (ed.), *Linguistics: the Cambridge survey* Vol.4. Cambridge: Cambridge University Press, 1-13.

McDavid, Raven I., Jr. 1979 (1942). Some principles for American dialect study. In William Kretzschmar, Jr. (ed.), *Dialects in culture: essays in general dialectology by Raven I. McDavid, Jr.* University: University of Alabama Press, 5-9.

Paulston, Christina B. 1976. Pronouns of address in Swedish: social class semantics and a changing system. *Language in Society* 5:359-86.

Pederson, L. 1971. Southern speech and the LAGS project. *Orbis* 20:79-89.

Petyt, K. Malcolm. 1980. *The study of dialect: an introduction to dialectology*. Boulder: Westview Press.

Preston, Dennis R. 1988a. Methods in the study of dialect perceptions. In Alan Thomas (ed.), *Methods in dialectology*. Clevedon: Multilingual Matters Ltd., 373-95.

Preston, Dennis R. 1988b. Sociolinguistic commonplaces in variety perception. In K. Ferrara, et al. (eds), *Linguistic change and contact*. Austin: Department of Linguistics, University of Texas, 279-92.

Romaine, Suzanne. 1982. *Sociohistorical linguistics*. Cambridge: Cambridge University Press.

Shuy, Roger. 1983. Unexpected by-products of fieldwork. *American Speech* 58:345-58.

Thomas, Alan (ed.). 1988. *Methods in dialectology* Clevedon: Multilingual Matters Ltd.

Trudgill, Peter. 1983. *On dialect: social and geographical perspectives*. New York: New York University Press.

Tucker, G. R. & Wallace E. Lambert. 1972. White and Negro listeners' reactions to various American-English dialects. In Joshua Fishman (ed.), *Advances in the sociology of language*, Vol. II. The Hague: Mouton, 175-84.

Walters, Keith. 1988. Dialectology. In F. Newmeyer (ed.), *Linguistics: The Cambridge survey*, Vol. 4. Cambridge: Cambridge University Press, 119-39.

Walters, Keith. 1989. Social change, and linguistic variation in Korba, a small Tunisian town. Unpublished dissertation: University of Texas, Austin.

Weinreich, Uriel. 1954. Is a structural dialectology possible? *Word* 10:388-400.

Weinreich, Uriel, William Labov, & M. Herzog. 1968. Empirical foundations for a theory of language change. In Winfred P. Lehmann & Yakov Malkiel (eds), *Directions for historical linguistics*. Austin: University of Texas Press, 95-188.

Wolfram, W. 1969. *A sociolinguistic description of Detroit Negro speech*. Washington, D. C.: Center for Applied Linguistics.

Wolfram, W. & Ralph Fasold. 1974. *The study of social dialects in American English*. Englewood Cliffs: Prentice-Hall.

Wolfson, Nessa. 1976. Speech events and natural speech. *Language in Society* 5:81-96.

Identifying and Interpreting Variables[1]

Walt Wolfram
North Carolina State University

Introduction

In one form or another, the linguistic and the social **variable** have now become widely recognized constructs in language variation studies. Although the emergence of the quantitative paradigm certainly had a formative influence on the development of these constructs, it would be wrong to conclude that their development was endemic to the quantification era in dialect studies. There is a sense in which earlier dialect geography studies employed the notion of the linguistic and social variable as well, whether or not it was recognized explicitly. For example, a traditional, qualitatively-oriented dialect study (e.g. Kurath and McDavid 1961) which delimited the vowel alternates [ə], [ɛ], and [i] as possible productions for the final vowel of a set of words such as *sofa* and *china* was ultimately no different in setting forth the parameters of a 'variable' than later, quantitatively-oriented studies that might measure the relative frequency of each of these variants as part of a study of systematic variability.

Notwithstanding its qualitative analogies and precursors, it was the quantitative measurement of variance and the correlation of this linguistic variance with a set of social factors or a set of independently defined linguistic factors that projected the notion of linguistic and social variables to the next stage of development. This approach now has evolved to the point where it is common to speak of the examination of linguistic and social variables as the core of language variation analysis. Furthermore, **variation analysis** has evolved as a subfield of sociolinguistics in its own right.

As the notions of the linguistic and the social variable have developed, a set of theoretical and methodological questions has also arisen. What exactly is the status of such units, linguistically and/or sociolinguistically? How does an analyst go about finding and defining sociolinguistic variables in conducting actual variation studies? Those of us who learned how to manipulate linguistic and social variables through painstaking trial and error procedures sometimes forget our struggles to define the units of analysis and the procedural decisions that guided our extraction of data related to these units. There are numerous small, but often critical decisions that need to be made in the process of delimiting variables -- decisions that may affect the resultant dialect profile in important ways. If principled decisions are not made at significant junctures in the analytical process, even the most sophisticated quantitative manipulations will not be able to save the analysis. As Labov (1969) put it:

> ....even the simplest type of counting raises a number of subtle and difficult problems. The final decision as to what to count is actually the final solution to the problem in hand. This decision is approached only through a long series of exploratory maneuvers (Labov 1969:728)

In this discussion, I will attempt to set forth some of these 'exploratory maneuvers'. My own research encounters and experience teaching students to conduct variation analysis has taught me that the presentation of elegant-appearing summaries of results found in published versions of variation studies are often far removed from the laboratory in which such analyses are conducted. In the process, some of the critical procedural and analytical decisions may be disregarded or camouflaged, making the analysis seem much cleaner than it actually is. This discussion may not detract from students' need to learn some of these lessons by jumping into the variation waters for themselves, but it should at least comfort them to know that the many small procedural and analytical choices they confront along the way are not inherently related to their own inadequacies. Indeed, fellow and prospective variationists who recognize the stages of variable definition and extraction should be better equipped than we were in our original fumblings in this analytical paradigm. At least that is my hope!

The Linguistic Variable

Before we discuss the procedural steps that typify the delimitation of linguistic variables, we need to consider the status of the constructs linguistic and social variable. What exactly is a linguistic variable as employed in the study of language variation and how does this unit relate to recognized structural units in the linguistic system? This is not a trivial question, particularly in light of the fact that linguistics is rightly preoccupied with defining and identifying structural units and relationships of various types. The **linguistic variable,** as used in language variation studies, is itself an abstraction; it is made up of a class of **variants** -- varying items that exist in a structurally-defined set of some type. In a sense, the relationship of the variable to its variants may be likened to some classic linguistic relationships, such as that between a morpheme and its allomorphs or a phoneme and its allophones, except that the relationship between a linguistic variable and its variants is not, by definition, a linguistically defined emic-etic one. It may be tempting to extend the notion of emic status to the linguistic variable as a sociolinguistic construct, but this takes us in a direction that is best left for another discussion. Our immediate concern is the basis for establishing the variable and its variants.

What is it that brings together the varying items of the variable? Operationally, these varying elements all occur in a linguistically-defined set of some type. The set may be a **structural category**, such as a particular morpheme category (e.g. third person singular present tense suffix), a **phoneme** (systematic or classical definition of a unit such as /θ/ in English), a **natural class of units** in a particular linguistic environment (e.g. final stop consonant clusters in word-final position), a syntactic **relationship** of some type (e.g. negative concord), the **permutation or placement** of items (e.g. presentential versus verb phrase placement of adverbs), or even a **lexical item** (e.g. the occurrence of the word *ain't* as a negativized auxiliary or copula form). The linguistic variable, then, is founded in a linguistically-defined unit of some type, although this delineation is fairly broad, ranging from syntactic relationships to particular lexical items.

The relationship of the variants of the variable to each other, however, seems to be another matter. The actual examination of language variation studies shows the variants to exhibit a range of relationships to each other. At least, this was the case in the original formulation of the linguistic variable (Labov 1966a,b; Wolfram 1969). In one case, variants might represent different structural categories, as in -Z third person occurrence/non-occurrence or the existence/nonexistence of a subject-verb concord pattern, while in another case, variants might exist within a significant linguistic unit, as, for example, allophones of a phoneme, (e.g. variants for word-final /t/ may be a glottal stop [ʔ], unreleased [ ], or flap [ɾ]). And variants of a variable could mix 'emic' and 'etic' units. In Labov's (1966a) original delimitation of vowel variants for the variable designated (eh) in New York City, the phonetic value ranged within and across phonemic boundaries. These variants were linguistically united by the fact that the varying productions occurred within the same set of words. In Labov's formulation of the (eh) variable, the different variants were even assigned weighted values for an overall scoring index without apparent regard for their phonemic status, as follows:

Phonetic Value		Score
[ɪᵊ]	=	1
[ɛᵊ]	=	2
[æ^]	=	3
[æ:]	=	4
[a:]	=	5
[ɑ:]	=	6

Understandably, linguists may feel uneasy when a class of varying structures does not respect the reified structural units of linguistics (for example, Labov (1966a:53) notes that 'it is irrelevant whether the vowel in question would structurally be assigned to /æ/ or /eh/ or even /ih/'); they should feel even more uncomfortable with a kind of weighted index which can completely obscure the distribution of linguistic variants, as the cumulative score on the Labov index for /eh/ does. For example, a speaker might obtain a score of 60 through a variety of numerical permutations (e.g. 10 tokens valued at 6 each = 60, but 6 tokens valued at 3 plus 8 tokens valued at 4 plus 2 tokens valued at 5 = 60 also). If ever there was a semblance of linguistic relationship between variants of the variable, such a scoring procedure may lose all track of this linguistic basis. Yet, we are left with the conclusion that the tabulation of the index score for the (eh) variable as defined by Labov certainly did show patterned co-variation with social variables. In fact, a cumulative index score for (eh) presents a very revealing, if not the most revealing, sociolinguistic profile for the community (cf. Labov 1966a). It is probably safe to conclude that the definition of the linguistic variable in early variation studies was largely motivated by the desire to reveal the most clear-cut pattern of social and linguistic co-variation. Certainly, it was more of a sociolinguistic construct than a linguistic one in the original formulation.

The advent of the **variable rule** (Labov 1969) changed the interpretation of the linguistic variable, although there has been little discussion of how the notion 'linguistic variable' in early sociolinguistic studies (e.g. Labov 1966a, 1966b; Wolfram 1969) related to the variable rule as it developed in later studies (e.g. Labov 1969, Cedergren and Sankoff 1974, Sankoff 1978, etc.). Remember that the relationship of the variants of the variable to each other was not linguistically principled in the original formulation of the linguistic variable. But a variable rule started with a conventional **optional linguistic rule**, with all the rights and responsibilities attendant to a linguistic rule. In essence, the variable rule simply expanded and redefined the notion of optionality to include constraints on its variability, maintaining that some of these constraints were linguistic in nature and some were sociological. In adopting a linguistic basis as the starting point for this rule, however, the 'variable' departed from its original definition in which the linguistic relationship of the variants to each other was irrelevant. We thus have two definitions of linguistic variable used by variationists, at least historically. The original version was a sociolinguistically motivated construct, established to set forth the co-variation of language items and social variables; the varying language items in this formulation had status apart from the linguistic rules or processes that governed them. The revised version was linguistically-based, as it was confined to linguistic rules that were enhanced by linguistic and social constraints on variability. In this definition, social constraints were simply added to linguistically-principled factors influencing variation.

As far as I can determine, the different goals of the two interpretations of the linguistic variable have not been discussed, and there remain issues to be resolved. It has not been demonstrated to my satisfaction that the version of the linguistic variable wedded to the variable rule necessarily leads to the most adequate SOCIOLINGUISTIC profile of linguistic and social co-variation. As mentioned above, the variants of the sociolinguistically-based linguistic variable may be configured linguistically in a variety of linguistic rules, variable or otherwise, and it just may be that the patterning of linguistic and social co-variation is most adequately indicated by a construct which is not confined to a single linguistic rule. For example, in my study of English among Puerto Rican and Black male youths in East Harlem (Wolfram 1974), I identified the following relevant variants of the morpheme final //θ// variable in words such as *tooth* and *both*. Some of these variants were further represented by several different phonetic realizations, or 'subvariants.'

Variant	Phonetic Realization
θ	[θ] [tθ]
f	[f]
t	[t̪] [ʔt] [ʔ] [ɾ]
∅	No phonetic realization, assimilated voiceless fricative
s	[s] [z] when not followed by sibilant

It should be clear that the linguistic path to the variants and subvariants involves a number of different rules, variable or otherwise. In fact, my summary discussion (Wolfram 1974:105-106) of the variants involved over 10 different phonological rules, including four classical variable rules. As enlightening as the presentation of these formal linguistic rules may be, it does not necessarily guarantee the most revealing picture of language and social variation in this community. And I see no inherent reason why it should. As Labov himself pointed out in his earlier studies (1966a), patterns of social variation are not held captive by linguistic boundaries. In fact, I would maintain that the most straightforward sociolinguistic profile in East Harlem derives from the correlation between the variants of (th) as set forth above and an independently defined set of social variables such as ethnicity, interethnic contact, and so forth; the variable rule picture is linguistically interesting, but not as sociolinguistically revealing, in my opinion (cf. Wolfram 1974:87-107). This observation does not detract from the need to formulate the precise linguistic rules accounting for varying phonetic realizations of the unit // θ //, but it suggests that the analysis of linguistic processes and the description of social and linguistic covariation may need to be separated.

I personally see a justification for both the linguistic and the sociolinguistic definitions of the linguistic variable, given different descriptive goals. I am not willing to discard the original definition of linguistic variable simply by adding social variables to variable linguistic rules, since this places social factors on a par with independent linguistic constraints in describing linguistic variability. We cannot simply assume that the incorporation of social factors with linguistically-principled processes will automatically provide the most sociolinguistically adequate description; on the contrary, it may turn out to be an unwarranted mixing of linguistic oranges with sociological apples. It still needs to be empirically demonstrated that the linguistic variable as originally formulated for the examination of linguistic and social covariation is no longer a viable sociolinguistic construct. We may have thrown out the sociolinguistic baby with the linguistic bathwater.

From a strictly methodological viewpoint, I also find the original version of the linguistic variable a convenient starting point in approaching language variation. If the goal of a study is sociolinguistic, it offers an essential sociolinguistic construct for correlating linguistic and social variation. If a study is primarily linguistic, it still provides a convenient heuristic for accessing variation, although data on variants admittedly may need to be manipulated for primary linguistic description. As we walk through the procedural steps of identifying and defining the linguistic elements in a study of language variation, we shall see that the notion of the linguistic variable continues to play a prominent operational role in focusing on our object of study.

The Social Variable

The other side of examining linguistic and social co-variation involves identifying the social variable. As typically used, the **social variable** refers to a varying social attribute or characteristic of some type. The basis for variance may range from some aspect of demographic background, such as geographic region, age, sex, or socioeconomic status, to social situations (e.g. setting, interlocutors), social relationships (e.g. social networks), and personality traits (e.g. conservative/liberal, ethnic consciousness). As with the notion of the linguistic variable, there were earlier precedents in dialectology for isolating various types of social variables in the examination of language variation. The delimitation of regional areas and the classification of speakers on the basis of factors such as age, sex, and the classic Linguistic Atlas Type I and Type II informants certainly set a precedent for delimiting the social correlates of linguistic variation.

Early correlational studies of social and linguistic variation seemed focused upon various background demographic variables in their delimitation of the social side of this equation. Fischer's (1958) early quantitative study of *ing/in'* variation in a New England village considered the sex of the speaker and socio-economic status, but it also included personality type and the formality of the occasion as social factors affecting variation. Labov's *The social stratification of English in New York City* included a number of traditional background demographic variables, with a few new wrinkles for sociolinguistic study, such as his development of the notion of contextual 'style.' My own original attempts to isolate social variables in the study of sociolinguistic variation (e.g. Wolfram 1969) were, in retrospect, too restricted to conventional demographic factors, as I considered variables such as status, age, sex, ethnicity, racial isolation, and style. Even with traditional demographic variables, there are questions about the validity of 'basic' social constructs and the operational definitions that guide co-variation studies of social and linguistic variables. For example, traditional, superficial socioeconomic status indices hardly do justice to the complexity of the construct 'social class' (Rickford 1986; Guy 1988).

More recent studies isolating social variables have focused on social relationships and interaction variables, following the lead of Milroy's (1980) **social network** analysis. Basic network description now has been adapted for diverse speech communities. For example, Walter Edwards (1986) has constructed a social network index for Detroit Eastside Black residents that includes characteristics such as the extent of kinship in the community, desire to stay in the area, participation in 'street culture,' and other traits that seem to define the network of relations in an inner-city community. At the same time, Eckert's (1988) examination of teen-aged peer cohorts in the Detroit suburbs uses a modified network analysis to classify adolescent subjects into 'jocks' and 'burnouts.' Other studies use mixed sets of variables; for example, Viv Edwards (1986), in her study of Black English in England, divides groups on the basis of social networks, lifestyles (e.g. Pentecostal Christian, Rastafarian, etc.), and five different types of intersituational variation (e.g. formal interview with white interviewer, formal interview with black fieldworker, peer conversation without interviewer present, etc.). The isolation of social variables for the examination of linguistic and social co-variation has certainly evolved greatly in an attempt to determine the most descriptively adequate fit between social and linguistic variables. Furthermore, examining the interactional effect of social variables has become increasingly sophisticated, typically involving multivariate statistical analyses of data. We certainly have come a long way from the examination of co-variation between simple descriptive tabulations of linguistic variants and various isolated demographic characteristics of subjects.

One of the persistent issues in studies of linguistic and social co-variation concerns establishing the 'best' fit between social variables and linguistic variation. Much of the earlier work in language variation took pains to establish an initial set of social variables which could be built into the research design. Thus, it was typical for studies to start with a representative sampling of speakers from pre-determined social groupings. This was criticized (e.g. Bickerton 1971; DeCamp 1971) as forcing linguistic variation into procrustean social groups when, in fact, language variation itself might be a more meaningful starting point for examining sociolinguistic variation. Recent advances in multivariate analysis, in particular, 'principal components analysis' (Horvath 1985), have rendered this point somewhat moot, but these advances do not negate the significance of setting forth possible social variables for manipulation to begin with, to say nothing of the need to ensure that these variables are adequately represented in the study of variation. The analysis of linguistic and social co-variation still can only be as good as the variables it has to manipulate.

With all the advances, there remain underlying theoretical and methodological issues related to the examination of co-varying social and linguistic variables. The search for underlying social explanation has now replaced the more superficial examination of background demographic variables, but this search can sometimes be elusive. It is relatively simple to show that a physically-based classification of speaker sex correlates with linguistic variation, but much more difficult to offer an explanation as to how the concept of **gender,** as a 'complex of social, cultural, and psychological phenomena attached to sex' (McConnell-Ginet 1988:76), should affect language variation. In a similar way, it may be easy to delimit contextual settings that reflect varying 'stylistic' points of language use, but this does not offer an underlying explanation of **why** this parameter should correlate with language variation. Attempts to examine the social psychological dynamics that underlie surface social variables, as Giles (1984) and Bell (1984) have done for style and McConnell-Ginet (1988) and Boe (1987), among others, have done for gender, should help move the social side of sociolinguistic inquiry to a new level of explanation, but this line of inquiry is also more empirically evasive.

If we extend the search for explanation to the correlation of social and linguistic variables, we also find limited progress toward a 'theory' of linguistic **and** social co-variation (see Kroch 1978 for such an attempt). Most effort in language variation studies has gone into the isolation of the most descriptive configuration of social and linguistic variables vis-a-vis explaining such co-variation. As creative as some of the correlational analyses may be, they still do not satisfy the ultimate urge to explain rather than simply describe. In fact, I personally feel that the current emphasis on variable **manipulation** simply through the production of more powerful computer programs runs the risk of turning variation studies into a type of methodological reductionism, camouflaged by the sophistication of the quantitative management programs. And, although this discussion is focused on the nitty gritty questions of methodological procedures in the delimitation of linguistic variables, method cannot afford to be ignorant of the theory that informs it. I personally think that it is important for language variationists to be good linguists and good sociolinguists, not simply good collectors of data or good number crunchers.

There are also persistent procedural issues with respect to the search and extraction process in language variation studies. Since the analysis of data can only be as good as the data provided by the extraction process, I will spend the remainder of this discussion 'walking through' these preliminary variable identification and extraction procedures -- procedures that may be overlooked but, in fact, constitute critical steps in the examination of linguistic variation.

The First Stage: Identifying Potential Variables

I have not always had the good fortune of knowing a great deal about the dialects I have investigated prior to the collection of a substantive sampling of speech. Perhaps this is a shortcoming on my part, but at least it has given me genuine empathy with the typical sort of 'Where do I start?' question asked by researchers/students confronted with their first set of audio or video-recorded conversational data. (I will not concern myself with the direct elicitation of structures, which requires considerable preliminary knowledge of the variety at the same time it provides only supplemental data for the examination of variable linguistic structures.) The data provided by a representative sample of recorded speech certainly will offer a range of potential variables for investigation, so the question of choosing variables for concentrated study becomes a practical issue.

The first step in the selection process involves **setting up a pool of potential variables** for examination. How do we come up with an inventory of variables? Most researchers don't describe this first step, so I can only report what we (e.g. Wolfram 1969, Wolfram 1974, Wolfram and Christian 1976, Wolfram, et al. 1979; Christian, Wolfram, and Hatfield 1983; Christian, Wolfram and Dube 1988) typically do. Given a set of tape-recorded conversational interviews, my colleagues and I start very simply; we listen to each tape and take notes about 'interesting' features. In most cases, this means structures that are not considered 'standard English,' structures that are different from what we are familiar with in other varieties of English, or common structures that may form the basis for comparing varieties. It is ultimately a very subjective procedure, and one that admittedly opens the door to our own linguistic biases. We try to guard against dialect ethnocentrism, but the fact remains that we start with our own 'informed' perceptions of what is different and interesting. The end result of this initial step is a set of notes for each recorded interview in the study. Following is a brief excerpt from an original set of notes for one subject in our Appalachian English study (Wolfram and Christian 1976). Each linguistic item is referenced by the counter number on the tape recorder.

These notes contain some general socially diagnostic variables (i.e. features we have found in a range of vernacular varieties, such as the regularized reflexive *hisself*), some regional lexical items (i.e. features that seem peculiar to the region, such as the lexical choice *raised up*), and some variable items that may be peculiar to the variety (i.e. the extensive use of *a*-prefixing as in *a-blowin'*).

Recorder Counter (Sony)	Example
506	if they can find 'em a good job
511	I was raised up in Princeton
529	'cording to what kinda job...
536	he works for hisself
569	seem to me like they're taking people's house
724	they poseta be on one side of the ridge
741	traps people's got set
805	used to throw rocks at this old ladyO and man's house
830	well, they just thought, it was, the wind was a-blowin'
841	this old lady and man's son was spozedta dies in this house
916	he's got his can and put him a pegleg on

Given the rich array of structures that often turns up in these preliminary observational notes, we may ask why some variables are good candidates for variation analysis and others are not. Part of the answer, of course, lies in the goals of the study, but it goes further than that. Some structures are better candidates for variation analysis than others. Of the structures cited in the above notes, two structures were eventually subjected to extended variation analysis (cf. Wolfram and Christian 1976 and Christian, Wolfram and Dube 1988), subject-verb concord and *a*- prefix, while other structures were included in qualitative notes about this variety (see the Appendix of Christian, Wolfram and Dube 1988); still others were put 'on hold' because of practical limitations as to what we could examine or because there were inadequate amounts of data for even preliminary structural observations.

What are the criteria that guide the analyst in choosing a linguistic structure for the examination of systematic variability? Although there are no rigid rules about this selection process, there are some practical considerations that guide most analysts. One of the preliminary considerations is the **relative frequency of the item.** Items that are rare, either because of the relative infrequency of the structure in ordinary conversation or because of conscious suppression in an interview situation are not good candidates for variation analysis. The structures themselves may be linguistically and/or dialectally fascinating and critical for a comprehensive descriptive profile, but if they don't occur with sufficient frequency they can hardly be tabulated in a study of variation. Rarely-occurring grammatical structures such as 'remote time *been*' (e.g. *He been lost the key*) or specialized *be done* constructions (e.g. *He'll be done jumped out the tub when I come in the room*) may be important structures for the qualitative investigation of Vernacular Black English, but their relative infrequency makes them poor candidates for examining systematic variability in this variety.

Since phonology consists of a relatively small, closed set of units which occur frequently, phonological structures are often favored for variation analysis over the more expansive domain of grammatical structures, but there are certainly grammatical structures that occur with sufficient frequency for such analysis. Parenthetically, we note that a researcher anticipating the analysis of particular grammatical variables may structure questions into an interview that are likely to increase the likelihood that certain items will occur. For example, talking about past time events will typically enhance the potential for past tense forms; similarly, talking with children about habitually occurring events such as current games is likely to enhance the potential for 'habitual' *be* in Vernacular Black English. Creatively manipulated conversational interviews help assure the occurrence of some types of grammatical structures, but there remain others that resist even the most creative elicitation strategies for one reason or another.

In choosing linguistic structures for variation analysis, it is also important to select **structures for which the parameters of variance can be defined.** Counting variants of a linguistic variable typically is conducted by tabulating the number of **actual** occurrences of a particular structure in terms of all those cases where a form might have occurred, or **potential cases.** For example, in order to set up a meaningful index of [ɪŋ]/[ɪn] variation, it is necessary to first establish the range of contexts in which the variants [ɪŋ] and [ɪn] potentially vary. In this case, the parameter for variation, unstressed *-ing* forms (e.g. *He went a-hunting*), I followed Krapp's (1925:268) observation that the prefix could occur with 'every present participle.' This turns out, however, to be a quite inaccurate basis for defining the linguistic contexts in which *a-* may occur. The structural conditions in which *a-* may be attached, are much more restricted, as *a-* attaches only to those cases of *-ing* which function as a verb or adverb (e.g. *He was running to the store* may attach an *a-*, but **The movie was shocking* may not) and only to forms not headed by a preposition (e.g. *He makes money building houses* may attach an *a-* prefix to *building*, but **He makes money by building houses* may not); there are also phonological restrictions on the potential attachment of the *a-*, as it attaches only to verbs beginning with a stressed syllable (e.g. *hámmering* versus **repéating*) and forms beginning with a consonant (e.g. *fighting* versus **acting*) (see Wolfram 1979 and 1980 for a more complete discussion of these parameters). The ultimate decision as to what constitutes a potential context for the variance of the *a-* is obviously premised upon a series of exploratory maneuvers which involve substantive qualitative linguistic analysis. This detailed analysis is a prerequisite for defining the parameters of any variation analysis.

Defining the parameters of variation may prove even more elusive in cases that involve semantically significant grammatical forms; in fact, some variationists (e.g. Lavandera 1978; Romaine 1981) have real reservations about including meaning-changing grammatical forms in the study of authentic variability. A classic illustration in this regard is the case of 'habitual *be*' in Vernacular Black English. If we assume that this form marks an aspectual category referred to as 'habituality' (e.g. Fasold 1972; Bailey and Maynor 1987), how do we define a 'potential' environment for the occurrence of *be*? We cannot simply count as potential cases for habitual *be* 'equivalent' structural forms such as conjugated cases *be*. The form *are* in a sentence such as *My ears are itching right now* is NOT a legitimate linguistic context for *be* usage (i.e. **My ears be itching right now*), according to most analyses of this form, whereas a form such as *My ears usually are itching* (i.e. *My ears usually be itching*) would be. As it turns out, some potential environments may entail structures not involving forms of *be* at all, as in the case of the habitual use of 'present' forms such as *Sometimes my ears itch*. And if we take into account the notion of speaker attitude as suggested by Myhill (1988), delineating a potential context for *be* occurrence becomes even thornier. When one study considers only a subset of present tense verb forms as potential cases for *be* (e.g. Myhill 1988) and another study considers conjugated forms of *be* while ignoring present tense verb forms other than *be* as potential cases for *be* (e.g. Bailey and Maynor 1987), the description of systematic variability for *be* may be drastically affected. The point is not to resolve here the issue of what constitutes a legitimate linguistic environment for tabulating actual cases of *be* in terms of potential cases, but to underscore the importance of defining the linguistic parameters for variation as a preliminary to the adequate measurement of variation. In reality, of course, variationists often go through a number of preliminary exploratory manipulations involving the parameters of variance before they are satisfied with their measurement of the variants. This is certainly legitimate, so long as one is working with readily retrievable and reclassifiable data. More about that later.

In setting forth a variable for investigation, it is essential to **codify variants in a way that is consonant with the goals of the study.** This may seem like an obvious step, but it is one worth noting, nonetheless. If the goal of the study is to determine patterns of social and linguistic co-variation, the variants need to be codified in a way that holds the most potential for revealing these patterns. If, on the other hand, the goal of a study is simply to describe detailed aspects of linguistic variation, then the coding of variants should reflect this fact. For example, in my analysis of the *th* variable introduced earlier, five distinct variants were set up initially, ranging from the 'standard' variant [θ] (including both the affricate [tθ] and [θ] to a stop (phonetically including an unreleased [t˺], glottal stop [ʔ], coarticulated glottal stop and unreleased stop [ʔt˺], and flap [ɾ], to a sibilant (phonetically including [s] and [z]). The rationale for delimiting the variants in this way was not founded originally in a hypothesis about the linguistic status of the variants, but in hypotheses about the distribution of forms for different social groups of Puerto Ricans and Blacks. I may not have been precisely right in my codification of variants for this purpose, but the ensuing analysis showed revealing patterns of distribution relating to the social factors examined in the study (cf. Wolfram 1974). Parenthetically, I would add that the variants eventually were formulated as conventional linguistic processes, although there were limitations and the coding of variants had to be reorganized somewhat for straightforward linguistic description. The goals of the study thus come into play in the codification of variants, a fact sometimes ignored by variationists. This is not a trivial observation, as it takes us back to our earlier discussion of the differing interpretations of the linguistic variable found in variation studies.

Practical considerations of reliability also have to guide the codification of variants. For example, I have trouble perceiving impressionistically the difference between an unreleased voiceless alveolar stop [t˺], a co-articulated unreleased stop and glottal stop [ʔt˺], and a glottal stop [ʔ] in word-final position from an audio recorded interview, so I realistically had to take that into account in delimiting the variants for the *th* variable I presented earlier. I can recall an analysis of phonetic vowel variation in Detroit speech by my colleague Ralph Fasold (Fasold 1968) in which two phonetic variants had to be merged after the fact (in this case, it was the difference between a lowered [ɛ˅] and a raised [æ˄] that had to be merged) because Fasold and I could not reach reasonable levels of agreement (above 85%) in our impressionistic transcription of the designated variants. Considerations of reliable variant coding are not often brought up in the literature on linguistic variables, but most analysts confronting the extraction of audio data have had to wrestle with this concern in a practical way.

Selecting linguistic variables for study involves considerations on different levels, ranging from descriptive linguistic concerns to practical concerns of reliable coding. To a beginning researcher, all these little decisions made in the process of defining variables may seem somewhat overwhelming; as the analyst becomes more secure, however, these decisions keep the process vibrant and intriguing.

The Extraction Process

While it might be nice to say that the extraction process mechanistically follows the preliminary definition of variables and variants, the realities of actual variable tabulation have taught me otherwise. In many cases, the definition of variables and variants comes from pilot attempts to extract data. There simply is no way that the analyst can anticipate all the questions that will arise in the extraction process and make principled decisions about these questions before beginning to extract data. That only happens in written reports of procedures for publication. In reality, the initial attempt to extract data often forces the researcher to go back, reorganize, and revise coding systems for variables. Perhaps the best overall advice that can be given in anticipation of this exercise is the need for the analyst to **make principled decisions, keep a record of each of these decisions, and then follow them procedurally in a consistent way.** Such decisions should also be reported in the presentation of results, following the researcher's creed to ensure replicability.

There are different ways to carry out the actual extraction process; some may extract data for a number of different variables while listening to a tape-recorded interview without the aid of a written typescript; others go to great lengths to prepare a reliable transcript that can then be used for the extraction of data. In one case reported by Poplack (1989), data was 'transcribed' right onto a computer data file. The initial investment of time and effort in Poplack's preparation of a reliable transcript for entry is enormous, and this approach seems quite limited for entering fine phonetic detail, but the dividends for the eventual analysis are also quite bountiful. Once the transcript data are entered, variables could be manipulated readily through the Oxford Concordance Program (Hockey and Marriott 1980). Such programs are attractive, and they may be the wave of the future in variation studies, but not all variationists have access to the fairly extensive resources (technological and human) needed to prepare data in this manner.

I personally have found it convenient to use a rough written typescript as a reference guide to locate structures for extraction while listening to a tape-recorded interview, but to limit the number of variables extracted during a single sitting. Listening to a recording for one or two variables at a time tends to ensure more reliable identification of relevant structures for tabulation, particularly if they are relatively frequent structures.

We can best illustrate the types of decisions to be made in the extraction process by examining a portion of an actual typescript for a variable which has been investigated frequently in variation studies, the classic case of word-final consonant clusters (see Guy 1980). The sample here comes from a transcript of one of our interviews conducted in connection with the study of Puebloan American Indian English (Wolfram, et al. 1979). Based on previous studies, it was determined that the parameters of variation for this variable were restricted to those clusters that shared voicing among the members of the cluster (e.g. it included clusters such as `[kt]` or `[nd]` but excluded for extraction clusters such as `[mp]` and `[nt]` since the former cases share voicing but the latter do not) and clusters in which the final member was a stop (e.g. it included `[st]` and `[nd]` but excluded `[ks]` and `[dz]`). In an initial step, a rough, standard orthographical transcript was used as a reference to locating those cases of potential consonant clusters that would be extracted from our listening to the actual audio recording of the interview. I want to emphasize that the written transcript is used only as a reference point to guide listening to the actual structures in question; it does not serve as the basis for the actual extraction of data. The original marking of a written transcript, prior to the actual extraction process, might look like the following, with appropriate candidates for our tabulation of cluster reduction noted here by underlining.

> Well, mo<u>st</u>, of the older teachers, you know, they really don't like that because, you know, they don't -- they can't understa<u>nd</u>. They don't understa<u>nd</u>, they really don't, you know, they ju<u>st</u> talk...

An immediate question arises. What exactly is extracted for each case? Is it enough to simply note whether the cluster is reduced or not, or must one note finer phonetic detail in terms of the cluster? Although some analysts have extracted data by simply counting the consonant cluster as reduced or not, I think this is an unwise move, since it presumes that all the relevant linguistic categories potentially affecting the incidence of the variable have been determined. Experience has taught me that some important hypotheses about linguistic parameters of variables should be expected to arise during the active extraction of data. Therefore, the linguistic form of the items being extracted should be retrievable for manipulation in terms of emerging hypotheses concerning linguistic constraints on variability. For most phonological cases, relevant linguistic factors relate to the phonetic composition of the item itself and surrounding phonological context, quite traditional concerns of phonology proper. In this light, we make an initial decision -- to transcribe phonetically (in this case, broad phonetic details seem adequate) the segment(s) of the cluster in question as well as relevant phonetic context. A data entry (on old-fashioned file cards or in a current automatic data processing program) for the first two clusters listened to is as follows:

... mo[s] [ə]f ...
... understa [n]/ [d]they

The phonetic detail transcribed here is hardly elaborate. It includes simply the realized segment of the cluster, in this case [s] and [n], respectively, and a broad transcription of the following context. If the phonetic production of the vowel preceding the cluster were outside the range covered by the standard orthography (e.g. if the o of most was [u] instead of [o], [ɔ], etc.), the vowel also would be recorded, but there is nothing exceptional in these cases. This decision, in itself, represents a tentative conclusion that the phonological context following the cluster is going to be more important as a linguistic constraint on variability than the context preceding the cluster. Notice also that a following pause is indicated (in this case, by / for intrasentential pause) as an important part of phonetic detail for the following context. As it turns out, the grouping of this pause in relation to the canonical shape of the following environment is an important aspect of delineating constraints on variability for word-final consonant clusters. If we did not attempt to record this detail reliably we would lack essential data for our analysis of systematic variability down the road. The principle here seems to be: **when in doubt, always opt to note more structural detail than less in extracting data, since it is easier to discard than to go back and record more data.**

The item *and* in the typescript raises a couple of different issues about extraction. One issue is the question of lexical exceptions. Does *and* behave like other types of word-final clusters, or is it a specialized lexical item whose 'basic' phonetic form is better treated as [Vn] than [Vnd]. If the form is categorically realized as a non-cluster by most speakers who exhibit authentic variability in other final clusters, this item should probably be set apart to be treated in some special way, either as a lexically-based constraint or a non-potential case for cluster reduction. In my earliest study of consonant cluster reduction, I decided to take no more than three cases of *and* so that overall figures of variability wouldn't be skewed by data on a cluster that turned out to be constrained lexically rather than by the kinds of structural phonological properties that constrain the variability of other word-final clusters. In later studies, I completely eliminated *and* from my tabulations of final clusters, convinced that it behaved in a way different from the way other types of consonant cluster reduction operated. Butters (1989) was quite right to point out that one reason his tabulation of final consonant clusters in his data from Wilmington, North Carolina, was not completely comparable to my earlier figures for Detroit, Michigan, speakers (Wolfram 1969) was due to the fact that I included cases of *and* in my tabulations and he did not. I hope that these little decisions in extraction do not make a significant difference in the measurement of consonant clusters as a case of systematic variation, but I cannot deny that it makes some difference. At least in this case, the procedure for inclusion and exclusion of items was set forth explicitly so that other analysts could come to their own conclusion. As Rickford, et al (1988) have pointed out, discussions of copula deletion in Vernacular Black English have not always been clear as to the basis for the deletion percentages (i.e. deleted forms in relation to contracted forms or deleted forms in relation to contracted plus full forms), leading to confusion about levels of copula deletion in different studies.

The case of *and* raises another issue concerning extraction, the type-token question. For example, a decision to include *and* as a potential instance of cluster reduction, followed by a further decision to take ALL cases of *and* in the spoken corpus, could end up severely distorting an overall profile of cluster reduction. In order to guard against this distortion, I adopted the following extraction procedure in my original tabulation of this variable:

> If the same word occurred more than three times, only the first three examples [i.e. first three starting in the second part of the interview, after the subject had become somewhat acclimated to the interview] were taken in order not to skew the data with too many tokens for one particular type. (Wolfram 1969:58)

To be honest, I have no idea if three tokens for each word type is an appropriate number for sampling the data, and I have since revised type-token procedures to be more sensitive to structural categories (e.g. three tokens for one word when followed by a vowel, three when followed by a consonant, etc.) vis-a-vis simple, lexically-based type-token considerations. The original decision was motivated simply by a concern about data that might potentially distort the nature of variation in consonant cluster reduction. **Attention to lexical exceptions and type-token ratios must be considered in the extraction of data in order to ensure the most representative picture of actual variation.** Such a concern is not simply a practical matter; attention to such factors is important in resolving bona fide linguistic controversies, such as the relation of lexical diffusion to the neogrammarian hypothesis (Labov 1981). I personally believe that many of the 'practical' decisions that need to be confronted during extraction end up focusing on central issues relating to the nature of language organization and variation.

The case of *just* in the above sample represents many of the same types of issues raised by *and*; it is often realized categorically in its reduced form (e.g. [ǰəs]) and, for most speakers, cluster reduction occurs in disproportionate frequency compared with word-final clusters in other items. If we assume that we are going to extract some cases of unstressed *just* as authentic cases of variation for final cluster (certainly an arguable case based on the previous discussion of *and*), we then need to confront another practical issue: the item *just* is followed immediately by a [t] in this case. Since the final item of an intact cluster in *just* also would involve a [t] (i.e. [ǰəst+tɔk]), an accurate transcription of the [t] of *just* is reduced to a judgment about juncture or the phonetic duration of the [t]. For the rapid conversation found in an interview, that involves a close, impressionistic call in transcription detail, one that is difficult to make reliably. Thus, I determined that 'clusters which were immediately followed by a homorganic stop were to be excluded from the tabulation ... because of the phonetic environment' (Wolfram 1969:58). **Issues of reliability must be confronted squarely in the extraction of data, and cases for which reliability cannot be attained should not enter into the measurement of variability.**

The question of reliability relates not only to the extraction of variants for a variable; it also relates to the identification of potential cases as well. In a study of tense marking in Vietnamese English (Wolfram and Hatfield 1984), Deborah Hatfield and I encountered numerous cases in which the question of obligatory tense marking was indeterminate; that is, the verb form might or might not have been judged as requiring marked past tense in the Standard English model we were using as the basis for determining obligatory past tense. For example, if an interviewer asks the question, 'How do people celebrate holidays in Vietnam?' and the subject replies 'When I am there I go to the celebration...,' the determination of obligatory past time marking for the English verbs *am* and *go* would be based in knowledge about the subject's past and present experiences, in addition to an assessment of the temporal setting of the conversational discourse. In identifying potential cases for marked past tense in one of our interviews (admittedly, one of the most difficult ones in the entire sample), Hatfield and I agreed on 513 cases which should have required past tense marking in English; at the same time, however, I included 53 additional cases of obligatory tense marking not included by Hatfield and she recorded 40 cases I had not marked for obligatory tense marking. The agreement level on cases of obligatory tense marking thus did not meet a reasonable cut-off point for reliable identification of potential cases, as we agreed only on 84.7 percent of the cases requiring obligatory tense marking. Our reliability problem was not, however, related to recording whether or not past tense was marked on cases we agreed on as obligatory contexts for past tense; for those 513 cases, there was over 95 percent agreement as to whether the form was actually marked or not. So in this case, the question of reliability was related not to whether or not past tense was marked, but was related to the cases to be extracted. Unfortunately, questions of this type often do not make it to the published version of an analysis (see, for example, Wolfram 1985), even though the multitude of little decisions made along the way may end up shaping the analysis in important ways. As mentioned previously, the failure to set forth such procedural steps violates the researchers' obligation to provide enough information for replication; it also makes other researchers feel that they must be the only ones confronting so many little decisions in their extraction of data, when, in fact, wc are all involved in these kinds of struggles in our search to uncover systematic variability.

Manipulating Linguistic Variables

There is only one more step to consider before turning the data over to the number crunchers, whether the number crunching consists of a current version of VARBRUL (see Sankoff 1988; Guy's contribution in this volume) or some other multivariate analytical procedure. This is the coding of categories for manipulation in the analysis. I have already mentioned the array of social variables that might be considered in the manipulation of data, so I will not repeat that here. Instead, I prefer to focus on the qualities that make for reasonable manipulation of linguistic variables.

First of all, **the coding and manipulation of 'independent linguistic constraints' in the determination of systematic variability should be linguistically-principled.** For example, if an analyst is to examine the effects of phonological context on cluster reduction, the classification of contexts should recognize phonetically natural classes of sounds, cluster composition, and phonologically reasonable categories of linguistic environment. In one of the most extensive analyses of variable constraints of cluster reduction processes, Fasold (1972) considered the canonical shape of surrounding items (e.g. consonant/vowel), types of linguistic boundary (e.g. morpheme, external word), natural phonetic classes of consonants (e.g. stop, spirant, sonorant), and suprasegmental environment (stressed/unstressed syllable) in examining linguistic constraints on variability. Whether or not we agree with Fasold's analysis and his particular formulation of the variable rule incorporating these constraints, we must concede that the coding of potential constraints is reasonable in terms of what we know about the organization of phonological structure.

The manipulation of categories in the search for linguistic constraints on variability clearly must take its cue from knowledge of linguistic organization. I would, for example, be skeptical of any analysis that united unnatural phonetic classes or violated universal dependency relationships in the permutative manipulation of independent linguistic variables. Solid qualitative categorization of linguistic phenomena obviously paves the way for determining systematic patterns of linguistic variability.

Finally, **the manipulation of variable linguistic data should be examined as a type of evidence for examining linguistic phenomena in its own right.** Variation should not only be informed by solid linguistic understanding, it should help us further our knowledge of language. The patterning of variability should be considered as a type of evidence which can be applied to broader questions of linguistic patterns, ranging from a metatheory of optionality in language to specific arguments for rule separation and collapsing (e.g. see Wolfram 1973; Guy and Bisol 1988; Sankoff and Rousseau 1989). In the best of linguistic worlds, the examination of linguistic variation should contribute to basic linguistic insight. Without maintaining respectable standards for linguistic conduct, I have grave reservations about the increasingly sophisticated models for handling quantitative linguistic data.

Our limited procedural excursion should have shown, at the very least, that counting variants is hardly the simplistic procedure it is sometimes made out to be. It requires the insight of solid linguistic reasoning in examining variable linguistic data, just as it should require an informed socio-psychological and socio-cultural perspective in examining the social side of language variation. As we go about defining variables and extracting data for these variables, we see that it also requires a good dose of common sense in making decisions that will allow authentic systematic variability to emerge. I know many professionals who possess extraordinary talents in one area or the other, but not many of us are blessed with the full complement of these capabilities. Perhaps it does take a special breed of person to conduct variation studies after all. Certainly, it brings together a full range of expertise and knowledge if it is to be done right.

Note

1 Thanks to Donna Christian, Ralph W. Fasold, Dennis Preston, and John Rickford for their comments on a preliminary draft of this manuscript.

References

Ball, Arnetha, Raina Jackson, Nomi Martin, & John R. Rickford. 1988. 'Don't count' cases in the analysis of the English copula. Paper presented at NWAVE XVII, Montreal, Canada.

Bailey, Guy & Natalie Maynor. 1987. Decreolization? *Language in Society* 16:449-74.

Bell, Alan. 1984. Language style as audience design. *Language in Society* 13:145-204.

Bickerton, Derek. 1971. Inherent variability and variable rules, *Foundations of Language* 7:457-92.

Boe, S. Kathryn. 1987. Language as an expression of caring in women, *Anthropological Linguistics* 29:271-84.

Butters, Ronald K. 1989. *The death of Black English: divergence and convergence in White and Black vernaculars.* Frankfurt am Main: Verlag Peter Lang.

Cedergren, Henrietta J. & David Sankoff. 1974. Variable rules: performance as a statistical reflection of competence, *Language* 50:333-55.

Christian, Donna, Walt Wolfram, & Nanjo Dube. 1988. *Variation and change in geographically isolated communities: Appalachian English and Ozark English. Publication of the American Dialect Society No. 74.* Tuscaloosa, AL: University of Alabama Press.

Christian, Donna, Walt Wolfram, & Deborah Hatfield. 1983. *Adolescent and young adult English of Vietnamese refugees*. National Institute of Education Final Report No. G-81-0122.

DeCamp, David. 1971. Toward a generative analysis of a post-creole speech continuum. In Dell Hymes (ed.), *Pidginization and creolization of languages*. Cambridge: Cambridge University Press, 349-70.

Eckert, Penelope. 1988. Adolescent social structure and the spread of linguistic change, *Language in Society* 17:183-207.

Edwards, Viv. 1986. *Language in a Black community*. San Diego, CA: College-Hill Press.

Edwards, Walter F. 1986. Vernacular language use and social networking in East-side Detroit, *Proceedings of Eastern States Conference on Linguistics*, pp. 117-128.

Fasold, Ralph W. 1968. A sociolinguistic study of the pronunciation of three vowels in Detroit speech, Unpublished manuscript.

Fasold, Ralph W. 1972. *Tense marking in Black English: a linguistic and social analysis*. Washington, D.C.: Center for Applied Linguistics.

Fischer, John L. 1958. Social influences on the choice of a linguistic variant, *Word* 14:47-56.

Giles, Howard (ed.). 1984. *The dynamics of speech accommodation* (special issue of the *International Journal of the Sociology of Language* 46).

Guy, Gregory. 1980. Variation in the group and the individual: the case of final stop deletion. In William Labov (ed.), *Locating language in time and space*. New York, NY: Academic Press, 1-36.

Guy, Gregory R. 1988. Language and social class, in Frederick J. Newmeyer (ed.), *Linguistics: The Cambridge Survey, Vol. IV: The Socio-Cultural Context*. New York, NY: Cambridge University Press, 37-63.

Guy, Gregory R. and Leda Bisol. 1988. Phonological theory and variable data, Paper presented at NWAVE XVII, Montreal, Canada.

Hatfield, Deborah H. 1986. Tense marking in the spoken English of Vietnamese Refugees. Ph.D. Dissertation, Georgetown University.

Hockey, S. and I. Marriott. 1980. Oxford concordance program. Version 1.0. Oxford, England: Oxford University Computing Program.

Horvath, Barbara M. 1985. *Variation in Australian English: The sociolects of Sydney*. New York, NY: Cambridge University Press.

Krapp, G. Phillip. 1925. *The English language in America*. New York: Frederick Unger Company.

Kroch, Anthony. 1978. Towards a theory of social dialect variation, *Language in Society* 7:17-36.

Kurath, Hans & Raven I. McDavid. 1961. *The pronunciation of English in the Atlantic States*. Ann Arbor, MI: University of Michigan Press.

Labov, William. 1966a. *The social stratification of English in New York City*. Washington, D.C.: Center for Applied Linguistics.

Labov, William. 1966b. The linguistic variable as a structural unit, *Washington Linguistics Review* 3:4-22.

Labov, William. 1969. Contraction, deletion, and inherent variability of the English copula, *Language* 45:715-62.

Labov, William. 1981. Resolving the Neogrammarian controversy, *Language* 45:715-62.

Labov, William, Paul Cohen, Clarence Robins, & John Lewis. 1968. *A Study of the non-Standard English of Negro and Puerto Rican Speakers in New York City*. Final Report No. 3288. U.S. Office of Education.

Lavandera, Beatriz. 1978. Where does the sociolinguistic variable stop? *Language in Society* 7:171-83.

McConnell-Ginet, Sally. 1988 Language and gender. In Frederick J. Newmeyer (ed.) *Linguistics: The Cambridge survey Vol. IV. Language: The socio-cultural context.* New York, NY: Cambridge University Press, 75-99.

Milroy, Lesley. 1980. *Language and social networks.* Baltimore, MD: University Park Press.

Myhill, John. 1988. The rise of *be* as an aspect marker in Black English Vernacular, *American Speech* 63:304-325.

Poplack, Shana. 1989. The care and handling of a mega-corpus: The Ottawa-Hull French project. In Ralph Fasold & Deborah Schiffrin (eds), *Language change and variation.* Philadelphia, PA: John Benjamins, 411-444.

Rickford, John R. 1986. The need for new approaches to social class analysis in sociolinguistics, *Language and Communication* 6:215-221.

Rickford, John R., Arnetha Ball, Renee Blake, Raina Jackson, & Nomi Martin. 1988. Rappin' on the copula coffin: theoretical and methodological issues in the variable analysis of contracted and deleted *BE* in BEV. Paper presented at NWAVE XVII, Montreal, Canada.

Romaine, Suzanne. 1981. On the problem of syntactic variation: a reply to Beatriz Lavandera and William Labov, *Working Papers in Sociolinguistics* 82. Southwest Educational Development Laboratory.

Sankoff, David, ed. 1978. *Linguistic variation: models and methods.* New York, NY: Academic Press.

Sankoff, David. 1988. Variable rules. In Ulrich Ammon, Norbert Dittmar, & Klaus J. Mattheier (eds), *Sociolinguistics: an international handbook of the science of language and society.* Berlin: Walter de Gruyter.

Sankoff, David and Pascale Rousseau. 1989. Statistical evidence for rule ordering, *Language Variation and Change* 1:1-18.

Wolfram, Walt. 1969. *A sociolinguistic description of Detroit Negro Speech.* Washington, D.C.: Center for Applied Linguistics.

Wolfram, Walt. 1973. Variable constraints and rule relations. In Ralph W. Fasold and Roger W. Shuy (eds), *Analyzing variation in language.* Washington, D.C. Georgetown University Press, 70-78.

Wolfram, Walt. 1974. *Sociolinguistic aspects of assimilation: Puerto Rican English in New York City*. Washington, D.C.: Center for Applied Linguistics.

Wolfram, Walt. 1979. Toward a description of *a*-prefixing in Appalachian English, *American Speech* 51:45-56.

Wolfram, Walt. 1980. *a*-prefixing in Appalachian English. In William Labov (ed.), *Locating language in time and space*. New York, NY: Academic Press, 107-42.

Wolfram, Walt. 1985. Variability in tense marking: a case for the obvious, *Language Learning* 35:229-53.

Wolfram, Walt & Donna Christian. 1976. *Appalachian speech*. Washington, D.C.: Center for Applied Linguistics.

Wolfram, Walt, Donna Christian, William L. Leap, & Lance Potter. 1979. *Variability in the English of two Indian communities and its effect on reading and writing*. National Institute of Education Final Report No. 77-0006.

Wolfram, Walt and Deborah Hatfield. 1984. *Tense marking in second language learning: patterns of spoken and written language in a Vietnamese community*. National Institute of Education, Final Report G-83-0035.

The quantitative analysis of linguistic variation

Gregory R. Guy
York University

1. Quantitative methods and dialect research

One of the attractions -- and one of the challenges -- of dialect research is the Janus-like point-of-view it takes on the problems of human language, looking one way at the organization of linguistic forms, while simultaneously gazing the other way at their social significance. This duality of focus is one of the charms that dialect research holds for many of its practitioners (myself among them), but it is also the source of certain fundamental methodological problems for the field. To shed light at the same time on both linguistic structure and social structure we are necessarily required to amass large amounts of data from many individuals; we must therefore confront problems of quality control and reliability, data handling and data reduction, and interpretation and inference. Hence it can be fairly said that all dialect research, whether geographic or social, is inherently quantitative. From the earliest results of empirical dialect studies over a century ago it has been obvious that rarely can we speak in categorical terms about the properties of dialects: isoglosses never bundle perfectly, each word has its own history, and there is no pristine dialect devoid of internal variation. Rather, we account for them in essentially quantitative terms: variability, tendencies, relations of more and less. Increasingly, therefore, dialect research has come to rely on the standard apparatus of quantitative methodology, including tabular and graphical methods for data display, summary statistics and inferential statistics, tests of significance and reliability, and quantitative analytical techniques.

These developments have been particularly pronounced in the area of speech community studies and sociolinguistic variation. This chapter will attempt to survey the principal quantitative methods in current use in this field, and briefly discuss how and why they are used. A particular interest will be those methods that help us explore the complex mapping between language and society. Thus will we strive to simultaneously illuminate both of the faces of the god of inherent variability.

2. Three steps in quantitative analysis

There are three principal phases in the course of any quantitative analysis, which may be summarized as data collection, data reduction and display, and data interpretation and explanation. Data collection deals with questions such as:

> How do we obtain our data?
> Do the data validly reflect the phenomena we are investigating?
> Is the data sample representative of the larger population?
> Are the procedures for obtaining data reliable and reproducible?
> What can be done to minimize bias in the data?

Issues such as these are obviously crucial to the successful outcome of any kind of dialect research, which is why they constitute a principal focus of the present volume. However, since such issues are dealt with extensively in other articles in the volume, they will receive limited attention here. In section 3 we will confine our discussion to two quantitative problems of data collection: sampling and reliability. The balance of the chapter will concentrate on the two remaining phases of quantitative research.

Data reduction and display deals with issues such as how we look at the data and summarize it. The methods employed here are intended to digest a large number of data points so as to make manageable the task of analysis and understanding, and to allow the identification of general trends and patterns. Familiar methods of this type from areal dialectology are the dialect map and the isogloss. Community studies have tended to rely on tabular and graphical methods, and 'maps' of an abstract nature. We explore some of these methods in section 4.

Interpretation and explanation is the phase in which we try to answer the question: What does it mean? Explanation, of course, is ultimately beyond the realm of methodology; satisfactory explanations will come from our knowledge and experience as linguistic scientists, and the theories we have developed about the nature of human language. But there are a variety of quantitative methods that can help us move toward that end, allowing us to draw inferences from the data, test hypotheses, and interpret the results. In this area lie quantitative measures of significance, correlation, and interaction and independence, as well as numerical parameters that quantify the magnitude and direction of various kinds of effects. Methods of this type will be discussed in sections 5 and 6.

3. Data collection: Sampling and reliability.

Although there are areas of linguistic studies where it is sometimes possible to collect all the available relevant data, dialect research is never so privileged. Rather, we must rely on a sample of the possible data, which means we have to confront all the usual quantitative problems associated with sampling. First there is the question of how subjects or tokens are selected for the sample. Care must always be taken that this procedure is not biased in any way that can potentially effect the variation being studied. Thus if one wished to investigate average human height, one would not draw all one's subjects from basketball teams, as this would surely yield biased results.

One of the best ways to ensure representativeness is to use a random sample. This is a sample which is constructed in a way that gives each potential subject or datum in the total population an equal probability of being included in the sample. An example of this would be a random sample of households with telephones which was constructed by making up telephone numbers from a random number table. Of course such a procedure would not give every speaker an equal chance of being included (those living in large households with one phone would have a lower probability than those who have their own phone lines, and people without phones would have a zero probability of being included), but for many purposes such a sample would be excellently representative. In community language studies, a random sampling procedure is not always ideal, but whatever method is chosen should pay attention to the problem of representativeness.

The sampling problem is intimately connected to the issue of significance, which is further discussed below. Significance statistics are mainly interpreted in terms of whether or not an observed distribution of data could be obtained just by sampling error from a population whose distribution is normal (or reflects some version of the null hypothesis). Thus if one found, say, that 15 out of 20 female informants used a particular dialect form, while only 5 out of 20 male informants did so, how likely is it that such a pattern could be randomly selected from a population in which men and women actually used the form with equal frequency? This is the kind of question that significance tests address.

Finally, the most fundamental question that always arises about sampling is sample size: how much data do we need? There is a simple answer: get as much data as you can. In quantitative studies, more is almost always better. But this answer is not very helpful. More specific answers are available in some cases from statistics, by working backwards from desired levels of significance, confidence intervals, and the like, but these techniques are beyond the scope of the present work. Interested readers are referred to statistical texts, such as Woods et al. 1986.

Reliability is another data collection issue that has a quantitative side. It refers to the question of reproducibility: if we did the same study over again, or if somebody else followed our procedures, would the same answers be obtained? In community studies that use more than one researcher, it is a preferred practice to conduct tests of inter-researcher reliability, to make sure that everyone is collecting the same kinds of tokens in the same way, applying the same criteria and analysis. Thus in Guy et al. 1986, a study of Australian English intonation, the five people involved in data collection and coding all listened separately to the same passages of text, and coded the intonations occurring therein according to the analytical scheme being used for the study. Where discrepancies were found, the group met together to discuss and resolve them, and the procedure was repeated until a point was reached where overall agreement among the raters regularly exceeded 90% and disagreements did not reflect any systematic biases on the part of individual researchers. This kind of test should be applied to any analytical framework as a check on the tightness of the definitions and the possible bias or inattentiveness on the part of the people doing the work. Even if only one researcher is involved, care should still be taken in this regard, for example by coding the same passage twice at different times to see if the same results are obtained. If the results are not fairly consistent, the significance of the whole study becomes somewhat questionable.

4. Approaches to reduction and display.

The general problem of data reduction is to find some summary of the data which minimizes unimportant detail and efficiently presents an overall picture of relevance to the researcher's interest, and does all this without significantly distorting the original data or obscuring important facts. Usually no single device will accomplish all of these ends, but there are a broad spectrum of techniques for the conscientious dialect researcher to choose from.

Choice of methods depends on several kinds of factors. First there are the characteristics of the original data points. Do the data represent information about different individuals or about a series of different linguistic productions by the same individual? Are the variables under study continuous (e.g. F1/F2 values for vowel articulations) or discrete (e.g. occurrence or non-occurrence of a syntactic construction, or deletion or retention of a phonological segment), and if discrete, are they binary, ternary, polynomial? Second there is the issue of the distribution of the observations. Are they tightly clustered, as in a 'normal' distribution, or clumped in a bimodal or polymodal pattern, or widely scattered? And finally, there is the problem of what one wishes to do with the results. What hypothesis is being examined? What point does one wish to make with these studies?

The most widely-used data reduction techniques are summary statistics, including the familiar measurements of central tendencies such as mean (the arithmetic average), median (the value which half of all the data points are higher than, and half lower) and mode (the most frequently occurring value of the variable). These are devices for finding the 'middle' of a dispersion of quantitative values. They are used primarily for continuous or interval data, and are useful to the extent that one can meaningfully talk about a 'middle' in the data distribution under investigation. Thus in a normal, 'bell-shaped' data distribution, the mean, median, and mode all have identical values, and meaningfully characterize the clustered nature of the pattern. In a skewed distribution with a few extreme outlying values, however, the mean will be markedly shifted, while the mode and median may be unaffected. And in a strongly bimodal distribution (one that shows two clumps of data points), the mean and median will simply characterize some point midway between the two modes, which may be completely uninteresting.

Comparable summary statistics for discrete (nominal) variables are also available. The best-known such method is the fraction of times some particular outcome is found in the data: for example, the fraction of consonantal pronunciations of postvocalic /r/ by a speaker, or the percentage of individuals who used some particular lexical item. Although the original events are discontinuous (one either uses or does not use the word), a fraction varies continuously over the rational numbers in the interval from 0 to 1. Such a number does not, of course, measure a 'central tendency' (a baseball player with a .250 average never gets one-quarter of a hit), but they do give a useful summary of the ratios of alternative outcomes.

In dealing with discrete variables that have more than two possible realizations, it is often found desirable to devise another type of summary statistic called an index. In such a case a fraction only shows the frequency of one of the outcomes, and gives no information about the distribution of the remaining cases across the other outcomes. An index, on the other hand, weights all the realizations in some way, so as to give a global measure. An example is found in Labov's treatment

(1966) of the (dh) variable in New York City, which can be realized as a stop [d], affricate [dð], or fricative [ð]. Assuming that the variants were socially rankable according to their 'nonstandardness,' Labov developed an index for this variable which weighted a fricative realization at zero, an affricate at 1, and a stop articulation at 2. The index score was computed as (((no. of stop realizations X 2) + (no. of affricates X 1))/total no. of realizations of the variable) X 100. On this scale, an individual who used all stops would receive an index score of 200, one who used all fricatives would get a score of 0, and mixed usages would get intermediate index values proportionate to their ratios of stops and affricates.

Indexes of this sort give a useful global summary of the distribution of ternary or polynomial variables, but attention should be paid to their assumptions and limitations. The example cited above assumes that the three realizations can be ranked in a scale, and that stop articulations can be meaningfully characterized as being twice as 'nonstandard' as affricate articulations of this variable. If such assumptions proved to be at odds with the social interpretation of these variants, the utility of the index would be undermined.

The endpoint of data reduction is usually some display of the data in a way that effectively demonstrates the trends that have been discovered. The principal display methods used in dialect research are tables, graphs, and maps. Tables give an effective one- or two-dimensional display of quantitative results, and since they present actual numerical values, they are maximally explicit and precise. However, they suffer several important limitations. First, if one attempts to illustrate with a table more than two dimensions influencing the variable, or more than one variable (e.g. to demonstrate co-variance), the table becomes very complex and difficult to interpret. Second, tables depend for their impact on the reader making comparisons of the various cells in the table, reading across rows and down columns. While the message they thus convey is explicitly present in the values, it may not be very salient or visually impressive.

The principal virtue of graphical displays is thus that they are graphic. They can be designed to make salient the relationships that are found in the data, to illustrate trends, show differences between various individuals, or groups, or variables; and to demonstrate covariance between different variables. They show proportions or ratios in an analog form that is more readily apprehended by the human eye.

Consider, for example, the line graph in Figure 1, which shows the rate of consonantal (as opposed to vocalized or 'r-less') pronunciations of post-vocalic /r/ in New York City (adapted from Labov 1966). In one graph it clearly illustrates the stratification of different social classes, and the style-shifting towards higher use of the consonantal variant (which Labov terms (r-1)) in more careful styles by all social classes. The same information could be displayed 'digitally' in a table, but it would be a complicated table with dozens of cells to be perused and compared, and would not yield with the same clarity the depiction of major trends that is so obvious in the graph.

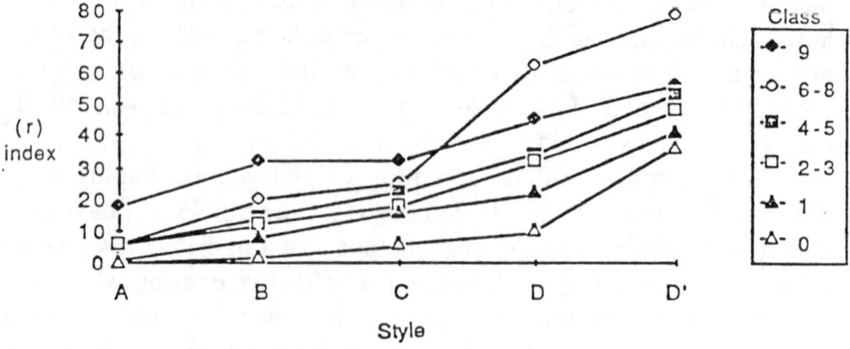

Figure 1. Class stratification of (r) in New York City (after Labov 1966:160)

Of course graphs involve their own limitations and assumptions. Line graphs such as Figure 1 imply that the axes are continuous dimensions, that it is meaningful to draw a line connecting the measured points which, in effect, extrapolates intermediate values. Is this true for the horizontal dimension in Figure 1? What do the points on the lines between, e.g. casual and careful styles mean? Is there a semi-careful style? For Labov these questions have favorable answers. He treats this stylistic dimension as a continuous variable of 'degree of self-monitoring' (which is at a maximum in the most formal styles). Thus a line graph is justified here. But for other data sets in which one axis is clearly a nominal (or even ordinal) variable, bar graphs are the preferred approach.

Another type of display that is particularly useful in showing covariance of two quantitative variables is the scattergram. Figure 2 shows an example taken from a study (Guy & Boyd 1990) of the rate of deletion of final /t,d/ in English in 'semi-weak' verb forms such as kept, told, etc. Each point plots an individual speaker according to two continuous variables: the speaker's age (horizontal axis) and the speaker's probability of deletion in such words (vertical axis). The points tend to fall in a line from upper left to lower right, demonstrating an inverse correlation between age and rate of deletion. The linear regression line drawn across the figure is a statistical device for measuring covariance of this sort.

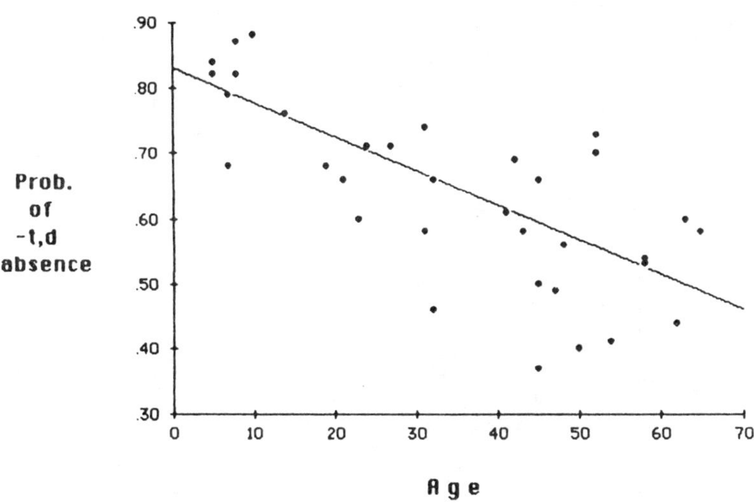

Figure 2. Probability of deletion in semi-weak verbs by age (Guy and Boyd 1990:8)

Probably the most widely used device in dialectology for data reduction and display is, of course, the map. Their use in general dialectology does not require further discussion here, for they have been considerably discussed in Part I of this volume, but one relevant use in community studies that deserves additional mention here is the quantitative map. Figure 3 is an example from East Anglia and the east midlands, showing the percentage of [U] in such words as *brother* and *us* for each the respondents surveyed.

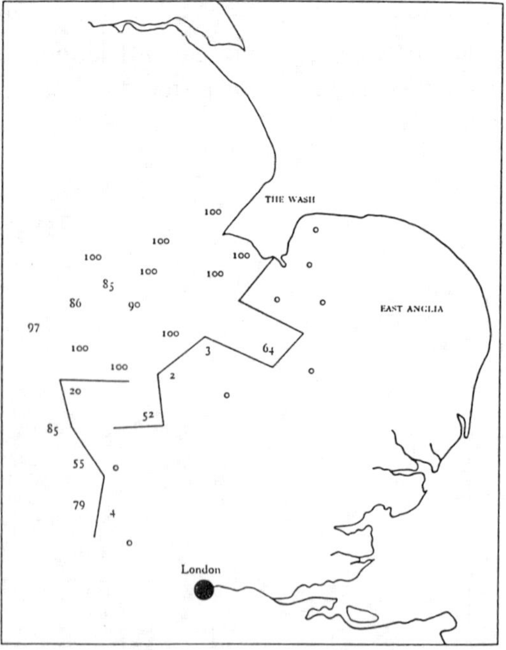

Figure 3. Quantitative dialect map (Chambers & Trudgill 1980:130)

The main virtue of maps is their graphic iconicity. They directly represent spatial relationships in a way that is interpretable in terms of the physical world. (Things close together in the world are close on the map; directional relationships are preserved, etc.) It has often been thought desirable to develop displays that have the same kind of iconic relationship to features of the (nonphysical) social or linguistic world, so that people who are socially or linguistically similar will be close together in the display, and directions in the display will have some straightforward relationship to social (or linguistic) dimensions. A variety of methods has been developed by which such abstract maps of 'social space' can be drawn. We will discuss one such method, principal components analysis, which has been put to use recently in community dialect studies.

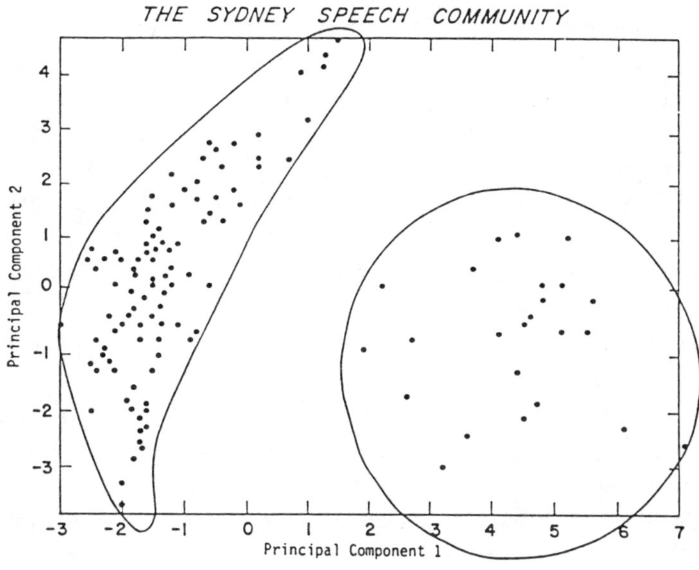

Figure 4. A principal components plot (Horvath & Sankoff 1987:190)

An example of a principal components ('Princom') display is shown in Figure 4, taken from Horvath & Sankoff's 1987 study of social dialects in Sydney English. The data points represent individuals in the study plotted in a scattergram according to the first two dimensions of an abstract linguistic similarity space computed by the Princom method. To develop such a display one first devises measures of a number of independent linguistic variables and computes these measures for each individual in the sample. In Horvath's data the measures were things like frequencies of use of particular phonetic realizations of vocalic and consonantal variables in the dialect (e.g. number of instances of use of the pronunciation [ay] for the vowel in 'high'). Each individual's linguistic usage is then 'described' by a series of these quantitative measures. The Princom procedure examines these measures for covariance and correlation, attempting to find a smaller number of abstract dimensions that will minimize variance in the sample. (We would not be surprised to find, for example, that speakers who used more nonstandard variants for the vowel in 'high' also used more nonstandard variants in the vowels of 'hay' and 'how.' To the extent that such a pattern was systematic, these measures could be combined into a single Princom dimension.)

The interesting result for dialect studies of such an analysis is that the distribution of individuals on the linguistic map thus created may correspond to meaningful social divisions. Thus in Figure 4 there are two relatively discrete clusters of individuals: a crescent-shaped cluster at upper left and a globular cluster to the right. These distributions correspond nicely to socially real groupings in the population: all the individuals located in the globular cluster are immigrants to Australia who are non-native speakers of English. Furthermore, within the crescent, individuals are distributed approximately according to social class (working class speakers falling toward the bottom, and upper-middle class speakers towards the top). Thus the linguistic map arrived at by Princom analysis yields a socially significant classification of the 'lects' found in the Sydney speech community.

5. Approaches to interpretation.

The ultimate goal of any quantitative study in dialect research is not to produce numbers (e.g., summary statistics), but to identify and explain linguistic phenomena. Thus we would like to be able to test hypotheses, compare alternative analyses, and develop models of the data from which we can make predictions. To this end one can draw upon another class of quantitative methods that are called inferential statistics. We will focus here upon two such methods widely used in community dialect studies: tests of significance and variable rule analysis.

There are a variety of tests of significance, but they usually reduce in the end to a statistic conventionally known as 'p,' which is the probability that the so-called 'null hypothesis' is true. The null hypothesis always states that nothing is going on: there is no relationship between the independent and dependent variables, and the observed distribution of the data is due merely to random fluctuation and sampling error. If this hypothesis has a low probability of being true, say p=.05 or .01, then the distribution is said to be statistically significant. This means that whatever effect or relationship is being investigated is probably a real one, because the likelihood of it being due to chance is very small: only one in twenty or one in a hundred.

Significance values can be derived from a variety of other statistical tests, such as the well-known chi-square test and the t-test. One of these, which also has another purpose, is the correlation statistic (r). It is used, like the scattergram display discussed above, to test whether two quantitative variables covary significantly. It is derived by characterizing a number of data points (in dialect studies these are usually individual informants) on two different numerical measures. The correlation statistic is then computed to show whether these two measures tend to go up together, or go down together, or vary independently of one another. A perfect direct correlation (r=1) is one in which the two values for each individual are always equal, or differ by the same amount. Thus they would fall along a straight line in a scattergram, with a slope of 1. Conversely, a perfect negative correlation (r= -1), occurs when an increase in one value is always associated with an equivalent decrease in the other value. When r=0, there is no correlation between the two values whatsoever. What one usually deals with, however, are values of r other than 1, 0, or -1. In such cases the statistic is an aid to understanding the nature of the relationship, showing whether things are weakly or strongly correlated, in a positive or negative direction, and since r values can be translated to p values, they will also help one to estimate the significance of a relationship.

It should be noted that all inferential statistics should be thought of as aids to the researchers' discovery process, hypothesis testing, and so on, rather than being considered definitive 'proof' (or disproof) of one's research question. Short of collecting the total sample of all relevant tokens (which is usually impossible, if only because the total set is infinite), we can never state categorically that a research hypothesis is true or false. In statistical terms this would mean obtaining a p value of zero or one, which cannot happen. We can say that the probability of the null hypothesis being true is extremely small or extremely large, but there is almost always some chance of being wrong.

Even so basic a concept as the criterion value -- a figure, like .05, which is used as the cutoff point for significance -- is actually arbitrary, and depends on what use one wishes to make of the answer. Conventionally, a value of .05 is widely used as the criterion of significance for the purpose of reporting results in scholarly papers in the social sciences. But this value is too strict for some purposes and too lax for others. If someone's life depended on the outcome (as, for example in medical research on the toxicity of a new drug), that person would probably want a much smaller chance of being wrong, say only .01 or .001. And at the other end of the scale, suppose one found on an initial approach to some problem a p value of .08 or .10. It would be foolish to abandon a hypothesis on the strength of this if it were promising for other reasons, theoretical or empirical. Under these circumstances one would normally take this as an encouraging outcome, and do further research on the problem, such as collecting more data, trying to remove possible sources of bias, controlling for intervening variables, or refining the definitions of the variables. A p value of .60 or .80 might discourage one from further pursuit of a line of inquiry, but such decisions should always be guided by our knowledge and theoretical expectations, and not based blindly on the statistical results.

6. Variable rule analysis

Variable rule analysis is a type of multivariate analysis which is now widely used in studies of linguistic variation. Its purpose is to separate, quantify, and test the significance of the effects of environmental factors on a linguistic variable. These conditioning factors may be either social (e.g. the effect of social class on the use of consonantal pronunciations of post-vocalic /r/ in New York City), or linguistic (e.g. the effect of the syntactic function of a relative pronoun on its realization as 'that' as opposed to 'which' or 'who').

Such questions can of course be approached more simply by compiling contingency tables, computing percentages, and applying statistical tests such as chi-square. Thus in our hypothetical examples above, one could compare the percentage of consonantal (r-1) pronunciations produced by middle-class New Yorkers with the percentage produced by working-class speakers, or the percentage of 'that' realizations of the relative pronoun in subject position with the percentage in object position. Given the availability and relative simplicity of such methods, what is the point of using a somewhat 'higher-tech' method like variable rule analysis?

The answer to this question lies in the superiority of multivariate methods over univariate methods for studying certain kinds of problems. When there are several different environmental factors affecting one linguistic variable, a series of tables showing these effects separately (e.g. the realizations of /r/ by sex, by social class, by speech style, etc.) can easily give distorted or even wildly misleading results if the data are not evenly distributed across all the independent variables. Since in linguistic data it usually happens that the data are in fact unevenly distributed, a multivariate analysis will give more accurate results, because while computing the effect of one independent variable, it explicitly controls for the effect of all other known independent variables.

Again, an example may help to clarify this point. Consider a hypothetical table (Table 1) for the pronunciation of /r/ in NYC which conforms to known patterns of class and stylistic distribution:

	Casual Style		Word List Style		Totals	
	#/total	%	#/total	%	#/total	%
Working class	1/20	5	40/100	40	41/120	34.2
Middle class	15/100	15	10/20	50	25/120	20.8

Factor values:

Working class	.43	Casual Style	.28
Middle class	.57	Word List Style	.72

Table 1: Use of consonantal (r-1) pronunciations of postvocalic /r/ in New York City (hypothetical example).

Comparing cell percentages in Table 1, it is clear that middle class speakers always use more consonantal (r-1) realizations than working class informants in comparable styles. But the marginal totals for the two classes seem to show exactly the opposite: higher use by the working class (34%, vs 21% for middle class)! This arises because the data for working class speakers are predominantly drawn from the more careful style D, in which all speakers use more (r-1), while the data for middle class speakers are predominantly drawn from the casual style A. The row totals constitute a univariate analysis, which cannot resolve problems of this nature. A variable rule analysis, however, controls for style while estimating the class effect, and correctly assigns factor values indicating higher use by the middle class. The factor values for style and class in these hypothetical data are given in the table (computed using MacVarb). They correctly show the working class as disfavoring (r-1): a value of .43, vs. .57 for the middle class.

Using VARBRUL. How does one actually go about doing a variable rule analysis in a community dialect study? The remainder of this section will be devoted to a discussion of the procedures for such a study. Interested readers are referred to the standard sources for further information (e.g. Labov 1969, Cedergren & Sankoff 1974, Guy 1975, 1980, 1988, Rousseau & Sankoff 1978). We will illustrate the steps in this process with examples from the author's work on English -t,d deletion (Guy 1977, 1980).

The first step is to identify a linguistic variable. This can be phonological, morphological, syntactic, or lexical, but one should always be aware of the fact that identifying something as a variable already involves certain theoretical assumptions or (implicit or explicit) claims. If we take two (or more) surface outputs as being alternants or variants of a single entity, this implies a claim that there is some point in the linguistic system where a choice is made between those two forms. While this is relatively uncontroversial in the area of phonological variables like English -t,d deletion, it has been a matter of some contention in the areas of syntax and lexicon (see e.g. Lavandera 1979, Romaine 1982). It should therefore be a prerequisite for any quantitative study of language variation that a clear and defensible position on the nature and locus of the variation has been achieved; pre- or a-theoretical research is as impossible in quantitative studies as anywhere else.

Identifying a variable includes defining the variants (what is and what is not a token of the variable under study) and determining the envelope of variation (where is it possible or impossible for the variable to occur). Categorical contexts (where there is no variation) and neutralizing contexts (where the variation is irrelevant or undiscernible), must be identified and are normally excluded from the analysis. In the case of -t,d deletion, the variable is taken as the occurrence vs. non-occurrence of apical stops in word-final consonant clusters (e.g. 'west side' vs. 'wes' side'). The envelope of variation was defined according to the lexicon of standard English: any word that contains a final -t,d after a consonant (other than /r/) in standard English pronunciation is treated as a candidate for the deletion rule. (Final sequences of consonant plus -t,d which could be produced by some other lexical process such as contraction were also excluded: e.g. 'can't,' 'won't.') No categorical contexts were identified, but a number of neutralization environments were excluded from the quantitative study, such as a following word beginning with a /t/ or /d/, on the grounds that one cannot reliably discern a systematic distinction between 'best time' and 'bes' time.' (See Wolfram, this volume, for a fuller discussion.)

Next one must postulate a model for the nature of the choice that governs the outcomes. Normally this is framed as a variable rule (Labov 1969), in which one proposes an underlying form as well as a generative rule which converts the underlying form in the course of a derivation to a different surface form. This rule may or may not apply (i.e. it applies variably). When it has applied in some derivation, the output of the rule appears on the surface, and when it has not applied, the input (or underlying form) appears. For -t,d deletion, we postulate that all lexical entries contain the full form with final /t/ or /d/, and that the tokens that omit this segment on the surface are the result of a variable deletion rule of the form:

/t,d/ --> <ø>/ C__##

Although the 'variable rule' of this sort has given its name to the analytical method we are describing, the method is not wedded to this notational framework. At a minimum it requires some model in which items are linked by a speaker's choice among them, but any theory which has such choice points can make meaningful use of this type of analysis. One way in which alternative models are nontrivially different is the treatment of ternary or polynomial variables. A single variable rule can successfully model only two possible outcomes; if more than two variants are involved, additional variable rules must be postulated. This is the way Labov handles contraction and deletion of the English copula, for example (1969), and he explicitly argues for an ordered sequence of a contraction rule followed by a deletion rule (which applies to the output of contraction) as being superior to other possible models, such as one in which deletion applies directly to the full uncontracted underlying form, or one in which the copula is not underlyingly present but is variably inserted.

In conjunction with the formulation of a variable rule (or other theoretical model of the variability), one must identify possible conditioning factors which may influence the choice among the alternants or the application of the variable rule. This is another place in which theory and knowledge of the workings of language guide the researcher to formulate reasonable hypotheses for investigation. It would be possible, of course, to investigate whether -t,d deletion was correlated with the phases of the moon or the speaker's initials, but no intelligent researcher would waste his or her time on such blind alleys (and no funding agency, one hopes, would finance such an enterprise). Rather, the kinds of hypotheses that have been pursued in connection with -t,d deletion are:

1) the preceding phonological environment: does deletion occur more often after /s/, or some other fricative, or a nasal, or another stop?

2) the following phonological environment: is deletion favored by a following consonant, or glide, or vowel?

3) the morphological status of the deletable segment: is there more deletion of the /t/ in 'missed,' or 'mist,' or 'lost'?

4) the stylistic context: do speakers delete more in formal or informal social settings?

These environmental factors are organized into factor groups (in the terminology of this method). Each factor group can be defined as a locus in the variable rule where conditioning occurs and consists of an exhaustive list of all the possible mutually-exclusive factors that could occur at that locus. Thus the factor groups are independent variables, and the factors in the group are the possible values of this independent variable. For a successful variable rule analysis, the factor groups must be established so that they are orthogonal and independent. That is, they must be cross-cutting, so that insofar as possible each factor in a group can co-occur with every factor in all the other groups. And each must represent a logically separate and isolable constraint.

In the case of -t,d deletion, the variables discussed above constituted the principal factor groups used in the analysis. The preceding environment factor group was analyzed according to manner of articulation of the preceding consonant: sibilants, other fricatives, nasals, laterals, and stops. The following environment factor group distinguished obstruent consonants (including nasals), liquids, glides, and vowels, and of course also made provision for a following pause. The morphological factor group distinguished monomorphemic words such as 'mist' (in which the final -t,d is part of the root morpheme), regular past tense verb forms such as 'missed' (in which the final -t,d uniquely represents the PAST morpheme), and semiweak verbs such as 'lost' (in which the final -t,d represents the PAST morpheme, but not uniquely as the same information is conveyed by a root vowel change). Finally, a stylistic factor group was defined according to whatever stylistic variation was identifiable in the available data. For example, we studied one informant for whom a massive amount of data was collected over several days and were able to distinguish stylistic variation between her business conversations at work and her private conversations at home.

A moment's thought will reveal that the factors in these groups are exhaustive (e.g. every following environment can be coded as one of the five factors in the relevant group) and mutually exclusive (no following environment can be coded as more than one of the factors in the group). The groups are also orthogonal (e.g. any morphological type can occur with any following environment) and logically independent (e.g. there is no reason to believe that formal speech will incline a speaker to produce more words with nasals preceding final -t,d).

Defining and codifying the factor groups actually represents a major part of the analytical work in a variable rule study. One should not expect to get the definitive analysis on the first attempt. Rather, as with most empirical research, one will formulate hypotheses, test them and refine them, perhaps discard some and develop new ones. This may lead to the incorporation of additional factors or groups into the analysis. There are two conflicting constraints that govern this process. On the one hand, there are advantages to making the first analysis (the codification of factors and factor groups) as exhaustive as possible, because this minimizes the chance of overlooking something which might turn out to be important, and because if an entirely new factor were added at a later stage, all the original data might have to be recoded. But this desire to be comprehensive from the outset must be weighed against the available time and resources for doing the research, and the amount of data that are available and can be collected. A highly detailed coding system takes more time to design, and more time to apply to each datum being coded, and needs more data to support the larger number of fine distinctions. But resources are always finite, and one should always have some results to show at the end of the project. There is no point in developing the ultimately subtle codification of factors if that means that (a) there is no time left to do the quantitative study, or (b) there is only enough time remaining to code an amount of data too small to give significant results for all the distinctions made, or (c) there is not in any case enough data obtainable on the issue at hand. Thus in every study one must arrive at a minimax solution balancing these two desiderata: do the most comprehensive analysis that can be brought to completion with the resources that are available.

Having identified a variable, and relevant conditioning environments, and formulated a model of the variation, one is in a position to actually code the data, i.e. to go through the collected corpus identifying tokens of the variable and classifying each one according to the coding scheme that has been devised. In a large study this will generate lots of data points with a great deal of information about each. Handling, storing, editing, and manipulating such quantities of information becomes a sizable task, which is facilitated by computerization. There are now several programs available for doing these operations.

For storing data, it has become preferred practice to compile the coded data in token files, that is, a file in which each token has a separate entry. In comparison with coding the data in tabular form and storing it cell-by-cell, the token format allows maximum recoverability: each data point can be traced back to its original source, if questions arise or recoding is necessary. (Unfortunately the format of these files has not been standardized across the various programs, so care should be taken before preparing such a file to ensure that it will be readable by the analysis program one intends to use.) Editing and correcting the stored files is done either by means of a dedicated program or a general text editor. The token file is converted to a cell file for Varbrul analysis (see below) by means of a dedicated routine in the analysis program.

One may also wish to perform various manipulations of the data in the course of an analysis, such as compiling summary statistics and cross-tabulations, recoding to combine or eliminate factors or groups, and partitioning the data set into subfiles or collapsing separate files.

The heart of a variable rule analysis is the estimation of the constraint effects and their significance. This involves calculating a factor value for each factor in the analysis, which is a number between zero and one that indicates to what extent and in what direction the factor affects the rate of application of the rule. These values pattern as follows: a value above .5 is a factor which favors the application of the rule, while a value below .5 indicates a factor which disfavors the rule, and a value exactly equal to .5 is a factor which has essentially no effect on the rule. Furthermore, a value approaching 0 indicates that the relevant rule (or choice) never applies in the environment of that factor (a 'negative knockout'), and a value approaching 1 indicates that the rule always applies in the environment of that factor (a 'positive knockout').

The factor values are calculated by the Varbrul program developed by Sankoff and Rousseau (Cedergren & Sankoff 1974, Rousseau & Sankoff 1978). This program utilizes an algorithm based on the 'maximum likelihood' procedure for estimating constraint effects. Several mathematical models have been proposed for relating the observed frequencies to the calculated factor values; the one that is currently preferred by most researchers in this field is the 'logistic' model. It may be summarized in the following formula (where P_i represents the factor value associated with factor i, P_0 represents an overall 'input probability' which sets the general level of rule application, and P_{ijk}... represents the probability of rule application in the environment of factors i, j, k...):

$$P_{ijk..}/(1-P_{ijk..}) = P_0/(1-P_0) \times P_i/(1-P_i) \times P_j/(1-P_j) \times \ldots$$

To do a Varbrul calculation, one prepares an input cell file -- in effect a table showing all the possible combinations of factors for which data were found, and for each of these cells, a fraction showing the number of realizations of the variant designated as indicating a 'rule application' against the total number of tokens (showing any variant) observed in that context. In other words, such a file contains the same kind of information as is shown in the hypothetical table of /r/ variation in New York City above (but without the marginal totals and percentages, as these can be computed by the program). Any one of the several versions of Varbrul can then compute from such a file a unique and replicable set of factor values showing estimates of the independent effects of all the factors used in the analysis.

Armed with these results, the final phase of the linguist's work begins: that of interpretation and explanation. The numbers are not the answer to any of our questions; they are just additional inferential statistics which we can use as empirical guideposts in our search for answers. Perhaps the most basic kind of inference to be drawn from the variable rule results is estimating the direction and magnitude of the factor effects. The factor values are interpreted according to the distribution of values described above. In the -t,d case, consider the results shown in Table 2 for the morphological factor group:

	Probability of deletion
Monomorphemes (e.g. mist)	.65
Past tense of semiweak verbs (e.g. lost)	.55
Past tense of regular verbs (e.g. missed)	.31

Table 2: Effect of morphological factors on -t,d deletion (Guy & Boyd 1990:7)

We conclude that -t,d deletion occurs most often in monomorphemic words, while past-tense forms strongly inhibit the rule, and semiweak verbs fall in between, but closer to the monomorphemes. Also, the spread of values in this group (their substantial divergence from the neutral value of .5) indicates that the effect is a strong one. An insignificant factor group will show values clustered around .5.

Another type of inference that can be drawn from such results is the elimination of insignificant factors and groups to wring out superfluous detail from the analysis. This is a basic goal of all attempts at explanation; by Occam's Razor, a theory is better to the extent that it minimizes explanatory principles and presents the most general account of the facts. In variable rule analysis this means discarding factor groups that do not make a significant contribution to the goodness-of-fit between the model and the observed data, and combining factors within groups to the extent that (a) they represent subdivisions of a more general category, and (b) are not significantly different from one another in factor value. In either case this is achieved by comparing the results of a run which includes the factor or group in question and one that eliminates it. For testing whole groups this process can be done automatically by a step-up/step-down procedure in versions 2S and 3 of Varbrul. For testing distinctions within a group, however, it must be donc by the researcher, because of criterion (a) above.

An instance of this problem can be found in the -t,d deletion case. In early studies of this variable, I made an additional distinction in the morphological factor group, between past tense (e.g. 'walked') and past participle ('have walked') forms. The factor values obtained were virtually identical for these two categories. Since the words in question were the same in internal morphological structure (the difference between the two categories is a functional one, due to the presence or absence of an auxiliary elsewhere in the sentence), a valid case could be made to combine them. I did so, with no significant decline in the goodness-of-fit measure. This result was interpreted as indicating that the distinction was not relevant to the operation of this rule. All subsequent analyses therefore combined the two categories into one.

A related type of inference that is drawn from these results is testing the significance of factor effects. The most powerful factors will account for a great deal of the variance in the sample, and their omission from an analysis will produce striking declines in the goodness-of-fit measure. Marginal effects will likewise produce marginal declines. In every case we can obtain a p statistic showing the significance of the factor or factor group.

The goodness-of-fit measure utilized in these procedures is the log-likelihood statistic (l.l.), which is computed for each run. To test the significance of any item (group or factor), one compares a run including the item with a run in which it is omitted. The change in l.l. between the two runs is proportional to one-half of a chi-square statistic. Thus one multiplies the difference in l.l. by 2, and looks up the result in a chi-square table, with the degrees of freedom being equal to the change in total degrees of freedom between the two runs. (The total degrees of freedom for any run can be calculated as the total number of factors minus the number of factor groups; thus when an entire group is eliminated the change is equal to the number of factors in the group minus 1, and when factors within a group are combined it is equal to the number of factors in the group before combination minus the number of factors after combination.)

Finally, we come to the last step. We have arrived at the most general analysis possible, eliminating superfluous factors so that only significant effects remain. We have comprehended the direction and size of those effects. What remains to be done is explanation. Why should the numbers be as they are? Why have our hypotheses been confirmed or disconfirmed? Of course, explanation lies outside of method, in the province of theory. Therefore I cannot enunciate any general principles as to how one goes about doing this, other than the ones provided by the philosophy of science. I will therefore conclude with one final example from the quantitative study of -t,d deletion: an attempt at explanation of the morphological results.

Why should -t,d deletion apply less often in past tense forms than monomorphemic forms, and why should semiweak verbs fall in between? Why is there no difference between past tense forms and past participles? The answer to the first question would appear to be essentially functional: deleting final -t,d from regular past tense verbs creates systematic surface equivalence to the present tense forms. The resulting potential for confusion should be disfunctional, and is therefore avoided. The rule thus deletes segments in inverse proportion to their functional load. This explanation also accounts for the intermediate position of the semi-weak verbs, where the -t,d carries some functional load, but another signal is available to convey the same information.

However, this explanation does not answer the second question, about the equivalence between past tense and past participial forms. The functional explanation would predict less deletion for the regular past tense forms, since the -t,d in participles has a very low functional load. (An utterance like 'I've miss' my bus' is unambiguously reconstructable.) How do we reconcile the two findings?

The answer, I would suggest, lies in the organization of language. Yes, there must be forces at work in language to maintain functional distinctions and avoid massive homonymy. But at the same time, there is ample evidence that the various components of the grammar such as the phonology and the syntax are relatively autonomous, and automatic in operation. It is therefore theoretically implausible to imply that a lowly phonological process like -t,d deletion should be made privy to high-level information about the syntax and semantics of the sentence. However, it is generally accepted that phonological processes are sensitive to morphological structure. In this case all the results can be accounted for by a morphological constraint on the deletion rule. The rule applies freely when no boundary precedes the final -t,d, but is constrained somewhat by a derivational boundary in the semiweak verbs, and heavily constrained by the inflectional boundary in the past tense and past participle forms.

However, these morphological distinctions are themselves essentially functional; they constitute a kind of grammaticalization of the functional/semantic distinctions. It is true that the rule is only directly affected by the morphology; where morphology and function disagree, the results follow morphology. But if we push the explanation one step further, asking why such morphological distinctions exist, we ultimately arrive at functional ends.

References

Cedergren, Henrietta & David Sankoff. 1974. Variable rules: performance as a statistical reflection of competence. *Language* 50:233-55.

Chambers, J. K. & Peter Trudgill. 1980. *Dialectology*. Cambridge: Cambridge University Press.

Guy, Gregory R. 1975. Use and applications of the Cedergren/Sankoff variable rule program. In Ralph Fasold & Roger Shuy (eds), *Analyzing variation in language*. Washington, D.C.: Georgetown University Press, 59-69.

Guy, Gregory R. 1977. A new look at -t,d deletion. In Ralph Fasold & Roger Shuy (eds), *Studies in language variation*. Washington, D.C.: Georgetown University Press, 1-11.

Guy, Gregory R. 1980. Variation in the group and in the individual: the case of final stop deletion. In William Labov (ed.), *Locating language in time and space*. New York: Academic Press, 1-36.

Guy, Gregory R. 1988. Advanced Varbrul analysis. In K. Ferrara et al. (eds), *Linguistic change and contact*. (Texas Linguistic Forum, Vol. 30). Austin: University of Texas, Department of Linguistics, 124-36.

Guy, Gregory R., Barbara Horvath, J. Vonwiller, E. Daisley, & I. Rogers. 1986. An intonational change in progress in Australian English. *Language in Society* 15:23-52.

Guy, Gregory R. and S. Boyd. To appear. The development of a morphological category.

Horvath, Barbara & David Sankoff. 1987. Delimiting the Sydney speech community. *Language in Society* 16:179-204.

Labov, William. 1966. *The social stratification of English in New York City*. Arlington, VA: Center for Applied Linguistics.

Labov, William. 1969. Contraction, deletion, and inherent variability of the English copula. *Language* 45:715-62.

Lavandera, Beatriz. 1979. Where does the sociolinguistic variable stop? *Language in Society* 7:171-82.

Romaine, Suzanne. 1982. *Socio-historical linguistics: its status and methodology*. Cambridge: Cambridge University Press.

Rousseau, Pascal & David Sankoff. 1978. Advances in variable rule methodology. In David Sankoff (ed.), *Linguistic variation: models and methods*. New York: Academic, 57-69.

Sankoff, David & William Labov. 1979. On the uses of variable rules. *Language in Society* 9:189-222.

Woods, Anthony, Paul Fletcher, & Arthur Hughes. 1986. *Statistics in language studies*. Cambridge: Cambridge University Press.

III. Group Studies

Variation theory and language contact:[1]

Shana Poplack
University of Ottawa

1.0. Introduction

This paper describes a variationist sociolinguistic approach to the study of language contact phenomena. In what follows we first briefly outline the basic notions informing the variationist framework, describe the key concepts and issues in current language contact research, and then proceed to explore how variationist sociolinguistic concerns may be applied to issues fundamental to the bilingual[2] inquiry. In so doing, we draw on our ongoing work on typologically similar and different language pairs: Spanish/English, French/English, Finnish/English, Tamil/English and Arabic/French in North American contact situations. Our focus is not on the results of these studies, but rather on illustration of 1) the conceptual, methodological and analytical problems arising in the course of these investigations, and 2) some of the solutions we have adopted to overcome them.

2.0. Variation Theory

The branch of empirical linguistics known as *variation theory* (e.g. Labov 1971, 1984; Sankoff 1982, 1988, G. Sankoff 1974, G. Sankoff & Labov 1985, Guy this volume, Wolfram this volume) involves a combination of techniques from linguistics, sociology, anthropology and statistics, among others, to scientifically investigate language use and structure as manifested in natural(istic) context. The variationist viewpoint on language may be characterized by its preoccupation with 1) accounting for grammatical structure in connected discourse, and 2) explaining the apparent instability therein of linguistic form-function relations (Sankoff 1988:141). In scientifically accounting for the production data contained in a speech sample, variationists seek to discover *patterns* of usage, which pertain to the relative frequency of occurrence or co-occurrence of structures, rather than simply to their existence or grammaticality.

The primary object of description of the variationist is the speech of individuals qua members of a speech community, i.e. informants specifically chosen (through ethnographic or sociological methods) to represent the major axes of community structure. Thus, an important aspect of any study in the variationist framework involves entrée into the speech community, where observation of language use in its socio-cultural setting is carried out. A specific goal of this procedure is to gain access to the *vernacular*, the relatively homogeneous, spontaneous speech reserved for intimate or casual situations. This is taken to reflect the most systematic form of the language acquired by the speaker, prior to any subsequent efforts at (hyper-) correction or style-shifting (themselves imposed by the combined pressures of group membership and the social meaning within that group of the linguistic options available). Since in almost every corpus of production data there are some linguistic elements that do not obey the normal constraints of the system, the analyst must be able to distinguish systematic from unsystematic heterogeneity. Another motivation for analysis of the vernacular is to provide a basis for establishing the nature of the system, against which we can subsequently assess what may be characterized as deviant with regard to it.

The structure of communication in the speech community is seen by variationists as realized through recurrent choices made by speakers at various interactional and grammatical levels (ibid.:151). The choice mechanism entails that given linguistic 'functions' may be realized in different 'forms.' Thus, it is fairly uncontroversial that the Caribbean Spanish plural marker *-s* may be produced as [s], [h] or ø; the French negative particle as *ne ... pas* or ø *... pas*; Vernacular Black English 3rd p. sg. copula as *is*, *-s*, or ø, and none of these choices involves differences in referential meaning. In order to account for the variant that was actually selected in a given situation, the variationist must determine why, where and when it was used, as well as by whom. As becomes apparent from examination of natural discourse collected in any speech community, the answers to these questions are themselves variable. Methods developed for dealing with this variability stem from the recognition that it is *inherent;* i.e. (in contrast to classic cases of 'allophonic' variation, for example) it cannot be factored out, no matter how closely the analyst specifies the context. This does not imply that such variability is unstructured. The variationist adopts quantitative techniques to uncover the systematic differences between speakers, often associated to some extent with one or more of age, sex, ethnicity, educational level, etc. Typically, each speaker will alternate among all the choices, but will manifest an overall *pattern* of variant frequencies consistent with that of other individual members of her group.

In conjunction with extra-linguistic influences, purely internal features of the linguistic environment will also play a role in determining variant choice. The use of multivariate or 'variable rule' analysis (e.g. Sankoff 1979, Rand & Sankoff 1988) enables the analyst to extract regularities and tendencies from the data, and thereby determine how selection of a linguistic structure is influenced by specific configurations of factors that characterize the environment in which it occurs. In this way it is possible to ascertain which features of the (social and linguistic) context favor or disfavor the occurrence of a form when all are considered simultaneously, and how strongly. The use of this methodology has succeeded in overcoming many of the analytical difficulties associated with intuitive judgments and anecdotal reporting used in other paradigms. This is particularly crucial in the study of bilingual and/or minority language situations, where normative pressures inhibit the use of vernacular or non-standard forms, and where 'categorical perception' on the part of the linguist/observer tends to inflate the importance of a form which may have in fact only occurred on a few occasions. In what follows we illustrate how these considerations may be applied to the bilingual context.

3.0. Concepts in Language Contact

Our own program of research on language contact involves the study of the linguistic processes by which forms from two or more languages may be combined as a result of their common use, the linguistic constraints on such combination, and its consequences for the structure of the languages involved. We have also sought to ascertain the social meaning of language choice as exemplified by speaker 1) behavior, 2) attitudes, and 3) perceptions.

We begin by defining our terms. We follow Weinreich (1968:1) in designating the individual as the locus of language contact, with the proviso that that individual be a bona-fide member of a bilingual speech community. Again following Weinreich (ibid.), we define *bilingualism* as the practice of alternately *using* (emphasis ours) two or more languages, and the individuals involved as *bilingual*. The usage requirement ensures that both languages are regularly accessed in normal interaction, and in the stable bilingual communities we have studied, speakers typically make use of both languages with the same interlocutors, in the same domains, and within the same conversational topic. Our focus on *intra-situational* language combination is at least partially motivated by the goal of obtaining data permitting the establishment of linguistic, in addition to other, constraints on its occurrence; situational language switching (as described by Gumperz 1982) may consist entirely of (monolingual) stretches of speech in one language followed by (monolingual) stretches in another, and thus provide no locus to observe the processes of combination which interest us.

Our studies have focused on adult bilinguals whose language repertoire is 'stable' in the sense that neither language acquisition nor attrition is involved in the contact situation, although each of the relevant languages will, of course, continue to manifest internal variability. This focus is not imposed by any theoretical dictate, but simply by the goal of describing the linguistic concomitants of *regular* interaction in two or more languages, to which the more labile behaviors of language learners or losers may ultimately be compared. Our emphasis on stable bilingual communities, as opposed on the one hand to communities undergoing language shift (e.g. Mougeon and Beniak 1991) or language death (e.g. Dorian 1981, 1989), and on the other, isolated individuals who happen to know two or more languages, but who are not (necessarily) constrained by group norms of usage (e.g. Woolford 1983, di Sciullo et al. 1986), is similarly intended to establish a baseline for *conventional* bilingual interaction against which other, perhaps idiosyncratic, behavior may be assessed.

The characterization of *bilingual* provided above imposes no *a priori* requirement as to degree of language proficiency required to be so classified (see e.g. Baetens Beardsmore 1982 on the difficulties inherent in such an assessment), and our studies have involved speakers of varying bilingual abilities when such individuals have been ascertained to represent core members of the bilingual speech community. Though level of bilingualism has not constituted a criterion for inclusion in or exclusion from our speaker samples, we regard the speaker's bilingual ability as a key explanatory factor of his actual linguistic performance. We thus take account of this factor by including it as an 'independent variable' in linguistic analyses of bilingual phenomena, as described in section (5.2.1) below.

Sustained contact between two languages may manifest itself linguistically in one or more of the following ways: code-switching, lexical borrowing on the community and individual levels, incomplete L_2 acquisition, interference, grammatical convergence, stylistic reduction, language death. Our understanding of these concepts has basically been informed by the classical and current literature in the field of language contact. Empirical quantitative analysis, however, requires us to operationalize these concepts such that they refer to mutually exclusive phenomena. Observation of their actual manifestations in discourse reveals that along with unambiguous instances of each, there exist other examples whose surface form does not permit ready classification as one or another result of language contact. We return to this issue below. The working definitions provided in what follows are based on unambiguous manifestations of these phenomena.[3]

Code-switching is the *juxtaposition* of sentences or sentence fragments, each of which is internally consistent with the morphological and syntactic (and optionally, phonological) rules of the language of its provenance. Code-switching may occur at various levels of linguistic structure (e.g. *sentential, intrasentential, tag*) and it may be *flagged* or *smooth*. Intrasentential switching may occur at *equivalence sites* (where permissible switch points are constrained by word order homologies between switched constituents), or, more rarely, consist of *constituent insertion* (where word-order constraints *across* switch boundaries need not be respected for eligible constituents). The internal structure of the constituent is determined by the grammar of one language, but its collocation in the sentence is determined by the grammar of the recipient language.

Borrowing is the *adaptation* of lexical material to the morphological and syntactic (and usually, phonological) patterns of the recipient language. We distinguish established *loanwords* (which typically show full linguistic integration, native-language synonym displacement, and widespread diffusion, even among recipient-language monolinguals) from *nonce borrowings* (which though identical to loanwords in linguistic manifestation, need not satisfy the diffusion requirement). Loanwords generally are indistinguishable from native-language material at all but the purely etymological level, fail to be recognized by speakers as being of foreign origin, and do not involve active *borrowing* per se in any but the historical sense, as they are transmitted naturally along with the remainder of the monolingual lexicon. Though nonce borrowings show the same patterns of morphological and syntactic integration as established loanwords (in contrast with code-switches, which remain *unintegrated*), they do require active access to the L_2 lexicon, and in this sense they resemble code-switches.

Convergence also involves the process of borrowing, although we reserve this term for the transfer of grammatical structure (e.g. plural marking, agreement rules, etc.) from one language to another. Unlike lexical borrowing, it does not involve *adaptation* of other-language material to recipient-language grammar, but consists rather of the *introduction* of (unadapted) other-language patterns into the recipient-language system. Also in contrast to lexical borrowing, which generally features an etymologically foreign form, convergence may involve no *visible* other-language material (as in e.g. the transfer of a word order). In fact, convergence need not involve any transfer at all: it may simply consist of the selection and favoring of one of two (or more) already existing native-language forms which coincides with a counterpart in the contact language (e.g. Klein 1980). (Other types of borrowing which do not involve surface indications of other- language material include *calquing* (e.g. Sp. *rascacielos* based on Eng. *skyscraper*) and *semantic shift* (e.g. Fr. *librairie* based on Eng. *library*)).

Though we have not actively focused on these in our research, we see *incomplete* L_2 *acquisition* as a (possibly fossilized) state of the language acquired through formal means and not used for normal interactional purposes, and *interference*, as the unpatterned, *idiosyncratic* manifestation of any of the above-mentioned language contact phenomena.

Stylistic reduction is the narrowing of the stylistic repertoire available to the individual, which may or may not be accompanied by concomitant expansion via incorporation of stylistic options from the other language. Stylistic reduction may also affect every level of linguistic structure available for style shifting, and may manifest itself as 1) undue preference for only one of several available variants of a variable, thereby obviating the choice mechanism and depriving that variable of its stylistic connotations (e.g. Lavandera 1978), or 2) continued use of all of the options, but failure to *distribute* them appropriately according to style (e.g. Gal 1984), or 3) preference for one or another member of a stylistically marked lexical doublet without reference to contextual appropriateness (Miller and Poplack, forthcoming). *Language death* is the gradual diminution of domains seen as appropriate to the use of L_2 until such time as none remain, and at different stages of this process, may or may not be accompanied by linguistic change due to contact (e.g. Dorian 1981).

Because code-switching, borrowing, incomplete language acquisition, and interference may result in utterances containing elements of two languages, each of these bilingual behaviors has at one time or another been used as evidence about another. And because convergence, stylistic reduction, and language death need involve no overt elements of the other language, they may remain undetected by any but the most systematic examination, except in cases where the resulting structure is clearly ungrammatical by the standards of one of the two contact languages. (e.g. Fr. *Je suis 14 ans* 'I am 14 years old'; as opposed to J'*ai 14 ans*, lit. 'I have 14 years'.). Long-term examination of these issues has led us to conclude that each of these mechanisms for combining material from two grammars within a single utterance results from different processes and is governed by different constraints (see also, e.g., Grosjean 1990). This observation is generally uncontroversial when it comes to unambiguous manifestations of these processes. The problem is that it is often difficult to infer synchronically which mechanism has produced a given utterance. As in the case of (monolingual) syntactic ambiguity, this is because different processes can result in the same surface string. Given present knowledge, it does not seem possible to identify *a priori* every token on a case-by-case basis. In section (5.3) below, we illustrate how variationist methodology, when applied systematically to corpora of bilingual discourse, with special attention to cases where the different mechanisms have *different* manifestations, can contribute to the resolution of this problem.

In ensuing sections we briefly address four of the methodological and analytical tenets associated with the variationist framework, insofar as they can be applied to issues in language contact. These are: 1) the use of appropriate data, 2) the selection of informants to ensure representativeness and the knowledge of what they represent, 3) the principle of accountable reporting, and perhaps most important of all, 4) circumscription of the variable context, or defining the object of study.

4.0. Methods

4.1. Appropriate data and collection procedures

The notion of appropriate data gained importance in variation studies when it became apparent that styles of speech other than the vernacular are often characterized by unsystematic hypercorrection *away* from the speaker's native speech patterns. Thus (monolingual) speakers may not only fail to produce underlying segments in contexts in which they are expected, but when attending to their speech they may also re-insert them non-etymologically (cf. Eng. *tuna-r-on toast*, Fr. *huit-z-autres* 'eight others,' Sp. *un sojo* 'an eye'). This behavior is particularly frequent when the variable involved is stigmatized, as the manifestations of language contact have been reported to be in most communities. We are not aware of reports of 'hypercorrect' bilingual behavior per se; what does seem to be the case is that in formal or awkward or other speech styles perceived to be inappropriate, those manifestations subject to conscious control tend to be avoided altogether. As an example, Table 1 shows that in the speech of one Puerto Rican informant, code-switching occurs at least four times as often in informal or vernacular speech situations, providing the interlocutor is also an ingroup member, as opposed to simply a fluent bilingual.

Speech Style	Number of code-switches	Number of conversation minutes	Average number of code-switches per minute
Formal (ingroup)	87	90	1
Informal (nongroup)	107	120	1
Informal (ingroup)	152	30	5
Vernacular (ingroup)	54	15	4
N = 400			

Table 1: Average number of code-switches per minute by speech style and group membership (after Poplack 1981)

When the interlocutor does not enable code-switching, for example by fulfilling the conditions of group membership and/or succeeding in establishing an interaction perceived to be appropriate for it, not only does it occur infrequently, but (in this particular case, though not shown in Table 1) the incorporations from English are largely restricted to nouns, and ethnically-loaded or untranslatable nouns at that (Poplack 1981), which are ambiguous as to their status as 'true' code-switches. So while the vernacular/ingroup data show a full gamut of intrasentential, intersentential and tag switching, English incorporations collected by the outgroup member (the author) were extremely limited.

Restricting the object of study to the 'vernacular' has not proved to exclude potentially important data associated solely with other speech styles. For one thing, certain bilingual behaviors (including code-switching, and to an extent, borrowing (Poplack, Sankoff & Miller 1988)) are themselves *hallmarks* of vernacular style. For another, and this has also been our experience with monolingual linguistic variables (with the possible exception of purely lexical ones), the data comprising the bulk of the other styles is *included* in the vernacular materials, while the reverse is not the case (e.g. here, informal styles include some noun incorporations, but formal styles show little or no intrasentential switching).

Perhaps the richest, most copious data on code-switching it has been our privilege to work with were the Puerto Rican Spanish/English materials collected by Pedro Pedraza in the course of nearly seven years of participant observation of a single block in East Harlem, New York. The sheer volume and quality of the data he obtained enabled us not only to detect many instances of rare switch types previously thought to be non-existent or not permissible (e.g. between pronominal subject and verb, between auxiliary and verb, switches of lone determiners, etc. (Poplack 1980, 1981)), but also enabled us to discover that even within a single well-circumscribed community, different *patterns* of code-switching could coexist, differentially employed by different groups of speakers. Since very few of us are permitted the luxury of investing several years in data gathering, we continue to experiment with ways of approximating that situation.

A basic methodological requirement of our studies of bilingual, minority and/or stigmatized language situations is that the raw data be collected by skilled interviewers who not only are, but are also perceived by informants to be, ingroup members, and whose own linguistic repertoires feature the same phenomena we are attempting to elicit. In our experience only interviewers with these characteristics are consistently capable of creating the appropriate interactional conditions to enable linguistic manifestations of language contact that are subject to conscious control.

The elicitation techniques employed within the interview setting do not take the form of direct questioning about the bilingual behavior in question, but are rather adaptations of the 'sociolinguistic interview' (e.g. Labov 1966, 1984; Labov et al. 1968, Sankoff & Sankoff 1973, Wolfram & Fasold 1974, Poplack 1979, 1989; Baugh 1979): a loosely structured set of topics preselected by the interviewer to mirror current, local and/or individual interests, minimally including childhood games, customs, folklore, recipes and narratives of personal experience. The interviewer is instructed to follow the informant's lead in topic shifting, and only introduces a topic when none appears forthcoming from the informant. The content of each interview will thus vary from informant to informant, but we find that a common core of subject matter generally recurs. Where information is required concerning language attitudes (questions which are by nature more formal), these may be asked at the end of the interview, or at a posterior meeting. The entire conversation is tape-recorded (with the permission of the informant), and constitutes the raw data for all subsequent analyses. As will be obvious from the description of our collection procedures, these interviews contain, in addition to (varying amounts of) data on the language contact phenomena of interest, ample attestation of at least one, if not both, of the (monolingual) codes in contact. In fact, it has been our experience that most bilingual phenomena are as a rule extremely sparse in running discourse (e.g. in our French/English materials, code-switches occur anywhere from not at all to 132 times in an interview, loanwords represent between 0.1% and 2.5% of the total lexicon employed by an individual, unambiguous cases of convergence are exceedingly rare, etc.). It is thus our policy to collect as *much* data as possible (sometimes up to five hours per informant), in the hopes of obtaining a sufficient number of spontaneous attestations of these rare phenomena.

The purely monolingual portions of the interview are also fundamental to the inquiry, as they play a crucial role in establishing whether a given feature is appropriately analyzed as resulting from contact. The codes entering into the contact situation may themselves show regional or non-standard features not found in normative varieties, which may or may not result from prior interlinguistic influence. For example, we would be obliged to consider a borrowed form like *afforder* rendered with a retroflex [ɹ] as failing to show phonological integration into French, if we were not aware that the retroflex variant had already penetrated the Canadian French phonological system, where it presently co-varies with apical [r] and velar [ʁ], even in French-origin words, and among French monolinguals. Though the retroflex variant may well be due to contact in the *historical* sense, considering it on a par with *synchronic* manifestations is tantamount to classing the voiced palatal fricative realization [ʒ] of ***garage*** in the speech of a contemporary French/English bilingual as due to influence from French. Admittedly, this is its ultimate source, but not within the lifetime of the speaker.

Communities may also evolve innovative compromise solutions to the problem of reconciling two languages, with no apparent counterpart in either of the monolingual codes. This is the case of double stress assignment to bisyllabic nonce loans in Canadian French: main word stress is assigned according to English rules, shifting stress to the left, while syllable stress is assigned according to French (e.g. *quíèt*). On the one hand, this pattern forms part of the stereotypical 'French Canadian accent' in monolingual English discourse, and so could be considered due to English influence, but on the other, its use in French discourse appears to be restricted to flagging nonce borrowings.[4] These kinds of facts are crucial for the decisions the linguist ultimately makes regarding the identification of a given phenomenon as resulting from language contact.

4.2. Selection of informants

We have been referring to ingroup and outgroup members, implying the existence of some entity one can be a member of, which in turn leads to the question of the optimal informants for a variationist study of language contact phenomena. It is uncontroversial that any speaker with any degree of knowledge of more than one language is theoretically capable of combining them in any way she chooses. There have been ample reports in the literature, usually in the guise of counter-examples to proposed constraints, of the learned use of foreign words and expressions, cross-language punning and other bilingual word-play observed among academics, family or friends. The variationist seeks to determine the actual *role* of such phenomena in the bilingual repertoire. A key component of the variationist research program (in monolingual as well as bilingual discourse) is to distinguish the isolated, and perhaps idiosyncratic, token from the regular patterns that characterize natural exchanges in the speech community.

It has been observed repeatedly that membership in a social network imposes clear restrictions on the behavior of members (e.g. Labov et al. 1968, Milroy 1980). Our studies of language contact phenomena within this framework have shown that such restrictions are not directly predictable from the typological relationship or other purely linguistic features of the languages in contact, and are often stronger than these would warrant. To cite but one example, in the Puerto Rican community in Harlem, code-switching is copious, transitions between languages are smooth, and it occurs at all possible switch boundaries, of which there are many, given the typological similarities between the languages. Moreover, no special rhetorical effect appears to be accomplished on the *local* level, i.e. by the *individual* switch (Poplack 1980, 1981, Sankoff & Poplack 1981). The situation differs markedly in the French/English bilingual communities in the Ottawa-Hull region of Canada. Here only a very small proportion of the code-switching is genuinely intrasentential. Instead of juxtaposing the two languages smoothly, Ottawa-Hull francophones draw attention to, or 'flag,' their switches, by different discourse devices: metalinguistic commentary, English bracketing, repetition or translation. In fact, just about every switch serves a rhetorical purpose, and to accomplish this purpose it must be flagged, and should not pass unnoticed (Poplack 1985). These differences cannot be ascribed to the linguistic configuration of the contact language pairs, since they are typologically very similar. For reasons detailed elsewhere (ibid.), we conclude that the different code-switching patterns stem from differences in community norms, which must be empirically established on a case-by-case basis.

Much of our work (as indeed, much of the sociolinguistic work in the field of language contact more generally) has been based on small-group studies, using standard social network methodology. As has been described by Milroy (1980, cf. also Poplack 1989), there is a major trade-off between the depth afforded by participant observation and the scope available from 'survey'-type studies (Labov 1966, Sankoff & Sankoff 1973), where potentially explanatory extralinguistic variables (e.g. age, sex, socioeconomic class, educational level, etc.) may be manipulated in ways not possible in the study of self-selected peer groups. In particular, a recurrent criticism of network studies concerns their possible lack of representativeness. In 1982, we began to confront this problem by supplementing our ethnographically-oriented studies of bilingual behavior with a large-scale study of bilingualism in the adjoining cities of (officially anglophone) Ottawa and (officially francophone) Hull, which together constitute the national capital region of Canada (Poplack 1989)[5]. One hundred and twenty francophone informants were selected using strict random sampling procedures and stratified according to age, sex, and minority vs. majority language status of the French language in their neighborhood of residence. Random sampling ensures that informants meeting predetermined quotas are fully representative of the (francophone) population of the region. Each sample member is also identified according to socioeconomic status, educational attainment, level of bilingual ability, and neighborhood of residence, and each of these factors is regularly incorporated as an independent variable into studies of her linguistic behavior. The inclusion of such factors in our linguistic analyses has enabled us to uncover sometimes unexpected extra-linguistic constraints on bilingual behavior which we could not have intuited, such as the finding that membership in the speech community is more important than bilingual ability in determining borrowing rates (Poplack 1988), or the social class constraint against established loanwords (Poplack, Sankoff & Miller 1988).

5.0. Data Manipulation

5.1. Transcription and handling of primary speech data

The raw data on which all our studies are based consist of tape-recorded naturalistic conversations containing (some) bilingual phenomena which will vary in type and degree according to the individual informant. The tape-recordings are typically searched exhaustively for a given feature (e.g. loanwords) and *all* instances of that feature are extracted for future analysis, in keeping with variationist analytical methods to be described in more detail in section (5.3). This procedure is then repeated for each subsequent feature under study.

Because the sheer size of the French/English corpus (approximately 3.5 million words) precludes repeated exhaustive searches, we resolved to transform these data into machine-readable form. This involved transcribing, correcting and entering the entire corpus onto computer, an undertaking which took several research assistants approximately three years of full-time work to complete. Space does not permit full explanation of the transcription protocol (see Poplack 1989); suffice it to say here that there is a major conflict between level of transcription detail and subsequent accessibility of the data, and the first crucial decision the analyst/transcriber must make concerns where the materials will be located on the continuum between them. In our French-Canadian data, for example, the word *père* is variously realized with a lowered, raised, or diphthongized [ɛ], and with a velar, apical or deleted [r]: [p ɛʁ], [pa^{I}r], [per], [pe ʁ], [pe], etc. Similarly, the loanword *high-rise* was produced as follows: [a: ɹáiz], [ai ráiz], [hái ɹ aiz], etc. Since each of these variant realizations may have different social meaning in the community, we initially wished to distinguish them in our transcription.

But accounting orthographically for numerous phonetic realizations of a single lexical item means that in a study involving just one of these words, its occurrences would have to be located under six or seven separate entries. When this is multiplied by the 17,000 or so lexical types occurring in the corpus, the number of sites which must be searched to extract lexically identical forms becomes unmanageable. To facilitate the automated treatment of the data and maximize accessibility we thus adopted a solution of standard orthography for our transcriptions while still preserving much of the pertinent variability. Our overall strategy was to represent variation resulting from the operation of phonetic or phonological processes in standard orthography, regardless of the actual pronunciation of the form (i.e. all of the realizations listed above were transcribed as *'père,' 'high-rise'*). If, on the other hand, the variant realization affected an entire morpheme (e.g. the variable deletion of [l] in *l'église*, as in (1), these were represented as produced.

(1) Puis j'étais mariée à (Ø< [l]) église catholique puis toute. (091/1147)[6]
'And I was married at the Catholic church and all.'

This transcription protocol extends to English interventions in the text: these are also transcribed according to standard English orthography, even if there is a current French alternative. Dialect orthographies like *bines* 'beans,' *filer* 'to feel' are represented by us as '*beans*,' '*feeler*' in the interest of better accessibility and reduction of homography. Because this is a bilingual corpus, we of course wished to flag interventions from English for purposes of automatic recognition. We initially attempted to distinguish unambiguous code-switches, unambiguous loanwords and intermediate forms. For tagging purposes, a code-switch was provisionally defined as any sequence of two or more English words, other than compound nouns (e.g. *science-fiction*, *real-estate*, *baby-sitter*), whose status must be established using other criteria, and proper nouns (e.g. *Born-again*, *Women's Lib*). Other lone lexical items of English origin known to be widely used in the region were considered for these purposes to be loanwords. Words whose status is doubtful (e.g. single French words calqued on English forms, such as *insulation*, *capabilité*, *déshonnête*, *dépressé*), or nonce loans (e.g. *patroller, expropriétait)* were to be classed in an intermediate category.

Perhaps not surprisingly in retrospect, the tagging procedure failed for all but the unambiguous code-switches. Since the transcribers were (of necessity) native speakers of the dialect(s) under study, it quickly became apparent that in most cases they were incapable of identifying many loanwords as etymologically English. As they were themselves accustomed to designating *sewer* as *sour* [suʁ], and *beans* as *bines* [bIn], etc., they had no reason to consider them less 'French' than other *canadianismes* like *char* 'car' (an example which, in contrast, was (erroneously) classed as borrowed). Moreover, with few exceptions, there was no way for the transcribers to determine which potential loanwords were in fact widespread, before having transcribed a few dozen of them. Since months could elapse between two encounters with the same loanword, and since it was not feasible during the transcription phase to keep counts of each of the 20,000 occurrences of borrowed forms (while at the same time applying other aspects of a detailed transcription protocol to thousands of other items), we were forced for the sake of consistency to leave borrowed items unmarked. So while we do in fact have statistics on the frequency and level of diffusion of every borrowed form in the corpus (Poplack, Sankoff & Miller 1988), these were only obtained after first extracting them *manually* by reading through the entire 3.5 million word document.

A number of automated data handling programs were run on the interview files, in particular, the Oxford Concordance Program (Hockey & Marriott 1980). Figures 1 and 2, reproductions of entries in the Ottawa-Hull French Concordance, illustrate the organization of the data in alphabetical order by lexical type, along with the total number of occurrences of each type (or keyword), followed by every instance of its occurrence in the corpus. Each occurrence is preceded and followed by its immediate discourse context and accompanied by an address (speaker number and line number in the complete transcript of his individual interview) to facilitate retrieval of additional contextual information when necessary. The frames presented illustrate, among other things, the occurrence of the noun *pad* and the verb *pack* in the guise of a borrowing (*elle voulait avoir un* ***pad*** 'She wanted to have a pad' (063/1853); *... rien dans une couple de rangées faut tu* ***packes*** '... you only have to pack in a few rows' (14/354)) and as part of an unambiguous code-switch (*you took my writing* ***pad*** (013/623); *Faut tu* ***pack*** *your own au Basics* 'You have to pack your own at Basics.' (014/356)).

Speaker #	Line #	Left context	Keyword	Right context
		KEYWORD →	pack 2	← N OCCURRENCES
014	355	(F) les affaires de même là? C' est, tu (A)	pack	your own (F) puis à Basics je le sais pas s' il
014	356	s' il faut tu ... Je pense que oui. Faut tu (A)	pack	your own (F) au Basics, oui. Ça va plus vite
		CS FLAG →	packboy 1	← CS FLAG
075	148	ils en ont une job. Quand même ça serait pa--	packboy	oubedonc livraison, ils- va- va dans les
			pack-boys 2	
SPEAKER # → 014	351 ← LINE # ON TRANSCRIPT	occupé là, bien il y a des fois qu' ils ont des	pack-boys	mais ... quand-qu' il y a pas assez de pack-boys
014	352	pack-boys mais ... quand-qu' il y a pas assez de	pack-boys	tu sais ... (1) Ça doit être long, je sais pas
			packe 1	
005	2197	des Anglais, on a un chauffeur puis le gars qui	packe	les tubs, puis toute le restant c' est toute
			packer 3	
007	1156	de besoin. (007) Vois-tu moi j' étais (A)	packer	and helper (F) moi dans le temps du- de l' armée
007	1168	toute la (068) place. Tu sais, tu appelais ça (A)	packer	and helper (F) dans le temps. (inc) du
031	3482	(031) Ah, j' étais ... Comment-ce tu appelles (A)	packer.	(2) Ouais? Puis ensuite de deça? C' est là vous
			Packers 2	
081	924	un peu d' argent. Quand mon père travaillait à	Packers	là, on- on vivait bien. (2) Mhm. (1) Mhm. (081)
081	926	je pense, trente-quatre. (1) Mhm. (081) ... À	Packers,	tu sais, sontaient maudits dans ce temps là
			packes 2	
014	350	pas au ... Loblaw' s là, non. Non, faut tu ...	packes	ton- tu sais quand c' est bien occupé là, bien il
014	354	est rien dans une (W) couple de rangées faut tu	packes. ← LOANWORD (UNMARKED)	Comme si les (A) express, (F) les affaires de
			packetait 2	
105	1761	buggy, ça brassait un peu. On appelait ça- ça se	packetait	hein tu sais, on- on disait que ça packetait, ça
105	1761	se packetait hein tu sais, on- on disait que ça	packetait,	ça descendait de deça des fois. Puis le monde

Figure 1. Ottawa-Hull French concordance for 'pack' (Poplack 1989)

		CS FLAG →		
			pad 7	
013	623	(013) Okay. ... (inc). (A) You took my writing	pad,	eh? You took everything, eh? (6) (inc) le
063	1853	commencé ses périodes. Puis elle voulait avoir un	pad.	Nous-autres c' est un pad. (1) Ouais. (063) Elle
063	1853	elle voulait avoir un pad. Nous-autres c' est un	pad.	(1) Ouais. (063) Elle demande pour un pad là-bas
063	1854	est un pad. (1) Ouais. (063) Elle demande pour un	pad	là-bas, un pad là-bas c' est un affaire pour
063	1854	Ouais. (063) Elle demande pour un pad là bas, un	pad	là-bas c' est un affaire pour écrire dessus. (1)
068	1690	me promenais sur la grande-rue puis icitte avec un	pad	tu sais là. Ah sainte! C' était tannant. Quand j'
068	1694	tu es Eulalie aujourd'hui? Je leur montrais mon	pad,	tu sais? Bon bien ils me flippaient la page puis
		LOANWORD (UNMARKED) ↗		
			padé 1	
080	158	jusqu' aller en-arrière du cou icitte là, toute	padé	(inc) là. (1) Oui. (080) Ça d' épais, je vous
				← INTERVIEWER
			PADI 1	
099	456	à cinquante longueurs de n-- natation tandis que	PADI,	ça c' est un association internationale
			Padre 1	
056	869	(2) Ah ouais, ouais. (056) Dans le camp. Puis le	Padre,	c'est lui qui était comme interp-- interprète
			Padre-Foot 2	
056	858	là, de (A) German storm troopers? (F) Un nommé	Padre-Foot,	lui il a gagné la (A) Victoria Cross, (F) la
056	865	(1) Ah. (056) Ah oui, (A) fighting-Padre.	Padre-Foot.	Foot. (2) Puis vous l'avez rencontré là-bas
			pads 4	SPEAKER # →
008	813	pour jouer au hockey pour- on s' usait- pour des	pads.	(2) Ty-vrai? (1) Ah oui? (008) Ouais, on mettait
054	652	se mettait des- des livres de téléphone pour les	pads.	(1) Hein? (054) Des gros livres de téléphone
080	156	là, c' était toutes des- c' était toutes des	pads	ça d' épais, tu sais en ouate là ... (1) Oui
105	731	catalogues de chez Eaton' s puis on faisait des	pads	pour le goaler. (rire). (2) Ah mon-Dieu ça se
			Paf 2	
033	119	puis Holland. Puis ils ont fermé la porte.	Paf!	(2) Puis ça- a ty été là votre dernière job
091	1758	a frappé avec sa main, ça se peut puis ça a fait	paf!	Il m' a pas maganée puis il m' a pas sauté sur

Figure 2: Ottawa-Hull French concordance for 'pad' (Poplack 1989)

5.2. Secondary or reported data

Other types of data which are crucially important to the interpretation of bilingual speech production include information on speaker 1) characteristics, 2) attitudes and 3) perceptions.

5.2.l. Sociodemographic speaker characteristics. In the course of the 'sociolinguistic interview' described above, an attempt is made to obtain as much information as possible on the sociolinguistic background of each speaker. This typically includes a detailed account of the speaker's residential, educational, employment and linguistic history, as well as purely demographic information. On the basis of these and other data culled from the interviews, each speaker in the Ottawa-Hull sample was assigned a score on an English Proficiency Index (interpretable as a rough measure of level of bilingualism, since all of the informants have native abilities in French). The index is based on a combination of differentially weighted factors correlated with proficiency, including number of years of English-medium instruction, self-reports of English competence and propensity to use English according to situation, domain and interlocutor. All of this information is distilled into a 'sociolinguistic profile' for each speaker, which can be used as an independent variable in the explanation of his linguistic behavior.

5.2.2. Language attitudes. As part of our study of the New York Puerto Rican community, a detailed language attitude questionnaire (consisting of some 200 questions) based on standard social psychological methods was administered to each informant (Attinasi 1979). In reviewing the responses to these questions, some of which were self-contradictory, and others, ill-understood, it became apparent that by administering a questionnaire, the researcher not only predefines the possible attitudes that can be elicited (for closed questionnaires), but also the particular areas in which the respondent is permitted to express them (even in response to open-ended questions). Moreover, the very act of asking questions is likely to provoke some answer, regardless of whether the response reflects an idea that would even have occurred to the respondent if the interview had not taken place. In an attempt to alleviate this problem in subsequent research, we exploited the fact that our French interviews were very long, and though generally not conducted in a question-answer format, tended to cover a number of topics related to the overall theme of francophone life in a bilingual setting.

From the conversations constituting the Ottawa-Hull corpus, we systematically extracted every overt remark that could be construed as reflecting an attitude about linguistic or ethnic matters, and proceeded, by content analysis, to exhaustively compare and group similar attitudes (Poplack & Miller 1985). We imposed no predetermined analytical or classificatory grid on them, but rather classed contrasting comments as a set of responses to some 'virtual' question. Over 100 such 'questions' emerged, many of them reminiscent of those familiar in traditional language attitude studies (e.g. Who speaks 'good' French? What do you think of two francophones who communicate in English?, etc.). Although not all informants provide a response to each, and some provide more than one, this method has the obvious advantages of not only revealing issues which are important to the informants, but of characterizing them in their own terms. Along with standard presentation of proportions of different answers to each question, we could also report what proportion of the respondents actually *brought up* the particular topic. This gives us access not only to opinions, but to the degree to which these opinions represent a real preoccupation of the bilingual informants in our sample. We were thus able to determine that though both minority and majority francophones manifest the same overt signs of linguistic insecurity (attitudes which are in fact pan-Canadian among the francophone populace), speakers residing in neighborhoods where French is the official and majority language reveal by their reported behavior and their preoccupations a covert linguistic *security* not shared by their minority counterparts, which is likely ascribable to the status of their language. Moreover, independent studies of the actual behavior of these groups show that these subtle attitudinal differences have identifiable linguistic correlates (Poplack 1988).

5.2.3. Speaker perceptions. Our linguistic analyses of the behavior of nonce borrowings and established loanwords have led us to consider them as two (quantitatively different but qualitatively parallel) manifestations of the same phenomenon, as distinct from code-switching. But the psychological validity of this analytical decision for the bilingual speaker remained uncharted. We thus proposed to evaluate listeners' subjective reactions to different configurations of borrowed words (Poplack, Clément, Miller, Purcell & Trudel-Maggiore 1988). Adopting the matched guise procedure, we constructed a test tape consisting of sixteen stimuli, each containing a single English-origin form corresponding to one combination of the linguistic factors revealed to be significant in our earlier studies of loanword usage: 1) level of phonological integration (integrated or non-integrated), 2) level of morphological integration (integrated or non-integrated), and 3) levels of 'lexical' integration, here defined in terms of date of attestation of the word in French-language dictionaries and of its current diffusion across the community, as determined by the actual frequency of the word in the Ottawa-Hull French corpus. The instrument was administered to local native francophones, along with a questionnaire testing the identification, translatability and acceptability of borrowed words in different configurations of linguistic and social characteristics.

Subjective reactions to stigmatized linguistic variants are notoriously unreliable as predictors of actual usage. This problem is compounded in the case of incorporations from one language into another, as it may be impossible to determine whether eventual rejection is structural (i.e. refers to the manner in which the constituent is incorporated into the language), lexical (i.e. refers to the fact that the constituent does not form part of the lexicon of the judges' linguistic variety), or contextual (i.e. refers to the fact that the incorporation may be inappropriate to the type of interaction instantiated by the stimulus utterance). We therefore sought to reduce as far as possible the artificiality and contextual inappropriateness often associated by subjects with the simulation of stimuli by actors. To do this, we used as a source for our stimulus data actual utterances extracted from the Ottawa-Hull French corpus. Samples of the stimuli are provided in (2).

(2a) Stimulus 1: *boys* [bɔ:Iz]
[-phonologically integrated] [-morphologically integrated] [attested before 1900] [widespread]

Pis l'homme qui sort avec les *boys* pis qui va à taverne pis qui rentre très tard, je trouve que tu retrouves ça ici. (026/882)

'And the man who goes out with the boys and who goes to the tavern and who comes home really late, I find that you find that here.'

(2b) Stimulus 3: *patroller* [patro:ˈle]
[+phonologically integrated] [+morphologically integrated] [unattested] [nonce]

Pis euh, fait que je peux pas voir pourquoi payer des gros salaires à ces policiers là, qui ont juste un mille carré à *patroller* là, tu sais? (019/1650)

'And uh, so I can't see why we should pay big salaries to those police officers, who have just one square mile to patrol, you know?'

The results of our study confirm and extend our earlier conclusions based on actual speaker behavior when using borrowed forms. A first important finding concerns the fact that subjects are often incapable of isolating an English-origin word in an otherwise French sentence if they have not been previously cued as to its existence, and this, regardless of the linguistic configuration of the word. Loanword identification appears to proceed as a lexical look-up operation. As might be expected, words categorized as forming an integral part of the French lexicon, i.e. those of long attestation and/or widespread diffusion, are identified as borrowed less frequently than unattested nonce borrowings. It is of interest, however, that the latter are still isolated less often than their widespread but unattested counterparts.

The linguistic configuration of the word assumes its role not for identification of the loanword, but for evaluation of the excerpt containing it. Speakers consistently rate borrowed forms more positively when they are integrated into French phonologically and morphologically, and this is true for each of the measures of acquiescence, affect, and surprisingly, normativeness. This pattern is as true of loanwords attested in French-language dictionaries since the turn of the century as of unattested nonce borrowings, lending further support to our decision to treat them together.

5.3. Data analysis

The discovery of linguistic patterns that hold for every speaker and every context is just as accessible to the intuitions of the variationist as to any other linguist. The difference arises when we deal with large quantities of natural speech data. There are correlations and variability from speaker to speaker and context to context that the variationist wants to account for that are less accessible to intuitions, and in fact, can only be clearly detected through quantitative analysis. These difficulties are exacerbated in the case of bilingual performance. For example, grammatical convergence which does *not* give rise to utterances which, when considered individually, are ungrammatical in the recipient language, but only to *preference* for an already existing structure with a counterpart in L_2, is a phenomenon which by nature eludes impressionistic observation. Similarly, there seems to be no self-evident way to intuit what it is that people are doing when they engage in intrasentential code-switching, by nature an aberration in terms of monolingual grammar. There are various strategies a speaker can adopt to minimize the clash between L_1 and L_2 phonologies, morphologies and syntax, and quantitative analysis can reveal which predominates in a given (social and linguistic) context.

Variationist linguistics (like other sciences of social behavior) cannot provide an immutable law for all eventualities. Linguists accustomed to observing natural interactions hear infelicitous or ungrammatical constructions produced by monolinguals on a regular basis. It is thus not surprising that the same holds true for bilinguals. Quantitative analysis seeks to reveal the actual role (or the proportion) of initially questionable utterances within the larger system, i.e. whether they are idiosyncratic, or what some would call performance errors, or community norms. It can also shed light on the features of the environment which condition the choice of a particular structure.

5.3.1. The principle of accountable reporting. Two analytical principles underlying a quantitative variationist analysis are relevant to the study of language contact phenomena. The first is the principle of *accountable reporting* (Labov 1966). This requires not only that *all* the relevant examples of a phenomenon in some data set be incorporated into the analysis, but also, all of the contexts in which it *could have* appeared, but didn't. The sum total of occurrences and non-occurrences of variant realizations in a given context together constitute the *linguistic variable*, the key construct underlying variationist sociolinguistics. Thus, in studying variability in copula expression, for example, the variationist's data base will be constituted not only of all examples in which the copula was absent (3a), but also of those in which it surfaced ((3b) and (3c)):

(3a) If anybody (**ø**) in the way, well they'll mash him up. (4/275)
(3b) She**'s** older than this boy. (3/211)
(3c) His name **is** Son and his title **is** Nunez. (2/198)

The most immediate application of this principle to the bilingual context is in the determination of the *impact* of the various contact processes on the recipient language grammar. Language contact is (implicitly or explicitly) linked with linguistic change, but change is not brought about by a single deviant utterance. Processes like convergence and loanword incorporation are by nature quantitative. To assess the true role of a presumed change in the grammar of the *language*, it is necessary to count systematically the proportion of its occurrence, the contexts it has affected, and the speakers to whom it has spread.

The principle of accountable reporting poses special problems for bilingual data. In variable rule terminology, the examples in (3b) and (3c) are known as 'non-applications' (of the copula deletion[7] 'rule'). But for at least some manifestations of language contact, no non-applications may be observed or inferred. In examining the claim (Klein 1980) that the Puerto Rican Spanish present reference system was converging with that of English, as evidenced by an increase in use of the progressive to refer to activity in progress at speech time, (an aspect also designated by the Spanish, but not English, simple present), it was a straightforward matter to extract from our bilingual corpus all morphologically simple and progressive present tense forms, and note for each, whether it referred to ongoing activity or to iterative/habitual actions or immutable truths. By comparing the proportions of different morphological forms used for each of these interpretations to each other and to both historical and synchronic monolingual Spanish data, it was possible to establish that no *increase* in the use of the progressive could be inferred, either over time or among those speakers with most bilingual ability in English. We thus concluded that if grammatical convergence were taking place in Puerto Rican Spanish, the present-reference system was not its locus (Pousada & Poplack 1982).

In terms of code-switching, however, the principle of accountability in its strict form is far more difficult to apply. This is because even if we could agree on where a true code-switch had in fact occurred, it is impossible to ascertain where one *could have* occurred but did not. This would require knowledge of the precise environments in which switching is permissible. Now since code-switching is first and foremost a discourse device, once the global situation is seen as appropriate, a code-switch is no more predictable at the *local* level than, say, a curse or a joke.

One way to resolve this is as follows: if we knew where code-switching was *prohibited*, as would be the case if there were purely syntactic restrictions on its occurrence, we could use this information to apply the principle of accountable reporting. In this connection, Sankoff & Poplack (1981) made use of the *equivalence constraint* on intra-sentential code-switching (Poplack 1980, 1981) which states that codes may be switched intrasententially only when the word order of both languages is homologous on either side of the switch point. On this basis we could determine the syntactic boundaries at which a code-switch was permissible (i.e. could have occurred) in addition to all those at which one actually *did* occur. We were thus able to estimate the *propensity* of switching at a given syntactic boundary. However, analysis of syntactic boundaries (even if limited to only permissible switch boundaries and even in a relatively short stretch of speech) is an extremely onerous task.

As far as borrowing is concerned, we have discovered no obvious way to determine the non-applications. Any content word in the language is fair game for borrowing (as to a far lesser extent, are function words). Only an infinitesimal number of them actually undergo this process, however, and still fewer proceed to achieve the status of established loanwords. We cannot predict which ones will be affected, since examination of the behavior of both nonce and established loanwords reveals that these do *not* tend to group naturally into specific semantic classes or to fulfill particular lexical 'needs' (Poplack, Sankoff & Miller 1988). Moreover, establishing the non-applications for loanwords would additionally require determination of the precise synonym(s) for every borrowed word. Even if this were feasible, there is no guarantee that any of them would appear in a given corpus, since in order for a lexical item to recur, a speaker must be talking about the thing to which it refers.

What we normally do in cases like these is extract the entire body of 'applications' (here, loanwords), and define a new 'dependent variable' within them. Poplack, Sankoff & Miller (1988) considered the entire corpus of 20,000 lone lexical items of English origin in French discourse. These potential candidates for loanword status were found to occur in four frequency categories in Ottawa-Hull French: *nonce* (used only once), *idiosyncratic* (used more than once but by a single speaker), *recurrent* (used more than 10 times) and *widespread* (used by more than 10 speakers), and we attempted to determine which were in fact true loanwords. This involved 1) locating a number of features associated with unambiguous loanwords (e.g. long-standing attestation, widespread dispersion, phonological, morphological and syntactic integration, recurrence, etc.) and 2) coding each token of each lexical type of English origin according to the extent to which it satisfied these criteria. We were thus able to draw a clear distinction between loanwords and code-switches, in terms of their linguistic and social characteristics. As part of the same analysis we discovered that 'loanwords' and nonce borrowings could not be distinguished linguistically at any but the quantitative level, and only showed minor differences in terms of the speakers who used them. This confirmed our decision to treat them as manifestations of the same process.

5.3.2. Circumscribing the variable context. Perhaps the most controversial issue in the study of language contact phenomena is circumscription of the variable context. The first step a variationist will take in assessing contextual effects on the occurrence of one or another variant of a variable is to define the envelope of variation. If we want to determine the factors that promote, say, 'dropping the g' in forms like *workin'/working*, we must first locate the environments in which choice between the alternate realizations is even an option. In reviewing the potential candidates (i.e. forms containing the sequence *-ing*), we immediately discard tokens like *thing*, *ring*, *bring*, while retaining ones like *laughing*, *something*. Under main word stress, *-ing* is never reduced, though when unstressed, it often is. Inclusion of *thing* and *ring* in our data would not only have the effect of artificially lowering the overall deletion rate in the materials, since these would now include many contexts in which deletion never occurs, but more seriously, would blur the constraint hierarchy, or the pattern of *conditioning*, of the deletion process. How does this apply to the bilingual context?

Even if the analyst should be fortunate enough to dispose of a corpus containing many manifestations of language contact, s/he must still determine whether the other-language material constitutes a code-switch, or is a borrowing, or some other consequence of language contact. As we mentioned earlier, in empirical studies, it is often impossible, in a given sentence, to tell which of these processes has taken place. Though their results may be superficially similar, we submit that these processes are subject to different constraints and conditions, and that failure to separate them can only lead to confusing results.

5.3.2.1. Code-switching vs. borrowing. The problem of distinguishing code-switching and borrowing has prompted a number of studies on the characteristics of loanwords (e.g. Haugen 1950, Mackey 1970; Poplack & Sankoff 1984; Poplack, Sankoff & Miller 1988). It is generally reported that loanwords are phonologically, morphologically and syntactically integrated into the recipient language, and are recurrent and widespread. For nonce loans, however, the extralinguistic characteristics of recurrence in the speech of an individual and widespread distribution in the community do not hold. How can loanwords be distinguished from code-switches when this process is prevalent?

Close inspection of the results of the borrowing process (i.e. long-attested loanwords) reveals that they share a number of characteristics: they tend to be content words which take the same inflections and occupy the same syntactic slots as corresponding native recipient-language words. In the synchronic bilingual context, these facts can help distinguish loanwords from their original forms in the donor language, which of course take different inflections, if any, and may even occupy different slots. Specific tests for loanword status will vary from one language to another, depending on the particular morphological and syntactic features available.

Sankoff, Poplack and Vanniarajan (1990) studied combinations of Tamil, an OV language, and English, a VO language. Because of the differences in word order between the two languages, any switch involving an object NP will of necessity violate the word-order patterns of one or both languages. Yet it is precisely in object position where most of the tokens of English origin (generally consisting of single nouns) are found. Why should this language pair show so many apparently ungrammatical combinations, when the accumulating evidence suggests that languages are generally juxtaposed intrasententially in such a way as to result in *grammatical* sequences? There are at least two possible responses to this question. The first is that the structural makeup of the languages involved is disparate enough to permit few grammatical combinations. Should speakers of language pairs like Tamil/English wish to engage in code-switching, they would thus have no choice but to produce ungrammatical utterances. The second is that the 'offending' items are not in fact code-switches. This is where determination of the status of these elements becomes crucial. In these cases, we systematically compare their linguistic behavior with that of *unambiguous* code-switches and *unambiguous* loanwords. In the Tamil case, our analysis revealed that most of the single nouns in object position show the properties of borrowing and not of code-switching, i.e. they are accompanied by Tamil function words and carry Tamil case-marking. The fact that not all of the English-origin words are case-marked, however, again raises the question of whether the remainder are code-switches violating English word order. Quantitative analysis of *both* English-origin and *native Tamil* direct objects shows that, on the contrary, case-marking is variable on native Tamil as well as on borrowed English nouns. Moreover, comparison of marking rates shows that they are remarkably parallel. The borrowed forms contrast sharply with genuine code-switches from Tamil into English, which carry no Tamil case-marking, are accompanied by no Tamil function words, and begin and end only at syntactic boundaries which are equivalent in Tamil and English.

5.3.2.2. Nonce Loans versus Flagged Switches. In a study of bilingual behavior in English and Finnish, another postpositional language with case-marking, (Poplack, Wheeler and Westwood 1987), we again find that most of the English-origin material in Finnish discourse, consisting of single nouns and compounds, occurs in precisely those sites where true switches into English should be excluded.

As in the Tamil data, however, the majority of these nouns follow a Finnish function word and/or take the appropriate Finnish case-marker, indicating they are borrowings and not code-switches. Unlike the Tamil illustration, case-marking is obligatory in Finnish, but a good proportion of the English-origin nouns in the data are not case-marked.

Upon closer inspection, however, it became apparent that the presence of bare English-origin nouns in Finnish tends to be associated with an abnormal rate of certain discourse phenomena: in particular, pauses, ratification markers and flags, which in some conversations seem to be entirely confined to a switch-signaling function. Strikingly, the distribution of case-marking and discourse flagging of English-origin single nouns tends toward complementary distribution. This confirms that most of these nouns (the case-marked ones) are nonce borrowings. The remainder are most logically treated as flagged, non-smooth single-word switches.[8]

5.3.2.3. Constituent Insertion. In a study of Moroccan Arabic/French bilinguals, Naït M'Barek & Sankoff (1988) found that by far the most frequent type of intrasentential language mixture is neither nonce borrowing, established borrowing, nor switching at equivalence sites, but rather insertion of a French NP, including at least determiner and noun, and optionally other elements, in a syntactic slot for an Arabic NP. For example, French DET + N is often inserted after an Arabic demonstrative or predeterminer *wahed*, contexts which take DET + N constructions in Arabic, but whose French counterparts would not permit the (second) determiner (see also Bentahila and Davies 1983). There are ten times as many NP insertions in all as there are switches at the equivalence site between Arabic DET and French noun.

That the process responsible for these data is NP insertion (rather than the equivalence switching predominant in the Puerto Rican data) is further confirmed by a greater statistical tendency for a second switch (back to Arabic) to occur after the French noun *only if this noun is in NP-final position.* If the NP continues, e.g. with an adjective or noun complement, then it is more likely to continue in French.

6.0. Discussion

The bilingual mechanisms discussed here are discretely different ways of solving the problem of combining material from two different languages. Each of them resembles the others in at least some aspect, and is distinctly different in another. Code-switching, constituent insertion and nonce borrowing are all (potentially) ways of alternating two languages *smoothly* within the sentence and in this, all contrast with flagged switching. Nonce borrowing differs from the other processes in that it involves syntactic, morphological and (variable) phonological integration into a recipient language of an element from a donor language, whereas the other processes all maintain the monolingual grammaticality of the sentence fragment as determined by the rules of the respective language of its provenance. Indeed, nonce loans differ from established loanwords only *quantitatively* -- in frequency of use, degree of acceptance, level of phonological integration, etc. Constituent insertion differs from equivalence-based switching in that word-order constraints *across* switch boundaries need not be respected for those constituents eligible to be inserted. Switching at equivalence sites is the only mechanism which does not involve *insertion* of material from one language into a sentence of the other -- once a switch occurs, the rest of the sentence may continue in the new language (although further switches are also possible), whereas the other mechanisms generally require a return to the original language immediately after the nonce loan, inserted constituent, or flagged switch.

From a methodological point of view, it may be difficult to ascertain which mechanism has produced a given utterance. It seems clear that determining the status of the ambiguous item depends crucially on its linguistic and social context of occurrence. We have attempted to illustrate how quantitative variationist methodology, when applied systematically to representative corpora of bilingual discourse, can contribute to the resolution of these superficial ambiguities.

Notes

1 A preliminary version of this paper was prepared for a workshop on concepts, methodology, and data sponsored by the European Science Foundation Network on Code-switching and Language Contact in January, 1990. We thank the European Science Foundation for providing a forum for stimulating discussion of many of the issues presented here, and gratefully acknowledge the support of the Social Sciences and Humanities Research Council of Canada for much of the research on which this paper is based.

2 Throughout this paper we use *bilingual* to refer to *multilingual* as well.

3 Needless to say, some of these definitions, particularly those concerning the distinction between code-switching and borrowing, remain controversial. For detailed justification of those presented here we refer the reader to, e.g., Poplack et al. 1987, 1988; Naït M'Barek and Sankoff 1988, Sankoff et al. 1990.

4 This remains to be systematically studied.

5 This project has been generously supported from 1982 through the present by the Social Sciences and Humanities Research Council of Canada.

6 Codes refer to speaker number and line number of her/his utterance in the Ottawa-Hull French corpus.

7 Alternatively, the analyst may posit that (3a) is a non-application of the copula insertion rule.

8 Note that this type of flagging differs from the functional (or discourse) flagging reported among French/English bilinguals in Ottawa-Hull. In the Finnish/English materials flagging is associated with *production* difficulties, most likely attributable to the fact that the Finnish speakers in our sample did not belong to a community in which borrowing and code-switching are a discourse mode.

References

Attinasi, J. 1979. Language attitudes in a New York Puerto Rican Community. In R. Padilla (ed.), *Ethnoperspectives in bilingual education research: Bilingual education and public policy in the United States*. Ypsilanti, MI: Eastern Michigan University, 408-461.

Baetens Beardsmore, H. 1982. *Bilingualism: basic principles*. Avon, England: Multilingual Matters Ltd.

Baugh, John. 1979. Linguistic style shifting in Black English. Ph.D. Dissertation. University of Pennsylvania.

Bentahila, A. and Davies, E. 1983. The syntax of Arabic-French code-switching. *Lingua* 59:301-330.

Dorian, Nancy. 1981. *Language death*. Philadelphia: University of Pennsylvania Press.

Dorian, Nancy. 1989. *Investigating obsolescence: studies in language contraction and death*. (Studies in the social and cultural foundations of language 7) Cambridge: Cambridge University Press.

Gal, Susan. 1984. Phonological style in bilingualism. In Deborah Schiffrin (ed.), *Meaning, form and use in context*. GURT 84. Washington, D.C.: Georgetown University Press, 290-302.

Grosjean, F. 1990. The psycholinguistics of language contact and code-switching. *Papers for the workshop on concepts, methodology and data*. Strasbourg: European Science Foundation Network on code-switching and language contact, 105-116.

Gumperz, John. 1982. Conversational code-switching. In his *Discourse Strategies*. Cambridge: Cambridge University Press, 59-99.

Haugen, Einer. 1950. The analysis of linguistic borrowing. *Language* 26:210-231.

Hockey, S. & Marriott, I. 1980. *Oxford concordance program*. Version 1.0. Oxford, England: Oxford University Computing Service.

Klein, Flora. 1980. A quantitative study of syntactic and pragmatic indicators of change in the Spanish of bilinguals in the United States. In William Labov (ed.), *Locating language in time and space*. New York: Academic Press, 69-82.

Labov, William. 1966. *The social stratification of English in New York City*. Arlington, VA: Center for Applied Linguistics.

Labov, William. 1971. Some principles of linguistic methodology. *Language in society* 1:97-120.

Labov, William. 1984. Field methods of the project on linguistic change and variation. In John Baugh & Joel Sherzer (eds), *Language in use*. Englewood Cliffs, New Jersey: Prentice-Hall, 28-53.

Labov, William, Paul Cohen, C. Robins, & J. Lewis. 1968. *A study of the non-standard English of Negro and Puerto Rican Speakers in New York City*. Philadelphia: U.S. Regional Survey.

Lavandera, Beatriz. 1978. The variable component in bilingual performance. Paper presented at GURT.

Mackey, W. F. 1970. Interference, integration and the synchronic fallacy. *Georgetown University round table on languages and linguistics 23*. Washington, D.C.: Georgetown University Press, 195-227.

Miller, C. & Shana Poplack. Forthcoming. Language contact and the stylistic repertoire.

Milroy, Lesley. 1980. *Language and social networks*. Baltimore: University Park Press.

Mougeon, R. & E. Beniak. 1991. *Linguistic consequences of language contact and restriction: The case of French in Ontario, Canada*. (Oxford studies in language contact). Oxford: Oxford University Press.

Naït M'Barek, M. & David Sankoff. 1988. Le discours mixte arabe/français: des emprunts ou des alternances de langue? *Revue canadienne de linguistique* 33:143-154.

Poplack, Shana. 1979. Function and process in a variable phonology. Ph.D. Dissertation. University of Pennsylvania.

Poplack, Shana. 1980. Sometimes I'll start a sentence in Spanish y termino en español: toward a typology of code-switching. *Linguistics* 18(7/8):581-618.

Poplack, Shana. 1981. Syntactic structure and social function of code-switching. In R. Duran (ed.), *Latino discourse and communicative behavior*. New Jersey: Ablex, 169-184.

Poplack, Shana. 1985. Contrasting patterns of code-switching in two communities. In Henry Warkentyne (ed.), *Methods V: Papers from the fifth international conference on methods in dialectology*. Victoria: University of Victoria Department of Linguistics, 363-386.

Poplack, Shana. 1988. Language status and language accommodation along a linguistic border. In Peter Lowenberg (ed.), *Language spread and language policy: Issues, implications and case studies* (GURT 1987). Washington, D.C.: Georgetown University Press, 90-118.

Poplack, Shana. 1989. The care and handling of a megacorpus: the Ottawa-Hull French project. In Ralph Fasold & Deborah Schiffrin (eds), *Language change and variation* Amsterdam: Benjamins, 411-444.

Poplack, Shana, R. Clément, C. Miller, K. Purcell, & M. Trudel-Maggiore. 1988. Peut-on entendre l'intégration d'un emprunt? Paper presented at NWAVE-XVII. Université de Montréal.

Poplack, Shana & C. Miller. 1985. Political and interactional determinants of linguistic insecurity. Paper presented at NWAVE XIV. Georgetown University.

Poplack, Shana & David Sankoff. 1984. Borrowing: the synchrony of integration. *Linguistics* 22:99-135.

Poplack, Shana, David Sankoff, & C. Miller. 1988. The social correlates and linguistic processes of lexical borrowing and assimilation. *Linguistics* 26,1:47-104.

Poplack, Shana, S. Wheeler, & A. Westwood. 1987. Distinguishing language contact phenomena: evidence from Finnish-English bilingualism. In P. Lilius & M. Saari (eds), *The Nordic languages and modern linguistics 6*. Helsinki, 33-56.

Pousada, A. & Shana Poplack. 1982. No case for convergence: the Puerto Rican Spanish verb system in a language-contact situation. In Joshua Fishman & G. Keller (eds.), *Bilingual education for Hispanic students in the United States*. New York: Teachers College Press, 207-237.

Rand, D. & David Sankoff. 1988. *GoldVarb*. Logistic regression package for the Macintosh. Montréal: Université de Montréal.

Sankoff, David. 1979. *Varbrul 2S*. In Poplack, 1979. Appendix B.

Sankoff, David. 1982. Sociolinguistic method and linguistic theory. In L. Cohen et al. (eds), *Logic, methodology, philosophy of science VI*. Amsterdam: North Holland, 679-687.

Sankoff, David. 1988. Sociolinguistics and syntactic variation. In Frederick Newmeyer (ed.), *Linguistics: the Cambridge survey*. New York: Cambridge University Press, 140-161.

Sankoff, David. 1990. Dramatically contrasting language mixture strategies in two communities of fluent Arabic-French bilinguals. Paper presented at NWAVE XIX. University of Pennsylvania.

Sankoff, David, M. Naït M'Barek, & C. Montpetit. 1987. VSO/SVO bilingual syntax. Paper presented at NWAVE XVI. University of Texas at Austin.

Sankoff, David & Shana Poplack. 1981. A formal grammar for code-switching. *Papers in linguistics* 14,1:3-45.

Sankoff, David, Shana Poplack, & S. Vanniarajan. 1990. The case of the nonce loan in Tamil. *Language variation and change* 2,1:71-101.

Sankoff, David & Gillian Sankoff. 1973. Sample survey methods and computer-assisted analysis in the study of grammatical variables. In Regna Darnell (ed.), *Canadian languages in their social context.* Edmonton: Linguistic Research Inc., 7-64.

Sankoff, Gillian. 1974. A quantitative paradigm for the study of communicative competence. In Richard Bauman & Joel Sherzer (eds), *Explorations in the ethnography of speaking*. New York: Academic Press, 1-36.

Sankoff, Gillian & William Labov. 1985. Variation theory. Paper presented at NWAVE-XIV. Georgetown University.

di Sciullo, A., P. Muysken, & R. Singh. 1986. Government and code-mixing. *Journal of linguistics* 22,1:1-24.

Weinreich, Uriel. 1968. *Languages in contact.* The Hague: Mouton.

Wolfram, Walt & Ralph Fasold. 1974. *The study of social dialects in American English.* Englewood Cliffs NJ: Prentice-Hall.

Woolford, E. 1983. Bilingual code-switching and syntactic theory. *Linguistic inquiry* 14,3:519-536.

A Perspective on African-American English

Guy Bailey
Oklahoma State University

1.0. Introduction

This paper presents a perspective on African-American English (more commonly called *Black English* [BE]) that draws on four decades of research into BE in its social context.[1] That research has focused largely on three questions about BE: its relationship to white varieties (whether differences between BE and white vernaculars represent basic structural differences or only surface ones), its origins (whether it derives from an earlier creole or simply preserves older features of English that have largely disappeared from white speech), and its current lines of development (whether it is becoming more or less like white vernaculars).[2] Although none of the questions has been completely resolved, linguists have reached a tentative consensus on the first two. Labov (1982) lists four generalizations which form the basis of this consensus:

1. The Black English Vernacular is a subsystem of English with a distinct set of phonological and syntactic rules that are now aligned in many ways with the rules of other dialects.

2. It incorporates many features of Southern phonology, morphology and syntax; blacks in turn have exerted influence on the dialects of Southern whites where they have lived.

3. It shows evidence of derivation from an earlier Creole that was closer to the present-day Creoles of the Caribbean.

4. It has a highly developed aspect system, quite different from other dialects of English, which shows a continuing development of its semantic structure (Labov 1982:192).

The third question is still a matter of hot debate. 'The divergence controversy,' as the debate over this issue has come to be known, is the focus of much of the current work on BE, including large-scale research projects in Philadelphia, East Palo Alto, California, Detroit, and Texas.[3]

Although controversy has long been the norm for work on BE, the divergence controversy is unique in several respects. First, the notion that the black and white vernaculars are diverging from one another (the divergence hypothesis) was proposed independently by two different research teams (Labov's in Philadelphia and Bailey and Maynor in Texas and Mississippi) using different research methods on different kinds of informants in widely separated locales. Second, while opponents in earlier controversies were usually divided according to sub-disciplinary specialities (with creolists opposed to dialect geographers and sociolinguists agreeing with neither), no such alignments exist with regard to the divergence. Finally, unlike the earlier controversies, which sometimes degenerated into bitter polemics, the divergence controversy has in general focused solely on linguistic matters. Opponents of the divergence hypothesis have criticized adherents' methodologies and have asked for more data (see, for example, Butters, 1989); in some instances, they have made substantial contributions to the knowledge-base on BE (e.g., Rickford, 1989; 1990). In general, proponents of the hypothesis have met these challenges by examining more data and exploring new methods (e.g., Bailey and Maynor, 1989). The approach and perspective developed here emerges from this context of challenge and response.

2.0. Why Divergence is Controversial

Perhaps the best way to begin answering the divergence question is by asking why it is controversial. Some of the controversy clearly results from the fact that the divergence hypothesis challenges the one point most linguists had always agreed on, regardless of their positions on other controversies. For the most part creolists, dialect geographers, and sociolinguists all agreed that whatever its origin, BE was gradually becoming more like white varieties. Scholars actually have provided little evidence for such an assimilationist position, but this common-sense notion has nevertheless had a powerful effect on our understanding of the evolution of BE.[4] The amount of data needed to challenge such a widely-held notion successfully is immense, even when little evidence for the notion exists. However, the fact that the divergence hypothesis challenges a widely-held belief by no means accounts for all of the controversy. In fact, three problems which have posed significant difficulties in resolving other controversies also impede the resolution of the divergence controversy.

The first problem is conceptual: what exactly is BE? As Bailey and Bernstein (1990) point out, BE has been defined in a number of ways, not all of them compatible. Dillard (1972), for example, simply defines it as the vernacular of 80% of the black population. Other scholars define BE in terms of its origins, and Butters and Nix (1986) and Butters (1989) argue for a conception of BE which is significantly broader and more inclusive than that of other linguists.[5] Needless to say, linguistic descriptions based upon these various conceptions of BE might differ from each other quite a bit. Moreover, none of these conceptions allows for the kinds of spatial and temporal variation in BE that Bailey and Maynor (1987; 1989) identify. After reviewing the morass of definitions of BE, Bailey and Bernstein (1990) suggest that the most useful conception is one based on the cultural contexts in which it occurs. Using the terminology developed by Labov (1972), Wolfram (1974), and Baugh (1983) as a point of departure, they suggest Black English Vernacular (BEV) as a cover term for the working class vernaculars that have been the focus of most linguistic research, with designations such as Baugh's 'street speech' and Bailey and Maynor's 'folk speech' used to specify the particular variety of BEV being studied. In addition to grounding BE within its cultural context, such a conception maximizes the possibility for truly comparable studies.

The notion of comparable studies suggests a second problem, one of methodology, which underlies much of the work on BE. Actually the methodological problem comprises two separate issues. The first regards representativeness. Most studies of BE focus on relatively small samples of informants usually chosen in a haphazard manner (i.e., convenience samples).[6] Given such samples, linguists have little way of knowing whether their results are representative of the larger black population or only of the small group being studied. The second issue involves interviewing techniques needed to overcome the 'observer's paradox.' Because BE can be a vehicle for establishing identities and bonds of solidarity, as outsiders linguists have no way of knowing for sure whether or not they are getting at the 'deepest vernacular,' the most casual style, the style speakers of BE use when they are not being observed.[7] Both of these concerns have been central to the evolution of sociolinguistics in general, and work on BE has been crucial in the development of sophisticated techniques for studying language in its social context.[8] However, neither of these methodological problems has been completely solved; any solution to the divergence controversy requires that they be addressed.

The third problem impeding the resolution of the divergence controversy is analytical. Much of the apparatus of quantitative sociolinguistics, including the variable rule (Labov, 1972), emerged from attempts to describe the linguistic structure of BEV, and counting the occurrence and nonoccurrence of features, of course, is crucial. Labov (1972) was careful to stress, however, that counting was not an end in itself but a means toward clarifying linguistic structure, of identifying 'orderly heterogeneity.' In fact, understanding the functions of variables in a system is a prerequisite to accurate counting. An example will illustrate the kind of problem that can develop when this prerequisite is not met. Butters (1989) lists the *get* passive as a feature which is expanding in both the black and white vernaculars, citing evidence from Feagin (1979) which shows that younger white Annistonians use more *get* passives while older ones use more *be* passives and from Labov et al. (1968) which shows that New York City blacks frequently use *get* passives. Butters' assertion that the *get* passive is expanding may well be right, but we cannot confirm the assertion by simply counting *be* and *get* passives. A careful consideration of passive contexts will show that the distributions of the *get* and *be* passives are not the same. Consider the following (1 and 4 from the Texas fieldwork):

(1) he was considered an old fool;

(2) *he got considered an old fool;

(3) he was called an old fool;

(4) he got called an old fool.

While *be* can occur in passives with either stative or nonstative verbs, *get* can occur only with nonstatives. Any corpus that includes a high proportion of statives will artificially inflate the frequency of *be* forms in a simple tally of passives. An accurate comparison of the frequency of the two types of passives, then, requires an analysis of their distributional properties first. Many crucial features, not only in the divergence controversy but also in the controversy over the origin of BE, are features that require close attention to their distributional properties and function within a larger system. (Copula absence and durative/habitual *be* are only the most obvious examples.)

3.0. An Approach to BE

The approach to BE described here directly addresses the conceptual, analytical, and methodological problems outlined above. Conceptually, the approach takes the perspective on BE outlined in Bailey and Bernstein (1990), focusing on the vernacular in its cultural contexts. The impact of the rural and urban contexts is of particular importance in the evolution of BEV. Analytically, the focus is on the functioning of forms in their larger systems. As creolists have pointed out for a quarter of a century, it is not the presence or absence of particular features but their function in a system that is of importance. The methodology of the approach requires a more detailed discussion.

Methodology

The methods described here emerge from a larger study of urbanization and language change (ULC).[9] ULC focuses on the linguistic effects of rapid movement from rural areas to towns and cities in Texas over the last century. Because urbanization in Texas has been occurring over such a long period of time, ULC includes a diachronic as well as a synchronic component. The diachronic component explores philological sources, a series of recordings made during the 1930s and 1940s with former slaves born almost a century earlier, an 'export dialect' of 19th century Southern American English (SAE) still spoken in Brazil, and the protocols of the Linguistic Atlas of the Gulf States (LAGS). The synchronic component, the principal source of the data used here, is designed to confront both of the methodological problems outlined above: getting data that approaches the vernacular as closely as possible and obtaining a representative sample so that inferences can be made about the entire population of an area. As a result, the synchronic component comprises two distinct efforts: extensive fieldwork in four Texas communities ranging in size from 150 to 2,000,000 and a statewide, random-sample survey of selected phonological and grammatical features.

The four communities which are the target of most of our fieldwork include Springville, a rural community of 150 located on the Brazos River in the heart of cotton country; Atmore, a town of 5000 which is the seat of the county where Springville is located; Bryan - College Station, the major retail and service hub for the Brazos Valley; and Houston, the major metropolitan area in East Texas.[10] These four communities are inextricably linked both by the flow of goods and services and by patterns of migration. Springville children attend school in the community through the 8th grade; they then attend a consolidated high school in Atmore. Atmore, which has a Wal Mart and large grocery store, is also the major source of entertainment and shopping for Springville residents. After high school, Springville residents frequently move to Atmore to work, and less often to Bryan/College Station. Atmore residents often work in Bryan/College Station or move there, while Houston provides occasional shopping and entertainment for all of the other communities. Moreover, Houston is often a destination for people in those communities who move elsewhere to work.

Currently, fieldwork is complete in Springville, near completion in Atmore and Bryan/College Station, and underway in Houston.[11] The network approach developed by Milroy (1980) provides the organizing principle for fieldwork in all of these communities. In Springville, for example, we began observing interaction among residents at the three major gathering places in the community: the general store/post office (the only store in the community), the school, and the beer joint. Using these observations, along with information from interviews with our contacts in the community, we identified the major sociolinguistic networks and used our contacts to gain access to these networks. We then tried to interview as many participants as possible in each network.

While we conducted typical sociolinguistic interviews (using the techniques developed by Labov) with all the informants, we have done three other things as well. First, we tried to interview all of the informants a number of times over a three-month period in several different settings. Second, we tried to interview all of the informants (adults as well as children) in peer group settings where peers interacted with each other rather than with fieldworkers. Third, in order to insure that we obtained data that typified the interaction of informants with each other rather than with fieldworkers, we made extensive use of what we call *site studies*. Site studies are studies not of individual informants but of strategic sites of linguistic interaction during a given period of time. In Springville they worked in the following manner. After we had been coming to the community daily for over a month, conducting individual and group interviews not only in private homes but also in the school, the beer joint, and the store (the most important site for linguistic interaction in the community) residents began to trust us (making us privy to much of the community gossip), expect us, and look for us in the store to talk to us. Soon our interviews became intertwined with the day-to-day business of the store, and we began to record a wide range of unsolicited linguistic interactions, including arguments, business transactions, and the routine conversations that make up much of the community's linguistic activity. In other words, we were recording the everyday linguistic activity that developed around a site rather than interviews with individuals. The data we obtained was exceptionally rich, so we decided to 'formalize' this site study approach and make it a primary component of our fieldwork. In order to do this, we simply began going to the store (or beer joint) and turning on the tape recorder (in plain view, of course). Sometimes we would sit and talk to whoever came in; at other times, we would leave or move about elsewhere in the store, returning periodically to change the tape. By the end of the day we had recorded an entire day's linguistic activity at a single site. The data that emerges from these site studies is remarkable in several ways. For one thing, much of the linguistic activity is directed toward someone other than the fieldworker. We are able to observe people *almost* as if they were not being observed. Second, because the interlocutors include a significant portion of the community, they provide us with a different interview setting for many of the informants who are interviewed individually and in peer groups. Finally, a much wider range of speech events occurs in these site studies than in typical interviews. As I point out below, the site studies provide linguistic data that cannot be easily obtained in other ways. As a result, site studies, along with multiple interviews and group interviews, have become a crucial part of our approach to field research in all communities.

This field research has enabled us to outline urban/rural linguistic differences, especially in BEV, and to trace the diffusion of urban innovations into rural areas in some detail (see, for example, Bailey and Maynor, 1989; Cukor-Avila, 1989b). However, making inferences about a larger population based on field research in four communities, regardless of the quality of the field work, is a risky proposition. In order to broaden the sample and make it representative of the state as a whole, we decided to conduct a large-scale Phonological Survey of Texas (PST) and Grammatical Investigation of Texas Speech (GRITS). These surveys are multi-faceted studies of phonological and grammatical variation in the state (see Bailey and Bernstein, 1989, for a more complete account), but their centerpieces are random-sample telephone surveys of the entire state. We obtained these samples by 'piggybacking' on the Texas Poll, a quarterly random-sample telephone survey of the entire state (similar to the Gallup or Roper Polls) which asks questions and gathers information for a variety of public and private agencies (see Bailey and Dyer, 1992, for a more complete discussion). By placing a series of questions designed to explore phonological and grammatical variation on several of these polls and by tape-recording one of them, we have obtained crucial linguistic evidence from a random sample of the entire state of Texas. Our questions on one poll investigate the following phonological variables: the merger of /ɔ/ and /ɑ/, the merger of tense and lax vowels before /l/, the monophthongization of /aɪ/, the loss of /h/ in /hj/ clusters and /j/ in /tj/ clusters, the constriction or lack of constriction in post-vocalic /r/, intrusive /r/, the interchange of /ɑɚ/ and /ɔɚ/, and the fronting/raising of the onset of /aʊ/. Our questions on another poll investigate the following grammatical features: *might could*, *fixin' to*, and positive *anymore*.

The virtue of data from a random sample is that it allows us to make inferences about a larger population with a high degree of confidence (95%), to determine the likelihood of sampling error (+/- 3% in our samples), and to perform a number of statistical procedures on the data. The results from this source of evidence throw the evolving relationship of the black and white vernaculars into sharp relief.

4.0. Results

The design of the research described here generates data for several kinds of conclusions. The data from fieldwork helps document the presence or absence of linguistic forms, suggests the variety of BEV in which those forms occur, and traces the spread of urban features into rural areas. The evidence from the surveys allows for inferences about the larger population of Texas and for tracing the spread of changes in a more global fashion.

4.1. The evidence from fieldwork

The field methods used here provide evidence on a number of crucial morpho-syntactic problems in BEV. For example, Rickford (1990) has noted the use of the past perfect for the simple past (as in *we had came around a corner*, and then, um, *we came around a corner, we had went home*) in the speech of adolescents but not of adults. Since in his data the feature occurs only in the speech of young adolescents, Rickford suggests that it may well be age-graded, disappearing from speech as children grow into adulthood. However, our evidence from the speech of young adults (born between 1945 and 1965) in Texas suggests a rather different situation. In a study of verbal *-s* in narratives that uses data from Springville, Cukor-Avila (1989c) notes a number of instances of the past perfect used for the simple past in the speech of a 29-year-old black female:

(1) So when B. come, uh he wanted to know where the money, 'cause see they <u>had</u> <u>owed</u> some bills, an' she didn' have any;
(2) An' then I went by St. Joseph, an' uh by the time I got there an' J. <u>had</u> <u>run</u> out there, I say, 'Well wha's wrong with R?'

Other examples of this structure in the speech of young adults include the following:

(3) When I was working at Billups me an' the manager <u>had</u> <u>became</u> good friends an' so she called me sister;
(4) An' one day I <u>had</u> <u>came</u> over here to the store an' tha's when B. <u>had</u> <u>wanted</u> to go to work.

At this point we have not examined this feature in enough of our data to know its precise status. We do not know whether older adults use it, whether children use it more often than young adults, or whether it has a special syntactic or semantic function. We do know, however, that the structure persists at least through the first two decades of adulthood and that if it is an age-graded feature, it does not become one until adults reach middle-age. Our data from site studies and adult peer groups should provide answers to all these questions eventually.

Our data from fieldwork also provides new evidence on the two syntactic structures which have been at the heart of the divergence controversy. Myhill and Harris (1986) and Labov (1987) argue that one way in which BEV is diverging from white vernaculars is in its use of verbal *-s*. They note that in Philadelphia BEV, verbal *-s* is coming to be used not as an agreement marker but as a narrative marker (or historical present). The most typical use of verbal *-s*, then, is the following:

(5) ... the li'l boy, he comes and hits me right? I hits him back now (from Labov, 1987).

What makes this use of *-s* divergent is not simply its occurrence as a narrative marker (although that use differs both from what Labov found in New York City and what we have found with older folk informants in Texas) but its use *primarily* as a narrative marker.[12]

The Texas data differs in several crucial ways from the Philadelphia data, as Bailey, Maynor, and Cukor-Avila (1989) show. In the speech of adolescents and young adults in Texas, *-s* rarely occurs as a narrative marker; in fact, it rarely occurs. The situation among older adults in quite different. Verbal *-s* occurs much more often in the third singular than it does in the speech of adolescents and young adults (comprising about 30% of the tokens), and it also occurs in the third plural (accounting for seven percent of the tokens there), an environment where it almost never occurs in the speech of the younger age groups. In black folk speech (BFS) in Texas, then, verbal *-s* is more frequent than in street speech, both in the singular and in the plural. However, the difference is not simply in frequency. While the occurrence of verbal *-s* in BFS is variable, it is not random. Bailey, Maynor, and Cukor-Avila (1989) show that a preceding noun phrase (NP) subject strongly favors the presence of *-s*, both in the third singular and third plural, while a pronoun (PRO) subject favors the absence of *-s* in both environments. The following examples (from Bailey, Maynor, and Cukor-Avila, 1989) illustrate the alternation of *-s* and *ø* in BFS:

(6) ... let's see how it <u>look</u> down there;
(7) My daughter, she <u>work</u> down the V.A. hospital;
(8) All of the folks <u>sits</u> up on the top of that hill;
(9) Myron and them<u>'s</u> got it.

This NP/PRO constraint also operates in white folk speech in Texas; in fact, it has operated in at least some varieties of white English since the 15th century.[12] Moreover, the NP/PRO constraint affects *be* as well as other verbs in both BFS and white folk speech (WFS) and again has done so at least since the 15th century. The use of *is* as a plural, which accounts for a fifth of all plural tokens in our sample of BFS (see Bailey and Maynor, 1985b), is strongly favored by a preceding NP, as in the following:

(10) earthworms <u>is</u> plenty hard to find;
(11) deer and squirrels <u>is</u> out there.

In black and white folk speech, then, an NP/PRO constraint competed strongly with number agreement for the function of verbal *-s* and *is*. Over time, however, the NP/PRO constraint has gradually disappeared in both BEV and white vernacular. As Bailey, Maynor, and Cukor-Avila (1989) point out, in white vernaculars the competition between number concord and the NP/PRO constraint has been resolved in favor of number concord, with *-s* and *is* used almost exclusively to mark third singular even in the speech of the most insular children. In BEV, on the other hand, the competition has been resolved as *-s* itself, the form used ambiguously for both functions, has been lost and *is* has been replaced by ɸ and unconjugated *be*.

Thus while the data from Texas does not include the widespread use of verbal *-s* as a narrative marker, it does show the divergence of BEV and white vernaculars. Earlier, both BFS and WFS had *-s* variably in the singular and the plural and had *is* variably in the plural. The competition between the NP/PRO constraint and person/number agreement accounted for much of the variation. In the later development of BEV and white vernaculars, the competition disappeared in both vernaculars, but it disappeared in different ways. In the white vernacular, person/number concord won out. In BEV the form used ambiguously for both functions either disappeared (in the case of verbal *-s*) or was replaced by another form (as in the case of *is*).

One of those forms that has been replacing *is* is invariant *be*, a second morpho-syntactic feature that has been pivotal in the divergence controversy. Bailey and Maynor (1987; 1989) and Bailey (1987) base their argument for divergence largely on changes in the distribution and function of invariant *be* (or be_2) in the speech of four groups of lower class black informants in the Brazos Valley area of Texas. These include urban teens and preteens (11-15 years old), elderly rural and urban informants (primarily over 60 years old), a group of former slaves born between 1844 and 1864, and rural teens and preteens who parallel the urban ones. Bailey and Maynor point out that although all four groups use the same set of forms (*am*, *are*, be_2, *is*, and ø) in the paradigm for the present tense of *be*, as Table 1 suggests, there is one striking discrepancy in the distribution of those forms. Table 2 shows that the distribution of all of the forms is quite similar for all four groups except in one syntactic environment -- before *V+ing*. Before *v+ing*, ø dominates in the speech of the slaves and elderly adults, but in the speech of the children be_2 competes strongly with ø, accounting for a plurality of forms with the urban children and nearly 40% of the tokens with the rural ones. An analysis of the meaning of be_2, ø, and the conjugated forms before *v+ing* indicates the reason for the high frequency of be_2 in this environment in the speech of the children. Table 3 shows the meanings of the present tense forms before *v+ing*. The adults and slaves make no distinction among the forms, but the children do, using be_2 for durative and habitual actions in this environment and ø and the conjugated forms for actions of limited duration ('true progressives') or for future time. In the speech of the children, then, be_2 seems to have developed both grammatical and syntactic constraints which it did not have in earlier varieties and which are not present in white vernaculars either. These new developments, Bailey and Maynor argue, represent divergence.

A close analysis of the situation among rural children (see Bailey and Maynor, 1989) demonstrates that the use of be_2 + *v+ing* for durative/habitual meaning is in fact an innovation and provides some in-

		Urban 11-15	Adults 25-45	Adults 50-100	Ex-slaves	Rural 11-15
Ist sing	am	120(83%)	161(94%)	369(96%)	85(95%)	19(83%)
	be	23(16%)	10(06%)	12(03%)	2(02%)	3(13%)
	is	0	0	2(0.5%)	0	0
	0	1(01%)	0	3(0.7%)	3(03%)	1(04%)
3rd sing	is	734(82%)	490(80%)	2000(90%)	159(88%)	180(78%)
	be	39(04%)	28(04%)	16(01%)	0	9(04%)
	are	121(14%)	92(15%)	194(09%)	22(12%)	42(18%)
Plural & 2nd sing	are	36(14%)	35(12%)	137(19%)	17(18%)	10(11%)
	be	73(28%)	26(09%)	44(06%)	4(06%)	18(21%)
	is	24(09%)	21(07%)	139(19%)	18(19%)	14(16%)
	0	130(49%)	205(71%)	407(56%)	55(58%)	45(52%)
Total		1301	1161	3323	365	341

Table 1: Person/number distribution of forms of the present tense of *be* in four varieties of Black English (Bailey and Maynor, 1989 [except data for adults age 25-45])

		V+ -ing	gonna	Adj.	Loc.	NP
Urban 11-15	is/are	14	11	73	67	86
	be	44	0	2	13	2
	0	41	89	25	19	12
Adults 25-45	is/are	20	13	75	50	91
	be	19	0	3	10	2
	0	61	87	23	40	8
Adults 50-100	is/are	34	27	82	73	91
	be	1	0	3	8	1
	0	65	73	15	20	8
Ex-slaves	is/are	29	0	69	77	87
	be	0	0	2	8	1
	0	71	100	29	15	12
Rural 11-15	is/are	16	0	67	62	84
	be	39	0	6	14	2
	0	45	100	27	24	14

Table 2: Syntactic constraints on present tense forms in the plural and 2nd and 3rd person singular (each form as a percent of the total number of tokens in a given environment) (Bailey and Maynor, 1989 [except data for adults age 25-45])

	Limited duration/ Future			Extended duration/ Habitual		
	is/are	be	0	is/are	be	0
Urban 11-15	29	5	65	3	77	20
Adults 25-45	24	2	74	25	50	25
Adults 50-100	21	0	79	20	6	73
Rural 11-15	73	0	27	11	45	44

Table 3: Meaning of present tense forms before *V + ing* (each form as a percent of the total number of tokens in a given environment) (Bailey and Maynor 1989 [except data for adults age 25-45])

sight into the diffusion of that innovation. At first glance, the data in Tables 1, 2, and 3 seems to show that rural children manifest the same tendency to use be_2 before v+*ing* for durative/habituals as the urban children do, although the tendency is not as strongly developed. In other words, the rural children represent a kind of intermediate step in the evolution of be_2, with those children clearly adopting the urban innovation. However, as Bailey and Maynor (1989) point out, such a conclusion is somewhat misleading. In fact, two distinct patterns coexist among the rural children: one group of children is adopting the urban pattern (these four account for all of the tokens of be_2 before v+*ing*) while another (the remaining 16) maintain the older rural pattern.[13] Moreover, the four who manifest the urban pattern all have close urban ties, either living in Bryan/College Station for short periods or visiting there regularly. While it seems clear that the urban pattern will eventually supplant the older rural ones, the rural pattern still persists even among insular teenagers.[14]

The data from rural children answers a number of questions raised about the status of *be*$_2$ in particular and the divergence hypothesis in general (see Butters, 1989, and the essays by Vaughn-Cooke, Wolfram, and Rickford in *American Speech* 62, 1987, for a discussion of these questions). First, it clearly confirms the existence of the pattern identified in folk speech. The differences in the distribution and function of *be*$_2$ cannot be simply a consequence of stylistic differences in data from various groups of informants. The urban and rural children were interviewed in precisely the same manner (in individual and peer group settings). Whatever biases and problems affect one group affect the other. Second, because the rural and urban children talk about the same topics and are asked the same questions, other potential problems, such as differences in subject matter, that might affect the occurrence of certain features are eliminated. In fact, Bailey and Maynor (1989) are able to illustrate the differences between the urban and rural patterns by presenting virtually identical sentences. Finally, the data from rural children shows how the social process of urbanization leads to the spread of the innovative pattern in the use of *be*$_2$. Nevertheless, even this data has not satisfied all of the demands of the critics of the divergence hypothesis. For one thing, many of these critics still suspect that the 'observer's paradox' has somehow prevented our obtaining data on *be*$_2$ before v+*ing* in the speech of elderly adults (again see Butters, 1989). For another, they want to see a distribution across three consecutive generations (i.e., in apparent time) that parallels the configuration for sound change in progress that Labov (1966) and others have identified (see Vaughn-Cooke, 1987). Finally, many of the critics simply want to see more data.

Our fieldwork in the Brazos Valley helps answer the first two questions, and PST provides a substantial amount of additional data -- data which will help us determine more precisely when divergence began. The peer group interviews with adults provide interviewing contexts that closely parallel our best fieldwork with children, while the site studies described above allow us to come fairly close to overcoming the observer's paradox. In fact, the peculiar structure of Springville has given us a number of opportunities to observe (but of course not to tape-record) linguistic interactions among residents before they were aware of our presence. These observations suggest that the data which emerges from our fieldwork is a reasonable approximation of the speech of the community. The data from the peer group interviews and site studies confirm the basic findings of Bailey and Maynor (1987;1989): children and teenagers, especially those with urban connections, generally use *be*$_2$ + v+*ing* to mark durative/habitual actions while the older adults never do. The site studies confirm that this difference is not simply a quantitative one. Some of the older adults in the sample use *be*$_2$ almost as often as the urban adolescents do. For example, *be*$_2$ comprises about 10% of the total number of present tense tokens among the urban children in our sample; among the elderly adults who use it most often, it comprises about 7%. The difference is not in the occurrence/nonoccurrence of *be*$_2$, but in its syntactic distribution. In the speech of the urban children 70% of all tokens of *be*$_2$ occur before v+*ing*; in the speech of the elderly adults who use it most frequently (i.e., in whose speech it comprises 5-7% of the tokens), it never occurs in that environment, and when it appears elsewhere it is used for a wide range of meanings (see the tokens in Bailey and Bassett, 1986, and Bailey and Maynor, 1987). Quite clearly, then, *be*$_2$ has a different morpho-syntactic function in the speech of children, and the difference cannot be explained as an artifact of the interview context.[15]

The evidence from a group of informants whom we have not analyzed previously, younger adults born after World War II, provides further confirmation of the fact that differences in the distribution and function of *be*$_2$ are not simply artifacts of the interview context. Perhaps more important, that evidence enables us to determine more precisely when divergence began. The second section in Tables 1-3 includes comparable data for a group of adults born between 1945 and 1965. The data suggests that this group of adults represents a transition stage in the use of *be*$_2$. The frequency of *be*$_2$ in the speech of the young adults (it comprises 6% of their present tense tokens) lies somewhere between that of the elderly adults (2%) and the urban children (10%), but more important, the tokens of *be*$_2$ in their speech occur primarily before v+*ing* (68%). Further, as in the speech of children, be_2 + v+*ing* is used to mark durative/habitual actions. As Tables 2 and 3 suggest, however, the tendency to mark durative/habitual actions with be_2 plus a present participle is not as well-developed in the speech of the younger adults. Only half of the tokens with durative/habitual meaning are marked with be_2 in the speech of younger adults, as opposed to more than three-quarters in the speech of the urban children. Nevertheless, the data from this 'middle generation' enables us to plot in apparent time the evolution of be_2 + v+*ing* as durative/habitual marker. Figure 1 plots the occurrence of this structure as a percentage of all progressives with durative/habitual meaning across three generations. The resulting configuration is quite similar to that which emerges in sound changes in progress, and when taken in conjunction with the evidence from rural children (see Bailey and Maynor, 1989) confirms that the use of be_2 + v+*ing* as a durative/habitual marker is a recent innovation.

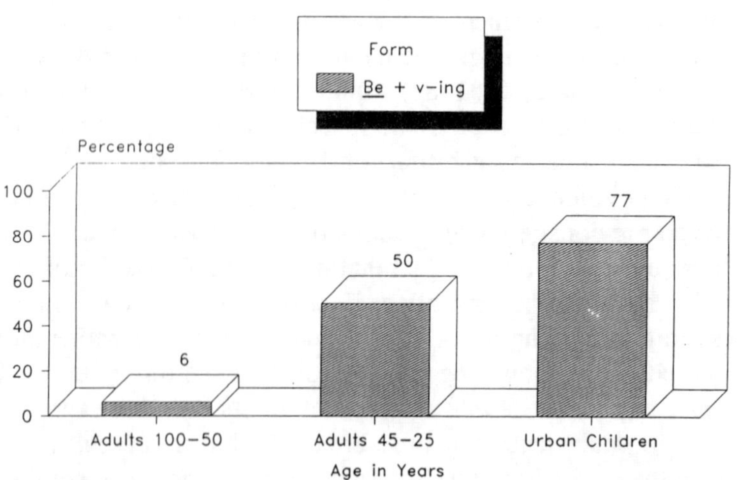

Figure 1: *Be* + *v-ing* as a percentage of all progressives with durative/habitual meaning

In some respects, the presentation of the data in Tables 1-3 and Figure 1 actually understates the generational differences in the use of *be*$_2$ + v+*ing*. *All* of the urban informants (and rural informants with strong urban ties) born after 1944 often use *be*$_2$ + V+*ing* to mark durative/habitual aspect; *none* of those born before that time do. A comparison of the *be*$_2$ tokens in the speech of two similar informants, one born in 1937, the other in 1945, illustrates this difference. Both informants are females with an eighth grade education, both are maids at Texas A&M University, both are grandmothers, and both live in the same area of Bryan, but the distribution of *be*$_2$ in their speech is different. The first informant uses five tokens of *be*$_2$, none before v+*ing*:

(12) Really, you <u>be</u> more partial to them [grandchildren] than to your own;
(13) I found in fast food restaurants people <u>be</u> dirty sometimes;
(14) Some of the girls wear them [boots] and they <u>be</u> turned down ... high-heeled boots, they <u>be</u> turned flat;
(15) FW: What causes those allergies?
INF: Well, all the growth and everything you <u>be</u> around....

The second informant uses 11 tokens, eight of them before v+*ing*. These tokens are remarkably similar to the ones we found among children.

(16) It <u>be</u> about three beers, two drinks and I <u>be</u> all right;
(17) FW: I always get up at 6:30;
INF: So Randy <u>be</u> getting in the bed [when] you <u>be</u> get up;
(18) [When] we was working at night, we <u>be</u> watching a cute little guy come in;
(19) ... 'cause we <u>be</u> going to bingo [every week];
(20) She <u>be</u> sitting up there [at work] and she <u>be</u> kerplunk;
(21) ... some went to $23 a month that she <u>be</u> getting here;
(22) [They] <u>be</u> fighting like R. and P.;
(23) I <u>be</u> doing those doctors [cleaning their offices].

Although they were born only eight years apart and are remarkably similar in their social histories, these two informants clearly represent two different stages in the evolution of *be*$_2$.

Even this comparison, however, understates the differences between the earlier and current use of *be*$_2$ to some extent. The informant born in 1937 may actually represent a kind of transition stage in the development of *be*$_2$, with the form in her speech having the semantic but not yet the syntactic properties of *be*$_2$ among the younger informants. A comparison of her tokens to the eight used by an informant born 20 years earlier (in 1917) suggests that in earlier BEV *be*$_2$ had not only a wider syntactic distribution than in current varieties, but also a wider semantic range. The eight tokens from the informant born in 1917 are as follows:

(24) That be a row here and tha's a row there;
(25) Tha's a piece of land over there where be a turn row betwixt it;
(26) They [chicken snakes] just be knotted up when they suck eggs;
(27) And May used to be the wet part of the year; it don't be now;
(28) Well, it don't be too many [thunderstorms] right around here;
(29) We hear tell in different places be, be storms;
(30) [If you] be sick and they wash your clothes they still want to pay for it;
(31) He be full [right now].

These tokens clearly show *be*$_2$ used for actions and states occurring at a single point in time (tokens 24, 25, and 31) as well as for habitual, durative, and permanent states and actions. This semantic and syntactic range is typical for BFS (see Bailey and Bassett, 1986). What seems to have happened over the last half century or so is that first the semantic range of *be*$_2$ became restricted to durative/habitual actions and then its syntactic distribution became restricted to positions before v+*ing*. In other words, *be*$_2$ has become grammaticalized as an auxiliary marking durative/habitual aspect. The development of *be*$_2$ as an auxiliary marking durative/habitual aspect provides black street speech with a grammatical category unavailable to white vernaculars or to BFS, and it also suggests that the current evolution of BEV reflects neither developments in white vernaculars nor a simple movement toward 'standard English.' Rather, that development (especially when viewed in light of changes in the use of verbal *-s*) suggests that the recent history of BEV reflects both the working out of internal structural pressures within BEV and the creation of speech communities where the use of language as a vehicle for affirming bonds of solidarity and establishing cultural identity takes precedence over a shift to standard English.[16]

4.2. The evidence from PST

Although Labov (1987) points out that the vowel systems of black and white Philadelphians are diverging, most of the debate over divergence has focused on morpho-syntactic systems. Further, since much of the evidence comes from intensive fieldwork with small segments of the population, the extent of divergence or convergence in the larger population is not clear. PST was designed in part to remedy these limitations by providing evidence on phonological change from a large-scale survey of the state of Texas. Although PST comprises four distinct components (a random-sample telephone survey of the entire state, a survey of high school students in nine communities, generational surveys of families in a number of communities, and systematic auditing of radio talk shows from around the state), this analysis focuses only on the first two.

Table 4 summarizes the data from the Texas Poll, while Figures 2 and 3 plot some of that same data graphically and add data from the student surveys. That data shows a number of ongoing phonological changes at different stages of completion in Texas speech. For example, the fronting and raising of /aʊ/ and the development of constricted allophones of postvocalic /r/ seem to be nearing completion (at least in white speech), while the merger of /ɔ/ and /ɑ/ and the spread of monophthongal /aɪ/ before voiceless obstruents are fairly recent phenom-

	Conservative	Innovative	Indeterminate	Total
/ɑ/ in lost	76.6	20.6	2.8	941
/ɑ/ in walk	76.7	19.9	3.4	944
[ɑI-ɑ] in night	73.6	23.2	3.2	942
/i-I/ in field	63.1	30.5	6.4	921
/e-ɛ/ in sale	61.9	34.0	4.1	924
/u-U/ in school	48.2	44.9	6.8	930
/hj-j/ in Houston	78.2	10.7	10.8	910*
[r] in Washington	12.7	83.5	3.9	909
/ɔ-ɑ/ in forty	5.0	91.9	3.0	934
/ə-ɚ/ in forty	16.1	79.0	4.9	942
/tj-tu/ in Tuesday	39.2	50.4	10.4	924
[ɑU-æU] in thousand	22.7	71.9	5.4	928

*Includes one response of [hustən] for Houston

Table 4: Summary of data from the Texas Poll, January, 1989 (percent of respondents using conservative and innovative forms for each feature and total number of responses for each) (Bailey, Bernstein, and Tillery, under review)

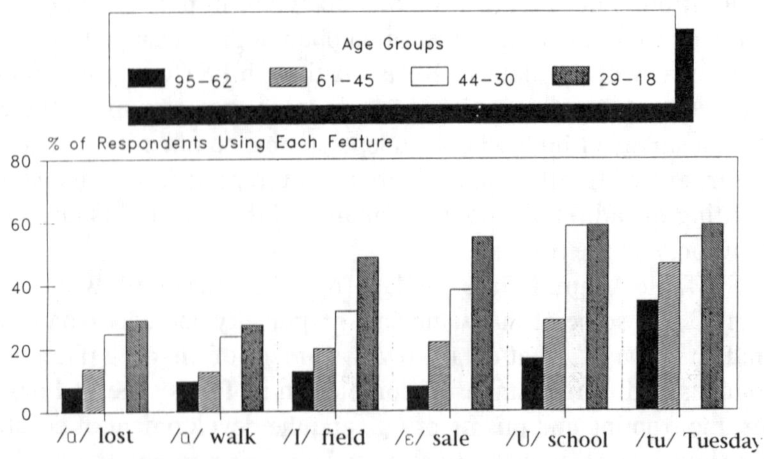

Figure 2: Innovative features in Texas speech (percent using innovative feature: ages 95-18; January, 1989 Texas Poll)

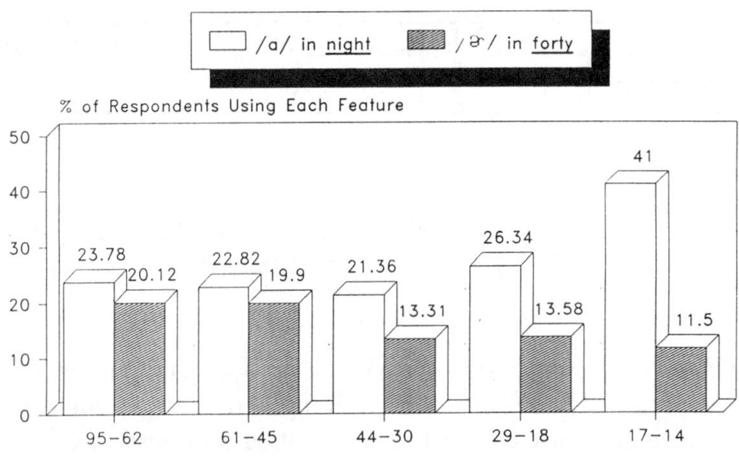

Figure 3: Two features of Texas speech (percent using features: ages 95-18, January 1989 Texas Poll; ages 17-14, student surveys)

ena. Figure 2 plots in apparent time five changes (the merger of / ɑ / and / ɔ /, the merger of tense and lax vowels before /l/, and the loss of /j/ after alveolars) that are occurring in many parts of the United States. Figure 3 plots two features traditionally associated with Southern Speech -- the loss of constriction in postvocalic /r/ and monophthongal /aɪ/ before voiceless obstruents. Although the first of these traditional features is gradually disappearing, the second has begun to spread quite rapidly. Thus while some of the phonological changes in Texas parallel developments elsewhere, others serve to maintain the regional distinctiveness of the state.

What is of most relevance here, of course, are the similarities and differences between black and white respondents to the Texas Poll. Table 5 provides the percentages of black and Anglo (i.e., non-Hispanic white) respondents who use innovative forms of seven variables (in eight tokens, since the merger of / ɑ/ and / ɔ/ is represented in both *lost* and *walk*).[17] As Table 5 shows, the figures for black and white respondents for the loss of /j/ after alveolars and the merger of /i/ and /I/

	lost	walk	field	sale	school	Tuesday	night	forty
Anglo	21	20	28	30	47	48	27	90
Black	4	1	27	35	20	51	10	39

Table 5: Percent of Anglo and Black respondents using innovative forms in the January, 1989 Texas Poll (rounded to nearest whole number) (Bailey, Bernstein, and Tillery, under review)

and /e/ and /ɛ/ before /l/ are remarkably similar, but the figures for the merger of /ɑ/ and /ɔ/, the monophthongization of /aɪ/ in voiceless environments, the use of constricted allophones of postvocalic /r/, and the merger of /u/ and /U/ before /l/, are all significantly different.[18] At first glance, these figures seem to confirm the scenario that Butters (1989) proposes: the speech of blacks and whites is converging with regard to some features and diverging with regard to others. However, such a scenario misses what is actually happening here. As Figures 2 and 3 indicate, these changes did not all begin, or to use Butters' criterion, become 'robust,' at the same time. The loss of /j/ after alveolars seems to have been well under way by the early part of the 20th century, while the merger of tense and lax vowels before /l/ became 'robust' before World War II.[19] Although a significant number of Texans have always used constricted allophones of /r/ and monophthongal /aɪ/ in voiceless environments, both of these features began to spread rapidly after World War II, and like merger of /ɔ/ and /ɑ/, their diffusion has accelerated during the last 30 years. If we examine black and white participation in phonological changes according to when those changes became robust, a striking pattern emerges. As Figure 4 (which plots black/white participation in phonological changes according to when they became robust and which adds data on the merger of /I/ and /ɛ/ before nasals) shows, with one exception, the merger of /u/ and /U/ before /l/, blacks and whites participate equally in changes that became robust before World War II but not in those that have become robust since the war.[20] In fact, post World War II changes seem to have had little influence on black speech. Thus while it is true that black and white speech are converging with regard to some features and diverging with regard to others, the convergent features are all older ones, the divergent features almost all recent ones. That, of course, is precisely what the divergence hypothesis holds.

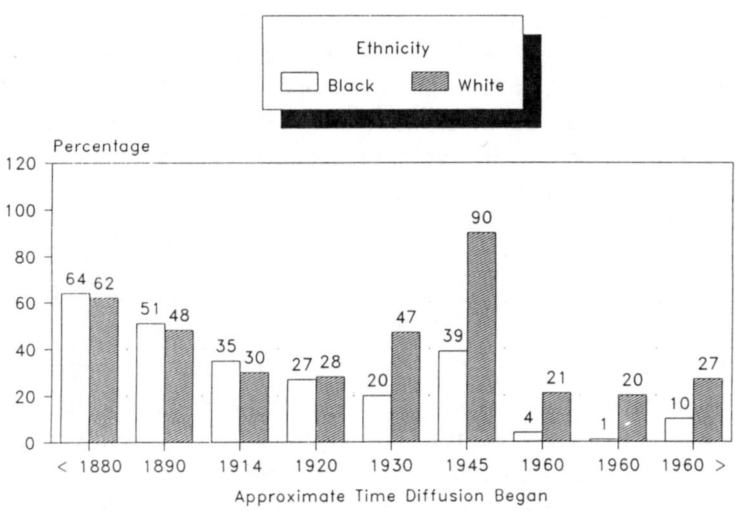

Figure 4: Changes in Black and White speech in Texas (percent using innovative form)

The data from PST becomes even more striking when viewed in light of the development of *be*$_2$ and verbal *-s* in BEV. As I pointed out above, the reanalysis of *be*$_2$ and the loss of *-s* seem to have occurred sometime around World War II. Remember that all of the urban informants (and rural informants with close urban ties) born after World War II use *be*$_2$ + v+*ing* to mark durative/habitual aspect; none of those born before that time do. Likewise, those born after World War II have very little verbal *-s* in their speech; those born before the war have *-s* variably both in the singular and plural, with its occurrence governed in part by the NP/PRO constraint. These developments, along with the fact that blacks do not participate in any of the phonological changes that have become robust since World War II, both provide strong evidence for the recent divergence of the black and white vernaculars and establish a time frame for that divergence. Before World War II, the black and white vernaculars were generally converging, as both blacks and whites participated in sound changes affecting Southern English and as each group assimilated features of the others' speech. (Whites for example, surely developed zero copula under the influence of BEV, and their extensive use of unconstricted allophones of /r/ may reflect that influence as well [see Feagin, 1989]). Since World War II, the black and white vernaculars have developed in different directions, with developments in one vernacular having little impact on developments in the other.

5.0. Conclusion

While divergence is clearly a major trend in black-white speech relationships, it would be a serious mistake to see it as the only trend. Significant numbers of African-Americans acquire varieties of English identical to those of comparable whites, and how many people speak some variety of BEV is not entirely clear. As Bailey and Bernstein (1990) point out, the linguistic situation among African-Americans has always been quite complex. Even in the middle of the 19th century, African-Americans used a number of varieties of English, with some speaking a creole, especially near the Georgia - South Carolina coasts, others speaking varieties identical to those of local whites, and many others speaking a range of varieties in between. The situation today is hardly less complex, with some blacks using one of the manifestations of BEV, others using varieties identical to whites, and still others using a range of varieties in between. Even BEV itself is quite complicated, showing both temporal and spatial (i.e., urban/rural) variation. In fact, much of the disagreement about BEV among linguists seems to stem from the failure to recognize the extent of the variation within BEV itself.

Linguists have also failed to give full due to the role that BEV plays in establishing cultural identities and reaffirming bonds of solidarity (see Rickford, 1990, for a discussion of these factors), perhaps because of their concern with the impact of BEV on the acquisition of 'standard English' in particular and on educational attainment in general. However, two decades of research on BEV suggest that acquiring 'standard English' is not the primary motive driving the evolution of BEV. As urbanization and its consequent segregation led to the development of new speech communities, the evolution of BEV came to be closely bound to the establishment of cultural identity and bonds of solidarity. If some educators regard it as dysfunctional in an academic context, its speakers clearly regard it as an asset within their culture.[21]

The major tasks of future research into BEV include sorting out the internal variation within BEV, i.e., identifying and describing the relationships among sub-varieties such as black folk speech and black street speech, and exploring the ways that BEV functions within its own culture. Like the earlier tasks of describing BEV, determining its relation to white vernaculars, and exploring its origins, these tasks will require innovative sampling and field methods, rigorous analytical techniques, and open minds that are receptive to unexpected results. As in the past, undertaking these tasks will not only provide insight into BEV in its social contexts but will also reshape the way we do dialectology.

Notes

1 The research for this paper was supported by grants from the National Science Foundation (BNS-8812552), American Council of Learned Societies, and Texas A&M University. I wish to thank Dennis Preston for his patience and help; Natalie Maynor and Cynthia Bernstein, who have been involved in this research from its inception; Patricia Cukor-Avila and Jan Tillery for providing exemplary fieldwork; Margie Dyer, who helped in the analysis of some of the data; and Jim Dyer, Director of the Texas Poll, without whose help the random sample would not be possible. While all of these people have made significant contributions to the paper, they are responsible for none of its flaws.

2 For an account of these controversies, see Bailey (1989) and the introductions to Montgomery and Bailey (1986) and Bailey, Maynor, and Cukor-Avila (1991).

3 The literature on the divergence controversy has become extensive over the last five years. The spring, 1987 issue of *American Speech* is devoted solely to this controversy; Butters (1989) and Bailey and Maynor (1989) provide fairly up-to-date literature reviews.

4 Actual *linguistic* evidence for convergence is remarkably sparse. Only Fasold (1976) and Vaughn-Cooke (1986) provide systematic attempts to document convergence, but Cukor-Avila (1989a) raises serious questions about the findings of Vaughn-Cooke.

5 Butters and Nix (1986) chide Fasold, Labov, Wolfram, and others for focusing 'on the speech of male adolescents from the most impoverished segments of the communities they examine....' In fact, most dialect studies focus on 'extreme cases' in order to establish a kind of baseline -- this has long been the practice in dialect geography. Speakers can then be described in relation to that baseline. In establishing a baseline of BEV, it makes sense to focus on those who participate most fully in the vernacular culture. That is precisely what sociolinguists have done. The fact that Butters apparently does not do this may account for the differences between his results and those of other studies of BEV in the South (Bailey and Bernstein, 1990).

6 Such samples are not necessarily bad. They often allow us to attack the observer's paradox in a way that more systematic samples do not and to identify variation that would otherwise go unnoticed. They only become problems when we attempt to make inferences about the larger population from them.

7 The fact that sociolinguistics provides no generally accepted way of demonstrating that data represents the 'deepest vernacular' makes it easy for us to dismiss each other's data by simply asserting that it does not represent the 'deepest vernacular.' Perhaps the best solution to this problem is to put the burden of proof on the skeptic: those who argue that a given corpus does not represent the vernacular have the responsibility to produce data that does.

8 The work of Labov shows the continual evolution of field methods designed to confront the observer's paradox. In the early New York City fieldwork (see Labov, 1966), Labov developed a series of different tasks to isolate contextual styles; in Philadelphia, he makes use of a member of the speech community as a fieldworker to explore the vernacular as deeply as possible. Our methods, described below, have as their purpose the same goal.

9 For a complete description of the methods of ULC, see Bailey and Bernstein (1989), Bailey and Dyer (1992), and Cukor-Avila and Bailey (1990).

10 Springville and Atmore are pseudonyms. In small communities, informants can sometimes be identified from the contents of some of the interviews alone, so in the interest of confidentiality, we use pseudonyms for the communities.

11 The primary fieldworkers for ULC include Patricia Cukor-Avila, Vivian Brown, Sherry Gleason, Kevin Glaspar, Kim Jennings Collier, Beverly Kerr, Lisa Abney Martin, Jan Tillery, and Bailey.

12 See Montgomery (1989) for an account of a similar, though not identical, constraint in Scottish English.

13 The existence of these two patterns can also be seen in the use of verbal *-s*. The rural children with urban ties use very little verbal *-s* while other children have vestiges of the older pattern.

14 See Cukor-Avila (1989b) for confirmation of this process.

15 Rickford (1990) confirms that be_2 is an innovative feature. The East Palo Alto study shows even more dramatic age differences than ours does.

16 Although Bailey and Maynor made this point in their initial account of divergence (1987:467), most discussions of this work focus on its arguments for the increasing segregation of blacks and whites (see Denning, 1989, and Rickford, 1990). However, Bailey and Maynor see the consequences of segregation not as linguistic divergence per se but as the creation of speech communities where establishing cultural identity and affirming bonds of solidarity become more important than a shift to 'standard English.' This is precisely the context where divergence might arise.

17 The other variables represent either completed changes, stable variation, or incipient changes that have yet to develop social meaning. For that reason they are not treated here.

18 The results of both the Duncan and Scheffe tests show that the differences between the responses of blacks and whites are significant at the .05 level (in most instances the .01 level) for /ɔ/ - /ɑ/, monophthongal /aɪ/, postvocalic /r/, and the merger of /u/ and /U/ before /l/. The differences for other features are not significant.

19 The presentation here actually understates the robustness of the merger of tense and lax vowels. Tillery and Kerr (1989) examine the merger in detail and show that it represents a long-term drift that, according to atlas records, was underway by the beginning of this century.

20 The reason why the merger of /u/ and /U/ before /l/ should be an exception is not clear, but it is interesting to note that black and white speech differ remarkably in processes affecting back vowels (such as fronting) in general. See Bailey and Benson (1989).

21 Baugh (1983) provides an excellent discussion of educational issues.

References

Bailey, Guy. 1987. Are black and white vernaculars diverging? *American Speech* 62:32-40.

Bailey, Guy. 1989. Black English. In William Ferris & Charles Wilson (eds), *Encyclopedia of southern culture*. Chapel Hill: University of North Carolina Press, 194-5.

Bailey, Guy & Marvin Bassett. 1986. Invariant *be* in the Lower South. In Bailey & Montgomery (eds), 258-79.

Bailey, Guy & Robert Benson. 1989. Chain shifts and mergers in the black and white vernaculars. Paper presented at the Southeastern Conference on Linguistics, Atlanta, GA.

Bailey, Guy & Cynthia Bernstein. 1989. Methodology for a phonological survey of Texas. *Journal of English Linguistics* 22:6-16.

Bailey, Guy & Cynthia Bernstein. 1990. The idea of Black English. *SECOL Review* 14:1-24.

Bailey, Guy, Cynthia Bernstein and Jan Tillery. Under review. The configuration of phonological change in Texas. *Language Variation and Change*.

Bailey, Guy & Margie Dyer. 1992. An approach to sampling in dialectology. *American Speech* 67,1:3-20.

Bailey, Guy & Natalie Maynor. 1985a. The present tense of *be* in southern black folk speech. *American Speech* 60:195- 213.

Bailey, Guy & Natalie Maynor. 1985b. The present tense of *be* in white folk speech of the southern United States. *English World-Wide* 6:199-216.

Bailey, Guy & Natalie Maynor. 1987. Decreolization? *Language in Society* 16:449-73.

Bailey, Guy & Natalie Maynor. 1989. The divergence controversy. *American Speech* 64:12-39.

Bailey, Guy, Natalie Maynor, & Patricia Cukor-Avila. 1989. Variation in subject-verb concord in Early Modern English. *Language Variation and Change* 1,3:285-300.

Bailey, Guy, Natalie Maynor, & Patricia Cukor-Avila. 1991. *The emergence of Black English: Texts and commentary*. Amsterdam: John Benjamins.

Baugh, John. 1983. *Black street speech: Its history, structure, and survival*. Austin: University of Texas Press.

Butters, Ronald R. 1989. *The death of Black English: Divergence and convergence in black and white vernaculars*. Frankfurt: Peter Lang.

Butters, Ronald R. & Ruth Nix. 1986. The English of blacks in Wilmington, North Carolina. In Montgomery and Bailey (eds), 254-63.

Cukor-Avila, Patricia. 1989a. Determining change in progress vs. stable variation in two studies of BEV. *SECOL Review* 13:92-123.

Cukor-Avila, Patricia. 1989b. The urbanization of rural BEV. Paper presented at the Southeastern Conference on Linguistics, Norfolk, VA.

Cukor-Avila, Patricia. 1989c. Verbal *-s* as a narrative marker? Paper presented at the Southeastern Conference on Linguistics, Atlanta, GA.

Cukor-Avila, Patricia & Guy Bailey. 1990. An approach to fieldwork in sociolinguistics. Paper presented at the Southeastern Conference on Linguistics, Tampa, FL.

Denning, Keith. 1989. Convergence with divergence: A sound change in vernacular Black English. *Language Variation and Change* 1:145-168.

Dillard, J.L. 1972. *Black English: Its history and usage in the United States.* New York: Random House.

Fasold, Ralph. 1976. One hundred years from syntax to phonology. In Sanford B. Steever, Carole A. Walker, & Salikoko S. Mufwene (eds), *Papers from the parasession on diachronic syntax.* Chicago: University of Chicago Press, 79-87.

Feagin, Crawford. 1979. *Variation in Alabama English: A sociolinguistic survey of the white community.* Washington, D.C.: Georgetown University Press.

Feagin, Crawford. 1989. Why southern states r-lessness? Paper presented at NWAVE XVIII, Durham, N.C.

Labov, William. 1966. *The social stratification of English in New York City.* Arlington, VA: Center for Applied Linguistics.

Labov, William. 1972. *Language in the inner city: Studies in the Black English vernacular.* Philadelphia: University of Pennsylvania Press.

Labov, William. 1982. Objectivity and commitment in linguistic science. *Language in Society* 11:165-202.

Labov, William. 1987. Are black and white vernaculars diverging? *American Speech* 62:5-12; 63-74.

Labov, William, Paul Cohen, Clarence Robins, and John Lewis. 1968. A study of the non-standard English of Negro and Puerto Rican speakers in New York City. Final report, Cooperative Research Project 3288, 2 vols. Philadelphia: U. S Regional Survey.

Milroy, Lesley. 1980. *Language and social networks.* Oxford: Blackwell.

Montgomery, Michael. 1989. Exploring the Roots of Appalachian English. *English World-wide.* 10:227-278.

Montgomery, Michael & Guy Bailey (eds). 1986. *Language variety in the South.* Tuscaloosa: University of Alabama Press.

Myhill, John & Wendell Harris. 1986. The use of verbal *-s* inflection in BEV. In David Sankoff (ed.), *Diversity and diachrony*, Amsterdam: John Benjamins, 25-31.

Poplack, Shana & Sali Tagliamonte. 1989. There's no tense like the present: Verbal *-s* inflection in early Black English. *Language Variation and Change* 1:47-84.

Rickford, John. 1987. Are black and white vernaculars diverging? *American Speech* 62:55-62;73.

Rickford, John. 1989. Continuity and innovation in the development of BEV *be*$_2$. Paper presented at NWAVE XVIII, Durham, N.C.

Rickford, John. 1990. Grammatical variation and divergence in vernacular Black English. In Marinel Gerritsen and Dieter Stein (eds), ICHL workshop on internal and external factors in syntactic change. The Hague: Mouton.

Tillery, Jan & Grace Kerr. 1989. The merger of tense and lax vowels before /l/. Paper presented at NWAVE XVIII, Durham, N.C.

Vaughn-Cooke, Faye Boyd. 1986. Lexical diffusion: Evidence from a decreolizing variety of Black English. In Montgomery and Bailey (eds), 111-30.

Vaughn-Cook, Faye Boyd. 1987. Are black and white vernaculars diverging? *American Speech* 62:12-32; 67-70.

Wolfram, Walt. 1974. The relation of white southern speech to vernacular Black English. *Language* 50:498-527.

Professional Varieties: The Case of Language and Law

William M. O'Barr
Duke University

A Personal Preface

Growing up and spending most of my pre-college years in South Georgia, it seemed inevitable that diversity in language would fascinate me. My parents, both Georgia natives themselves, came from different regions. Mother, whose world was Savannah and its orb, eloped with Father who had grown up in the Appalachian foothills. I sometimes imagine that their speech differences implanted alternative templates in my brain. As a child, I was forever asking which was the right way to say something, and why what seemed the same things often had many names.

Thus I was primed for the linguistic diversity inherent in the larger world around me: of Whites and Blacks, of Baptists whose talk about and to God differed from even Methodists whose church stood almost within sight, of women (who were often teachers) and men (who seldom were), of farmers and of town folk, of the educated and the illiterate. My maternal grandfather, first a local politician and later a representative in the General Assembly, seemed to have his own special way of talking about public life. His skill with language was heroic. Once a grammar school teacher took us on a field trip to the courthouse, only two blocks from school, but warned us in advance of the heavy and unpleasant talk we might hear as youthful citizens observing some trial in progress. The florid description of a shotgun being fired, of 'guts dripping from a man's side into a washtub,' are as alive today as when I first heard them. My maternal grandmother, the family's bastion of high cultural learning, had two impressive bookcases in her living room: one with classics of western literature, another with the piano compositions of what I thought were all the composers who ever lived. She, who had taught Latin in a one-room school as the century turned, had her own rules about language, of what could be said, of when, and to whom. And these were rules that never could be broken, no matter what, or so I thought. Once I made the mistake of referring to a Black woman as a 'lady,' only to be corrected and told that there were no Black ladies, only Black women. I was instructed that such things would be clear when I grew up.

Nearly half a century later, I feel a tug of early experience. Each of us could write a linguistic autobiography, and our divergent stories would be united by tales of early awarenesses that provoked us to seek ways of comprehending language as we have known it.

Language Varies -- But So What?

Many disciplines turned attention to the study of language variation in the 1960s. For some, this complemented the more fashionable quest for language universals. For others, it was the preferred alternative focus that dealt with the issues of language use. Studies of language variation by anthropologists, sociologists, and linguists in the 1960s were not, of course, the first studies of variety in language. However, the breadth of this new scholarship moved beyond the restrictions of previous boundaries. These emergent interests spawned a large number of studies, many of which suffered the shortcoming of failing to justify descriptive work in terms of theoretical goals.

Sociolinguistics, *sociology of language*, and *ethnography of communication* became different lines of inquiry. They corresponded roughly to efforts to explain linguistic variation as socially conditioned, to treat language as a generative component of the social system, and to document and compare language use in community life. These distinctions correspond generally to disciplinary differences. Linguists used society to help explain language; sociologists attempted to legitimize language as worthy subject matter; and anthropologists began to treat language and communication as aspects of culture deserving attention.

The flurry of work in all these fields yielded many good studies. It soon became clear to linguists that language variation not only could be, but ought to be explained with reference to social distinctions among speakers, contexts, and topics. Concepts like free variation became relegated to discussions of the history of linguistic theory. Even language change was reconceptualized sociolinguistically. Linguistics relied heavily on social coordinates to explain variation.

By contrast, sociologists used language instrumentally to explain social processes. Nationalism, ethnicity, and community were conceived as matters involving intersections between language and society. In addition to macrosocial issues, face-to-face interaction was also reexamined with reference to the medium through which it occurs. The study of conversation emerged as a sociological specialization.

In addition to supplying precedents for fieldwork methods to others, anthropologists undertook their own field investigations of language. In some instances, this meant including considerations of language within broader investigations of culture. In others, it meant treating language as the primary object of study rather than the instrumental means through which culture was examined.[1] Ethnographies began including more materials on language and communication. Ethnographies of speaking, a new genre of field studies, focused attention directly on these matters. Language use was shown to vary cross-culturally, but the complexity of differences across cultures led to no single conclusion about which aspects varied and which did not.

Other scholars, whose own interests did not tend to focus directly on language, found the general contributions of scholarship linking language and society useful but questioned the importance of proliferating studies that only seemed to document yet other instances of language variation. They soon tired of distributions of phonology in American cities, of descriptions of repair sequences in conversational interactions, and of greeting patterns in another tribal culture. There were good reasons for continuing such studies within the various disciplines, but those investigating society more broadly began to ask: So what? Behind this question was a growing dissatisfaction with linkages of this new information to more general questions.

Studying the Consequences of Language Variation in Legal Contexts

Although studies relating language and society were well established by the early 1970s, there were no studies of significance and certainly no body of theory relating language variation to professional or institutional contexts. The LSA Summer Institute of Linguistics at the University of Michigan in 1972 brought together an extraordinary number of scholars working on language in context. It provided intellectual support, assessed cumulative knowledge, and helped set future agenda. Public lectures and formal courses ranged broadly: pidgins and creoles, pragmatics, conversation, variable rules, etc. The base was solid; the horizons of theory were moved; and the good times rolled.

The Institute included no courses on language in institutional contexts except for Charles Ferguson's lectures on language and religion. For me, this served as an import foil to develop research questions about language in the domains of politics and law. As he examined varieties of religious language, data recording techniques, and theoretical goals, I attempted to extrapolate from his insights. By the end of the summer, I had formulated some ideas about how I might study language and law.

My interest in these issues had earlier roots, the most immediate of which were my two years in Tanzania in the late 1960s. The linguistic diversity of the rural community where I had worked *required* coming to terms with language in order to study the legal system. This was a matter of practical necessity, not simply a predilection or choice. The society I studied had been designated a 'tribe' by the British in 1928. Two languages with many regional varieties were indigenous to the homeland. This internal diversity was supplemented by Swahili (the national language of independent Tanzania) and English (a school language that had many uses among the educated). It was not possible to deal with substantive matters in the local legal system without also dealing with the intricate linguistic context in which it operated. In addition, these people employed a formalized system of double-talk to deceive outsiders. These conventions had uses well before the colonial period, but they also served in the contemporary political context. Near the end of my fieldwork, I had begun to appreciate these matters and their significance in social life. Language was more than an instrumental mechanism for conducting political life in the villages where I worked; it was a key to explaining options, strategies, and outcomes in public affairs. My experiences in East Africa prompted questions about language and law and constituted a filter though which I listened during the summer of 1972.[2]

The Nature of Legal Language

Back home in my own university's library, I found that most of the scholarship dealing with legal language up to that time had focused primarily on writing. Mellinkoff's *The Language of the Law* (1963) was a wonderful compendium of the history of modern American legal language. He explained the origins of couplets like *give* and *bequeath*, *acknowledge* and *confess*, and *break* and *enter* as originating in the conjunction of the Anglo-Saxon and French-Latin traditions that made up English law after the Norman Conquest. He detailed the history of legal verbosity in the centuries-old tradition of paying copiers by the page and offered other insights that help explain how modern legal language developed. Still, his work was focused almost entirely on the written language of the law. Neither he nor other scholars had considered in any detail varieties of language spoken in courtrooms and other contexts.[3]

The ethnographic guidelines for studying speech, articulated first by Dell Hymes (1974) and followed by many others, proposed a series of issues to investigate in studying spoken legal language: differences in speech corresponding to roles, genres appropriate for some contexts but not others, and distinctive features of speech events like trials, hearings, or conferences. These were useful guidelines and served as a scout's handbook.

Together, the scholarship of Ferguson, Mellinkoff, and Hymes pointed out possibilities, but it provided neither specific precedents nor direct guidance.

Getting Started

Treating the courtroom as a foreign environment had certain advantages. No formal legal training (and thankfully no personal encounters with the law) made this posture relatively easy. I began observation much as I had in Africa. It was initially helpful to start with an empty notebook and the simple expectation that the language of the court would, in course, virtually inscribe itself on the pages. This attitude also helped me in understanding what seemed important to the lawyers, witnesses, jurors, judges, and other court officials.

But I was not really a blank slate. Both anthropology and linguistic studies defined issues of importance: social structure, language repertoires, interaction. And my past professional and personal experiences oriented me as well. A few pages into my notebook, the marks of these issues began appearing in the margins around my observational notes.

After two weeks or so, I had a sense of what I thought was especially interesting: language strategies used to influence jurors and judges. I was curious about how the manner of presenting information might determine the outcome of trials. Theoretical precedents from anthropology concerning pragmatic strategies (e.g., the work of F. G. Bailey [1969]) and from sociolinguistics (i.e., the non-random nature of language variation) guided my thinking. Within a few weeks, I conjoined observation and theory in a proposal to NSF seeking funding for the study of courtroom language.

I was spared any serious criticism from skeptics who either thought I couldn't or shouldn't investigate such matters and blessed with support from the Law and Social Science Program to initiate empirical study of courtroom language and its effects on legal decisionmakers. I assembled a team of researchers at Duke and UNC-Chapel Hill to combine skills and insights from several disciplines. Anthropological field methods were joined with the theoretical questions of linguistics and tempered by issues of concern to the law. Social psychologists were engaged to design and conduct experimental studies assessing the effects of variable presentational styles. Ethnography and experimentation were made partners in a joint research venture (O'Barr and Lind 1981).

A summer of observation and audio tape recording in trial courtrooms yielded more than 150 hours of legal language in use. Guided by theoretical concerns in linguistics, practical questions posed by lawyers, and our own sense of what seemed important, four major issues were selected for intensive study. These were: 'powerless' language (stemming from Robin Lakoff's initial claims about gender differences in American English), hypercorrection (encouraged by Labov's work on this topic), simultaneous speech (stimulated by conversation analysts and their studies of overlaps and gaps in everyday conversations), and narrative versus fragmented testimony (predicated on the conflicting assumptions of trial lawyers that witnesses ought to be encouraged to give lengthy narratives or alternatively to be highly constrained).[4]

Although the specifics of the studies varied, they yielded a common finding: namely, that variation in speech style did have massive effects on legal decisionmakers. The multidisciplinary team, which I named the Duke Law and Language Project, worked together to describe language use in the courtroom and to assess the impact of language variation on the recipients of talk. Most importantly, the combination of disciplines helped answer the broader questions of why people talk differently and what difference it makes when they do.

These studies of language in the courtroom helped demonstrate the consequential nature of language diversity in social settings. However, the consistent finding across a series of variables raised troubling questions about the law itself. Particularly disturbing was the degree to which legal decisionmakers altered their opinions about the relative credibility of witnesses on the basis of variation in their presentational 'styles.' In charging the jury, the judge specifically empowers its members to decide upon the relative credibility of those who testified. Our work showed that manipulating presentational style could alter relative credibility and thus provided empirical evidence for the fragility of the concept of justice in American law.

More Recent Concerns

In the past decade, linguistic inquiry has increasingly focused on discourse as an interesting and appropriate level of analysis. This shift has occasioned two kinds of insight into language processes: the discovery of previously overlooked phenomena that occur at levels of organization higher than the sentence, and the understanding of discourse-level aspects of phenomena previously studied only at the sentence or subsentence level. Research on language and law has been affected by this shift in interest. New aspects of language in legal settings have been discovered and investigated. For example, by focusing on litigant narratives in small claims and more formal courts, the Duke-UNC research group has been able to study differences between lay and legal structures of argumentation, standards of proof, and concepts of evidence (O'Barr and Conley 1985).

In addition to discovering entirely new issues that arise at the level of discourse, there have also been investigations of the degree to which features of legal language studied at one level are manifest at other analytic levels. Again, in the case of the Duke-UNC group, it has been possible to show relations between certain speech styles characteristic of speakers with particular social backgrounds and the structure of their accounts given in small claims courts (O'Barr and Conley 1985; Conley and O'Barr 1990).

Further funding from NSF made it possible to study such accounts in seven cities in three states. From these, we have discovered significant dimensions of difference in the stories people tell in court. Most importantly, we have found that some litigants organize their accounts narrowly around specific issues of the violation of legal rules, such as contract violations or damaged property. Other litigants tell further-reaching stories when given the license to do so. Their accounts are about social relations gone sour, about neighborhood or family difficulties, and about the complex web of interactions within which legal problems emerge. We have termed these two kinds of accounts *rule-oriented* and *relational*.[5]

In contrast to the earlier study where we felt positivistic confirmation of ethnographic findings would be helpful in establishing the credence of our claims, we have elected to proceed in a more interpretive manner in order to build models of the *rule* and *relational* orientations that characterize the legal discourse of lay litigants. We expect researchers may wish to study these differences experimentally in order to assess the impact of such variation on legal decisionmakers.

Law and Language Studies More Generally

At the end of the 1980s, an assessment of the state of scholarly knowledge about law in legal contexts yields a very different finding than was the case in the early 1970s. In addition to the work my colleagues and I have been doing at Duke and UNC, many other researchers representing several disciplines have conducted innovative and significant work in American and other legal settings. Three important review articles have chronicled and assessed this work: Danet (1980), Levi (1982), and Brenneis (1988). Because of the excellence of these review essays and their appended bibliographies, the greatest service I can provide is to recommend them to scholars who have not already relied on them for guidance. Together, they show that linguists and social scientists have devoted considerable attention over the past two decades to language in the domain of the law both in the English-speaking courts of the United States and Britain and in the courts and legal systems of other countries. However, the questions asked and the methods employed are so diverse as to defy simple or easy categorization. All share the common interest in linking language use with the functioning of the institutions of the law. Given this diversity of interests and approaches, it seems unlikely that any single method will be used in such studies or that any common paradigm or general theory will be advanced. Rather, it is the case that, unlike the situation twenty years ago, there are many good models of sound and interesting work for other scholars to use in developing their own research questions about language and law. There is every reason to believe that, now established as a legitimate field of inquiry, we can expect additional studies that help us understand better the relations between language and the institutions of law.

Special Issues in the Study of Law and Language

Language and law studies have produced at least three special, and perhaps unique, sets of issues that are not likely to be shared by language studies in other contexts: (1) access to the study of language in legal domains is a complex matter because only some situations are public while others are highly confidential; (2) the applications of linguistic knowledge in the law has resulted in complex issues as increasing numbers of linguists act as out-of-court consultants and in-court expert witnesses; and (3) guaranteeing the rights of non-native speakers of official court languages (as well as the deaf and other language-impaired persons) has emerged as a legal issue.

Other Professional Contexts

Finally, language and law as an area for the study of language in a professional domain must be understood as part of a larger movement among linguists and social scientists to study language in other such contexts as education, business, and medicine where the issues associated with research have important similarities and differences.

Notes

1 The studies in Bloch (1975) represent this latter shift in emphasis. David Turton's contribution is an especially forceful criticism of the conventional attitude within anthropology toward language and makes a strong case for the value of direct attention to language (Turton 1975).

2 These concerns are also discussed in O'Barr (1975) and O'Barr (1983).

3 Chapter 2 of O'Barr (1982) contains an extensive discussion of the history of written legal language as contained in Mellinkoff and related studies.

4 These studies are reviewed in detail in Chapter 5 of O'Barr (1982). The antecedents of our work on 'powerless' language can be found in Lakoff (1975). Labov (1972) reviews his research on hypercorrection which stimulated our investigations of this topic. Sacks, Schegloff, and Jefferson (1974) is the classic introduction to conversation analysis and was the basis for the lectures given by Sacks and Schegloff at the 1972 LSA Summer Institute. Advice on courtroom tactics is contained in trial practice manuals which are discussed at length in O'Barr (1982), 31-38.

5 *Rules versus relationships: The ethnography of legal discourse* (Conley and O'Barr 1990) describes our findings in detail.

References

Bailey, F. G. 1969. *Strategems and spoils.* New York: Schocken.

Bloch, Maurice (ed.). 1975. *Political language and oratory in traditional society.* New York: Academic Press.

Brenneis, Donald. 1988. Language and disputing. *Annual Review of Anthropology* 17:221-37.

Conley, John & William M. O'Barr. 1990. *Rules versus relationships: The ethnography of legal discourse.* Chicago: The University of Chicago Press.

Danet, Brenda. 1980. Language in the legal process. *Law and Society Review.* 14:445-564.

Hymes, Dell. 1974. *Foundations in sociolinguistics: An ethnographic approach.* Philadelphia: University of Pennsylvania Press.

Labov, William. 1972. Hypercorrection as a factor in linguistic change. In William Labov, *Sociolinguistic Patterns.* Philadelphia: University of Pennsylvania Press, 122-42.

Lakoff, Robin. 1975. *Language and woman's place.* New York: Harper & Row.

Levi, Judith. 1982. *Linguistics, language, and law: A topical bibliography.* Bloomington: Indiana University Linguistics Club. (Mimeographed).

Mellinkoff, David. 1963. *The language of the law.* Boston: Little, Brown.

O'Barr, William M. 1975. Language and politics in a rural Tanzanian council. In William. M. & J. F. O'Barr (eds), *Language and politics,* The Hague: Mouton.

O'Barr, William M. 1982. *Linguistic evidence: Language, power, and strategy in the Courtroom.* New York: Academic Press.

O'Barr, William M. 1983. The study of language in institutional contexts. *Journal of Language and Social Psychology* 2:241- 251.

O'Barr, William M. & John M. Conley. 1985. Litigant satisfaction versus legal adequacy in small claims court narratives. *Law and Society Review* 19:661-701.

O'Barr, William M. & E. Allan Lind. 1981. Ethnography and experimentation -- Partners in legal research. In B. D. Sales (ed.), *The Trial Process.* New York: Plenum.

Sacks, Harvey, Emanuel Schegloff, & Gail Jefferson. 1974. A simplest systematics for the organization of turn-taking in conversation. *Language* 50:696-735.

Turton, David. 1975. The relationship between oratory and the exercise of influence among the Mursi. In Maurice Bloch (ed.), *Political language and oratory in traditional society.* New York: Academic Press.

IV. Special Topics

Folk Dialectology

Dennis R. Preston
Michigan State University

Dialectologists have been principally concerned with differences in speaker performance and have hoped that studies of such performance will help illuminate the principles of language change. Although it is true that Nineteenth Century Herderian notions of the folk provided justification for purely synchronic and cultural interpretations, such redirection did not change the understanding that the basic data of the discipline remained the noises, arrangements, and meanings produced by respondents (see Francis, this volume).

Social psychologists drew attention to receivers as well as producers by studying language attitudes. That trend was incorporated into sociolinguistics, where respondents were used as reactors to as well as performers of variation. In all such studies, however, it was still the noise of speakers' performances which was used to elicit responses. Perhaps the initial use of different languages in attitude studies made later scholars accept the uninvestigated premise that respondents' attention to differences in form was the principal source of judgments. Later monolingual studies showed that respondents' attitudes were shaped even by forms of which they had no overt awareness. In Labov (1966), for example, respondents rated performances which contained fewer realizations of post-vocalic (r) much lower on a job appropriateness scale but were unable to indicate what linguistic feature was used in their evaluation.

This chapter will suggest that overt folk notions of language, based on neither production of nor response to forms, provide a helpful corollary to both production and attitude studies of regional (and other) varieties. Folk linguistics has generally been reported anecdotally and serves usually as a foil to the 'correct' linguistics professionals want to present to neophytes. Hoenigswald (1966), however, makes the strong claim that knowledge of the folk categories of language at every level of analysis serves not only folkloristic, anthropological, and applied ends but also general linguistic ones. In particular, folk notions of language might themselves be shapers of directions for change and clues to otherwise apparently unmotivated choices in such change.

Hoenigswald's plea for the study of folk linguistics has not gone completely unheeded. The ethnography of communication (e.g., Hymes 1972) has legitimized the study of the awareness of and regard for the shape and uses of language in standardized speech communities. Anthropologists and folklorists have been at work investigating folk linguistics in other societies for some time (e.g., Stross 1974), but such efforts had not been made in Western European cultures (and ones derived from them) until very recently.

What has been done in folk linguistics rarely served dialectology. Only the simplest questions had been formulated and asked: Where do dialect boundaries exist? What sorts of speech are contained within them? How distinct are they? Two traditions exist which approach or suggest approaches to these concerns. First, work in linguistic geography in The Netherlands has sought to determine respondent belief about the distinctness of neighboring areas (Rensink 1955); that work prompted similar investigations in Japan (e.g., Grootaers 1959) and resurfaces from time to time in current European work (e.g., Kremer 1984). Applications of this degree-of-difference technique in the United States are illustrated in part 3 below. Second, cultural geography provides qualitative and quantitative models for folk dialectology. Information about respondents' perceptions of the surrounding physical space has been determined by having them draw maps of it, and predefined regions (e.g., states) have been rated by respondents for such characteristics as desirability of residence, political climate, job opportunity, and so on. Both techniques have been used in folk dialectology and are illustrated in parts 1 and 2 below. Gould and White (1972) provide a good introduction to these *mental mapping* techniques, and Preston (1989) summarizes both the linguistic and cultural geographical backgrounds of folk dialectology. This paper reports on recent developments and extensions of these techniques.

1. Draw a Map

The most straightforward way of discovering what respondents believe about area is to have them draw maps. In the first attempt to use this technique in dialect study, I asked students at the University of Hawaii to 'draw maps of the areas of the United States where people speak differently' (Preston 1982). I also asked them to label the areas they outlined with the name of the variety of English spoken there or, if they did not know or use one, with the label they usually assigned the speakers who lived there.

A word about a false start -- not critical of students at the University of Hawaii, for it has proved to be a difficulty wherever this work has been done in the United States. Since physical and political boundaries might prejudice results, I first used a blank map of the United States for elicitation.[1] The resulting confusion was so great that it was necessary to use a map with state lines or allow respondents to consult a detailed road map. I understand that there is a movement afoot to improve geographical knowledge, but, for the time being, folk dialectology research is confounded with folk geography.

Figure 1 is an example of one young Hawaiian's map and Figure 2 another's. The detail of the first must somehow be combined with the paucal information of the second in arriving at a composite; I first used a simple technique. Each respondent's boundary for each area was treated as an isogloss. When the 'isoglosses' from all respondents for one area were overlaid by hand drawing, 'bundles of isoglosses' were identified and taken to be that group's mental map outline of the dialect area under consideration. Figure 3 shows how thirteen southern Indiana respondents' overlapping boundaries were used to determine the dialect area 'Northern' for them. There is little disagreement on the eastern and northern limits; similarly, many respondents set the southern limits at the Michigan, Wisconsin, and Minnesota southern boundaries, although the majority include a small portion of northern Iowa. The map does not show it, but a slightly larger number of respondents included all of Minnesota at the western boundary, so the final determination was as is shown in Figure 4, in which the results of similar composite-making for all areas are displayed.

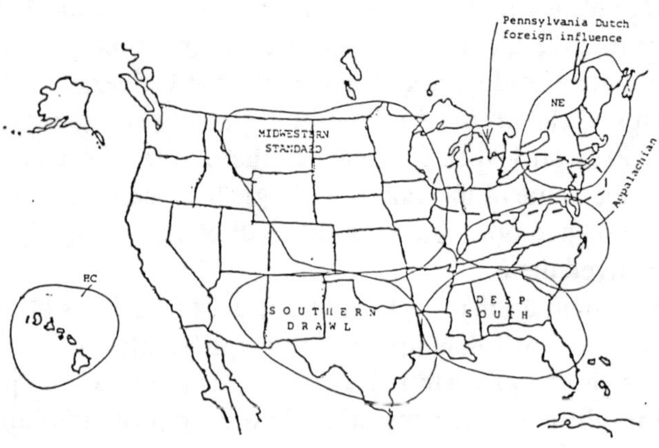

Figure 1: A Hawaii respondent's hand-drawn map of U. S. dialect areas showing considerable detail

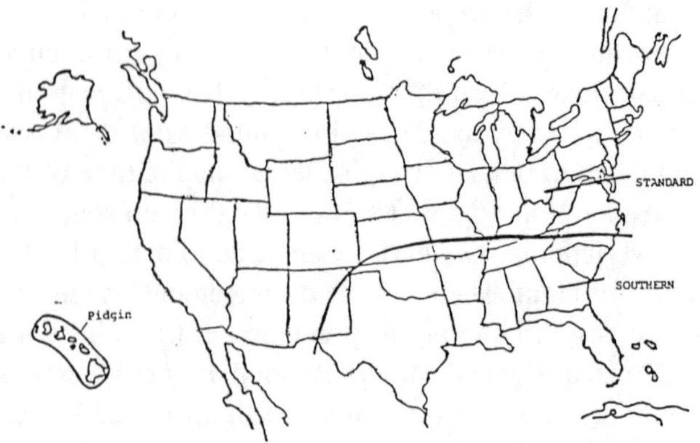

Figure 2: A Hawaii respondent's hand-drawn map of U. S. dialect areas showing little detail

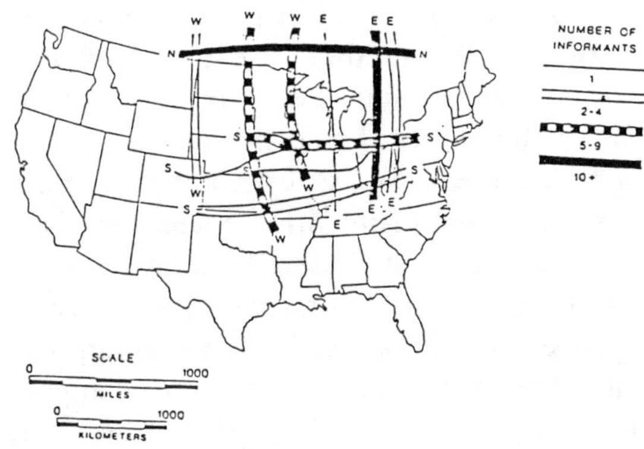

Figure 3: The computation of the 'Northern' speech area as drawn by thirteen southern Indiana respondents

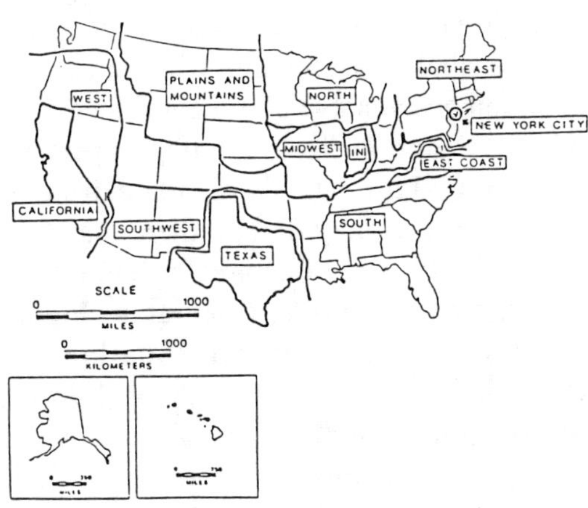

Figure 4: A map of U. S. dialect areas as perceived by southern Indiana respondents, each area determined as in Figure 3

Preston (1986) compares and contrasts five such maps from the perspectives of Hawaii, southern Indiana, western New York, New York City, and southeastern Michigan with one another, with production dialect maps, and with maps of nonlinguistic aspects of cultural geography. These studies suffer considerably, however, from limitations imposed on the number of respondents by the laborious hand-tracing of boundaries and, therefore, from a lack of sociolinguistic depth: the small number of respondents makes it impossible to investigate gender, generation, class, or ethnic differences. Once it was seen that respondents from many different areas used the same very general cognitive template for area identifications, a way of determining isoglosses for larger numbers of respondents was devised. The outlines of each respondent's areas were traced onto a digitizing pad which fed the coordinates activated by this tracing into a computer program keyed to a standard map. This technique allows automatic compilation of composite maps based on large numbers of respondents and on demographically appropriate subdivisions of them.[2]

The dotted area in Figure 5 shows the composite of 138 southeastern Michigan respondents' outlines of the dialect area 'Southern.' Such representative composite maps depict an area where fifty percent of the respondents agree; a higher percentage of agreement will considerably reduce the area, reaching, eventually, what one might call the 'core' (Figure 6); a smaller percentage will increase the area, reaching eventually one of unconscionable size, contributed by perhaps only one or two respondents (Figure 7). Testing different percentages of respondent agreement will reveal if relatively regular expanding and decreasing concentric lines emerge. If they do not, there may be a barrier beyond which even 'liberal' outliners of an area will not go or an extent from which even 'conservatives' will not withdraw. Figure 8, which illustrates agreement on the boundaries of 'Southern' for seventy-five percent of these Michigan respondents, shows how more conservative respondents have regularly reduced the dimensions of 'Southern,' (in contrast to the larger area shown in the fifty percent agreement of Figure 5), but Figure 9, which illustrates ninety-one percent agreement, shows that the coastal extent of 'Southern' is stronger than that of any other direction. Since the fifty percent composite (Figure 5) includes the coastal territory, there is no need to revise it, but recognition of such tendencies plays an important role in interpretation, here, perhaps, indicating a folk knowledge of the east to west direction of historical spread of American dialects.

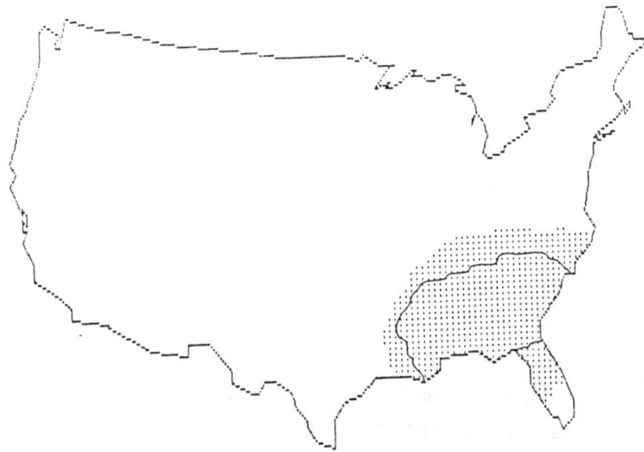

Figure 5: Michigan (dotted area) and Indiana (solid line) respondents' representations of the 'Southern' speech area at a 50% agreement level

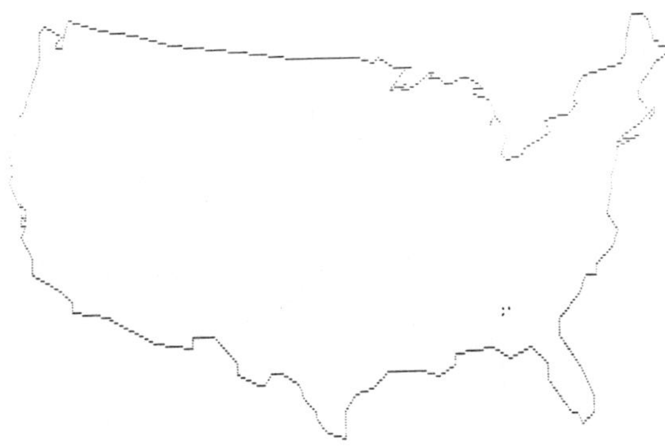

Figure 6: Michigan respondents' representation of the 'Southern' speech area at a 96% agreement level

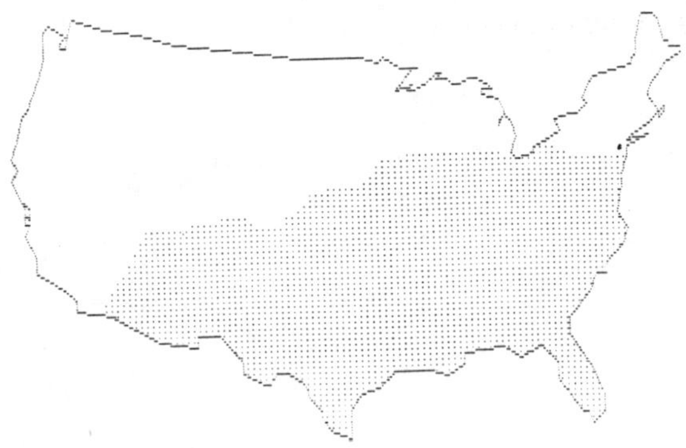

Figure 7: Michigan respondents' representation of the 'Southern' speech area at a 0.7% agreement level, showing areas included by even one respondent

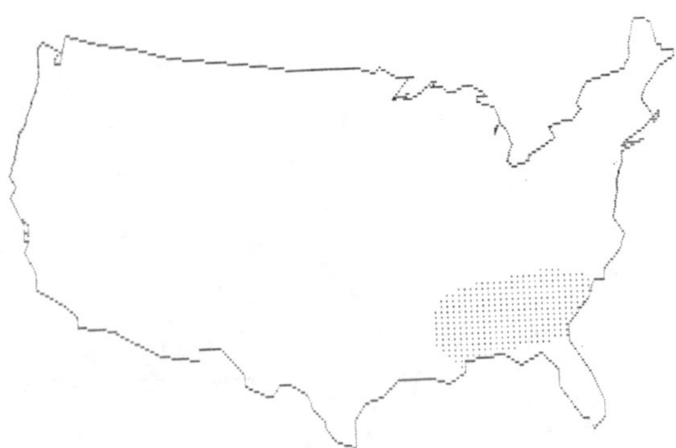

Figure 8: Michigan respondents' representation of the 'Southern' speech area at a 75% agreement level

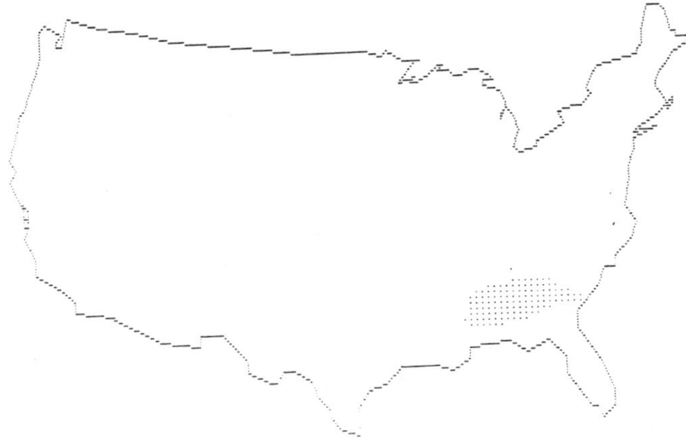

Figure 9: Michigan respondents' representation of the 'Southern' speech area at a 91% agreement level

A consideration of all the regions drawn and an extraction of the composite for each allows compilation of a mental map of dialect areas for a particular set of respondents. Figure 10 shows such a map for 147 southeastern Michigan respondents, and Figure 11 allows comparison with a similarly derived map from 123 southern Indiana respondents. (The solid line in Figure 5 shows even more dramatically the much smaller area regarded as 'Southern' by Indiana respondents.) As suggested above, these maps may be contrasted not only with one another but also with production dialect maps and with maps of other cultural geographical findings.

Since computer processing permits a larger sample, subdivisions of populations may be investigated, introducing a sociolinguistic dimension (Chambers, Chapter 5, this volume). Figure 12, for example, contrasts the youngest (20 and under, dotted area) and the oldest (60 and over, solid line) Michigan respondents' characterizations of 'Southern.'[3] The fifty year old decade stands about half way between

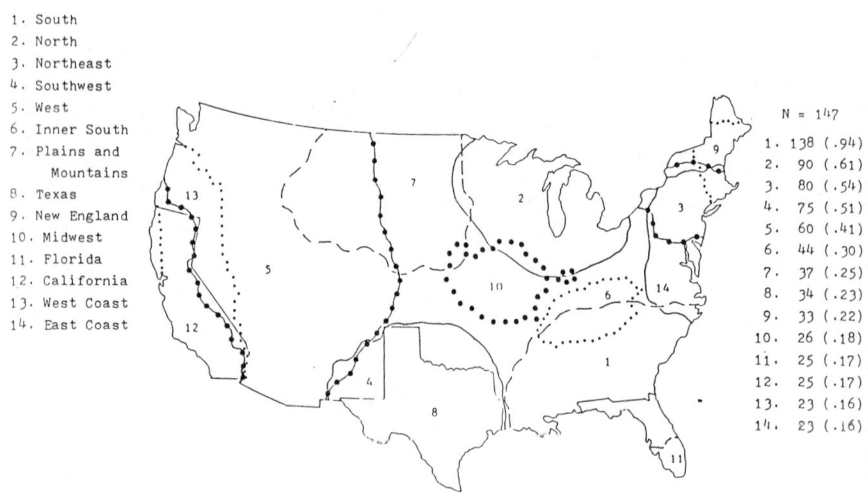

Figure 10: Michigan respondents' computer-generated mental map of U.S. speech regions

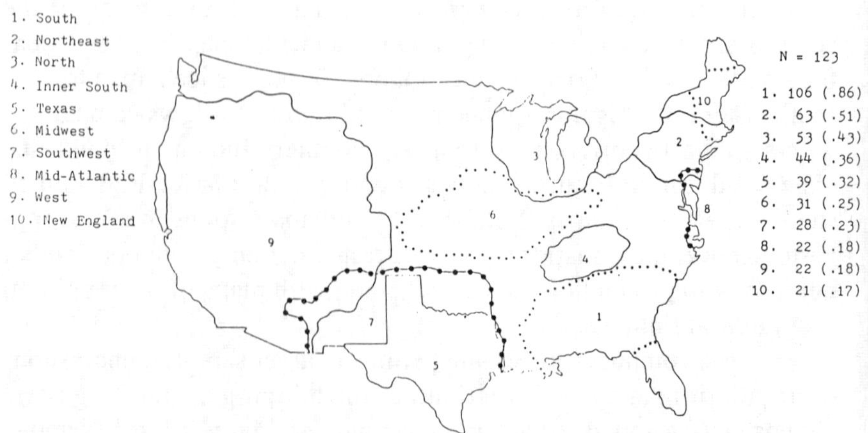

Figure 11: Indiana respondents' computer-generated mental map of U.S. speech regions

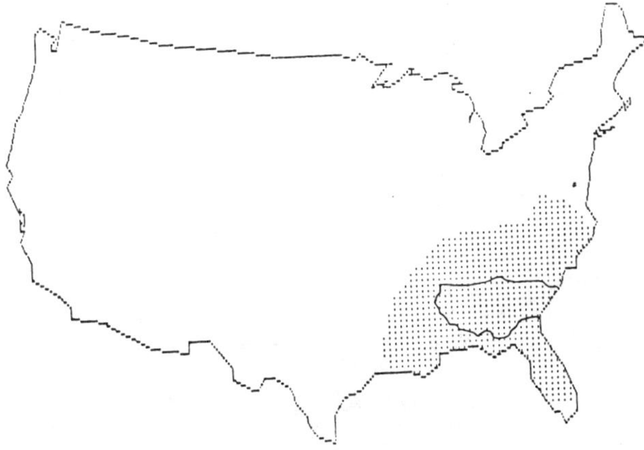

Figure 12: Youngest (dotted area) and oldest (solid line) Michigan respondents' representations of the 'Southern' speech area (both at the 50% agreement level)

these extremes, but there is no significant difference between the youngest respondents' outline and those in the twenty, thirty, and forty year old decades. The Indiana respondents reveal a similar (though not so dramatic) difference. It remains to be seen if this is age-graded -- which implies that older raters draw a smaller 'Southern' (perhaps smaller areas in general[4]) -- or a change in the perception of the extent of the speech area 'Southern' for both Indiana and Michigan raters.

Although gender differences in the map-drawing task have not proved interesting, social status provides additional contrasts. Figure 13 contrasts lower middle (dotted area) and upper middle (solid line) class perceptions of 'Southern' for Michigan respondents. Although working class respondents outline a slightly smaller area than the lower middle class, there is little difference between the middle and lower-middle class representations. Like the oldest respondents, the upper middle class tend to isolate a more core-like area. The interpretation of these social status differences is not immediately clear.

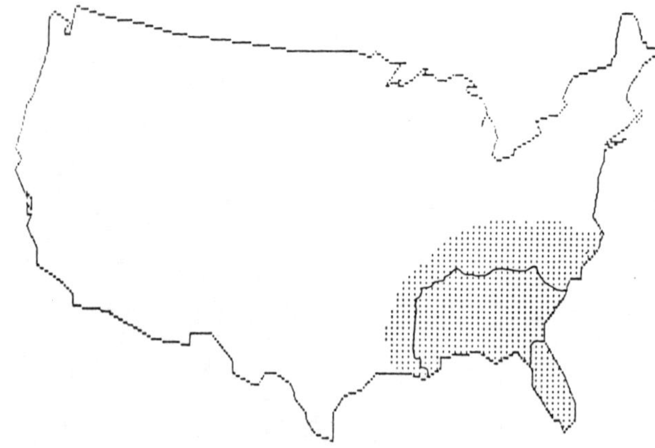

Figure 13: Lower middle class (dotted area) and upper middle class (solid line) Michigan respondents' representations of the 'Southern' speech area (both at the 50% agreement level)

From these comparisons, it appears that some of the sociolinguistic commonplaces determined in production data studies (change, age-grading, social stratification) are paralleled in this perceptual task, and continued comparison of subgroups for different regions and with data derived from other studies (see below) may reveal other parallel patterns.

2. Area Ratings

In recognizing regional speech areas, nonlinguist respondents use protocols other than their perception of purely linguistic differences. My Hawaii study of hand-drawn maps (Preston 1982) cataloged the labels which were assigned to areas and residents of areas and found that midwestern and inland northern speech areas were most often assigned such positive labels as 'standard,' 'regular,' 'normal,' and 'everyday.' In fact, all areas except the South were assigned some such positive label at least once. It was also the case that these Hawaii respondents as well as those in every other area investigated showed a much higher proportion of respondents who identified a 'Southern' speech area than any other. Figure 10, for example, shows that .94 of the southeastern Michigan respondents identified the 'Southern' speech area; the closest competitor ('Northern') was outlined by only .61 of the same population. Similar results can be seen in Figure 11 for the Indiana respondents. These results suggest that 1) regard for language correctness plays a role in areal distinctiveness and 2) areas perceived as least correct have greatest distinctiveness.

A second, less powerful trend emerged from a more careful examination of labels. Such positive labels as 'standard,' 'normal,' and 'everyday' were often contrasted with 'high-falutin',' 'very distinguished,' and 'snobby' (the latter usually associated with northeastern varieties). In addition, some positive labels did not refer to correctness at all: e.g., 'friendly' and 'down-home.' These data suggested that respondents were distinguishing between 'correct' and 'pleasant' varieties, a trend not unlike the pattern of ratings given local versus RP varieties in much of the work carried out by Giles and his associates in Great Britain (e.g., Ryan, Giles, and Sebastian 1982) -- a nonlocal, standard variety may rank high for education, status, competence, industriousness but low for honesty, warmth, friendliness. A local or nonstandard variety (or varieties) often has these ratings reversed.

To sample these notions directly, I asked Michigan and Indiana respondents to rank the fifty states, New York City, and Washington D.C. for 'correctness' and 'pleasantness' on a scale of one (least) to ten (most). Few respondents complained about this task; the relativist position so often taken by linguists, however morally unreproachable, was not that taken by the respondents. They complained that they did not have information about this or that state, but the ranking was for them a reasonable task and apparently represented opinions overtly held about the sites where better and worse, pleasant and unpleasant English was spoken in the United States.

Figures 14 and 15 show that for both sets of respondents the areas most definitely associated with incorrect English are the South and New York City; they are the only areas which have mean scores

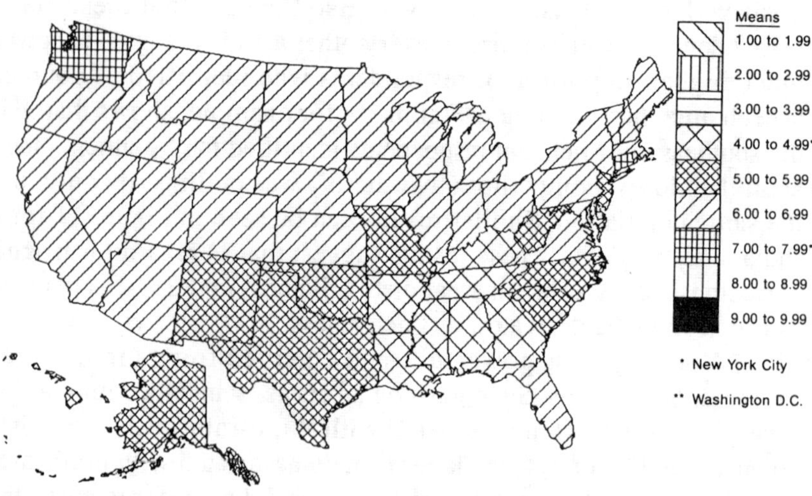

Figure 14: Southern Indiana ratings of 'correct' English on a scale of 1 to 10 (where 1 = least correct)

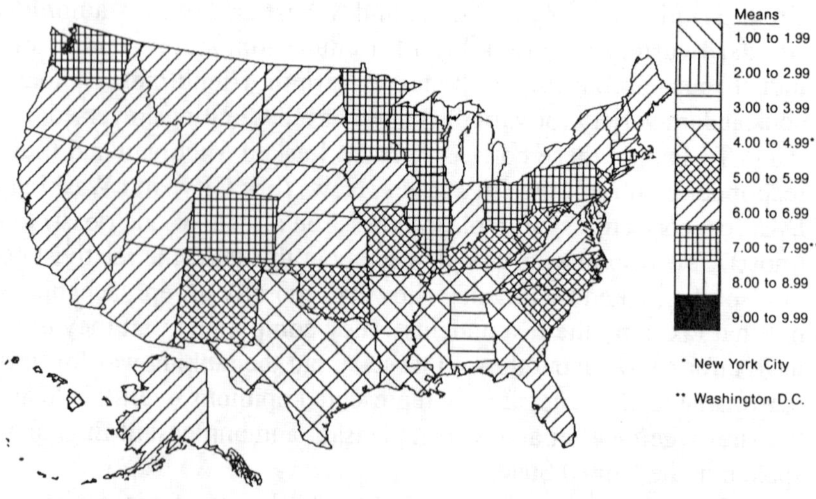

Figure 15: Southeastern Michigan ratings of 'correct' English on a scale of 1 to 10 (where 1 = least correct)

within the range 4.00 -- 4.99 (and for Michigan raters Alabama dips even into the 3.00 -- 3.99 range). Areas which border on the South and New York City are given ratings in the 5.00 to 5.99 range, and their low ratings may be accounted for by noting their proximity to the lowest-rated areas. The other two sites falling in that range, -- Alaska (only for Indiana respondents) and Hawaii -- must be interpreted differently. It is most likely that for many respondents the caricature of non-native speakers for these two regions may be very high. Unfamiliarity is an unlikely reason for the low rating since these respondents are just as likely to be unfamiliar with some of the plains and mountain states (e.g. Montana and Idaho) which fall in the 6.00 -- 6.99 range.

Turning to the other end of the scale, Michigan raters see themselves as the only state in the 8.00 -- 8.99 range, exposing considerable linguistic self-confidence. Indiana respondents, however, rate themselves in the generally acceptable 6.00 -- 6.99 range, but clearly regard some other areas (Washington, D.C., Connecticut, Delaware, and Washington) as superior. This lower ranking of the home area must indicate some small linguistic insecurity. The Michigan ratings in Figure 15 suggest at least one of the sources of that insecurity. Those raters allow surrounding states to bask in the warmth of Michigan's correctness: Wisconsin, Minnesota, Illinois, Ohio, and Pennsylvania (all nearby states) earned ratings in the 7.00 -- 7.99 range. Indiana, however, which actually shares a boundary with Michigan (as some of the above-mentioned states do not) is rated one notch down, in the 6.00 -- 6.99 range. Two interpretations are available. Either Indiana is seen by Michigan raters as belonging to that set of states farther west which earn ratings in that range, or, much more likely, Indiana is seen as a northern outpost of southern speech. It is almost certainly this perception of Indiana as a site influenced by southern varieties (an historically and descriptively accurate perception for much of Indiana) which produces its linguistic insecurity. That Indiana respondents classify themselves along with Michigan, Illinois, Wisconsin, and other Great Lakes states in the 6.00 -- 6.99 range in their own rating (Figure 14) may be interpreted as their attempt to align themselves with northern rather than southern varieties in order to escape the associations which form the basis of their insecurity. On the other hand, the narrower range of ratings provided by the Indiana respondents (4.00 -- 7.99) compared to the Michigan raters (3.00 -- 8.99) may indicate a more democratic view of correctness in general, a corollary to the Indiana raters' relatively greater linguistic insecurity.

Other high ratings by both groups include some of the New England area, the older site of correctness and one perhaps even associated with English English. Quite unexpectedly, Washington, D.C. earns a high rating from both, an indication, perhaps, that the center of government is seen as an authority on matters linguistic. Seldom mentioned in popular discussions of correctness, however, is the west, but it is assigned generally high ratings by both Indiana and Michigan respondents. There appears to be, for both sets of respondents, a sense of a leveled, unremarkable, but essentially standard speech to the west.

A factor analysis of thc ratings provides a more subtle way of grouping together areas rated similarly. Figure 16 shows the factor analysis of the correct ratings from Indiana and Figure 17 the same results for Michigan. The strongest factor group (#1) for both groups is the rather large western area to which both assigned high but not the highest ratings. The second strongest factor group for both areas is the low-rated south, and, for Indiana residents, it reaches up to include the local area, a further, more subtle indication that Indiana linguistic insecurity stems from associations with southern speech. This same factor group is peculiarly divided for Michigan respondents; in addition to a small group of southern states, there is a continuum of New England, Mid Atlantic, and Great Lakes States in this category. Even these areas are broken up by a small number of idiosyncratic groups. These analyses suggest that the Indiana raters have a greater consistency in their perception of correctness as a geographical phenomenon. The third factor group for Indiana is a New England -- Mid Atlantic stretch; the fourth a generally southwestern group of states; the fifth New York and New York City, and the sixth an interesting confirmation of the suggestion that Alaska and Hawaii might be rated lower on the basis of their being perceived as sites with a high concentration of non-native speakers. Their being joined by New Mexico in a factor analysis makes that interpretation much surer.

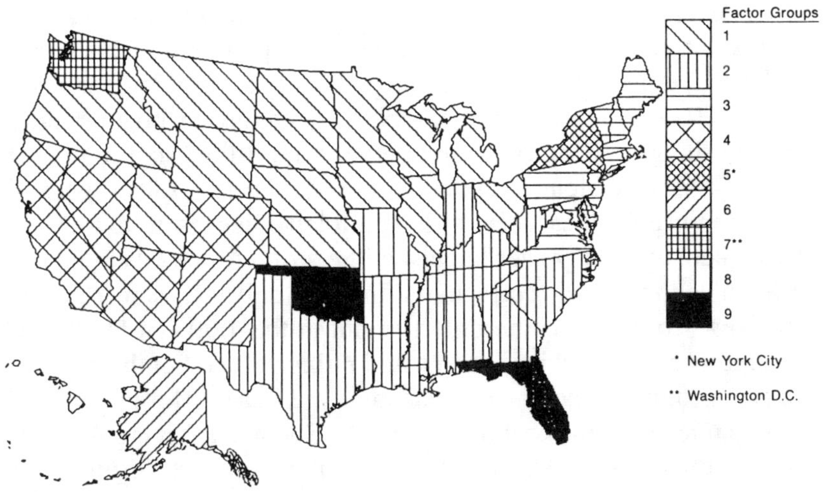

Figure 16: Factor analysis of southern Indiana 'correct' ratings

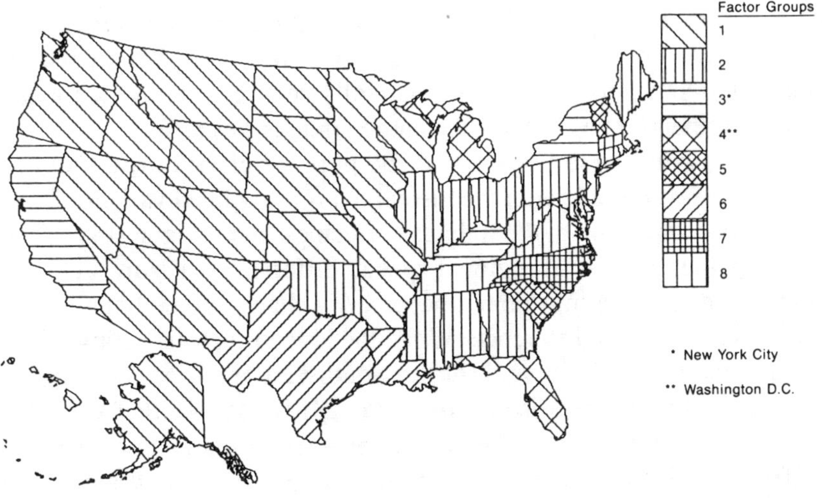

Figure 17: Factor analysis of southeastern Michigan 'correct' ratings

Figures 18 and 19 display the ratings of Indiana and Michigan respondents respectively for 'pleasant' speech. The suggestion by Giles and associates that local speech is affectively preferred seems strongly confirmed, especially in the Indiana perceptions. Only Indiana is rated in the 7.00 -- 7.99 range for pleasantness, and the Michigan raters put only Washington, Colorado, and neighboring Minnesota in the same 7.00 -- 7.99 range along with their home site. These results suggest that the preference for local speech along affective lines is more focused in areas where there is greater linguistic insecurity. At the other end of the scale, in contrast to the correctness findings, only a few areas are rated low. New York City is the only site put in the 4.00 -- 4.99 range by both Indiana and Michigan raters, and ratings of the South, similar for the two groups in the correctness task, are very different here. The Michigan respondents continue to rate the South low, giving Alabama a score in the 4.00 -- 4.99 range, but the Indiana raters, although they find the South incorrect, do not find it so unpleasant. In fact, New Hampshire, New Jersey, New York, and Delaware are a much larger pocket of unpleasant speech areas from the point of view of Indiana speakers. For Michigan speakers this eastern unpleasantness is associated only with New York City and immediate surroundings.

Factor analyses of these pleasant ratings confirm that Indiana speakers do create a little pocket (along with Illinois) for themselves, but Michigan raters, more linguistically secure, extend the pleasant rating of their home site over the entire Great Lakes area.

How do these facts about the perception of correctness and pleasantness coincide with the mental maps of regional variation?

A comparison of the Indiana correctness map (Figure 14) with the Indiana mental map of regional speech differences (Figure 11) shows that correctness ratings do not necessarily change at the boundaries of perceived regional difference. While the low correctness ratings for the South and Outer South and for the Southwest are very good matches between the two representations, the Midwest, North, West, New England, Northeast, and East Coast, all seen as distinct speech areas, differ very little in their correctness ratings. Different dialect areas, then, may have equal status so far as correctness is concerned, but, as suggested above, some areas are clearly inferior, and it seems that infe-

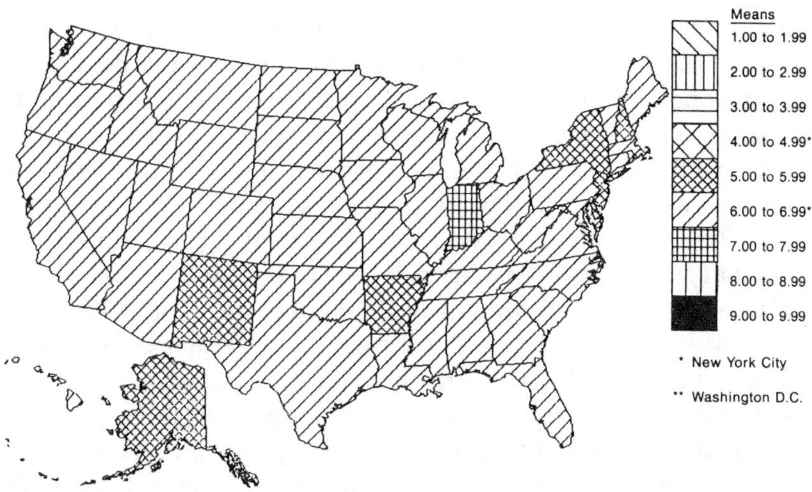

Figure 18: Southern Indiana ratings of 'pleasant' English on a scale of 1 to 10 (where 1 = least pleasant)

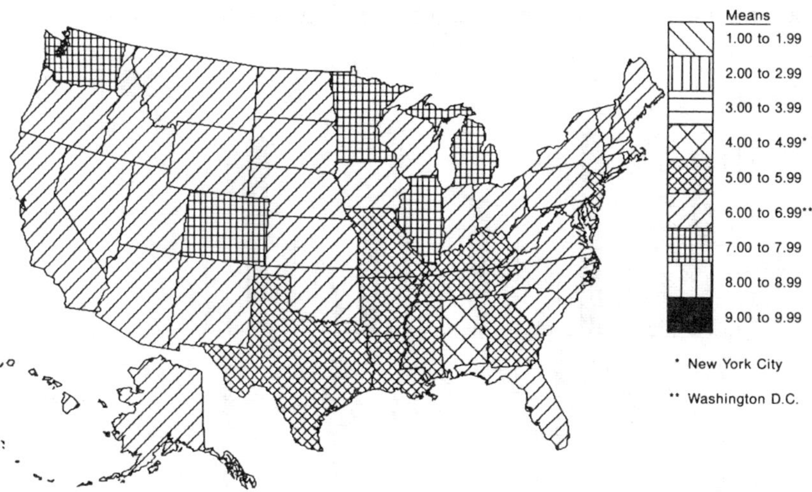

Figure 19: Southeastern Michigan ratings of 'pleasant' English on a scale of 1 to 10 (where 1 = least pleasant)

riority is more consistently identified. Although historico-cultural and linguistic facts make the South salient, it is not risky to suggest a relationship between the perceptual salience of the South in the respondents' taxonomies of where dialect areas exist and their low ratings of that area. Note that the second most salient area for Indiana respondents (51%) and the third for Michigan respondents (54%) is the 'Northeast' -- the area where New York City, also poorly rated, lies.

The Michigan perception map (Figure 10) does not mirror the differentiated levels of correctness in the Great Lakes area (Figure 15), for Indiana is combined with Michigan, Minnesota, Illinois, Wisconsin, and Ohio in a 'North.' On the other hand, the greater complexity of rankings in the Michigan correctness study is paralleled by greater complexity in areal distribution in the Michigan hand-drawn maps in general. Greater overlapping appears, corresponding to the more confused factor analysis groupings shown in the Michigan ranking studies (e.g., Figure 17) and suggesting that areas with greater linguistic self-confidence show less perceptual uniformity and consistency.

Subgroup behavior in these tasks is revealing. Upper middle class Indiana respondents give higher and middle and lower middle class raters lower correctness ratings, as shown in Figure 20.

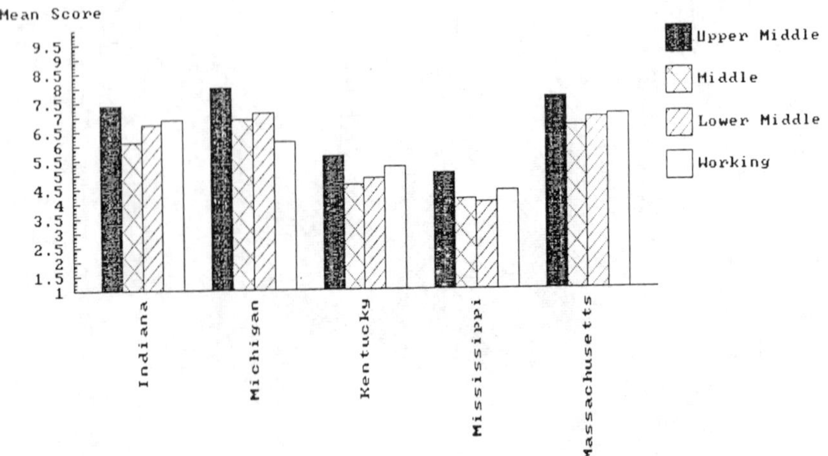

Figure 20: Southern Indiana 'correct' ratings of selected states by social status

This tendency is true for stigmatized (Kentucky and Mississippi) as well as approved (Massachusetts and Michigan) areas and applies to the local area (Indiana) as well. (This tendency also extends to the Indiana ratings of 'pleasant' speech.) Such class stratification in correctness ratings may reflect middle and lower middle class linguistic insecurity, manifested here in generally lower ratings. Interestingly enough, Michigan raters, from an area of greater linguistic security, do not show this stratified rating. Since these data suggest a parallelism to 'hypercorrection,' it will be important to ask if these tendencies are stable or involved in change. Apparent time scores of Indiana ratings for correctness do not indicate change in progress, suggesting that the mildly hypercorrect patterns of middle and lower middle class (and, to a lesser degree, female) raters may be relatively stable phenomena. In fact, the pattern of Indiana ratings for southern speech suggests age-grading rather than change (Figure 21). Since neither younger nor older speakers participate in the everyday world of work (Chambers and Trudgill 1980: 91-2), the prescriptive attitudes of the community which reflect negative evaluations of southern speech mean least to them, and the amelioration of their rankings on the correctness task follows an age-graded, curvilinear pattern.

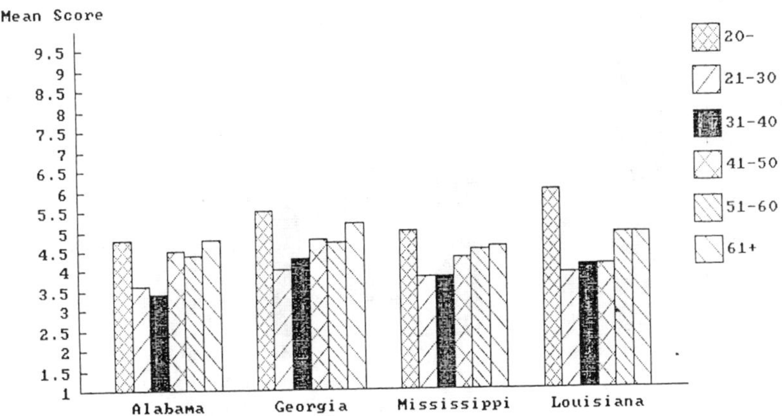

Figure 21: Southern Indiana 'correct' ratings of selected southern states by age

In addition to such age, gender, and class variation in performance and attitude, sociolinguists have observed ethnic diversity. Blacks, for example, were found to have less linguistic insecurity and less awareness that New York City speech was stigmatized by outsiders (Labov 1966: 351-2). On the other hand, their attitude towards southern speech was harsh:

> When I was very young, and used to hear about some of the things that happened in the South, I had a physical reaction, as if my hair was standing on end ... and if I would hear a white Southerner talk, I was immediately alerted to danger, and so I could never see anything pleasant in it. (Labov 1966: 352)

Similarly, blacks in southeastern Michigan rate the local area high, even higher than long-term white residents, but their ratings of southern speech, although low, are not lower than white Michigan respondents' ratings of the same areas (Figure 22).

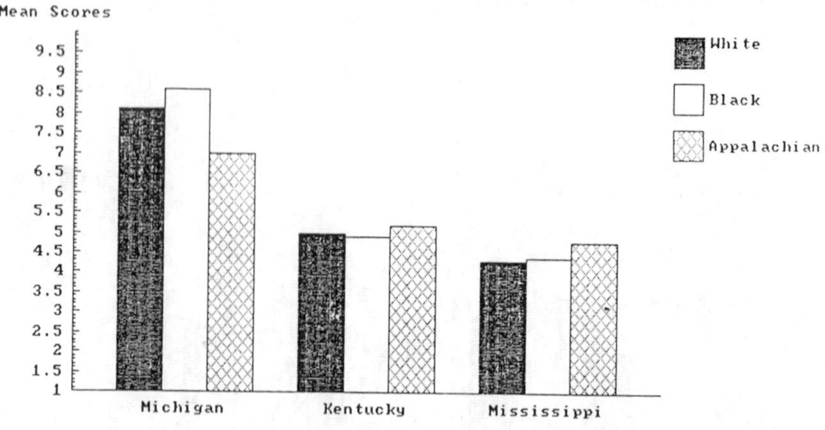

Figure 22: Southeastern Michigan 'correct' ratings for selected states by ethnic group

From this perspective, blacks in Michigan share local attitudes to a greater extent than immigrant Appalachians do. For example, Michigan raters with Appalachian backgrounds assign Michigan itself a rather lower correctness score than do the black and long-term white residents. In fact, the Michigan Appalachian rating (7.0) is not strikingly different from the assessment of Michigan given by Indiana raters (6.8). In addition, their ratings of southern areas are not as harsh as those assigned by the black and long-term white Michigan respondents. In this case, attitudinal convergence is stronger across racial lines than across a line which divides recent immigrants who come from a stigmatized speech area (Appalachia) from long-term local white residents in a relatively prestigious one (Michigan).

A more careful look at the Appalachian Michigan ratings shows, however, that dramatic change is beginning. Figure 23 is a display of apparent time data for Michigan Appalachians' ratings of those same areas shown above in Figure 22.

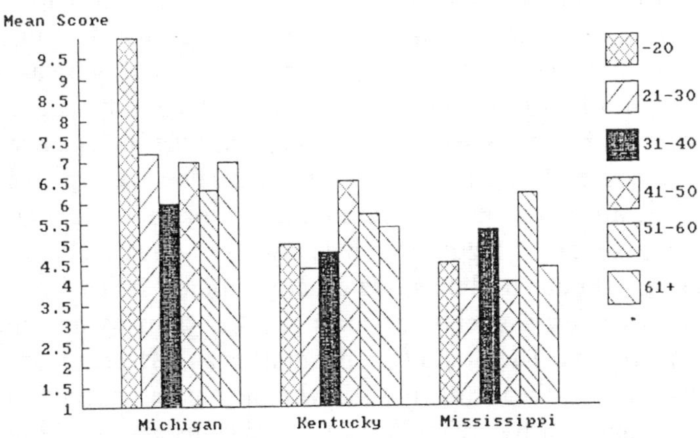

Figure 23: Michigan Appalachian 'correct' ratings of selected states by age

The youngest Appalachians' high regard for the local variety might be 'contact hypercorrection' and may be a painful indicator of their desire for local acceptability. The home area, here Kentucky, although clearly downgraded by all six age groups is more dramatically disapproved of by the youngest, whose scores are even lower than their age pairs from Michigan in the ratings of Kentucky.

These ratings tasks reveal the importance of prescription and affective attractiveness in the perception of regional varieties and further illustrate the importance of demographically broad samples in determining patterns of change.

3. Area differences

A third task rates the degree of difference respondents perceive between their own and others' use. Areas of the United States were rated as 1 (no difference), 2 (slightly different), 3 (different), and 4 (unintelligibly different); the mean score ratings were divided into four groups as follows: 1.00 - 1.75, 1.76 - 2.50, 2.51 - 3.25, 3.26 - 4.00. Figures 24 and 25 illustrate the responses from the two groups under consideration. Again, Indiana linguistic insecurity emerges. Although in the correctness task the Indiana raters grouped themselves with areas to the north (Figure 14), avoiding connection with the South, insecurity surfaces here (as it did in the factor analysis) since the Indiana respondents do find a degree of difference between themselves and speakers to the north. The difference ratings from Indiana look more like the Indiana pleasantness ratings (Figure 18) since only the two latitudinally contiguous states (Ohio and Illinois) are exactly similar.[5] Indiana respondents do not, however, associate difference from their own speech with nonstandardness. The South (rated worst) is as different from Indiana speech as the Northeast (rated well, with the obvious exception of New York City and nearby areas). In fact, Massachusetts, rated high, is the only area with unintelligibly different speech. Michigan respondents are much harsher on the South and do seem to associate extreme difference with nonstandardness. The core of the South (Louisiana, Mississippi, and Alabama) is rated both most different and most incorrect.

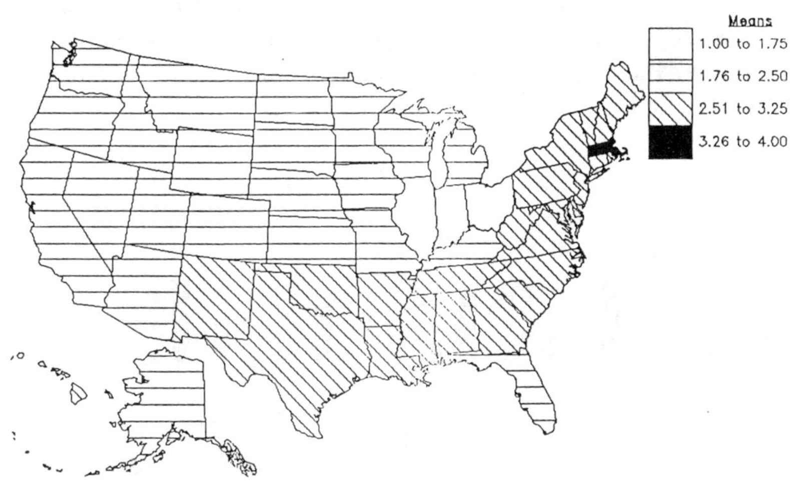

Figure 24: Southern Indiana ratings of degree of difference on a scale of 1 to 4 (where 1 = same, 2 = slightly different, 3 = different, and 4 = unintelligibly different)

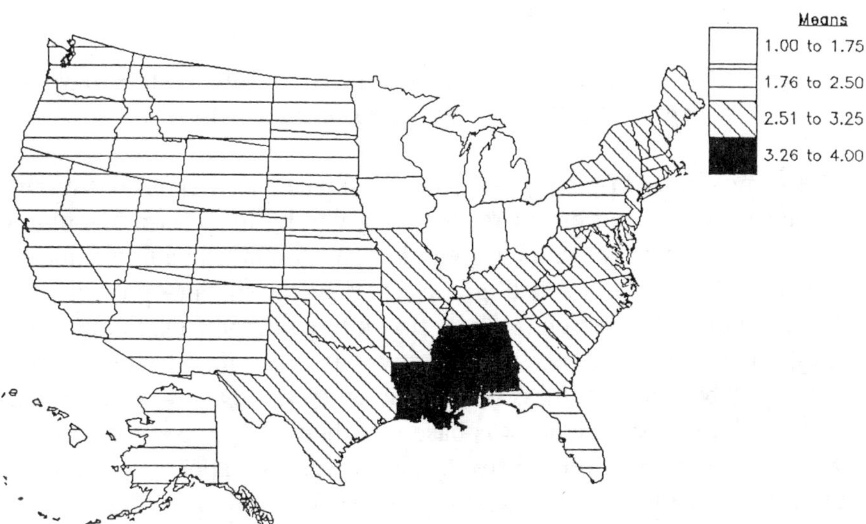

Figure 25: Southeastern Michigan ratings of degree of difference on a scale of 1 to 4 (scale as in Figure 24 above)

These difference ratings confirm and challenge some of the earlier suppositions concerning sociolinguistic commonplaces in perception data. Figure 26 shows ratings of Kentucky by age for various respondents.

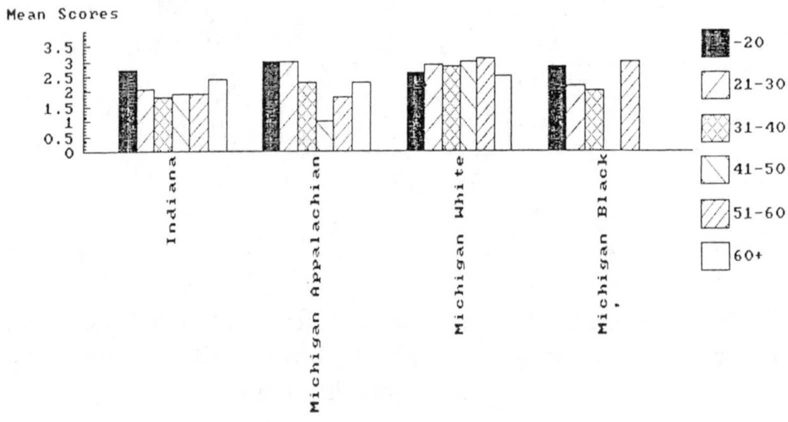

Figure 26: Southern Indiana and southeastern Michigan (subgroup) degree of difference ratings for Kentucky by age

The convergence of younger Michigan Appalachian responses with the relatively stable pattern of responses given by long-term Michigan white respondents is again apparent, but an age-graded pattern emerges for the three 'southern-based' groups (Indiana, Michigan Appalachians, Michigan blacks) which, at least for Indiana responses, is not what might have been predicted. Above it was assumed that the age-graded pattern of better correctness ratings for southern areas by younger and older Indiana respondents was based on their failing to participate in working community prejudices, but in Figure 26 it appears that working-age groups feel less strongly that Kentucky is different. Perhaps the dominance of Louisville as the local metropolitan area for these Indiana respondents will not allow working people to ignore the similarity of speech on both sides of the river, so the difference ratings are necessarily lower. Paradoxically, the community prejudice against a less prestigious variety is strongest in those same respondents. Does this reveal a tension between large-scale regional prejudice against Appalachian speech and a desire to be dissociated from it on the one hand and local recognition of the extensive speech similarity between southern Indiana and northern Kentucky on the other? This apparent disharmony (and perhaps others in such studies) might be reconciled by recent work in vantage theory (e.g., MacLaury 1987), which suggests that differential labeling of the same facts may represent different vantage points from which such facts are viewed. In this case, Indiana and Kentucky are different when affective domains are activated (many hand-drawn maps, correctness, pleasantness) but similar when neutral or practical protocols are used (degree of difference). That explanation does not at all account for the fact that Michigan blacks and Appalachians also show age-graded responses to Kentucky, with youngest and oldest respondents finding a greater degree of difference.

In general, however, the perception of difference task showed less demographic variation than any of the others, but work in other areas and further investigation of these data may reveal patterns worth analyzing.

4. Area identification

How accurately can respondents place voice samples from different regions, and how might the boundaries which emerge from that task correspond to those already established?

Figure 27 shows the sites at which recordings were made for the recognition test; the voices (all short samples from interviews with well-educated, middle-aged males) were played in random order and the respondents identified each voice with a site. Assigning the sites the numbers one through nine (from south to north) allowed calculation of mean scores for the task. If each voice were recognized perfectly by each respondent, the scores would read simply, 9.00, 8.00, and so on from north to south. The actual scores were as shown in Table 1.

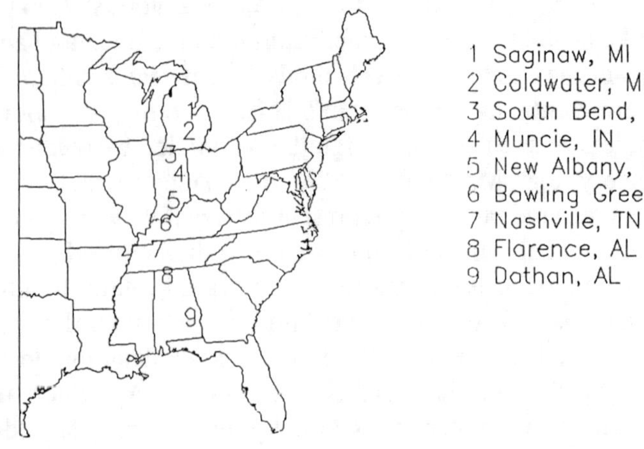

Figure 27: Identification task voice sample sites

	Site	Michigan Respondents	Indiana Respondents	Perfect ID Score
1	Saginaw MI	7.0	6.6	9.00
2	Coldwater MI	6.6	6.3	8.00
3	South Bend, IN	6.2	6.4	7.00
4	Muncie, IN	5.5	6.1	6.00
5	New Albany IN	5.3	5.8	5.00
6	Bowling Green KY	4.1	5.1	4.00
7	Nashville, TN	3.5	3.8	3.00
8	Florence, AL	3.1	2.6	2.00
9	Dothan AL	3.7	2.5	1.00

Table 1: Mean scores for Indiana and Michigan regional voice identifications

If the distance between mean scores indicates the distinctiveness heard between samples, then a convention of calling a .50 or greater difference a 'minor' boundary and a difference of 1.00 or greater a 'major' one is reasonable. Based on those calculations, a taxonomy of the respondents' areas of acoustic differentiation of United States dialects (along a north-south dimension only) is as shown in Figures 28 and 29.

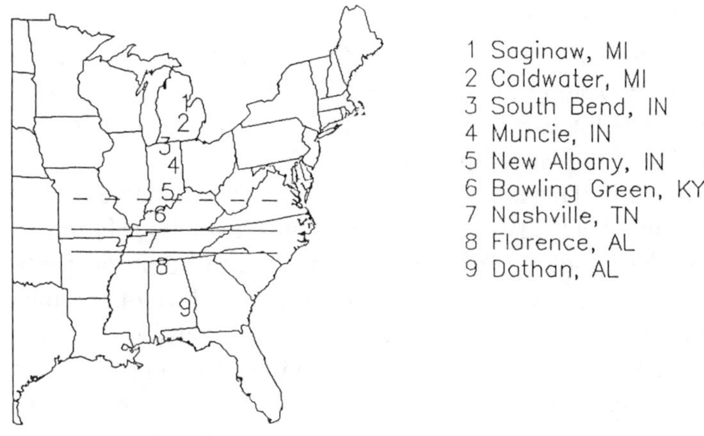

Figure 28: Southern Indiana identification task 'boundaries'

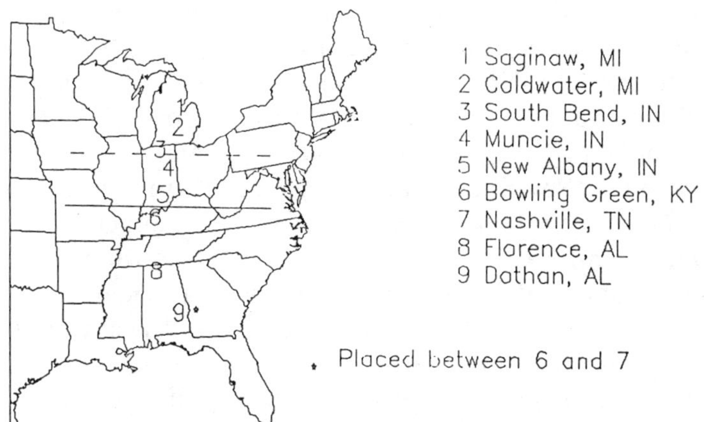

Figure 29: Southeastern Michigan identification task 'boundaries'

Both sets correspond (and fail to correspond) in interesting ways to the data gleaned from the earlier tasks. Although Indiana residents claim to distinguish a 'North' from a 'Midwest' in their hand-drawn maps (Figure 11), there is no evidence that they hear any such difference strongly. The Michigan respondents, however, who show a similar distinction in the composite of their hand-drawn maps (Figure 10), do have a minor boundary between voice samples #3 and #4. Though both groups distinguish an 'Outer South' from the 'South,' only the Indiana respondents have strong boundaries there. Nevertheless, it would be premature to suggest that the boundary between, say, sites #7 and #8 is the same distinction as the one which exists between those two regions on the hand-drawn composite (Figure 11).

The Indiana respondents hear one minor and two major southern distinctions, but it is the Michigan hand-drawn map (Figure 10) which has an overlapping 'Outer South' and 'South,' providing a three-way rather than two-way division. In summary, the Indiana hand-drawn composite (Figure 11) results in a four-way division along the north -- south continuum between areas #3 and #4, #4 and #5, and #7 and #8; the Indiana identification task (Figure 28), however, places major boundaries only between areas #7 and #8 and between #6 and #7. Another boundary (albeit minor) between #5 (the home site) and #6 serves, perhaps, to cut off local speech from anything that might be regarded 'Southern.' Indiana speakers, in yet another expression of linguistic insecurity, may want to indicate that they belong to a large, undifferentiated 'North,' not to any of the several areas of 'South' which they cut off below them. Michigan respondents have only one major boundary (Figure 29), between #5 and #6, a differentiation between the 'South' and everything else. This major division falls precisely in the area where both groups have a 'trough' in their hand-drawn generalizations -- a sort of no-man's land which arises where two perceptually different areas are seen as particularly distinct. The difference here is that the Michigan respondents hear that distinction strongly; Indiana respondents do not. The secondary distinction for Michigan respondents (Figure 29) in the identification task (between areas #3 and #4) is almost certainly a part of their awareness of the difference between 'North' and 'Midwest,' even though their hand-drawn generalization does not have a 'Midwest' which reaches far enough east to be an actual part of the particular north -- south continuum of voices being discussed here.

When the identification task is compared with the degree of difference task, the Indiana residents (Figure 24) are again those who make the greater number of subdivisions along the north -- south dimension. The Michigan difference boundary between Indiana and Kentucky (Figure 25) is precisely in the place where the major Michigan identification boundary (between areas #5 and #6) falls. Although the degree of difference task shows an even more radically different 'Deep South' for Michigan respondents, their identification task does not reflect that. In the degree of difference task (Figure 24), the Indiana respondents make sharp subdivisions between Michigan and Indiana (areas #2 and #3 on the identification task), between Indiana and Kentucky (areas #5 and #6 on the identification task), and between Kentucky and Tennessee (areas #6 and #7 on the identification task). The latter two are parallels to differences heard in the identification task, but the first comes much closer to the distinction heard by the Michigan respondents but not taxonomized in the hand-drawn or degree of difference tasks.

How do these data compare to the ratings? The Indiana respondents' correctness map (Figure 14) is simple. There is a generally correct 'North' (everything above the Ohio River assigned a score in the 6.00 -- 6.99 range) and a generally incorrect 'South' (all in the 4.00 -- 4.99 range). The cut is precisely at the minor boundary in the identification task (between #5 and #6) which severs the home area from the 'South.' The Michigan correctness map (Figure 15) shows, however, a five-stage decrease along the line investigated in the identification task -- Michigan 8.00 -- 8.99, Indiana 6.00 -- 6.99, Kentucky, 5.00 -- 5.99, Tennessee 4.00 -- 4.99, and Alabama 3.00 -- 3.99. Michigan respondents have a caricature of increasingly incorrect southern speech -- the farther south, the more incorrect. The Indiana respondents, although they too negatively evaluate southern speech and are careful to cut themselves off from nearby varieties of it, more simply dichotomize the middle part of the United States into a correct 'North' and incorrect 'South,' perhaps, again, reflecting the need for greater compartmentalization among those with greater linguistic insecurity.

A similar stratification recurs in the pleasant task. There are essentially only two dimensions for the Indiana respondents; a most pleasant home area and not unpleasant surroundings, including a 'South' which fares not better or worse than a 'North' (Figure 18). The Michigan respondents, however, have a clearly stronger negative caricature of southern voices along this affective dimension (Figure 19). Local speech is most pleasant (7.00 -- 7.99), Indiana less so (6.00 --6.99), Kentucky and Tennessee even less so (5.00 -- 5.99), and Alabama as bad as New York City (4.00 -- 4.99).

Perhaps the identification task shows simply that respondents hear more differences in areas which are closer to home. The Indiana respondents have internal southern divisions; the Michigan respondents have internal northern ones. The other tasks, however, reveal that regional speech differences which are heard as most distinctive do not necessarily correspond to the mental maps the same respondents have for dialect distribution and distinctiveness nor to the areas which are derived from their judgments of the correctness and pleasantness of varieties.

An apparent time study of these data suggests further interesting details. Figure 30 (Indiana) shows that strong or secondary southern boundaries (around #6, #7, and #8) exist for all groups over 30. The 21-30 group places a strong boundary between #5 and #6 (where only a weak one exists for the oldest respondents and the 51-60 age group, although the latter shows an uncharacteristic number of displacements). The youngest Indiana respondents continue to show this major boundary between #5 and #6, but they do away with the lower southern distinctions and introduce a northern one not found in any of the other southern Indiana age groups. Figure 31 (Michigan respondents arranged by age) offers parallels and contrasts. Michigan respondents do not as frequently use major boundaries in general, but their secondary boundaries, at least for middle aged respondents, often divide the same southern territory (e.g., at site #7) so frequently divided by Indiana respondents. More interesting, however, is the similarity of the youngest Michigan and Indiana respondents' maps. Except for minor details, these maps significantly agree and suggest a change in the perception of U.S. speech boundaries into four distinct regions, although they do not exactly conform to those posited by students of production dialectology.

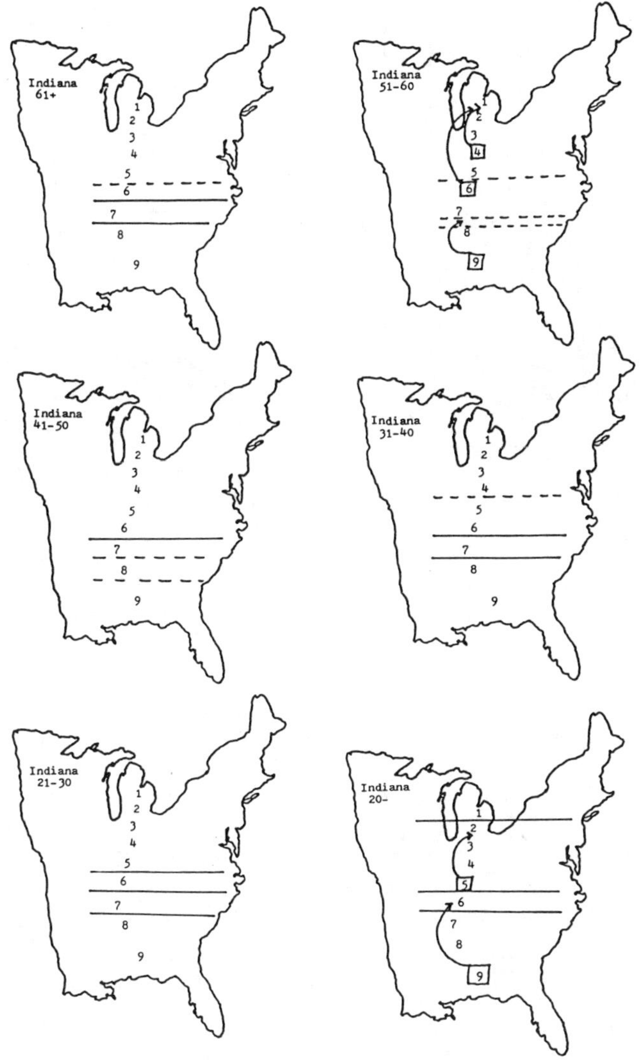

Figure 30: Indiana identification task 'boundaries' by age

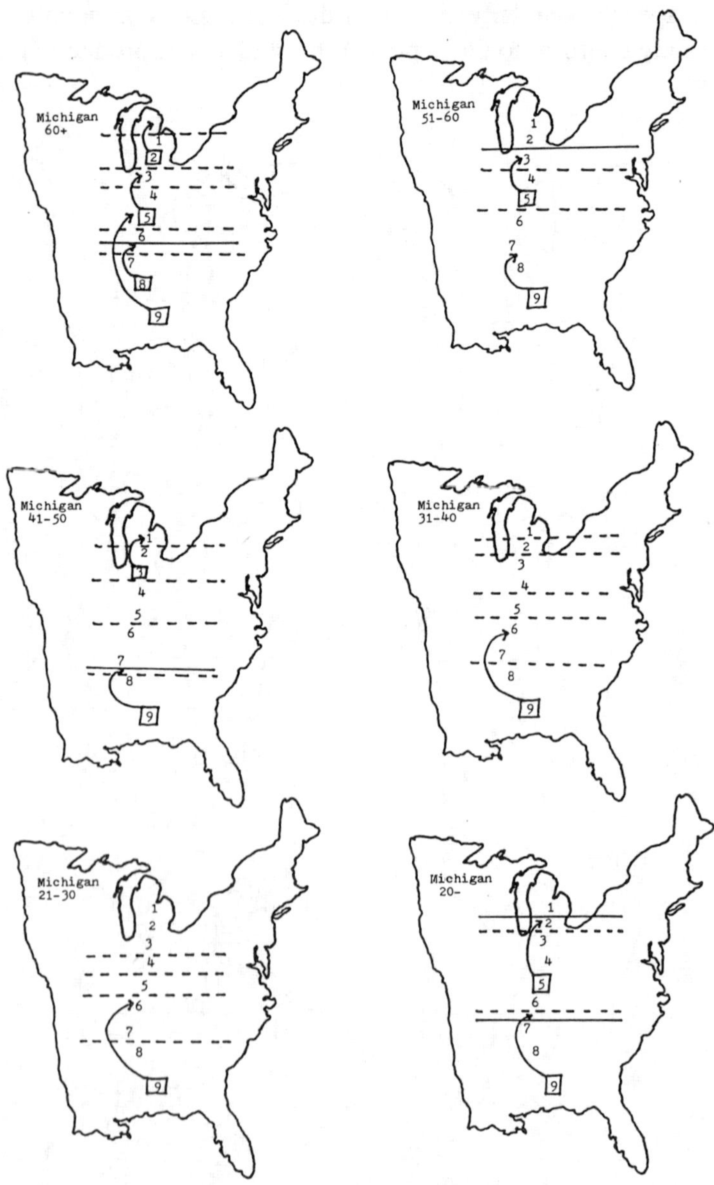

Figure 31: Michigan identification task 'boundaries' by age

Variation in folk dialect data suggests many of the characteristics of production data -- apparent time change and age-grading, social stratification, hypo- and hypercorrection, gender related trends, linguistic insecurity, and divergence and convergence of contact groups. On the other hand, some of these parallels may not precisely mirror specific findings from production sociolinguistics. For example, the Indiana and Michigan similarities in dialect identification among youngest speakers may be an importation from popular culture phenomena rather than reflections of on-going change in lower-level local perceptions and categorizations. Just such indications, however, may be clues to the factors which lurk behind the social motivations for perceptual change, and those changes may constitute a part of the impetus for change in language itself.

5. Interviews

The essentially quantitative approaches taken in the above four studies may be supplemented by 'grounding' (i.e., post-task discussions with the respondents), by interviews concerning nonlinguists' general views of language diversity, or by participant-observation in the speech community. Although the study of these data is in progress, some representative samples of Michigan interviews are reported here.[6] In this first sample, respondents illustrate that 'North' and 'South' are the principal distinctions in American English, and a nonnative graduate student fieldworker asks explicitly where they believe standard English is spoken:

Participants:[7]

H=Taiwanese male linguistics graduate student, age 34

G=White female southeast Michigan computer programmer, age 32, (D's significant other)

W=Taiwanese female, about age 30 (H's spouse)

S=White male southeast Michigan high school student, age 15 (D's son)

D=White male southeast Michigan social worker, age 40 (S's father, G's significant other)

H: But which city you think is the - standard English for, I mean, from-
[
D: From from well - we think, yeah, we think the Midwest.
[
S: ( )
[
G: Detroit. ((laughs))

H: Midwest?
[
S: The Midwest no, cause dad Cal- I I've been to California=
[
D: ( )
[
G: California-

S: =a lot more than you, California talks the same way as here. There's no accent. I can't tell the difference.
[
D: Right - that's true I can't either when I'm in California.
[
S: So like the the Western - the North, North and the South=
[ ]
D: They talk a little slower though.

S: =would basically be the two accents, with little tiny dialects here and there.

G: That's true.=

S: =Like the New Yorkers ((laughs)).

. . . .

H: Oh you know what, I've always thought Northern part English is standard. So, that's wrong right?

```
G: I think so Northern English.
          [
D:         (             ) - Yeah I think so.
                                        [
S:                                       Yeah North- Northern=
                                                          [
D:                                                         I=

S: =English.

D: =think that's correct.

H: Northern part English is c- is standard English=

D: =Yeah, yeah.
      [
G:     That's right - what you hear around here.
             [
S:            Yeah standard.
                                        [
D:                                       Because that's what you
hear on the TV - like newscasters. If you listen to the - the=
         [
H:        ((laughs))

D: =national newscast of the national news  - on Channel 7 som-=
                                          [
G:                                         Uh huh

D: =they sound they sound like we: do, they they sound sort of
Mid- Midwestern --(        )
```

It is important to note in this exchange that 'midwest' often isolates an area labeled 'North' in the maps presented so far (e.g., Figure 10). Composites of hand-drawn maps, however, were based on the areas outlined by the respondents rather than on the labels given them. For these respondents 'North' and 'South' are the principal American English speech areas, and 'North' is the land of correctness. Note, however, that one of the 'little tiny dialects' is New York City, and at the hiatus in this passage, all the participants (and the fieldworker) participate in their impression of New York City pronunciations of 'New York.' This more informal approach would at first seem to confirm only the salience of local and nonstandard areas for speakers with low linguistic insecurity, but later content in this same conversation is revealing.

```
H:                                So you can tell this guy from
uh what maybe I mean - just listen his accent.

S: (.hhh) You can tell whether he's from the North or the South=
          [
H:         (              )
                                                [
D:                                               (   ) Yeah - yeah

S: =but not which particular area,
                                [
D:                               (                  ) Western States=
                                               [
H:                                              (    ) just the part
North part South part

D: = uh (   ) particular ways of talking too=
         [
S:        Right.

G: =(  ) they're kind of southern.

D: Yeah, that's true.

G: I mean you wouldn't think of North Dakota (           )
                                                    [
D:                                                   Usually Texas
is pretty distinct.

G: Colorado's not (     ) distinct.

D: No, Colorado (   ).

G: Texas is, but that's Southern.

D: Yeah.

H: Texas is Southern (     ).

G: Yeah.

H: (   ) you say that California English is the same - accent=
                                                     [
```

```
S:                                              As here

H: =here?

S: Yeah. - California is the same accent
     [
D:    (             )
              [
H:             So in in this case how do you -  distinguish=
                                                [
S:                                               You can't (  )

H: =from this guy for instance he may be from California (    )
                                              [
S: =tell the difference                        OH: You could
possibly tell the difference from the slang words they use.

 . . . . . . . . . . . . . . . . . . . . . . . . . . . . . . .

S:                                 Yeah they they might have
the same accent but use different terms for things, like s-
'pop', we call it like 'pop' here, (.hhh) Andrea's from- my
sister's been in California for a long time, they call it 'soda'
out there.
```

At first, only southerners and northerners seem distinct. 'D' continues to push for the idea that 'Western' is salient, but 'North Dakota' and 'Colorado' are used as examples of places no different from Michigan (see Figure 25). 'Texas' is different, but it is 'Southern.' The fieldworker reminds the respondents that they claimed earlier that California was also the same as Michigan and asks if there is no way to tell these regions apart. Interestingly enough for professional dialectologists, only after this prodding does 'S' come up with the idea of lexical difference, the previous discussions being restricted, apparently, to phonology ('accent' -- the term preferred by nearly every folk respondent for pronunciation differences). Since the map-drawers were given instructions to draw boundaries around areas where people 'speak differently,' it is worth wondering, in light of this interview evidence, what linguistic level was guiding the task. After this lexical possibility is recognized, an example is extensively discussed with further interesting results.

G: [[Or and I don't know when I hear people say 'soda' I think=

H: [[(   )

G: =they're trying to be up- sort of upper crust or snobbish or=
[
S: (   )

G: =something yeah.

H: Oh upper crust means the same
[
G: Putting on airs:, well I think it's putting on airs really.

S: It could be=

H: =Oh ah this is very interesting, you mean if you - you would think the people say - 'soda' is from upper class (   )

S: [[I (   ) - not really

G: [[No not really not the upper class so much as as people who try to look sophisticated like - traveled a lot or something.
[
S: When you-

S: When you hear someone using like - no slang, perfect English=
[
H: (   )

S: = you would think of - upper class.

G: Um hum.
[
S: (.hhh) You know always talking - in perfect English and using like their full vocabulary, - always always
[
H: How- how do you define perfect=
[
G: Very (   )

H: =Engl- I mean.

S: Um - perfect grammar uh - you wouldn't cut words short uh=
[[
H: ( ) ah perfect
[
G: like=

```
S: =there would probably, yeah, you wouldn't say 'goin', you=

G: =you wouldn't say 'goin'
                                            [
H:                                           Wouldn't say 'going'

S: =would say 'going.' You'd hear that, you'd hear the 'g' at=
                          [
H:                         'Going'

S: =the end, 'going'. -  (.hhh) You know they'd-
                      [
W:                    'Going'.
                                               [
H:                                              Everybody's very
clear or something?

S: Yeah, it'd be - very clear - you know - and probably s- semi-
slow.

G: Probably, yeah.
                [
S:               Y- you know to make sure they would get it all
out, if you heard someone talking like that you'd probably think
they had lots of money or something.
```

After 'G' suggests that people who say 'soda' are upper-crust, a more thorough discussion of class stratification ensues. 'G' asserts throughout that there is a kind of pretense in such use, but 'S' appears to believe that the features he enumerates (slower and more distinct pronunciation, large vocabulary, no slang) isolate upper class speakers, not hypercorrectors.

Ethnicity in speech plays a large role in these interviews, as it did not in the earlier tasks. The comprehensibility of African-American English is one of the topics of the following:

Participants:

N=White female linguistics graduate student southeastern Michigan, age 26.

E=White male telephone lineman southeastern Michigan, age 45

D=White female sales clerk southeastern Michigan, age 45 (E's spouse)

E: I don't really think you'd notice it.

N: A southern accent?
[
E: Honestly. Unless it's a real deep southern accent. And a Texas accent is not necessarily- really southern. - Not what I=
[
D: Yeah but you=

E: =consider southern.

D: =notice people who have an accent. I mean like working at the store people will come there, and I couldn't tell if they were saying 'white' or 'wide' you know when they were asking for shoes.

E: Yeah but that's black not white people.
[[
D: They want- No no. It wasn't black people. It was not black people if I recall they were- they were white people

E: You know like the time I was standing outside-
[
D: ((clears throat)) In fact I think I can understand black people a whole lot better than some of the white southern people.
[
E: But I had that time when I was standing outside the office there and I kep- you know- and he kept saying - you know 'Atwood' and here he was saying 'Edward.'
[
D: Edward

N: Oh ((laughs))

E: And I said 'No: damn it. T. Edward T.,' and he says 'That's right. Atwood T.'

N: Oh ((laughs))

```
D: But no I- I-
              [
E:             I was standing out in the cold and this guy is
getting paid about two bucks an hour, and I'm standing there
making about eight or ten waiting for him to push a button so I
can get in the office and do my work. And I couldn't- He=
                                     [
N:                                    Oh because-
                                                  [
D:                                                 ID himself-

E: =couldn't understand me and I couldn't understand him,
```

This conversation first shows what both the Indiana and Michigan mental maps (Figures 10 and 11) show, that Texas is a separate dialect area, at least not a part of the 'South.' 'E,' however, relates an anecdote to support his point about the unintelligibility of African-American English; this ethnic and the preceding social status data are important supplements to the quantitative data reported on above.

6. Conclusion

These several approaches have illustrated the results of cognitive linguistic mapping, the mapping of correctness and related affective dimensions, and interviews aimed at eliciting overt linguistic notions, at least in United States English and for nonlinguists. Such folk concepts represent strongly held, influential beliefs in the linguistic life of large and small speech communities.

Such a multidimensional approach to what are ultimately folk linguistic questions provides a surer consideration of the limited data of language attitude surveys and an important supplement to the much more general study of production differences. It serves, therefore, to help build a more complete and accurate picture of the regard for language use and variety within a speech community, a goal shared by applied, theoretical, and ethnographic approaches to language study.

Notes

The newer work reported on here has been supported by two National Science Foundation Grants (BNS-8417462 and BNS-8711267) for which I am extremely grateful. Needless to say, the findings and opinions expressed here are my own.

1 The work in Japan mentioned above (e.g., Grootaers 1959) concludes that the perception of speech differences is based on physical and political boundaries nearly exclusively and is, therefore, of no use to dialectologists. Even if this contention were true, sociolinguistic and ethnographic uses of such information would still justify its investigation.

2 More technical detail of this process is given in Preston and Howe (1987).

3 One might justifiably complain that the number of older raters is very small, but a map of the extent of where even one respondent in this age group drew the area is smaller than the fifty percent realization of the under twenty decade.

4 This tendency exists, in fact, for a number of areas and may represent an interesting proclivity for older respondents to isolate a more core-like territory and/or to tolerate more undesignated areas on their maps in general.

5 In fact, although the map does not show it, many Indiana raters made so bold as to say that northern Kentucky was 'the same.'

6 Analysis of post-task interviews with Michigan and Indiana respondents and of wider-ranging conversations with Michigan respondents are in progress. Reports of these findings will be more elaborately detailed in Preston (in progress) and Preston and Niedzielski (in progress).

7 Conventions used in the transcripts are the following:

a) 'LAN' (loudness or contrastive stress)
b) '[[' (speech begins at the same moment)
c) '[' (between lines, next speaker overlaps)
d) ']' (between lines, end of next speaker overlap)
e) '((laughs))' (noises, transcriber comments)
f) '[ ]' (phonetic representation)
g) 'wit-' (word is cut off)
h) '( )' (unintelligible portion)
i) '(went)' (possible interpretation)
j) ' - ' (untimed pause)
k) 'well:' (length, repeated if necessary)
l) '(hhh)' & '(.hhh)' (audible breath out and in respectively)
m) '.' ',' '?' (final, pause, and rising intonation)
n) '=' (linked speech, no pause)

References

Chambers, J. K. & Peter Trudgill. 1980. *Dialectology*. Cambridge: University Press.

Gould, Peter & Rodney White. 1972. *Mental maps*. Harmondsworth: Penguin.

Grootaers, Willem. 1959. Origin and nature of the subjective boundaries of dialects. *Orbis* 8:355-84.

Hoenigswald, Henry. 1966. A proposal for the study of folk-linguistics. In William F. Bright (ed.), *Sociolinguistics*. The Hague: Mouton, 16- 26.

Hymes, Dell. 1972. *Foundations in sociolinguistics*. Philadelphia: University of Pennsylvania Press.

Kremer, L. 1984. Die niederländisch-deutsche Staatsgrenze als subjektive Dialektgrenze. In Grenzen en grensproblemen (Een bundel studies nitgegeren door het Nedersaksich Instituut van der R. U. Groningen ter gelegenheid van zijn 30-jahrig bestaan = Nedersaksich Studies 7, zugleich: Driemaandelijske Bladen 36), 76-83.

Labov, William. 1966. *The social stratification of English in New York City*. Arlington: Center for Applied Linguistics.

MacLaury, Robert E. 1987. Co-extensive semantic ranges: different names for distinct vantages of one category. In Barbara Need, Eric Schiller, & Anna Bosch (eds), *CLS 23: Papers from the 23rd annual meeting of the Chicago Linguistic Society*, Chicago: Chicago Linguistic Society, 268-82.

Preston, Dennis R. 1982. Perceptual dialectology: mental maps of United States dialects from a Hawaiian perspective. *Hawaii Working Papers in Linguistics* 14,2:5-49.

Preston, Dennis R. 1986. Five visions of America. *Language in Society* 15:221-40.

Preston, Dennis R. 1989. *Perceptual dialectology*. Dordrecht: Foris.

Preston, Dennis R. In progress. The perception of language variation.

Preston, Dennis R. & George Howe. 1987. Computerized studies of mental dialect maps. In Keith M. Denning, Sharon Inkelas, Faye C. McNair-Knox, and John R. Rickford (eds), *Variation in language: NWAV-XV at Stanford*. Stanford: Department of Linguistics, 361-78.

Preston, Dennis. R. & Nancy Niedzielski. In progress. Folk linguistics in southeastern Michigan.

Rensink, W. 1955. Dialectindeling naar opgaven van medewerkers. *Amsterdam Dialectbureau Bulletin* 7:20-3.

Ryan, Ellen B., Howard Giles, & Richard J. Sebastian. 1982. An integrative perspective for the study of attitudes toward language variation. In Ellen B. Ryan & Howard Giles (eds), *Attitudes towards language variation*. London: Arnold, 1-19.

Stross, Brian. 1974. Speaking of speaking: Tenejapa Tzeltal metalinguistics. In Richard Bauman & Joel Sherzer (eds), *Explorations in the ethnography of speaking*. Cambridge: Cambridge University Press, 213-39.

The Patterning of Variation in Performance

Charles L. Briggs
Vassar College

1. Introduction

Establishing variation as a linguistic issue worthy of serious study has not been not a trivial matter.[1] Such powerful determiners of linguistic agendas as Saussure and Chomsky limited the scope of linguistics to, in Chomsky's famous phrase, concern with 'an ideal speaker-listener in a completely homogeneous speech-community' (1965:3) or, as Saussure put it, 'a number of impressions deposited in the brain of each member of a community, almost like a dictionary of which identical copies have been distributed to each individual' (Saussure 1959/1916:19). *Parole*, or, in Chomsky's lexicon, performance,[2] was 1) accidental, unpredictable, and unsystematic and 2) accordingly not susceptible to (or deserving of) linguistic inquiry. It would, in any case, yield no insights into the fundamental nature of language or lend itself to the development of theory.

Alternative views of the relationship between structure and variation in language were, however, also clearly articulated early in the twentieth century. Sapir (1921) argued in *Language*, for example, that study of variation can greatly assist us in grasping the nature of linguistic patterning. His approach to grammar was less oriented toward the search for a cognitive lowest common denominator lodged in the mind of all speakers than a heterogeneous conjunction of competing norms (cf. Hymes 1973; Silverstein 1986). Sapir also argued that patterning extends beyond the level of languages as wholes to embrace social groups (1929) and individuals (1927, 1928). Published in the same year as Sapir's *Language*, Jakobson's (1972/1921) first significant publication, an essay on the Russian poet Khlebnikov, sought to fashion a linguistic approach to the science of literature. He not only drew attention to differences between everyday and poetic language and contrastive varieties of the latter, but he pointed to a dialectical relationship between competing patterns as a dynamic force that fuels language change. Nonetheless, the centrality of structural and generative perspectives relegated the study of variation largely to the periphery of mainstream linguistics. While dialectology was clearly alive and well, its fruits were seldom incorporated into 'mainstream' bodies of theory and methodology.

The work of Hymes and Labov in the 1960s changed the placement of variation within linguistic study in two ways. First, these writers attempted to create an institutional nexus for the study of variation, one that would render it a vital facet of linguistic inquiry. Their promotion of the terms *sociolinguistics* and, for Hymes, the *ethnography of speaking* provided a tangible -- that is, lexical -- space for work on variation. The manner in which each author expanded the scope of linguistics was nonetheless contrastive. Labov (1966, 1972a, 1972c) explored the nature of variation in terms of units identified by traditional modes of analysis (phonology, morphology, semantics, and syntax). Paying careful attention to questions of sampling and the contextual parameters of data elicitation, he developed quantitative means of gauging the relationship between particular linguistic features and socioeconomic factors. Gumperz (1962, 1971) pushed for greater analytical rigor in defining speech communities, particularly with respect to the interaction of linguistic varieties. Fishman (1966) expanded the scope of empirical research on variation to include nation states and even larger units of analysis. Hymes (1971c, 1974) stressed the need to look beyond the domains investigated by received analyses in documenting the full range of forms and functions within a given speech community. In concluding the article that set the ethnography of speaking in motion, he urged anthropology to draw on linguistics and at the same time to 'formulate its own ethnographic questions about speech and seek to answer them' (1964:48).

Secondly, Hymes and Labov incorporated methodological insights, respectively from ethnography and sociology, in countering the common equation of variation with 'deviation' or 'error.' Hymes

(1964:46) specifically countered the characterization of speech that emerges from the Saussurean dichotomy in his 1964 article on 'The ethnography of speaking': 'Structure and pattern have been treated in effect as pretty much the exclusive property of language (*la langue* : *la parole*) ... Speaking, like language, is patterned, functions as a system, is describable by rules.' Hymes and Labov sought to demonstrate that the study of *parole* also falls within basic scientific -- and certainly linguistic -- interest in structure and systematicity. Hymes argued that 'with regard to description of a single case there should be concern to find invariance (a sociolinguistic system) and, as between cases, a concern to find variation, or diversity, of use and function' (1974/1967:78). Labov's proposal (1966:91) for the quantitative study of variable rules was developed in order to overcome the fact that 'stylistic variation has not been treated by techniques accurate enough to measure the extent of regularity which does prevail.'

The need to overcome the structuralist (à la Saussure) and transformationalist bias against the study of variation has engendered opposing tendencies in sociolinguistics and the ethnography of speaking. The desire to show that language use is systemic, patterned, and rule governed is opposed by interest in discovering the unique and emergent dimensions of linguistic forms and functions; since the latter are indexically grounded in interaction, they cannot be explained by general rules and structures alone. As Bauman (1987) has recently noted, the tension between these two foci has not received sufficient attention. I would suggest that the redefinition of performance that emerged in the early to mid-1970s constituted an attempt to turn these opposing concerns into related components of a common theoretical framework. This shift is apparent in a transformation of the relationship between the terms 'performance' and 'competence' from a theoretical opposition to an empirically complementary relationship, a shift that is evident in papers by Hymes (1971a, 1971c) and in Bauman and Sherzer's (1974:7) definition of performance as 'the interplay between resources and individual competence, within the context of particular situations.'

This new definition of performance thus directed attention specifically toward the rapprochement between shared resources and patterns on the one hand and individual abilities and unique communicative events on the other. In 1975, both Bauman (1975) and Hymes (1975) presented definitions of performance that stressed the way that the role of performer entails an assumption of responsibility to an audience for a display of communicative competence in which both form and content are subject to evaluation. Hymes brought stylistic patterning into the picture in two ways, focusing not only on how performance organizes linguistic diversity but also on 'the systematic study of variation in performance' (1975). In his introduction to a collection of essays on ethnopoetics, Hymes reiterated the importance of studying both individual details of particular works and more abstract aspects of patterning through 'persistence in seeking systematic covariation of form and meaning' (1981:10).

In 1971, Hymes argued that 'certain lines of folkloristic research,' particularly the study of performance and genre, '... are essential to the progress of the trend in linguistic research called "sociolinguistic"' (1971b:42). These folkloristic leads have given rise during the intervening years to a body of cross- and often multi-disciplinary research that has greatly advanced our understanding of these areas. I believe that a volume which celebrates the centenary of the American Dialect Society by pointing to the advances that have been made in the study of linguistic diversity provides a fitting occasion to return, nearly twenty years later, to the issue that engaged Hymes. I hope to show that the study of performance and genre offer important insight into the patterning of linguistic variation from the level of minute formal alternations to that of the organization of vast stretches of discourse which emerge in a wide range of contexts and, in some cases, over substantial periods of time. I will proceed to explore, however, some recent discoveries that point to the need to go beyond the received concepts of genre and performance in order to account for important types of variation. In keeping with the orientation of the volume toward the illustration of concepts through presentation of empirical studies, I will report results from an ongoing study of Warao, a native language spoken in eastern Venezuela.

2. Investigating Warao performance

Some 22,000 Warao live in the delta of the Orinoco River in northeastern Venezuela and adjacent regions. *Warao* is an autochthonous designation meaning 'lowland people,' which contrasts with *hotarao* 'dry land people,' a term used in reference to any non-Warao, especially non-indigenous Venezuelans (criollos).

The delta consists of small pockets of land that are separated by innumerable branches of the Orinoco. Until the 1920s and early 1930s, most Warao lived in the swampy interior by fishing and exploiting the starch of the *ohidu* 'moriche palm' (*Maurita flexuosa*). Shortly after the arrival of the Capuchin missionaries in the 1920s, a group of Warao from the Sakobana River introduced the cultivation of *ure* 'ocumo chino tuber' (*Colocasia sp.*) (see Heinen 1975; Heinen and Ruddle 1974). Rapid expansion of this cultigen prompted most Warao to move from the moriche forests to the river banks, and this change made the Warao much more available to criollos for wage labor.

The bulk of my research has been conducted with Warao who live in the Mariusa River in the Central Delta. The Mariusa people were among the last group to emerge from the moriche swamps and take up residence along the riverbanks. Several local groups continue to live in the moriche swamps. The Mariusans do not cultivate *ocumo chino* or any other crops; they subsist instead on gathering moriche starch, fruit, larvae, and other forest products, fishing, hunting, and digging for crabs. Some fish are sold to criollo traders and fisherman for cash, and flour and other consumer products are purchased. The population continues to be migratory, moving between the moriche swamps, the mouth of the Mariusa river, and various village sites up river in keeping with the availability of resources.

Given the presence of dialect variation between deltaic regions, I also conducted several months of research in Murako and K^wamuhu, two adjacent communities to the south near the Guayo Mission, and I spent shorter periods of time in other areas. The residents of Murako and K^wamuhu rely almost entirely on agriculture and fishing; the extraction of moriche starch plays almost no role in subsistence. A bilingual school is located in Murako, and stores, a mission, and a clinic are available in Guayo (about 30 minutes by motorized canoe). Contrastively, schools, stores, clinics, and missions are absent in the Mariusa region. This is not to say that Mariusa is 'traditional' while Murako and K^wamuhu are 'acculturated' -- Spanish bilingualism is still quite limited in Murako and K^wamuhu, and Warao discourse genres are clearly evident.

The relationship between discourse and authority in Warao communities is closely connected with the role of male political leaders and medico-religious practitioners; these two types are referred to collectively as *aidamo* 'leaders.'[3] Political officeholders are usually headed by the *kobenahoro* 'governor' who is assisted by one or more *kabitana* 'captain,' *bisikari* (from the Spanish *fiscal*), and *borisia* 'policeman.' An *aidamo* known as the *dibatu* (from *dibu-* 'to speak'), serves as an orator. Other communities utilize such officials as the *komisario* 'commissioner' or *komando* 'commando' (the latter derived by association with the Venezuelan military). Many groups of officials also exercise authority over households and small hamlets that are located nearby. *Aidamo* oversee projects undertaken by the community as a whole, such as maintenance of the *hoisi* 'bridges' and management of the small fishing or rice cultivation projects that ideally produce income by selling the harvest to *hotarao* 'criollos.' They are also responsible for maintaining order; when conflicts arise, it is their duty to organize and officiate at a *monikata nome anaka* dispute mediation event (cf. Briggs 1988c). 'Counseling,' which plays a major role in *monikata nome anaka*, also emerges in pre-dawn soliloquies and dialogues as well as in other settings.

Warao medico-religious practice embraces three major types of specialists, the *wisidatu*, *hoarotu*, and *bahanarotu*;[4] becoming a competent practitioner of any variety involves mastery of a number of different types of sung or chanted ritual texts as well as the use of sacred rattles, *wina* cigars, and other paraphernalia (cf. Barral 1964; Olsen 1973; Wilbert 1972, 1987). Contexts of performance range from individual curing sessions to large-scale festivals in which the arrival of ancestral spirits is celebrated by residents from a large area (termed the *nahanamu*). Shamanistic discourse is linguistically quite complex in its reliance on an esoteric lexicon, complex poetic and musical structures, special modes of interpretation, and a heightened use of performativity. Practitioners possess the power to kill or cure, and their actions provide a perennial conversational focus in Warao communities.

Another central focus of Warao discourse is storytelling, and this includes both *dehe nobo* 'narratives of the ancestors' and *dehe hido* 'narratives of recent events.' Performing both types of narratives is a predominant leisure-time activity, and storytelling also plays an important role in ceremonial greetings (Briggs 1988a). Narrating *dehe nobo* is closely connected with one type of magico-religious practice, that of the *hoarotu*, because traditional narratives provide access to invisible realms that are manipulated through the use of *hoa*, songs that can help or harm. (I will return to this point later.) In general, only men generally perform *dehe nobo*;[5] while women can perform *dehe hido*, they seldom do so in public settings when men are present.

3. Genre and variation

As Hymes pointed out in 1971, folkloristic emphasis on the importance of oral genres offers an important boon to sociolinguistics 'because it can direct attention to essential features of language that are now neglected or misconceived in linguistic theory' (1971b:47). The concept of genre is crucial for studying variation in that genres shape units of speech, some of which are exceedingly long and complex, in accordance with phonological, morphological, lexical, syntactic, and pragmatic relations. A distinction drawn by Ben-Amos (1976/1969) between 'analytical categories' and 'ethnic genres' has exercised a formative influence on research in this area. While he characterizes analytical categories (such as epic, *Märchen*, and so forth) as tools for scholarly classification and comparison, Ben-Amos defines ethnic genres as forming part of 'a grammar of folklore' that captures the 'emic' system utilized by the members of a speech community in producing and interpreting discourse. Each genre, which must be discovered ethnographically, 'is characterized by a set of relations between its formal features, thematic domains, and potential social usages' (1976/1969:225). A great deal of research between the 1970s and the present has been directed toward discovering particular genres and systems of genres and their relationship to types of speech events, social roles, interactive settings, and the like (see Abrahams 1976/1969, 1985; E. Basso 1985; K. Basso 1979; Bauman 1983, 1986; Ben-Amos 1976; Brenneis 1978, 1988; Briggs 1988b; Caton 1990; Duranti 1983; Feld 1982; Glassie 1982; Gossen 1972, 1974; Hanks 1984; V. Hymes 1987; Labov 1972b, 1972c; Kuipers 1990; Opland 1983; Seeger 1987; Sherzer 1983, 1990). Since genres pattern speech on a number of levels simultaneously, they provide excellent opportunities for discovering complex and far-reaching co-occurrence relations (Ervin-Tripp 1972). Clearly, genres do not simply consist of packages of formal-functional relations that can be selected at will, something like taking a record off the shelf and placing it on the turntable. Access to genres is patterned by and in turn patterns such social characteristics as gender, social class or rank, age, and ethnicity as well as a host of contextual variables. Looking at who uses a token of which genre with whom when and where -- as well as at the social consequences of performances -- thus provides a great deal of information regarding the social and cultural patterning of form and function.

I will illustrate the power of genre to pattern a wide range of formal and functional discourse parameters with a narrative and a shamanistic song, both of which describe the sun's path across the sky. First the story. *Hokohi hakitane* 'Origin of the sun' is an important *dehe nobo* 'narrative of the ancestors.'[6] Quite briefly, the narrative concerns the way that the Warao struck a bargain in mythological times with a neighboring group, the Isawana (or Siawani, in other versions). The land inhabited by the Warao was perpetually shrouded in darkness, and it was accordingly nearly impossible to subsist. The Isawana youth who owned the sun had hung it no higher than the roof of his house, so it illuminated only the area in which his own people lived. Although the Warao man befriended him, the Isawana youth would only share the sun's light if the Warao sent him a virgin daughter as a bride. The elder of the Warao's two daughters left for the house of the Owner of the Sun, but she was raped en route by the Hoidatu, a spirit person whose name suggests his propensity for deflowering virgins. The younger daughter successfully reached the house of the Owner of the Sun. After consummating the marriage, the Owner placed the sun, now properly packed into its basket, high in the sky. Having nothing to regulate the speed at which it traveled across the sky, however, the sun moved far too quickly, producing unbearably short days. The Warao father and the Isawana youth accordingly tied a small morrocoy turtle behind the sun, and this 'pet' or 'companion' slowed him down considerably. The normal diurnal pattern was thus established, concomitantly providing a basis for gauging the passage of time. The myth goes on to describe the apprenticeship of two Warao to an Isawana master craftsman who taught them how to weave baskets, thus accounting for the introduction of this mainstay of Warao material culture. The narrative ends with a description of a subsequent battle between the cannibalistic Isawana and the Warao.

Santiago Rivera, *kobenahoro* 'governor' of the Mariusa region, performed *Hokohi hakitane* during a central ritual celebration, the *nahanamu*; an elderly visitor, Carlos Gómez, served as his respondent. Mr. Rivera frames the narrative as the version that his late Uncle Lorenzo told him, and he prefaces the performance with the question he posed to his uncle.[7]

Text 1 *Hokohi hakitane* 'Origin of the Sun'
Santiago Rivera, *Kobenahoro* 'Governor' of Mariusa (SR)
Carlos Gómez (CG)
Nabaribuhu, Mariusa region, 9 July 1987

1 SR Ine akotai tai denokoae,
1s 3s-REL 3s ask-PAST
So I am the one who asked him,

2 "Daku, tamaha hokohi hakitane katukane?"
uncle this sun exist-INF how
"Uncle, how was it that the sun came to exist?"

3 "Ine warate.
1s tell-FUT
"I'll tell it. [response of uncle to Mr. Rivera; frames narrative as reported speech of the uncle]

4 Hokohi hakitane,
sun exist-INF
When the sun came into existence,

5 oko hokohi isiko yahakanaerone,
1p sun with arrive-PAST-although
even though there was sunlight when we descended [from the sky],

6 ama tai oko otemo yahakanaerone,
now 3s 1p far-from descend-PAST-although
when we descended from way up there,

7 ama oko imahana eku katoanae diana.
now 1p darkness inside 1p/PAT-throw-PAST already.
later we were thrown into darkness.

8 Warao asibia imahana eku katoanae yama.
people half darkness inside 1p/PAT-throw-PAST HEARSAY
Half of the people were thrown into darkness, it's said.

9 Imahana eku katoanae,
darkness inside 1p/PAT-thrown-PAST
We were thrown into darkness,

10 awarao asibia kotai diana, hokohi isiko bahinae diana.
3-people 3-half REL already sun with remain-PAST already
half of the people stayed where there was still sunlight.

11 Tane monika Warao era,
thus equal people many
There were just as many people there.

12 Hokohi arotu akotai ote sabukaitu hanoko kobó.
sun 3-owner 3-REL far somewhat-INTENS house appear-PAST
The house of the owner of the sun could be seen fairly far away.

13 Tata ahanoko yewará neburatu,
there 3-house finish-PAST youth
The youth finished his house there,

14 harihari koitayahawitu.
flute play-PRES-DUR-INTENS
he's really playing his flute loudly.

15 Tai diana, harihari hisaka diana.
3s already flute one already.
He already had a real harihari flute.

16 Tai diana ekoitaya kotai neburatu diana.
3s already CAUS-play-PRES REL youth already.
It's the youth who's already playing it.

17 Ahanoko kobó,
3-house appear-PAST
His house became visible,
18 munawaraha amunawaraha habahabí."
paint one's eyebrows-DUR 3s-paint one's eyebrows-DUR paint-PAST
he was painting and painting his eyebrows."
19 Dakuma are nome tai diana, yo no sé,
uncle-PAT 3-narrative true 3s already (Spanish: I don't know)
Whether my uncle's story is true or not, I just don't know. [Spoken by Mr. Rivera to current audience.]
20 ine tamaha, ine dehe nokonaha, ine tamaha ine.
1s this 1s narrative hear-NEG 1s this 1s
I myself never heard this story, not I myself.
21 "Tamaha dehe tai, tamaha mare," sa.
this story 3s this 1s-story say-PRES
"This story here, this is my story," [my uncle] said.
22 CG Tai, tai diana.
3s 3s already
That's it, that's it now.
23 SR "Mare diana."
1s-narrative already
"It's my story now."

In these opening lines, Mr. Rivera sets the scene in two ways. First, he asserts the authority of the narrative by stating that he learned it directly from his dead uncle. Secondly, he introduces the dilemma that motivates the story's plot. He alludes to the descent of the Warao from their initial home in the sky, the subject of another well-known narrative (cf. Barral 1959:139-40), and the subsequent loss of sunlight by the ancestors of the present-day Warao. This description presages the journey made by one Warao to the house of the owner of the sun and his efforts to induce the owner to place the sun it its proper location in the sky.

I will contrast this brief segment of the *dehe nobo* with the beginning of one of the most important shamanistic songs, a *hoa* that focuses on the movement of the sun across the sky. It is referred to as *Hokohi awaba miana* 'The killing-song of the sun's death.' It was sung in a Mariusa community by an accomplished *hoarotu* shaman, Rafael

García. Mr. García served as one of the two teachers who taught a Warao from another region and me the beginning steps in becoming a *hoarotu.* This involves singing key texts repeatedly until the apprentice has learned them, in addition to learning how to ingest smoke from long, palm-leaf cigars; this ensemble of practices facilitates achievement of an ecstatic state in which contact with spirits is possible (cf. Wilbert 1972, 1987). Note that the lexemes used in *hoa* are highly presupposing, conveying a tremendous amount of information in brief poetic lines. I will accordingly provide a free translation of each line following the interlinear glosses. Lexemes that lack referential meaning are not translated.

Text 2 *Hokohi awaba miana* 'The killing-song of the sun's death'
Rafael García
Mariusa Akoho, 26 June 1989

1. **mianá mianá, namí**
mianá mianá namí
[invocation of spirit power to kill], namí
2. **mianá, namí**
mianá namí
[invocation of spirit power to kill], namí
3. **mianá, namí**
mianá namí
[invocation of spirit power to kill], namí
4. **mianá** hokonamo, **namí**
mianá beginning namí
[invocation of spirit power to kill] of the beginning, between earth and sky, namí
5. hokonamo, **namí**
beginning namí
in the beginning, between earth and sky, namí
6. hokonamo karari, namí
beginning dispersal, namí
[the light], its dispersal from the beginning, between earth and sky, namí
7. hiariawará, **namí**
2s-origin namí
this, your origin, namí

8. hiariawará, namí
   2s-origin namí
   this, your origin, namí
9. hokonamo tata tiori, namí
   beginning there sun namí
   there, in the beginning, between earth and sky, [your origin], sun, namí
10. manobo tiori, namí
   body sun namí
   the body of the sun, namí
11. mianá, namí, namí
   mianá namí namí
   [invocation of spirit power to kill], namí, namí
12. tiori, namí, namí
   sun namí namí
   the sun, namí, namí
13. tiori ahoko anamo abatoko, namí
   sun 3-whiteness 3-container 3-pendulant, namí
   the sun, the pendulant of the container of the light, namí
14. abatoko, namí
   3-pendulant namí
   its pendulant, namí
15. abatokó, namí
   3-pendulant namí
   its pendulant, namí
16. hokonamo ekuk^{w}ané, namí
   beginning from inside namí
   from inside of the beginning, between earth and sky, namí
17. abatokona ahiobona, namí
   3-pendulant 3-sweat-NOM namí
   its pendulant, its profuse sweating, namí
18. ahiobona, namí
   3-sweat-NOM namí
   its profuse sweating, namí
19. tiori ahok^{w}onamo ahiobona, namí
   sun 3-beginning 3-sweat-NOM namí
   the sun, its beginning, between earth and sky, its profuse sweating, namí
20. manobó tiori, namí
   body sun namí
   the body of the sun, namí

21. hokʷonamo **ekukané, namí**
beginning from inside namí
from inside of the beginning, between earth and sky, namí
22. **tatane ahokona hokoná, namí**
there 3-dawn-NOM dawn-NOM namí
there, its dawning, the dawning, namí
23. tata **hokoná, namí**
there dawn-NOM namí
there, the dawning, namí
24. kaiyukané **tiori** ahiobo, **namí**
simultaneous sun 3-sweat namí
in that moment the sun, its sweat, namí
25. ahiobo, **namí**
3-sweat namí
its sweat, namí
26. **tiori aniaroná, namí**
sun 3-reflection namí
the sun, its reflection, namí
27. **aniaroná, nanamí**
3-reflection nanamí
its reflection, nanamí
28. **tiori aniaroná, nanamí**
sun 3-reflection nanamí
the sun, its reflection, nanamí
29. ahiobo, **namí**
3-sweat namí
its sweat, namí
30. ahiobo, **namí**
3-sweat namí
its sweat, namí
31. **aniarona** kaiyukane hokonamo **nisimahá, namí**
3-reflection simultaneous beginning embrace namí
in that moment [of dawning], the embrace of its reflection from the beginning, between earth and sky [illuminates the heavens], namí
32. hokonamo **nisimahá, nanamí**
beginning embrace nanamí
from the beginning, between earth and sky, its embrace [illuminates the heavens], nanamí
33. **ateori anabai, nanamí**
3-body 3-sunbeams nanamí
from the sun's body, beams of light, nanamí

34. **anabai anaisimo namí**
3-sunbeams 3-redness namí
its brilliant red beams of light [shoot upwards], namí

A wide range of formal and functional contrasts are evident between the *hoa* song and the *dehe nobo*. One of the most striking differences is lexical: *hoa* draw on a specialized lexicon that is shared, by and large, by *wisidatu*, *bahanarotu*, and other practitioners, but which is virtually unintelligible to the uninitiated. While the everyday lexicon (hereafter EL) is seen as denoting all that is evident through ordinary modes of perception, *anobahatu aribu* 'curer speech' (hereafter CL, for curer lexicon) distinguishes the invisible, spiritual essences of entities. Some specialized items are formed by prefixing 'everyday' lexemes with such forms as *ana(e)-* and *aoko-*, which are referentially vacuous. Other items in CL bear no formal resemblance to their EL equivalents. I have identified all tokens of CL in Text (2) through the use of boldface type.

CL terms are often quite complex semantically; many simultaneously denote a visible phenomenon, its contemporary invisible character, and the basis of its supernatural efficacy. *Hoa* also use lexemes that appear in the EL but which are semantically contrastive when used in *hoa*. *Hokonamo*, for example, refers in EL to the 'principal root' of a plant, the 'ancestor(s)' of a local group, or to the 'origin' of a natural object, cultural practice, or the like. In CL, *hokonamo* refers to one of two houses that are visited by initiates into *hoarotu* practice through shamanistic dreams. Located on the horizon near the points at which the sun rises and sets, the *hokonamo* contain the 'masters' of every type of *hoa* spirit, and practitioners must obtain their cooperation in order to use a particular *hoa* in curing or inflicting.[8] *Dehe nobo* contrast with *hoa* in that *dehe nobo* draw entirely on EL, while *hoa* make extensive use of CL. This difference is tied to a basic contrast in the participant structures (Philips 1972) of the speech events in which they are performed. For *dehe nobo*, the primary audience consists of the human beings who are listening to the narrative, even though spirits may overhear as well. Since performances of *dehe nobo* do not contain techniques for controlling spirits, code-switching into CL would invite disaster by attracting malevolent spirits and giving them free rein to wreak havoc in the community. As curative *hoa* are sung, both a patient and one or more relatives are generally present. They are, nevertheless, not the intended addressees, and often they are not paying much attention to the *hoa*. Indeed, unless these individuals are shamans, they will be unable to understand most of what is sung. Even when they can understand, they do not serve as respondents. On those rare occasions in which *hoarotu* perform simultaneously, each sings a distinct *hoa* (Olsen 1973:143). Shamans generally go off by themselves to sing *hoa* in the killing or inflicting mode. In the case of *dehe nobo*, on the other hand, an audience is necessary, and one or more individuals nearly always serve as respondents.

As is often the case with specialized lexicons (cf. Dixon 1971), CL and EL share a common grammatical system. Note, however, that this statement is only true at the level of structure. The *distribution* of certain grammatical classes in *hoa* and *dehe nobo* is highly contrastive. While each line of the *dehe nobo* ordinarily contains one verb, *no verbal constructions whatsoever are evident in this hoa.* The plethora of personal pronouns in the *dehe nobo* point to the emphasis that is placed on sorting out agent-patient relations. Rich use is also made of temporal and spatial deixis in making sense of the relationship between events in *kaina mate hidoma* 'the time when our world was still being formed' as well as the manner in which the mythic actions are represented in the formal/functional patterning of the narrative. A broad array of suffixes that mark tense/aspect distinctions appear in *dehe nobo*. Forms are marked for past, present, and future, and the basis for calculating tense relations itself shifts between the time of the reported events and that of the performance.[9] The durative/non-durative opposition also plays a key role in indicating the relationship between events. The non-durative past suffix *-ae* prevails in lines (1-10); here the emphasis is on the background to the story. Once the events that form the focus of the narrative begin to unfold in subsequent lines, a durative past tense that consists of a stress shift to the last syllable of the verbal stem is common. (*Kobó* appears in lines 12 and 17, *yewará* in 13, and *habahabí* in 18.) Note that while this form is common in narrative, it appears much less frequently in other types of discourse. The grammaticalization of time, space, and person is complemented by the extensive use of gesture that characterizes performances of *dehe nobo*.

An examination of the *hoa* transcript will quickly reveal that all these forms are absent. Gesture does not compensate for the lack of verbal morphology -- *hoarao* generally stare blankly off into space while they sing. While their hands lie still while singing *hoa* in pedagogical or inflicting contexts, their hands are engaged in massaging the patient when they sing to cure. An interesting correlation is evident in this suppression of verbal morphology. If we order the different songs sung by *hoarao* in terms of their performative capacity for dominating potentially malevolent spirits (i.e., from a song for curing a minor cut to one for removing a powerful *hoa*), the number of verbal constructions diminishes to zero.[10] This fact provides a splendid puzzle for Austin's (1962) equation of performativity with 'explicit primary performatives' in which the referential content of the verb denotes the illocutionary force of the speech act, pointing again to the difficulty involved in using the speech act framework as a basis for cross-linguistic research. In the Warao case, one of the most trenchantly performative uses of the language involves no verbal constructions![11]

Clearly discernible poetic lines are evident in both *hoa* and *dehe nobo*, but the features used in segmenting them are clearly contrastive. Most importantly, musical patterning plays a fundamental role in *hoa* and *no* role in *dehe nobo*. This particular *hoa* utilizes four pitches, C, D, E, and F. Each poetic line is tied to a musical phrase that begins on either D or F and ends on the principal tone, C. Lines are not all characterized by the same sequence of pitches. The interval in any given line can be as little as D to C (e.g., line 2) or as much as F to C (e.g., line 1), and longer lines often involve three pitch descents. (The sequence in line 12 is F F D F F F F F D F E C C C). Nevertheless, all lines begin above the principal tone, and they do not reach the principal tone until the end of the line. The end of each line is also characterized by a decrease in intensity. Verbally, each line ends with *namí* (or *nanamí*), indicating that the performance is oriented toward teaching, practicing, or displaying rather than killing or curing.

In *dehe nobo*, a number of phonological features demarcate lines. Each line has a discrete phonological curve that includes a rise and a fall in pitch. While the peak may occur at any point after the initial syllable, the line-final syllable is generally uttered on the lowest pitch. Lines occasionally end on a medial pitch, indicating either emphasis (as with *era* 'many' in line 11) or a high degree of cohesion with the following line (cf. Woodbury 1985:182). While lines are ordinarily separated by pauses, the absence of a pause provides a device for establishing a high degree of cohesion between lines, particularly those describing closely related sequences of action. Grammatically, most lines contain one verb. Since Warao is a verb-final language,[12] lines generally end with a verb, an evidential particle, or an adverb.

A final axis of contrast between *hoa* and *dehe nobo* pertains to the manner in which performances are contextualized. While contextualization is at work in both genres, differences are apparent with respect to what Silverstein (1976, in press) has referred to as explicit metapragmatics. While metapragmatics constitutes 'a system of signs for stipulating, by standing for, the use of the signs in context' (in press), explicit metapragmatic signs denote language use by virtue of their referential content. *Dehe nobo* are highly reflexive in that narrators comment frequently in the course of the performance on the story and the manner in which it is unfolding. In this short passage, Mr. Rivera uses three *verba dicendi* that refer to the performance (*wara-* 'tell') and reception (*noko-* 'listen' or 'hear') of this story as well as his solicitation of the narrative (*denoko-* 'ask'). This section of the narrative also contains two discourse particles. While *yama* 'HEARSAY' is an evidential, *sa* 's/he says' is a quotative that has evidential implications. These two forms are only a fraction of the rich inventory of evidentials and related forms that are commonly used in *dehe nobo*.

By framing the narrative *vis-à-vis* the manner in which he learned it from his uncle, Mr. Rivera renders the performance dialogic in a special sense -- here two performances unfold simultaneously. Just as the uncle's performance is embedded within the current one, such that the entire *dehe nobo* is framed as quoted speech, the authority of the present performance is contingent on its location in a series of linked speech events that presumably began when the world was still assuming its present shape. Mr. Rivera returns in (19) to this point, noting that his only means of assessing the truth of the story is through reported speech -- he neither saw the events (as in a personal narrative) nor received them from spirits in a dream. His authority for performing the story rather hinges on that of his uncle, who has entered the status of 'ancestor.'

Other types of explicit metapragmatics provide evaluative commentary on characters and actions or take presupposed elements of the narrative and render them explicit (cf. Babcock 1977 on metanarration). A leading character in the story is Hoidatu, the sex fiend who rapes virgins. Mr. Rivera notes *tai hebu* 'he's a spirit,' and, code-switching into Spanish, *ése diablo* 'he's a devil,' making it explicit both that Hoidatu is not human and that he is a malevolent character. Another metapragmatic focus is on conversational exchanges that are embedded in the narrative. When the Warao first meets the Owner of the Sun, he asks: 'What will we call each other now?' He proposes establishing a quasi-kinship relationship: 'we will call each other *waraotu* now.'

One of the most interesting examples of metanarrative commentary in the performance follows the point at which the oldest daughter, who has been promised in marriage to the Owner of the Sun, is raped by the Hoidatu. After she identifies herself, the following dialogue takes place.

Text 1, continued
Hokohi hakitane 'Origin of the Sun'
Santiago Rivera, *Kobenahoro* 'Governor' of Mariusa (SR)
Carlos Gómez (CG)

24 SR "Diana miwanae," taturu.
already1s-CAUS-penetrate-PAST AUX-DESID
"He already broke my hymen," that's what she should have said.

25 Ah! Debunae, "ihi totuanara?" tanae yama.
ah say-PAST 2 hymen-INTERR AUX-PAST HEARSAY
Damn! He said, "Are you a virgin?" it's said that he asked.

26 Diana diboto anibakaida kotai diana debunatao.
already in response girl-AUG REL already say-NEG-PAST
But the young woman did not respond to him then.

27 Debunae, debunae,
say-PAST say-PAST
He spoke to her, he spoke to her,

28 dibakitane diana.
say-INF already
so that she would tell him.

29 Dibaturu diana, dubuhida sabuka tane.
say-DESID already rapid-AUG somewhat AUX-GER
She could have told him rather sooner.

30 Anae yama diana, anae, aho! totuana mituru monidawitu.
become night-PAST HEARSAY already damn hymen see-DESID impossibly-ITENS
They say that night fell then, night fell and damn! and he was really anxious to see her hymen.

31 Imahanu takore, waraotuma dumo hakotai nabakaboi diana, nabaká, nabaká,
darkness AUX SIMULT people-COLL leave-to-get-food-GOAL AUX-REL arrive-GER already arrive-PAST arrive-PAST
When darkness fell, the people who had gone to the forest for food were already arriving, and they kept arriving and arriving;

32 nabaká takore, imahanau totuana mikitane.
arrive-PAST AUX-SIMULT darkness hymen see-INF
When they had arrived, the darkness brought the time to see her hymen.

33 Ama suatane imahanau, imahanau.
now like this darkness darkness
Right away it became dark, very dark.

34 Dianawitu totuana miae;
already-INTENS hymen see-PAST
He looked immediately for the hymen;

35 totuana toroae sa obonokore, iwanae.
hymen thrust-PAST QUOT want-COND penetrate-PAST
he wanted to thrust himself through her hymen, it's said, but it was already broken.

36 CG Karah-!
Damn!

37 SR "Sina? Sina hiwanae?"
who who 2s-penetrate-PAST
"Who was it? Who broke your hymen?"

38 Totuana oatu waranaka takitane $k^{w}$are, debunaha, debunaha, debunaha, debunaha.
hymen take-AGENT tell-NEG AUX-INF for say-NEG say-NEG say-NEG say-NEG
So that [women] would never tell anyone who it was that broke their hymen, she said nothing, said nothing, said nothing, said nothing.

When the Owner of the Sun discovers that she is not a virgin, he asks her repeatedly for the name of the culprit, but the girl refuses to answer. After the Owner of the Sun reports this failure of dialogue to her father, Mr. Rivera's uncle comments that this is why Warao women never respond when asked for the identity of their first sexual partner. Note that Mr. Rivera is quoting not only his uncle's rendition of the narrative but the way his uncle commented on this passage in the reported performance. These lines also point to another important dimension of the metapragmatics of *dehe nobo*: metanarrative commentary provides a vehicle for delineating the impact of narrative episodes on the contemporary Warao world.

In contrast to what we have seen for *dehe nobo*, explicit metapragmatics plays almost no role in performances of *hoa*. While practitioners are keenly aware who taught them a particular *hoa*, no overt reference is made to previous performances. Explicit commentary is similarly missing, and the tremendous body of information that is presupposed by *hoa* is not explicated. The relationship between the processes that are occurring in invisible realms and the wake-a-day world is similarly not explained. This does not mean that such connections do not exist. To the contrary, the efficacy of *hoa* hinges on the way that the texts refer simultaneously to the archetypal actions of each *hoa* in the *hokonamo*, the movement of a particular token as it is sent by the shaman into or out of an individual's body, and the physical symptoms that are experienced by the victim or patient. Similarly, such crucial features of performances as the use of special voice timbres, musical patterns, and spatial and temporal restrictions -- in addition to the special lexical and grammatical patterning that I described earlier -- are crucial dimensions of the implicit metapragmatics of *hoa*. These elements are not, however, accorded explicit metapragmatic commentary during the performance.[13] In short, the reflexive element that plays such an important role in *dehe nobo* is virtually absent in *hoa*.

4. The metapragmatic encompassment of genre

I argued in the preceding section that discourse genres provide powerful means of patterning variation. As illustrated by a discussion of *hoa* and *dehe nobo*, genres provide extensive relations of co-occurrence with respect to prosody, lexicon, morphology, and syntax. The metapragmatic elaboration that characterizes *dehe nobo* and the absence of metapragmatics in *hoa* point to quite different processes of inserting these two types of discourse into social life. Genre thus provides us with a conceptual tool for grasping a vast range of types of formal and functional patterning.

Recent research suggests, however, that both theoretical and empirical constraints emerge when the concept of genre is treated as a *deus ex machina* for explaining variation. Indeed, genres do not provide formal-functional cookie cutters that render discourse homogeneous within a particular genre and entirely discontinuous with speech that lies outside of it. It is accordingly necessary to complement the concept with other theoretical tools in order to achieve an understanding of important types of variation. In the following section I will return to the narrative concerning the sun in order to illustrate the extent of the variation that can characterize different performances within the same genre and, in this case, even of the same narrative. I will go on to suggest that an examination of the metapragmatic constitution of performances can help us understand this sort of intra-generic variation.

4.1 Metapragmatics and genre

In turning to intra-generic variation, different performances produce quite different formal and functional patterns within tokens of the same genre. Some of the most interesting data in this regard that have emerged from my work on Warao involve different performances of the same *dehe nobo*. Recall the performance of *Hokohi hakitane*, the *dehe nobo* of the origin of the sun (Text 2). The 'governor' of the Mariusa region, Santiago Rivera, performed this text just before the beginning of the closing rituals of the crucial *nahanamu* ritual cycle. Two men with important positions served as his respondents -- Diego Rivera, the principal *wisidatu* shaman of the *nahanamu* and leader of the local group that sponsored it, and Carlos Gómez, a distinguished visitor. Most of the ritual specialists who were assembled for the *nahanamu* sat in and around the house, comprising an audience of about 30 men. His rendition must certainly be characterized as full performance, that is, an assumption of authority for a masterful display of communicative competence (cf. Bauman 1977; D. Hymes 1975).

Mr. Rivera performed the same narrative a month and a half earlier in Mariusa Akoho, the community that stands over the water at the mouth of the Mariusa River. Having just returned from a site up river, Mr. Rivera went to visit a close friend, Manuel Torres, who is also a powerful *hoarotu* shaman. While the previous performance emerged near the apex of ritual time, this one came in the course of a mundane visit that centered on the purchase of sugar. After an exchange of greetings and mock insults, Mr. Rivera and Mr. Pérez told a series of *dehe hido* -- narratives about recent events, particularly concerning which Mariusa residents had been inflicted by shamanistically-induced illness and who had tried to cure them. When Mr. Rivera proposed *dehe nobo warakí* 'let's tell narratives of the ancestors,' the two began to challenge each other to tell *dehe nobo*. Mr. Rivera finally took up the gauntlet and began telling 'The origin of the sun.' Mr. Pérez not only repeated Mr. Rivera's line-final words and phrases, but he proffered a number of lines before Mr. Rivera uttered them.

When they reached the point at which the older daughter takes the wrong path and ends up at the Sex Fiend's house, the two began a short joking sequence. Mr. Rivera and Mr. Pérez then continued with the narrative until they reached the point at which the daughter is rejected by the Owner of the Sun due to her loss of virginity. After condemning the Sex Fiend (Hoidatu), they joked that the Mariusa people were all becoming sex fiends.[14]

Text 3 *Hokohi Takitane* 'Origin of the Sun'
Dyadic Type
Manuel Torres (MT)
Santiago Rivera, *Kobenahoro* 'Governor' Mariusa region (SR)
Mariusa Akoho, 26 May 1987

SR Totuanae, barí taturu dihana,
totuana obonoya sarone dihana.
MT Aaaah!
SR Hoidatu ebe yahikitane?
MT Caraj-
SR Totuana iwanae dihana.
Totuana rokotuma.
MT Oko Mariusarao eku nakakitane dihana.
SR Oko Mariusarao kokotuka hoidatu.
(laughs)
MT Yatu monika yana ine.
Ine hisamika hoidatu yana tae ine.
Ine totuana iwanaha tihi, ine hoidatu ana.
SR Yatu totuana iwaya tai,
hoidatu tane warate.
MT hoidatu.
SR Daku dibuya kotai, daku,
"totuana iwanae tamaha?"
MT Warao sina tai "hoidatu" tane wahite?
SR "Yo no sé -- hoidatu -- yo no sé."
MT Ihi dihana hoidatu bahite ihí.
SR Ine yana, korisa iné.
Imahanau, miae.
Totuana iwanae,
"sina hiwanae?"
"Hoidatu maiwanae."
"No, no, no, no, no,
bahinu."
Dihana ihi totuana, totuana nok^{w}abukane hakitane,
qué wina!
Ote tai mate hobia mohoro.
Ayukaha tai, Hoidatu ekidakore, totoanae hese hakuna.
"Ama,
hidahia inatabau."

Bahinae,
tata turá.
"Totuana manokabukanae."
"Sina totuana hiwaní?"
"Maiwanae Hoidatu, Hoidatu.
MT Ah hah!

English translation

SR Since her hymen had been broken, she should have just=
returned home.
since he wants her with her hymen intact.
MT Aaaah!
SR Why did she lie down with the sex fiend?
MT Hell!
SR Her hymen was already broken!
Lovers of hymen.
SR All us Mariusa people have gotten to be like that already.
All us Mariusa people have become sex fiends.
(laughs)
MT I am not am not like you.
I am the only one who has not become a sex fiend.
Since I have not broken any hymen, I am not a sex fiend.
SR [Since] you are the ones who break hymen,
You will be called sex fiends.
MT Sex fiend.
SR My uncle tells me, my uncle,
"Is this the one who broke your hymen?"
MT Now who is going to deserve the name "sex fiend?"
SR "I don't know -- sex fiend -- I don't know."
MT You yourself will be called sex fiend, you yourself.
SR Not I, surely not I.
Night fell, he saw her.
Her hymen was broken,
"who broke your hymen?"
"Hoidatu broke my hymen."
"no, no, no, no, no,
go back home."
This is why you will never find any hymen, any hymen,
damn!
I guess that fellow over there is still drinking.
If there had never been a Sex Fiend, [women]=
would still have their hymen intact.

```
        "Now,
         send  me your younger sister."
      She returned home,
       she arrived there.
        "He didn't find my hymen intact."
        "Who broke your hymen?"
        "It was broken by Sex Fiend, Sex Fiend."
MT                                                      Ah hah!
```

Mr. Pérez teases Mr. Rivera, saying that his friend had indeed become a sex fiend while he, Mr. Pérez, was the only Mariusan to reject this role. Mr. Rivera then again assumes the voice of his uncle in asserting that they should call anyone who has sex with a virgin a 'hoidatu.' Returning to the narrative, the two men continue only as far as the point at which the sun is placed in its proper role in the sky, leaving out the second half of the narrative (in which the Warao learn to weave baskets but are also forced to fight the cannibalistic Isawana). While Mr. Rivera told this part in full during the *nahanamu* gathering at Nabaribuhu (in which Text 1 was recorded), the second performance ended at this point, and the two men returned to measuring sugar and counting money.

A third rendition of the story in which Mr. Rivera also participated contrasts even more sharply with the first performance. Larger Warao households, such as Mr. Rivera's, are generally composed of uxorilocal extended families. Married daughters and their husbands and children often live, as in this case, in houses attached to that of the parents-in-law. In the evenings, Mr. Rivera's sons-in-law are generally joined by his unmarried sons for conversation and storytelling. When *dehe nobo* are recounted, the role of the narrator is generally not assumed by one individual but is passed from one person to the next. The other participants are more than respondents; they continually proffer lines, which the current narrator either accepts, incorporating them into his own narrative style, or rejects. A great deal of metanarrative discourse emerges in which elements of the story and the style in which it is being narrated are discussed and, not infrequently, contested. Mr. Rivera joined the fray on 2 June 1987, sharing the role of narrator with two of his sons, Tomás and José, and two of his sons-in-law.

As the story began to unfold, Mr. Rivera engaged in an argument with his sons and sons-in-law concerning the proper point at which the narrative should begin and whether the Warao descended from the sky into sunlight or darkness.

Text 4 *Hokohi Takitane* 'Origin of the Sun'
Acquisition oriented dialogue
Santiago Rivera (SR)
José Rivera (Santiago's son) another primary narrator (JR)
Tomás Rivera, older son of Santiago (TR)
Sons-in-law (SO)
Mariusa Akoho, 2 June 1987

```
SR Oko, oko atuhe sanamataya,
   otemo kayahakahana,
   oko naoaha akotai.
JR                                             Ine a sabana,
                                                  ama ine,
                                            tamaha dehe ine.
SR                                                   Mate.
JR                              Kobukakitane makautubukore.
                                          Tatukamo yana mate,
                                       dehe otemo waraya mate,
                                           dehe waranu mate.
   Akariatamo,
    otemo huieka oko nanakanae akotai.
   Nanakakoré dihana,
    oko imahana eku nakaera dihana?
    nanakakoré akotai.
SR    Hokohi, hokohi eku, hokohi eku.
JR    Hokohi eku, ama . . . hokoma/
SR    /hokohi hokoma,
      hokohi hatanae dihana.
TR    ((Ama, tamaha hokohi/))
JR    /Ama, tamaha hokohi, ama,
      imahana eku nakaha akotai,
          katukane takitane oko imahana eku nakaeba oko akotai?
SR                                  Hokohi eku nakaerone asabaná/
JR                  /Nokabasabaya oko imahana eku nakae mohoro.
SR                                        Nakaekatá, tai dihana.
```

SO Asida mi? Asida.
TR Atae oko imahana eku nakaerá!
SO Mi?
SR Ama oko/
TR /Tamaha dehe akotai Warao sina areheba tamaha akotai?
Atae oko imanana eku nakaha akotai.
JR Anaka obonobú anaka;
hokohi hakitane.
TR Ah, nome.
JR Ama oko waranae,
ama oko waranae hokohi hakitane.
TR Ah, nome, nome, nome.

English translation

SR Long ago we, we were suffering,
since we arrived from up there,
those of us who had come.
JR I [think] this way's bad,
now it's my turn,
I'm [going to tell] this story.
SR Not yet.
JR I'm going to tell it because you are telling me to do so.
[The story] still isn't up to there yet,
the story is still told from back there
still keep telling it.
In the very beginning,
we descended from that place up there.
Once we had descended,
we descended into the darkness, right?
having descended to there.
SR Sunlight, into the sunlight, into the sunlight.
JR Into the sunlight, now ... in the daytime/
SR /in the sunlight in the daytime,
there was already sunlight, it is said.
TR ((This sunlight was later/))
JR /Later, this sunlight was later,
we fell into darkness,
how is it that we fell into darkness?
SR Since we fell into the sunlight, this [version] is bad./
JR /Perhaps it was afterwards that we fell into the darkness.
SR Of course we fell [into darkness] afterwards, that's it.

SO That's wrong, see? That's wrong.
TR We fell into the darkness again!
SO See?
SR Later we/
TR /Whose story is this anyway?
This story is about how we again fell into the darkness.
JR Let's think about it, let's do;
[it's the story of] the transformation of the sun.
TR Ah, that's true.
JR We told it that time,
we told about the transformation of the sun.
TR Ah, that's true, that's true, that's true.

One of the dimensions of contrast between *dehe nobo* and *hoa* that I emphasized above was that of contextualization. I argued that explicit metapragmatics, in which the referential content of language is used in characterizing pragmatic dimensions of language use, forms an important characteristic of *dehe nobo*, but is almost entirely lacking in *hoa*. I would like to return to the issue of metapragmatics in showing that the three performances of 'The origin of the sun' contrast markedly in the role that explicit metapragmatics plays in each.[15]

In the first performance (which took place in the course of the *nahanamu* rituals), Mr. Rivera retained control over the interaction as the narrative unfolded, and he alone served as narrator. His respondents were limited to repeating lines that he had already uttered. This type of performance is accordingly deemed *monologic* by Warao. When Diego Rivera attempted to initiate a joking exchange after the rejection of the elder daughter by the Owner of the Sun, Santiago Rivera cut him off. Several individuals tried to bring the performance to a close in view of the imminence of the closing rituals of the *nahanamu*, but Mr. Rivera silenced them by noting: *ine mate waraya* 'I'm still narrating.' Other metapragmatic signals, as I noted above, centered on the connection between this performance and the one in which Mr. Rivera learned it from his uncle. Mr. Rivera did not allow the ongoing interaction to spill over into the narrative, incorporating the setting of the performance into the narrative action. He rather drew on explicit metapragmatics in attempting to draw his audience out of the here and now and transport them imaginatively into the realm of *kaina mate hidoma* 'our world was still being formed.'

In the second, *dyadic* example, no audience was there to be creatively controlled. The performance only involved Mr. Rivera and Mr. Pérez, and they sat at very close quarters. While I was present, sitting some distance away, they never made eye contact with me, nor were any remarks directed to me. They forgot, it emerged later, that my small cassette tape-recorder was still operating. In the performance, contextualization of the narrative was largely patterned by the nature of the larger speech event in which it emerged -- a meeting between old friends. The connections between the narrative action, the present setting, and contemporary Mariusa were richly exploited. Lines were shorter, and less narrative detail was given. The poetic patterning itself was less regular, and parallelism was less prominent; the metanarrative exchanges between Mr. Rivera and Mr. Pérez were not marked poetically. The story, in short, became a conversational resource for the ongoing negotiation of a friendship between two friends, much like Western Apache humorous portraits of 'the whiteman' (Basso 1979).

The third example is *pedagogical*; in this case, younger men who were far from competent narrators were learning how to perform *dehe nobo*. The focus was not on the time when 'our world was still being formed' or the ongoing social interaction. The metapragmatic signs rather centered on the storytelling process itself. The way that Mr. Rivera interacted with his sons and sons-in-law during the narration contrasted dramatically with the much more submissive posture of the younger men during a preceding discussion of subsistence-related concerns. Mr. Rivera's version of *Hokohi hakitane* was openly challenged as incomplete and inaccurate.

In short, I was fortunate to have recorded the same *dehe nobo* in three tellings, each of which accorded a central role to the same individual. The results suggest that the three narrating events differ in far more than length and degree of detail, even though these differences are certainly apparent. Rather, the highly contrastive participant structures that are apparent in the three renditions are tied to substantial formal and functional differences in the metapragmatic grounding of the narrative. Highly contrastive definitions of the communicative functions of telling a tale emerge in moving between authoritatively invoking the primordial world, solidifying an old friendship, or disclosing the narrative process in the guise of learning a *dehe nobo*.

It is illuminating to compare these differences in the metacommunicative dimensions of the three tellings with respect to the metapragmatic locus of the performance and the relationship that is established between different facets of the performance. In the monologic case, Mr. Rivera constitutes the era in which 'our world was still being formed' as the metapragmatic center of the performance. Explicit metapragmatic discourse centers on placing the audience members in this world and explicating the relationships that obtain within it. Metapragmatics thus provides a means of enhancing the *distance* between contemporary society and the mythical realm. Mr. Rivera's attempts to prevent interruptions build a shield against the explicit penetration of the ongoing social setting into the realm of narrated events. This movement toward the mythic domain is so pronounced that insofar as the narrative is explicitly embedded in a social interaction, it is the performance by Uncle Lorenzo that interactively grounds the performance.[16] Note that this performance itself forms part of the world of *kaidamotuma* 'our ancestors.'

In the dyadic performance, on the other hand, the locus lies in *both* narrated and narrating events. As in the monologic performance, a great deal of time is devoted to describing the moral geography of the *kaina mate hidoma* world. Equal attention was devoted, however, to the contemporary world and to the relationship between the narrators. Rather than separating mythic past from interactive present, explicit metapragmatics provided a means of exploring the relationship between them. Just as contemporary Warao temporarily joined the ranks of mythological characters ('All us Mariusa people have gotten to be like that already'), the mythic identities became part of the social world for days after the performance as Mr. Rivera and Mr. Pérez jocularly accused a number of their relatives of being sex fiends.

In the case of the pedagogical performance, explicit metapragmatics does not bring either *kaina mate hidoma* or contemporary Warao society into focus. The explicit metapragmatic locus is rather placed in the act of storytelling itself, exploring the narrative qua textual entity, the process of transmission, and the competence of the narrators. The decontextualization and recontextualization of narrative becomes not just a means of providing access to the mythic realm, as in Mr. Rivera's characterization of his Uncle's performance in the monologic type, but a central and explicit focus. In the acquisition-oriented performance, the legitimacy of Uncle Lorenzo's version as a basis for narrative authority is challenged by Mr. Rivera's sons and sons-in-law through an assertion of the superiority of a performance by another narrator. The third type thus uses a discussion of storytelling as a means of organizing the metapragmatics of a storytelling session.

These contrasts provide us with a basis for returning to our discussion of the limitations of genre as an analytic tool. The appearance of a translation of Bakhtin's (1986) essay on 'The problem of speech genres' has sparked additional interest of late on genre. Bakhtin characterizes the genre as a 'relatively stable' whole that corresponds to 'particular conditions of speech communication' and 'a particular function' (1986:64). Generic styles, he continues, are 'inseparably linked' *inter alia* to 'types of relations between the speaker and other participants in speech communication.' While this strict correspondence between participant structures, formal patterning, and functional parameters may be more characteristic of some genres and some speech communities, the Warao data show that this characterization of genre will only prove adequate once the role of metapragmatic frameworks in shaping formal and functional patterning is taken into account. The distinction, say, between *dehe nobo* and *hoa*, does account for a great deal of systematicity in discourse that fall under one of these two rubrics. Nevertheless, generic patterning is not sufficiently powerful to account for precisely the sorts of 'particular conditions of speech communication' or 'particular contacts between the *meanings* of words and actual concrete reality' that Bakhtin had in mind (1986:86, 87; emphasis in original). I have argued that the Warao data can be explained with greater depth and precision when the role of explicit metapragmatics is taken into account.

4.2. *Variation within the same performance*

I have argued that genres provide powerful means of patterning variation. In the previous section I showed that generic patterning cannot explain important aspects of the formal and functional patterning evident within bodies of discourse that fall within clearly defined genres. I now want to suggest that metapragmatic frameworks do not constitute sets of formal-functional relations that necessarily render discourse homogeneous *within* performances. This does occur in certain genres; *hoa* songs for curing exhibit little formal or functional heterogeneity within performances.[17] In women's ritual wailing, on the other hand, variation with respect to what is sung at any given point and how the singers' voices are coordinated is patterned sequentially and contextually.

Both the genres that I have examined up to this point are dominated by men. A few postmenopausal women become shamans, and women occasionally become recognized narrators of *dehe nobo*. Contrastively, ritual wailing is almost exclusively the purview of women. When an individual dies, female relatives perform *sana* or *ona*, texted songs sung while weeping, until after the burial ends.

Wailers repeat a simple *refrain* that consists of 1) *ma-* 'my' + a kinship term, 2) a formula expressing loss, such as *ihi sana, me* 'oh pitiful you!' or *momoae* 'you left me,' followed by 3) *ma-* 'my' + a kinship term, to which a referentially-vacuous and prolonged final *-o* is suffixed. They also sing *textual phrases*, longer stretches of discourse that tell *inter alia* of the deceased, his or her life, the victim's relationship to the wailer and other members of the community, and the circumstances that lead to the death. Textual phrases generally include between 15 and 25 syllables. The alternation between refrains and textual phrases is patterned in part by the participant structure. One woman takes the lead at a time, sitting next to the corpse; this role starts with the closest relative (generally the mother) and then moves to more and more distant kin. This individual will produce most of the textual phrases. While the lead sings textual phrases, the other lamenters generally sing their refrains, hold the final *-o*, or remain silent. As the lead takes up her refrain, another singer (generally the woman who held the principal role prior to the entrance of the current lead) will produce textual phrases, many of which will reflect the themes introduced by the lead. As I discuss elsewhere (1989), the voices are also coordinated in terms of voice quality (especially timbre) and pitch.

This relationship does not, however, hold constant over the full course of the wailing, which generally lasts about a day. The number of wailers varies from two or three to twenty. Similarly, the degree of coordination of the voices in terms of the refrain vs. textual phrase alternation, voice quality, and pitch varies along a continuum that stretches from polyphony to near cacaphony, i.e., from tightly interwoven to virtually unintegrated. This type of variation is largely shaped by the relationship between the ritual wailing and other dimensions of mortuary ritual. Each event in the progression toward the burial heightens the emotional intensity of the wailing. Many of these actions, such as the completion of the coffin, the placement of the corpse into the coffin, closure of the coffin, and preparation for departure to the burial grounds, are controlled by the men. The women are responsible for placing objects associated with the deceased next to the body and inserting poison into the corpse, a technique that can purportedly kill the shaman responsible for the death when his *hoebu* spirits return to suck the victim's blood.

When these ritual actions are not imminent, the intensity of the wailing often diminishes to such an extent that the principal singer only intones an occasional textual phrase, while other wailers alternate refrains with silence. When an event is about to take place, the emotionality of the mourners suddenly rises, the number of wailers increases, the volume of their singing increases, and numerous women begin to sing textual phrases at the same time. Ritual wailing thus moves from coordinated polyphony to virtual cacaphony repeatedly in keeping with the integration of song into the mortuary ritual as a whole. A movement toward the cacaphony end of the continuum sometimes occurs, even in the absence of any external stimulus, when a principal singer's textual phrases are so charged with affect -- and social criticism -- that the intensity of other women's wailing is heightened as well. This movement, patterned by the way that ritual wailing emerges in performance, provides a central dynamic in the cultural construction of mourning.

All of this communicative activity falls under the aegis of *sana*. Both the formal and functional patterning of the wailing and the quite different responses that it elicits from listeners at various junctures between the death and funeral are, however, highly contrastive. In order to explain such variation, it is necessary to expand the focus in three ways. First, *sana* are sung, not spoken, and the complex musical polyphony evident in performances as multiple women sing structures the formal patterning and thematic content of discourse. Second, neither music nor speech can be seen apart from non-musical and non-linguistic activity. While building coffins, shrouding corpses, and filling their mouths with poison are not considered part of *sana*, these actions play a crucial role in moving ritual wailing along a continuum of affective and performance intensity. Third, one cannot grasp *sana* apart from their larger historical and social contexts. Textual production and reception are patterned by social structure as kinship shapes participant structures. Genealogy is, however, not all that is at stake -- texts and interpretations are also shaped by awareness of the events that have brought relatives into relations of cooperation or conflict. I am not simply arguing for a microscopic analysis that deems every imaginable linguistic and socio-cultural factor relevant. I rather want to make the case that some of the basic dimensions of the formal/functional patterning of discourse that have been attributed to genre may be better explained when we place genre into a larger pragmatic framework that includes such elements as music, movement, material culture, social structure, and history.

4.3. Inter-generic relations in performance

While I argued above that genres constitute important frameworks for patterning the production and interpretation of discourse, I want to point out some of its limitations as a conceptual tool. These pertained to the importance of systematically patterned variation within tokens of the same genre (4.1) and variation within single performances (4.2). In this section I will examine the incorporation of formally and functionally contrastive genres within the same speech event. Accounting for the patterning of inter-generic relations will entail going beyond a conceptualization of genres as isolated, objectified wholes.

Bakhtin (1981, 1986) opened up a fascinating area of investigation in pointing to the complexity of intergeneric dialogicality in literature. He points to ways in which the heterogeneity of discourse is increased not simply by the inclusion of distinct voices and ideological stances but by the juxtaposition of different genres, each of which imposes competing formal and functional constraints. Such writers as Abrahams (1985), Bauman (in press), and Dorst (1983) have explored oral genres in which a token of one type is embedded in a token of another. A number of such examples are available in Warao discourse, and I will focus on one in which the interaction of antithetical ways of speaking is crucial.

When a serious conflict erupts in a Warao community, one of the disputants or a relative may come to a member of the *aidamo*, the local leaders, and present the dispute publicly. If the *aidamo* consider the situation sufficiently serious, they will call together all of the disputants in one of their houses at night. In a dispute mediation procedure known as a *monikata nome anaka*, each of the involved parties tells her or his side of the story; relatives or other members of the community may serve as witnesses or advocates. The *aidamo* who is in charge of the proceedings controls turn-taking, and he (all *aidamo* are male) often provides a response to each narrative.

Two formally and functionally distinct types of discourse emerge in *monikata nome anaka*. One, which is designated with the verb stem for narration (*wara-*), is used by the disputants in recounting the events that led up to the conflict and the dispute itself and in assessing its impact on the community. The second, which is referred to as *dibu moa-* or *deri-* 'to counsel,' is exhortative rather than narrative speech. While it is used primarily by the *aidamo* in counseling the participants as to how they should act in such situations, male disputants often quote their own use of 'counseling speech' in attempting to prove that they had attempted to avert the conflict by counseling their wives, children, or younger relatives.[18]

'Narrating' and 'counseling' differ on a number of formal grounds. First, narrators usually quote the 'bad speech,' meaning angry, provocative discourse (often including taboo words or epithets) that gave rise to the fight; such speech is, on the other hand, reported only indirectly -- if at all -- in counseling. This difference is part of a general tendency to embed metapragmatic descriptions of particular utterances and actions in narratives, while counseling speech focuses on normative and general characterizations of speech events (e.g., 'when a man and a woman are getting married, we tell them, "X" ...'). This contrast is especially apparent in the use of deictic elements, particularly temporal and spatial deictics, and tense/aspect forms (cf. Briggs 1988c). The deictic complexity of these narratives becomes greater and greater as the proceedings continue; as narrators provide their own accounts of crucial events, they draw on the stories told by previous disputants and witnesses, thus increasing their indexical complexity. The counseling discourse of *aidamo*, on the other hand, seldom provides a resource for the construction of conflictual narratives.

Narrating and counseling constitute discourse modes that are used in a wide range of other speech events. If *aidamo* can engage these competing modes dialectically in *monikata nome anaka*, this very heterogeneity provides the key to dispute mediation, enabling the disorder to emerge in dramatic terms against the backdrop of authoritative, socially ordering speech. Variation, in short, is not only present -- it is *constitutive* of *monikata nome anaka* as a performance mode, and it provides the basis for mediating conflict.

The interaction of genres plays a contrastive if no less important role in ritual wailing. Rather than juxtaposing two modes of discourse, *sana* provide a generic framework for incorporating segments drawn from a host of different genres. I noted above that women are generally not accorded the right to perform *dehe nobo*, and only rarely do women act as shamans. Since the *aidamo* are exclusively male, women cannot officiate at *monikata nome anaka*, although they can serve as disputants and witnesses. In the course of singing textual phrases in *sana*, however, women appropriate the words of whomever they please, drawing on whichever speech events seem relevant. Wailers not only quote the public and private pronouncements of *aidamo* and shamans -- they parody and criticize them as well. If women were to draw on the power of reported speech as a means of attacking shamans in any other setting

-- or if men were to do so in any context -- they would be likely targets for supernatural sanctions. While the *sana* frame does not always preclude acts of retribution by shamans, it does provide an occasion in which women are *expected* to reveal with complete candor the truth surrounding a particular life and death. *Sana* thus provide an extremely broad framework in which utterances drawn from the full range of Warao discourse can be subjected to critical scrutiny (see Briggs, in press, b).[19]

I have argued that *monikata nome anaka* and *sana* both accord a central role to the interaction of genres. Interestingly, many Warao with whom I discussed these two types of performances described both as ways of establishing the truth and of mediating interpersonal conflict. The question arises as to whether this interaction of genres and speech events is something unusual. Certainly *sana* and *monikata nome anaka* do provide special cases simply in terms of the degree to which metapragmatic dimensions of discourse are used in making these connections explicit and indexing their centrality to the discourse. Bakhtin's work has attuned us to the degree to which discourse is built dialogically through the incorporation of speech that emerges in other times and places (1981; Volosinov 1973/1930). A substantial body of recent scholarship has focused on reported speech (cf. Bauman 1986, in press; Briggs 1990, in press, b; Hill 1983; Lucy, in press; Philips 1986; Silverstein 1985; Urban 1984). Researchers have pointed *inter alia* to the role of reported speech in increasing the formal and ideological heterogeneity of discourse by juxtaposing voices and speech events. Haring (1988) recently coined the term 'interperformance' as a means of elucidating the way that performances frequently build on preceding performances.

I want to suggest that such dialogicality does not emerge simply in special types of performances -- it rather constitutes a fundamental property of the performance process. Richard Bauman and I recently proposed a framework that attempts to account for the tendency in performances to incorporate past speech events and to render themselves particularly susceptible to appropriation in subsequent acts of communication (1990). We argue that central to performance is the process of entextualization, the framing of discourse as text through the use of poetic patterns that foreground form and create complex relations of cohesion. Texts become cohesive linguistic units that are segmentable from their contextual surroundings. This is not to suggest a return to a 'text-centered' view that reifies the text as analytically independent of 'the context.' The point is to view questions of form and function, content, style, and context from a more agent-centered perspective. Our goal is to signal the importance of the transformational processes entailed in the reception of performances and the incorporation of such discourse -- necessarily modified in significant ways -- in future discursive acts. The idea is that it is necessary both to closely examine discourse as it emerges in a particular setting as well as to illuminate the way that form and function are shaped by past and future speech events, social and political-economic frameworks, and the like.

Note that genre plays a central role in this process by virtue of its capacity for creating structural expectations regarding the way that units of formally and functionally distinct discourse (e.g., build ups and punch lines) are organized sequentially into identifiable wholes (e.g., jests and anecdotes); they provide templates for the production and interpretation of discourse. Performance texts exhibit a two-sided relationship to the situations in which they emerge; they are simultaneously contextualized by virtue of their indexical connections to elements of the context and highly susceptible to *decontextualization*, segmentation from a particular interaction for possible use in a variety of future settings. Decontextualization goes hand-in-hand with recontextualization, the transformation of texts in the process of inserting them in subsequent speech events.

We argue, then, that poetic entextualization plays a crucial role in performance in that it connects a given stretch of discourse with an ongoing process of recontextualization, both as the recipient of past utterances and as a resource for shaping future speech events. In the case of both *sana* and *monikata nome anaka*, the explicit metapragmatic devices that figure among the formal constituents of these genres clearly point to the participants' rights to recontextualize what has been said before. In the case of these two types of discourse, however, the role of genre is not unitary or fixed. Successfully performing either ritual wailing or dispute mediation discourse entails the creation of complex and dynamic relations between contrastive genres. Hanks (1987) draws on Bourdieu (1977a, 1977b) in demonstrating that colonial Mayan written genres were less fixed templates than flexible 'schemata' that were creatively adapted and transformed in practice. The Warao data similarly suggest that it is less fruitful to envision genres as unitary, isolated, and rigid cookie cutters for discourse than as powerful communicative resources that are constantly reshaped and rearranged in practice. These materials point to the need to place genre alongside other schemata that shape entextualization as well as decontextualization and recontextualization if we are to adequately grasp the role of generic patterning.

The very generic parameters of *sana* and *monikata nome anaka* thus require that participants look beyond the parameters of the ongoing speech event and the genre itself. This transcendence points both into the past, as other types of discourse that emerged at different times and in other places are incorporated and, in anticipating future recontextualizations, into the future as well. Decontextualization and recontextualization do not simply extract 'the same' story, lament, or the like from one setting and plop it down in the middle of a new set of circumstances. These processes rather build dynamism and indexical density into discourse by creating explicit and implicit relations between multiple bodies of discourse. While the linguistic implications of these operations are thus profound, their effects are at the same time social and political in that they place discourse within overarching relations of social power.

5 Conclusion: poetics and the dynamic character of language

I want to suggest that this perspective on entextualization, decontextualization, and recontextualization speaks to the relationship between performance, genre, and variation in three ways. First, I argued above that performance patterns variation within genres and between different phases of performances. I later proposed that this entextualization process renders discourse decontextualizable vis-à-vis its contextual surroundings. This points to the way that performance affects not just the constitution of isolated speech events but the connections between uses of language that can extend over long periods of time, extending from long before until long after the performance itself. As Bauman and I argue, this notion provides a useful antidote to microcosmic analyses of performance -- and of language use in general -- that reify context and overlook the ways performances are related to broader linguistic and social processes (see Limón and Young 1986). Warao ritual wailing and dispute mediation point quite effectively to the fact that performances do not draw exclusively on discourse that is framed as performance; they appropriate discourse not only from a wide range of genres but from a host of private and prosaic interactions. These examples also show how such performances can have a significant effect both on future performances (in a variety of genres) as well as on everyday discourse and conduct within communities. Performances provide means of organizing variation across discourse contexts by virtue of their ability to pattern the heterogeneous types of speech that often appear within them.

This perspective suggests, secondly, that linguists are not the only persons who take a keen interest in linguistic means of patterning variation. Warao frequently discuss the way that geography, gender, social rank (especially *aidamo* vs. *nebu* 'worker'), age, genre, interactional setting, and other factors are related to phonological, lexical, grammatical, and pragmatically based variation. Folk linguistics (see Preston, this volume) does not emerge in response to queries by fieldworkers alone -- it forms an essential part of discourse itself. I find that this interest in variation is particularly apparent in two types of settings. I have emphasized the way that explicit metapragmatics plays a central role in many types of performance.[20] I similarly argued in the previous section that just as performances draw on preceding speech events -- discussions, arguments, planning sessions, rehearsals, other performances, and the like -- they shape subsequent events, such as reports, criticisms, enactments of consequences, and other performances. This antecedent discourse often foregrounds aspects of the formal patterning, referential content, communicative functions, and contextualization of the speech that preceded it. Analyses of variation between speakers and performances are similarly often used in assessments of the communicative competence of participants.

Why, we might ask, is performance so closely connected with folk linguistics? As Jakobson (1960) and others have argued, the poetic function foregrounds form, drawing attention to the entextualization process itself. As Bauman (1977) and Hymes (1975) have emphasized, when poetically-elaborated speech emerges in performance, the assumption of responsibility by the performer for a display of communicative competence and the potential uses of language in transforming social relations and shared perceptions are foregrounded. (See also Myers and Brenneis 1984.) The formal and functional parameters of particular genres or types of speech events themselves can similarly be held up for critical assessment (cf. Briggs 1988c; Keenan 1973). In short, reflection on the objectification of language in entextualization and the communicative functions that accrue to such poetic patterning is hardly extrinsic to performance. Performance thus provides a unique window on 'folk' understandings of variation and the role that this type of linguistic reflexivity plays in communication. It also suggests that native speakers should be considered partners in understanding language structure and use rather than as unreflective mass-producers of linguistic data.

Third, a long tradition in the study of language, which includes such figures as Herder and Vico as well as Sapir, the Russian 'Formalists,' and the Prague School, suggests that poetics has a central role to play in the study of language (cf. Friedrich 1979, 1986). Sklovskij emphasized that 'the device of making it strange' (*priëm ostranenija*) renders poetic language an important force in shaping the dynamic character of language (cf. Erlich 1980/1955:176-78), and Jakobson (1972/1921, 1960, 1981/1968) detailed some of the ways in which this process takes place at phonological, lexical, morphological, and syntactic levels. Hymes (1971b) extended this argument to embrace language use, suggesting that genre and performance have a central role to play in the ethnography of speaking. Drawing on the Warao data, I have attempted to show that performance-based perspectives can reveal a broad range of types of variation from micro to macro when they are used in systematically examining variation between genres, between different performances that draw on the same genre, within different phases of a particular performance, and in the interaction of genres within a given performance.

These results suggest that two opposing tendencies have thus far limited the broader significance of performance-oriented analysis. On the one hand, the aestheticization of performance -- either by focusing exclusively on poetically elaborated features (such as parallelism, special formulae, phonological regularity, etc.) or by failing to consider texts that lack a high density of such elements -- severs the study of performance from other facets of linguistic study just as it obscures crucial dimensions of formal and functional patterning. Restricting the scope of analyses to investigations of neatly bounded performances that seem to fit nicely within the confines of a single genre will, in my estimation, impose similar theoretical, methodological, and empirical limitations. On the other hand, the *a priori* rejection of poetically elaborated discourse and performance-oriented analysis, whether adopted by conversation analysts or transformationalists, deprives researchers of powerful tools for investigating a broad range of types of linguistic patterning. I suggest by way of conclusion that the sorts of issues I have discussed in this article point to both the value of recent reformulations of *genre* and *performance* as resources for linguistic analysis as well as the need to continue expanding the theoretical and comparative base of the research.

Notes

I would like to thank the residents of the Mariusa region as well as those of Murako and Kwamuhu for their patience and friendship. Rosalino Fernández, Tirso Gómez, and Librado Moraleda generously assisted me in transcribing and translating the texts. I benefited from discussions with H. Dieter Heinen, Julio Lavandero, Andrés Romero-Figueroa, and Johannes Wilbert. Barbara Fries, Dell Hymes, and Dennis Preston provided close readings of a previous draft, and I am most grateful for these gifts of time and thought. My thinking about performance and related topics in the last few years also reflects collaborative research that I have conducted with Richard Bauman. I appreciate the support of the Universidad de Oriente in Cumaná and the Instituto Venezolano de Investigaciones Científicas in Caracas. Financial support was provided by a sabbatical leave and Mellon Grant from Vassar College, a research grant from the Linguistics Program, National Science Foundation, and a fellowship from the National Endowment for the Humanities, all of which I deeply appreciate and gratefully acknowledge. A return to the delta in 1989, kindly funded by a grant-in-aid from the Wenner-Gren Foundation for Anthropological Research, Inc. enabled me to recheck the transcripts and conduct additional research.

1 My emphasis on the term 'variation' in this essay reflects the overall concerns of the volume. I will be using the term in a broader sense than is often the case in the literature. I am certainly not restricting 'variation' to correlations between particular phonological, morphological, or syntactic features and specific sociological variables. I am clearly interested in types of formal and functional patterning that are often referred to with such terms as 'discourse,' 'textuality,' 'style,' and 'poetics.'

2 This is, of course, not to suggest that Saussure's distinction between *langue* and *parole* maps perfectly onto Chomsky's opposition of competence and performance. As Newmeyer (1986:72) notes, Chomsky's notion of competence embraces larger units (particularly the sentence), and he is more concerned with generative rules than a finite set of elements and relations. Chomsky's ultimate interest is also not in *languages* as discrete systems but in Universal Grammar. Nevertheless, both dichotomies are ranked hierarchically in such a fashion that variation and its connection with the social world is banished from the realm of serious linguistic inquiry.

3 'Aidamo' is unmarked for singular vs. plural.

4 Two notes of caution should be pointed out concerning these terms. First, other types of practitioners are present as well. (See, for example, Wilbert's 1981 discussion of the *naharima* or 'rain shaman.') Second, the referential range of the terms varies between delta regions. In some areas, for example, *hoarotu* is often used as a general term for medico-religious practitioners.

5 A very few women in Mariusa, Murako, and Kwamuhu become performers of *dehe nobo*, particularly after menopause. In some regions, however, female narrators are more common.

6 See Briggs (in press, a) for a fuller analysis of this narrative. Wilbert (1964:64-67) presents another version.

7 Criteria used in segmenting lines in both the *dehe nobo* and the *hoa* song are discussed below. The following abbreviations are used in the interlinear glosses:

-	separates morphemes
1s	first person singular
1p	first person plural
3	third person (unmarked for singular vs. plural)
3s	third person singular
AGENT	agentive
AUG	augmentative
CAUS	causative
COLL	collective
COND	conditional
DESID	desiderative
DUR	durative
FUT	future
GER	gerundive
INF	infinitive
INTENS	intensive
INTERR	interrogative
NEG	negative
NOM	nominalizer
PAT	patient
PRES	present
REL	relative pronoun
SIMULT	simultaneous (*-kore* also signals conditional)
(( ))	text enclosed in double parentheses is difficult to decipher
/	slashes at the end of one line and the beginning of another indicate overlap.

8 Wilbert (1972) suggests that there is only one *hokonamo*, while my consultants spoke of two. Given the fact that each shaman must dream the shamanistic cosmology into existence for himself if he is to gain power, individual differences are common. The divergence between our data may also be due to the fact that Wilbert conducted most of his fieldwork on these topics in the Winikina area, while my research was undertaken in Mariusa.

9 In this performance, three loci are apparent. The time that Uncle Lorenzo told the story to Mr. Rivera serves as a temporal locus in this narrative in

addition to the time of the performance and that of the era 'in which our world was still being formed.'

10 There is, however, one crucial exception to this generalization: Performances that are geared to inflicting *hoa* end with an *ayakana* section in which the shaman marks limited use of imperative forms in commanding the *hoa* spirit to 'grab' the victim.

11 My use of the term "verbal constructions" rather than "verbs" is motivated by the fact that many roots in Warao are, as Osborn (1966:253) notes, noun-verbs. Some roots that are clearly verbs do appear in *hoa*. Rather than taking verbal affixes, however, they generally receive a nominalizer, *-na*.

12 Osborn (1966) argues that Warao is an SOV language, while Romero-Figueroa (1985) suggests that the unmarked order is OSV.

13 Such terms as *miana* and *otonomari* present a special case. The former invokes the shaman's power to inflict *hoa*; the latter provides a sort of taking aim (for inflicting or curing) at a male victim or patient. (*Otonomaro* is used for women.) Shamans are clear, however, that these terms do not *refer* to the process of invoking spirits or to male/female victims or patients -- they have no semantic content. Thus, while their communicative functions are purely pragmatic, they seem to lack a metapragmatic dimension.

14 I have not included morpheme-by-morpheme translations for these texts; it is unnecessary for making the argument given here. In the transcription and translation I have placed lines that advance the narrative events on the left-hand side and the metapragmatic interventions on the right margin.

15 For a more detailed analysis of these performances, see Briggs (in press, a).

16 It should be noted, however, that the performance is clearly grounded in the social interaction through the use of implicit metapragmatics.

17 See Olsen (1973) for an analysis of the consistency in musical patterning within curing performances of *hoa*.

18 Women can appropriately 'counsel' their children or younger relatives. Women accordingly occasionally use 'counseling speech' in dispute mediations when the disputants are their social inferiors.

19 One exception here is that shamanistic discourse is represented through indirect discourse alone. Wailers go into great detail regarding which shaman killed whom and why, but they do not quote CL (curers' lexicon) items or even summarize the symbolic content of *hoa* or similar forms.

20 Note the qualifier; it is important to recall that explicit metapragmatics is conspicuously absent in a few genres, such as *hoa*.

References

Abrahams, Roger D. 1976/1969. The complex relations of simple forms. In Dan Ben-Amos (ed.), *Folklore genres*. Austin: University of Texas Press, 193-214.

Abrahams, Roger D. 1985. A note on neck-riddles in the West Indies as they comment on emergent genre theory. *Journal of American Folklore* 98:85-94.

Austin, J. L. 1962. *How to do things with words*. Oxford: Oxford University Press.

Babcock, B. A. 1977. The story in the story: metanarration in folk narrative. 'Supplementary Essay' (Chapter 7) In Richard Bauman, *Verbal art as performance*. Prospect Heights, IL: Waveland Press, 61-80.

Bakhtin, M. M. 1981. *The dialogic imagination*. Ed. Michael Holquist, trans. Caryl Emerson & Michael Holquist. Austin: University of Texas Press.

Bakhtin, M. M. 1986. *Speech genres and other late essays*. Ed. Caryl Emerson & Michael Holquist; trans. Vern W. McLee. Austin: University of Texas Press.

Barral, P. Basilio María de. 1959. *Guarao guarata: Lo que cuentan los indios Guaraos*. Caracas.

Barral, P. Basilio María de. 1964. *Los indios guaraunos y su cancionero: historia, religión y alma lírica*. Madrid: Departamento de Misionología Española, Consejo Superior de Investigaciones Científicas.

Basso, Ellen 1985. *A musical view of the universe: Kalapalo myth and ritual performances*. Philadelphia: University of Pennsylvania Press.

Basso, Keith H. 1979. *Portraits of 'the whiteman': linguistic play and cultural symbols among the Western Apache*. Cambridge: Cambridge University Press.

Bauman, Richard. 1975. Verbal art as performance. *American Anthropologist* 77:290-311.

Bauman, Richard. 1977. *Verbal art as performance*. Prospect Heights, IL: Waveland Press.

Bauman, Richard. 1983. *Let your words be few: symbolism of speaking and silence among seventeenth-century Quakers*. Cambridge: Cambridge University Press.

Bauman, Richard. 1986. *Story, performance, and event: contextual studies of oral narrrative*. Cambridge: Cambridge University Press.

Bauman, Richard. 1987. The role of performance in the ethnography of speaking. In Richard Bauman, Judith T. Irvine, & Susan U. Philips (eds), *Performance, speech community, and genre. Working Papers and Proceedings of the Center for Psychosocial Studies*, No. 11. Chicago: Center for Psychosocial Studies, 3-13.

Bauman, Richard. in press. Contextualization, tradition, and the dialogue of genres: Icelandic legends of the Kraftaskáld. In Alessandro Duranti & Charles Goodwin (eds), *Rethinking context.* Cambridge: Cambridge University Press.

Bauman, Richard & Charles L. Briggs. 1990. Poetics and performance as critical perspectives on language and social life. *Annual Review of Anthropology* 1959-88.

Bauman, Richard & Joel Sherzer (eds). 1974. *Explorations in the ethnography of speaking*. Cambridge: Cambridge University Press.

Ben-Amos, Dan. 1976/1969. Analytical categories and ethnic genres. In Dan Ben-Amos (ed.), *Folklore genres*. Austin: University of Texas Press, 215-42.

Ben-Amos, Dan (ed.). 1976. *Folklore genres*. Austin: University of Texas Press.

Bourdieu, Pierre. 1977a. The economics of linguistic exchanges. *Social Science Information* 16:645-68.

Bourdieu, Pierre. 1977b. *Outline of a theory of practice.* Trans. by Richard Nice. Cambridge: Cambridge University Press.

Brenneis, Donald. 1978. The matter of talk: political performances in Bhatgaon. *Language in Society* 7:159-170.

Brenneis, Donald. 1988. Telling troubles: narrative, conflict and experience. *Anthropological Linguistics* 30:279-91.

Briggs, Charles L. 1988a. Análisis sociolingüístico del discurso Warao: notas preliminares sobre las formas seculares. *Montalbán* 20:103-20.

Briggs, Charles L. 1988b. *Competence in performance: the creativity of tradition in Mexicano verbal art.* Philadelphia: University of Pennsylvania Press.

Briggs, Charles L. 1988c. Disorderly dialogues in ritual impositions of order: the role of metapragmatics in Warao dispute mediation. *Anthropological Linguistics* 30:448-91.

Briggs, Charles L. 1989. 'Please pass the poison': the poetics of dialogicality in Warao ritual wailing. Conference on lament, Austin, Texas.

Briggs, Charles L. 1990. History, poetics, and interpretation in the tale. In Charles L. Briggs & Julián José Vigil (eds), *The lost gold mine of Juan Mondragón: a legend from New Mexico performed by Melaquías Romero.* Tucson: University of Arizona Press, 165-240.

Briggs, Charles L. In press, a. Generic versus metapragmatic dimensions of Warao narratives: who regiments performance? In John Lucy (ed.), *Reflexive language: reported speech and metapragmatics*. Cambridge: Cambridge University Press.

Briggs, Charles L. In press, b. 'Since I am a woman, I will chastise my relatives': gender, reported speech, and the (re)production of social relations in Warao ritual wailing. *American Ethnologist.*

Caton, Steven. 1990. *'Peaks of Yemen I summon': poetry as cultural practice in a North Yemeni tribe*. Berkeley: University of California Press.

Chomsky, Noam. 1965. *Aspects of the theory of syntax*. Cambridge, MA: M.I.T. Press.

Dixon, R. M. W. 1971. A method of semantic description. In Danny. D. Steinberg & Leon A. Jakobovits (eds), *Semantics: an interdisciplinary reader in philosophy, linguistics, and psychology*. Cambridge: Cambridge University Press, 436-71.

Dorst, John. 1983. Neck-riddle as a dialogue of genres. *Journal of American Folklore* 96:413-33.

Duranti, Alessandro. 1983. Samoan speechmaking across social events: one genre in and out of a fono. *Language in Society* 12:1-22.

Erlich, Victor. 1980/1955. *Russian formalism: history-doctrine*. The Hague: Mouton.

Ervin-Tripp, Susan. 1972. On sociolinguistic rules: alternation and co-occurrence. In John J. Gumperz and Dell H. Hymes (eds), *Directions in sociolinguistics: the ethnography of communication*. New York: Holt, Rinehart, and Winston, 213-50.

Feld, Steven. 1982. *Sound and sentiment*. Philadelphia: University of Pennsylvania Press.

Fishman, Joshua. 1966. *Language loyalty in the United States*. The Hague: Mouton.

Friedrich, Paul. 1979. *Language, context, and the imagination: essays by Paul Friedrich*, ed. Anwar S. Dil. Stanford, Cal.: Stanford University Press.

Friedrich, Paul. 1986. *The language parallax: linguistic relativism and poetic indeterminacy*. Austin: University of Texas Press.

Glassie, Henry. 1982. *Passing the time in Ballymenone*. Philadelphia: University of Pennsylvania Press.

Gossen, Gary H. 1972. Chamula genres of verbal behavior. In Américo Paredes and Richard Bauman (eds), *Toward new perspectives in folklore*. Austin: University of Texas Press, 145-67.

Gossen, Gary H. 1974. *Chamulas in the world of the sun: time and space in a Maya oral tradition*. Cambridge, MA: Harvard University Press.

Gumperz, John J. 1962. Types of linguistic communities. *Anthropological Linguistics* 4:28-40.

Gumperz, John J. 1971. *Language in social groups: Essays by John J. Gumperz*, ed. Anwar S. Dil. Palto Alto, CA: Stanford University Press.

Hanks, William. 1984. Sanctification, structure and experience in a Yucatec Maya ritual. *Journal of American Folklore* 97:131-166.

Hanks, William. 1987. Discourse genres in a theory of practice. *American Ethnologist* 14:668-692.

Haring, Lee. 1988. Interperformance. *Fabula* 29:365-372.

Heinen, H. Dieter. 1975. The Warao Indians of the Orinoco Delta: an outline of their traditional economic organization and interrelation with the national economy. *Antropológica* 40:25-55.

Heinen, H. Dieter & Kenneth Ruddle. 1974. Ecology, ritual and economic organization in the distribution of palm starch among the Warao of the Orinoco Delta. *Journal of Anthropological Research* 30:116-38.

Hill, Jane H. 1983. The voices of Don Gabriel. Paper presented at the Annual Meeting of the American Anthropological Association, Chicago, Ill.

Hymes, Dell. 1964. Introduction: toward ethnographies of communication. In John J. Gumperz and Dell H. Hymes (eds), *The ethnography of communication, American Anthropologist* 66(6)2:1-34.

Hymes, Dell. 1971a. Competence and performance in linguistic theory. In R. Huxley and E. Ingram (eds), *Acquisition of language: models and methods*. London: Tavistock, 3-28.

Hymes, Dell. 1971b. The contribution of folklore to sociolinguistic research. In Américo Paredes & Richard Bauman (eds), *Toward new perspectives in folklore, Journal of American Folklore* 84:42-50.

Hymes, Dell. 1971c. Sociolinguistics and the ethnography of speaking. In Edwin Ardener (ed.), *Social anthropology and linguistics*. London: Tavistock Publications, 47-93.

Hymes, Dell. 1973. The scope of sociolinguistics. In Roger Shuy (ed.), *Sociolinguistics: current trends and prospects*. Washington, D.C.: Georgetown University Press, 313-33.

Hymes, Dell. 1974. Why the linguist needs the sociologist. In *Foundations in sociolinguistics: an ethnographic approach*. Philadelphia: University of Pennsylvania Press, 69-81.

Hymes, Dell. 1975. Breakthrough into performance. In Dan Ben-Amos & Kenneth S. Goldstein (eds), *Folklore: performance and communication*. The Hague: Mouton.

Hymes, Dell. 1981. *'In vain I tried to tell you': essays in Native American ethnopoetics*. Philadelphia: University of Pennsylvania Press.

Hymes, Virginia. 1987. Warm Springs Sahaptin narrative analysis. In Joel Sherzer & Anthony C. Woodbury (eds), *Native American discourse: poetics and rhetoric*. Cambridge: Cambridge University Press, 62-102.

Jakobson, Roman. 1960. Closing statement: linguistics and poetics. In Thomas A. Sebeok (ed.), *Style in language*. Cambridge, MA: M.I.T. Press, 350-77.

Jakobson, Roman. 1972/1921. Die neueste Russische poesie: Erster entwurf. In Wolf-Dieter Stempel (ed.), *Viktor Chlebnikov. Texte der Russischen Formalisten, Band II, Text zur Theorie des Verses und der poetischen Sprache*. München: Wilhelm Fink Verlag, 18-135.

Jakobson, Roman. 1981/1968. Poetry of grammar and grammar of poetry. In Stephen Rudy (ed.), *Selected writings, vol., III, Poetry of grammar and grammar of poetry*. The Hague: Mouton, 87-98.

Keenan, Elinor O. 1973. A sliding sense of obligatoriness: the polystructure of Malagasy oratory. *Language in Society* 2:225-43.

Kuipers, Joel C. 1990. *Power in performance: the creation of textual authority in Weyewa ritual speech.* Philadelphia: University of Pennsylvania Press.

Labov, William. 1966. *The social stratification of English in New York City.* Arlington, VA: Center for Applied Linguistics.

Labov, William. 1972a. *Language in the inner city: studies in Black English vernacular.* Philadelphia: University of Pennsylvania Press.

Labov, William. 1972b. Rules for ritual insults. In David Sudnow (ed.), *Studies in social interaction.* New York: The Free Press, 120-69.

Labov, William. 1972c. *Sociolinguistic patterns.* Philadelphia: University of Pennsylvania Press.

Lavandero, Julio & H. Dieter Heinen. 1986. Canciones y bailes del ritual de la Nouara. *Montalbán* 17:199-243.

Limón, José E. & M. Jane Young. 1986. Frontiers, settlements, and development in folklore studies, 1972-1985. *Annual Review of Anthropology* 15:437-460.

Lucy, John, ed. In press. *Reflexive language: reported speech and metapragmatics.* Cambridge: Cambridge University Press.

Myers, Fred R. & Donald Lawrence Brenneis. 1984. Introduction: language and politics in the Pacific. In Donald Lawrence Brenneis & Fred R. Myers, *Dangerous words: language and politics in the Pacific.* New York: New York University Press, 1-29.

Newmeyer, Frederick J. 1986. *The politics of linguistics.* Chicago: University of Chicago Press.

Olsen, Dale. 1973. Music and shamanism of the Winikina-Warao Indians: songs for curing and other theurgy. Unpublished Ph.D. dissertation, University of California, Los Angeles.

Opland, Jeff. 1983. *Xhosa oral poetry.* Cambridge: Cambridge University Press.

Osborn, Henry A., Jr. 1966. Warao II: nouns, relations, and demonstratives. *International Journal of American Linguistics* 32:253-61.

Philips, Susan U. 1972. Participant structures and communicative competence: Warm Springs children in community and classroom. In Cortney B. Cazden, Vera P. John, & Dell Hymes (eds), *Functions of language in the classroom.* New York: Columbia University Teachers College Press, 370-94.

Philips, Susan U. 1986. Reported speech as evidence in an American trial. In Deborah Tannen & James E. Alatis (eds), *Languages and linguistics: the interdependency of theory, data, and application* (Georgetown University Round Table on Languages and Linguistics 1985). Washington, D.C.: Georgetown University Press, 154-70.

Philips, Susan U. 1987. The concept of speech genre in the study of language and culture. In *Performance, speech community, and genre*, by Richard Bauman, Judith T. Irvine, & Susan U. Philips. Working Papers and Proceedings of the Center for Psychosocial Studies, No. 11. Chicago: Center for Psychosocial Studies, 25-34.

Romero-Figueroa, Andrés. 1985. OSV as the basic order in Warao. *Linguistics* 23:105-21.

Sapir, Edward. 1921. *Language: an introduction to the study of speech.* New York: Harcourt, Brace and World.

Sapir, Edward. 1927. Speech as a personality trait. *American Journal of Sociology* 32:892-005.

Sapir, Edward. 1928. The unconscious patterning of behavior in society. In C. M. Child, Kurt Koffka, John E. Anderson, et al. (eds), *The unconscious: a symposium.* New York: A. A. Knopf, 114-42.

Sapir, Edward. 1929. Male and female forms of speech in Yana. In St. W. Teeuwen (ed.), *Donum natalicium schrijnen.* Nijmegen-Utrecht: N. v. Dekker and van de Vegt, 79-85.

Saussure, Ferdinand de. 1959/1916. *A course in general linguistics.* Trans. by Wade Baskin. New York: McGraw-Hill Book Company.

Seeger, Anthony. 1987. *Why Suyá sing: a musical anthropology of an Amazonian people.* Cambridge: Cambridge University Press.

Sherzer, Joel. 1983. *Kuna ways of speaking.* Austin: University of Texas Press.

Sherzer, Joel. 1990. *Verbal art in San Blas.* Cambridge: Cambridge University Press.

Silverstein, Michael. 1976. Shifters, linguistic categories, and cultural description. In Keith H. Basso & Henry A. Selby (eds), *Meaning in anthropology.* Albuquerque: University of New Mexico Press, 11-55.

Silverstein, Michael. 1985. The culture of language in Chinookan narrative texts; or, on saying that...in Chinook. In Johanna Nichols & Anthony Woodbury (eds), *Grammar inside and outside the clause.* Cambridge: Cambridge University Press, 132-71.

Silverstein, Michael. 1986. The diachrony of Sapir's synchronic linguistic description; or, Sapir's 'cosmographical' linguistics. In William Cowan, Michael K. Foster, Konrad Koerner (eds), *New perspectives on Edward Sapir in language, culture, and personality.* Amsterdam: John Benjamins, 67-106.

Silverstein, Michael. in press. Metapragmatic discourse and metapragmatic function. In John Lucy (ed.), *Reflexive language: reported speech and metapragmatics.* Cambridge: Cambridge University Press.

Urban, Greg. 1984. Speech about speech in speech about action. *Journal of American Folklore* 97:310-28.

Volosinov, V. N. 1973/1930. *Marxism and the philosophy of language.* Trans. by Ladislav Matejka & I. R. Titunik. New York: Seminar Press.

Wilbert, Johannes. 1964. *Warao oral literature.* Caracas: Editorial Sucre.

Wilbert, Johannes. 1972. Tobacco and shamanistic ecstasy among the Warao of Venezuela. In Peter Furst (ed.), *Flesh of the gods: the ritual use of hallucinogens.* New York: Praeger, 55-83.

Wilbert, Johannes. 1981. The Warao lords of rain. In G. Buccellati & C. Speroni (eds), *The shape of the past: studies in honor of Franklin D. Murphy*. Los Angeles: University of California, Los Angeles, 127-45.

Wilbert, Johannes. 1987. *Tobacco and shamanism in South America*. New Haven, CN: Yale University Press.

Woodbury, Anthony 1985. The functions of rhetorical structure: a study of Central Alaskan Yupic Eskimo discourse. *Language in Society* 14:153-90.

Appendix: Resources for Research

Michael D. Linn
University of Minnesota -- Duluth

Dialectologists and social linguists have been collecting speech samples of one sort or another as long as there has been an interest in language variation. These samples are usually kept in the possession of the collector and often other scholars and laymen have not known where they are or if they are available for duplication or examination. In time the original record of the fieldwork is forgotten or the location of its archive is not generally known. Sometimes excellent collections have disappeared with the demise of the original director. Unfortunately, once a collection is lost the data cannot be replaced, at least not until we have time travel.

Fortunately, there has been an increased interest in preserving older collections of speech samples. Donna Christian, from September 1983 through May 1986, collected representative tapes and information on approximately 200 extant archives in the United States and reported on their whereabouts in *American English speech recordings: A guide to collections*, Washington, D. C.: Center for Applied Linguistics, 1986. Speech variation that is available from commercial sources is noted in Michael D. Linn and Marrit-Hannele Zuber's, *The sound of English: A bibliography of language recordings*, Urbana, IL: NCTE, 1984.

Because of space constraints, this appendix will not include entries found in either of the above two bibliographies unless they are of special significance such as Frederic Cassidy's *Dictionary of American Regional English*, Roger Shuy's *Detroit dialect study*, or Joseph Mele's *U. S. A. dialect tape center*. While the Christian study emphasizes the newer sociolinguistics archives, this one emphasizes the collection of the earlier Linguistic Atlas of the United States and

Canada archives. In this way, these two collections complement each other.

Selection

The entries in this guide to research were limited to those archives which are housed or collected in the United States and Canada. In addition, these collections are available to interested scholars and are housed either in private collections or in public or university libraries.

Organization

The archives denoted in this guide to research are listed in alphabetical order so that those who know the name of the collection they wish to find will be able to do so easily. At the end of the description of these collections, there is an index of dialects and varieties that lists the number of the archive which houses each.

Archives

1. American-Hungarian in South Bend, Indiana. Director: Dr. Miklos Kontra, utca Korosi Csoma, 35.V.66., H-1105 Budapest, Hungary. Collected between 1980 and 1981, informants of Hungarian descent were interviewed in East Chicago, Illinois; Pittsburgh, Pennsylvania; Toronto, Ontario; and South Bend, Indiana in both English and Hungarian. Informants are divided into 'old timers,' (those who came to the United States before World War II), displaced persons after World War II, and post-1956 refugees. Some second generation (those born in the United States) are also interviewed. The interview instrument combines the techniques of Shuy, Wolfram and Riley, *Field techniques in an urban language study*, Washington, D. C.: Center for Applied Linguistics, 1968 and Lee Pederson, An Approach to Urban Word Geography, *American Speech*, vol. 46. The interview contains free

conversation, picture elicitation, oral elicitation of vocabulary items, reading of both word lists and texts, and a listening test. Transcripts are available and a copy of the collection is located in the Linguistics Institute, Hungarian Academy of Sciences, P.O.B. 19, H-1250 Budapest, Hungary. Send inquiries to the director.

2. Archive of Folk Culture. Director: Joseph C. Hickerson, American Folklife Center, the Library of Congress, Washington, D. C. 20540. This collection is the most comprehensive one in the United States, probably in the world. It houses over 35,000 tapes, disks, cylinders, and wires. Most dialects in the United States, regional, social and ethnic, are represented, as well as many other dialects from much of the rest of the world. The American speech archives collected by the Center for Applied Linguistics under the direction of Donna Christian are housed here. Detailed descriptions are available upon request with some material commercially available. Write for information. Appointments are necessary for listening to recordings.

3. Avis Collection of Recordings of Canadian English. Director: A. M. Kinloch, Department of English, University of New Brunswick, Bag Service #45555, Fredericton, NB, Canada, E3B 6E5. Collected in 1960 by the late Walter S. Avis and his students, all provinces of Canada are represented as are the three types of Linguistic Atlas informants. The material consists of approximately seventy reel-to-reel tapes and seventy cassettes. A four minute prose passage, 'Harry's House,' written by Avis, was read by each informant. Cataloguing is still being done. The collection is housed in the Audio-visual Department, Kierstead Hall, 3rd floor, University of New Brunswick. Access is controlled by Kinloch. Special arrangements to use the material or to obtain copies can be made with Kinloch.

4. Center for German Speech Islands in America. Director: Professor Wolfgang Moelleken, German Department, State University of New York at Albany, Albany, New York 12211. An ongoing project, the collection of which began in 1964, this study is examining the varieties of German as they survive in speech islands in the United States,

Canada, and Mexico. The interviews are taped and some are transcribed. Available for scholarly research. Send inquiries to the director.

5. Collection of Newfoundland Speech. Director: William J. Kirwin, Department of English, Memorial University of Newfoundland, St. John's, Newfoundland, Canada A1C 5S7. Collected from 1960 through 1980, this collection is limited to Newfoundland and Labrador. All tapes and speakers are indexed and filed by community. There are field worksheets with phonetic transcriptions of responses. The tapes are filed in alphabetical order by community name. There is insufficient staff for routine copying, but serious scholars should send inquires to the director.

6. Colorado Linguistic Atlas Collection. Director: Harold Kane, English Department, Box 226, University of Colorado, Boulder, Colorado 80309. This collection has 68 informants, mostly from rural areas and small Colorado towns. These Linguistic Atlas type interviews were collected from 1948 to 1952, primarily by Marjorie Kimmerle. There is a description sheet for each informant and each town. Completed forms of phonological, morphological, and lexical items are coded to area and informant. There are also fifteen tapes. The collection is stored at the Western Archives Collection, Norlin Library, University of Colorado, Boulder, Colorado 80309. For access to the collection or for copies contact the director.

7. Detroit Dialect Study. Director: Roger W. Shuy, Linguistics Department, Georgetown University, Washington, D. C. 20057. Collected by Walter Wolfram, William K. Riley and nine others, each fieldworker transcribed his own tapes. These tapes were collected during the summer of 1965. Using a stratified random sample (see Shuy, Wolfram and Riley, *Field techniques in an urban language study*, Center for Applied Linguistics, 1968), to insure statistically significant representation of black and white, middle and working class, and male and female informants, seven hundred and twenty Detroit residents were interviewed. Forty-five minute audio tape recordings on 3/4 inch reels

and phonetic transcriptions were made for each informant. The interview included free conversation, an Atlas style questionnaire, and a reading passage (see Shuy, Wolfram, and Riley above). The material is stored in the Linguistics Department at Georgetown University. Special arrangements to use the material or to obtain copies can by made by writing to the director.

8. Dialect Survey of Southern England. Director: Hans Kurath. Sixty-six interviews were done by Guy S. Lowman in 1938-39 and six more by Henry Collins in 1966 of informants in the area southeast of a line from The Wash to the Bristol Channel. These records are phonetic transcriptions done in the Linguistic Atlas format without tape copies. The abridged worksheets are based on those used in the Linguistic Atlas of the Middle and South Atlantic States. The material is housed with the Linguistic Atlas Project, University of Georgia Special Collections, Department of English, University of Georgia, Athens, Georgia 30602 under the supervision of William Kretzschmar, Jr. A microfilm copy is available from the Photoduplication Services, Joseph Regenstein Library, University of Chicago, 1100 East 57th St., Chicago, Illinois 60637.

9. Dictionary of American Regional English (DARE). Director: Frederic G. Cassidy at 6125 Helen C. White Hall, Department of English, University of Wisconsin, 600 N. Park, Madison, WI 53706. The records of 2752 informants cover all fifty states and were collected by eighty fieldworkers who did direct interviews which included free conversation and a reading of 'Arthur the Rat.' There are 1002 questionnaires and 1843 audio tapes that are filed alphabetically by state, speaker and community. A *DARE* brochure is available on request. The questionnaire is available for $10.00. Use of *DARE* material is restricted to scholarly use at the *DARE* headquarters. Requests and questions should be directed to the director.

10. Eastern Townships Oral History. Director: Thomas Martin. Approximately 120 cassette tapes of free conversation about subjects such as the Great Depression and World War II were collected by

students of Champlain Regional College from residents of the eastern townships of Quebec from 1977 - 1979. Many of the informants are of Scottish, Irish or English ancestry. Transcripts and outlines are available, as are the tapes. For information, write to Anna M. Grant, Special Collections, Laurie Allison Room for Special Collections, John Bassett Memorial Library, Bishop's University, Lennoxville, Quebec, Canada J1M 1Z7 or telephone (819) 569-9551 Ext. 358.

11. Einar Haugen Collection of Recordings of American Norwegian Speech. Director: Einar Haugen, 45 Larch Circle, Belmont, Massachusetts 02178. Collected from 1936 through 1952, these 250 American Norwegian informants are primarily from Wisconsin and parts of Iowa and Minnesota. All of the material has been transcribed, some from recordings on to reel-to-reel tapes. One set is in the Director's possession, another at the Language Archive at Indiana University and a third set (made on cassettes) at the University of Oslo. Most of the material is in free conversation and narrative modes. Copies are available through the Harvard Language Center, Boylston Hall, Harvard University, Cambridge, MA 021138. The results and parts of the questionnaire with some complete narratives, as well as some single sentences, are printed in *The Norwegian language in America* by Einar Haugen, Philadelphia: University of Pennsylvania Press, 1953 and Bloomington: Indiana University Press, 1964.

12. Far Eastern Townships Phrase Book. Director: Lewis J. Poteet, Department of English, Concordia University, 1455 de Maisonneuve Blvd. West, Montreal, Quebec, Canada H3G 1M8. Beginning in 1968 and continuing today, the director has recorded his observations of twenty to twenty-five word phrases that reflect the English speech of Lennoxville, North Hatley, Scotstown, Megantic, and Sawyerville, Quebec. Copies are available upon request. The method is described in Lewis J. Poteet, *The South Shore phrase book*, Hantsport, Nova Scotia: Lancelot Press, 1983.

13. Influence of English on the Language of the Tirilones. Director: Lurline H. Coltharp, 4263 Ridgecrest, El Paso, Texas 79902. Collect-

ed from 1961-1963 by the director, these twelve reel-to-reel tapes of the Spanish of the forty-seven informants whose language was described in *The tongues of the Tirilones: a linguistic study of a criminal argot* (University of Alabama Press, 1965) by the director. Transcriptions are available for six of the tapes. The questionnaire, based on the phonetic division made by Tomás Navarro Tomás in *Manual de Pronunciación Española*, includes free conversation. The collection is stored in the library at the University of Texas at El Paso, El Paso, Texas 79968 as part of the Lurline H. Coltharp Collection. Questions should be directed to the director or the librarian in charge of the Lurline H. Coltharp collection.

14. Linguistic Atlas of the Gulf States (LAGS). Director: Lee Pederson, Department of English, Emory University, Atlanta, Georgia, 30322. These 1121 informants from the states of Florida, Georgia, Tennessee, Alabama, Mississippi, Louisiana, Arkansas, and Texas were recorded from 1968 through 1983. Nine hundred and fourteen were selected for primary analysis. The worksheet is in the Linguistic Atlas format with revision by Pederson to capture specific Southern speech characteristics. While the primary emphasis of *LAGS* is rural speech, there are 205 urban supplement items for the investigation of urban speech. The informants were divided into three chronological and educational groups: under twenty with high school education, under forty with college education, and over sixty with elementary education or less. Both male and female and black and white informants were tape recorded. The 5300 hours of taped recordings have been transcribed and are available, along with the protocols, from University Microfilms International, 300 N. Zeeb Road, Ann Arbor, MI 48106. In addition, files and mapping programs are available for IBM and compatible microcomputers. For fuller details see Pederson's *Linguistic Atlas of the Gulf States*, vols 1-3, University of Georgia Press, 1986-1990. Five more volumes are being edited for publication. While not part of the LAGS project, fieldwork is also being planned, under way, or completed for Colorado, Idaho, Montana, New Mexico, Nevada, and Utah. Scholars can have access to the materials at Emory University or at the Linguistic Atlas Project, University of Georgia Special

Collections, Department of English, University of Georgia, Athens, Georgia 30602, under the supervision of William Kretzschmar, Jr. Interested scholars should write to either Pederson or Kretzschmar.

15. Linguistic Atlas of the Middle and South Atlantic States (LAMAS). Director: William Kretzschmar, Jr., the Linguistic Atlas Project, University of Georgia Special Collections, Department of English, University of Georgia, Athens, Georgia 30602. Collected from 1933 - 1974, these 1216 records cover the area from the St. Lawrence Valley to the northeastern corner of Florida and from the eastern tip of Long Island to the confluence of the Ohio and the Big Sandy Rivers. All records made before 1950 were transcribed by the original fieldworker during the interview. Those made after 1950 were transcribed from tape. The Middle Atlantic States include New York, New Jersey, Pennsylvania, Ohio, and West Virginia, as well as southeastern Ontario. The South Atlantic States include Delaware, Maryland, Virginia, North Carolina, South Carolina, Georgia and eastern Kentucky. There is also a collection of reference works presented by Hans Kurath and a collection of recordings made in the 1930's. For the methodology see Hans Kurath, *Handbook of the linguistic geography of New England, 2nd* ed., with index prepared by Audrey Duckert, New York: AMS Press, 1972. For further information, write to the director.

16. Linguistic Atlas of New England (LANE). Director: Hans Kurath. From 1931-33, four hundred and sixteen informants were interviewed in 213 communities in the New England states: Massachusetts, New Hampshire, Connecticut, Vermont, New York (Long Island), Rhode Island, and Maine. Southern New Brunswick was also included. The responses to the 750 item questionnaire were recorded in phonetic transcription without benefit of electronic recording. However, some supplementary aluminum records made from 1933 - 39 and some tape recordings made from these aluminum records still exist. For the methodology used see Hans Kurath, ed., *Handbook of the linguistic geography of New England*, with index prepared by Audrey Duckert, New York: AMS Press, 1972. For a detailed description see Hans

Kurath, et al., director and editor, *The Linguistic Atlas of New England*, 6 vols, Providence Rhode Island: Brown University Press, 1939-1943. The original field books and the list manuscripts from which the Atlas was published are housed with the Linguistic Atlas Project, University of Georgia Special Collections, Department of English, University of Georgia, Athens, Georgia 30602, under the supervision of William Kretzschmar, Jr. A microfilm copy is available from the Photoduplication Services, Joseph Regenstein Library, University of Chicago, 1100 East 57th St., Chicago, Illinois 60637. Write to either depository for further information.

17. Linguistic Atlas of the North Central States (LANCS). Director: Originally the late Albert H. Marckwardt, now under the direction of William Kretzschmar, Jr. These 564 field records with tapes of 107 interviews include the states of Wisconsin, Michigan, Illinois, Indiana, Ohio, and Kentucky and the southwest section of the province of Ontario. The interviewing instrument was a modified version of the worksheet used in the Linguistic Atlas projects. Some interviews have been electronically recorded. The collection was done from 1933 through 1978. The original field books and the list manuscripts are housed with the Linguistic Atlas Project, University of Georgia Special Collections, Department of English, University of Georgia, Athens, Georgia 30602, under the supervision of William Kretzschmar, Jr. A microfilm copy is available from the Photoduplication Services, Joseph Regenstein Library, University of Chicago, 1100 East 57th St., Chicago, Illinois 60637. Write either depository for further details.

18. Linguistic Atlas of Oklahoma. Director: Originally the late William R. Van Riper now under the direction of Bruce Southard, English Department, Oklahoma State University, Stillwater, Oklahoma 74074. Using the Linguistic Atlas format, fifty-seven Oklahoma male and female informants of types one through three were tape recorded between 1960 and 1962. Transcriptions were done by Raven I. McDavid, Jr. The eight-hundred item interviews were based on the Atlas format developed by Kurath and revised by Marckwardt with some innovations to reflect Oklahoma speech. Copies are available

from the University of Chicago MSS on Cultural Anthropology, Photoduplication Center, Joseph Regenstein Library, University of Chicago, 1050 E. 57th St., Chicago, Illinois 60637. Additional copies are housed at the Department of English, Oklahoma State University with the Director and at the American Folk Life Center, Library of Congress, Washington, D. C. 20540.

19. Linguistic Atlas of the Pacific Coast. Director: David Reed, Department of Linguistics, 2016 Sheridan Road, Northwestern University, Evanston, Illinois 60201. Collected from 1952 through 1959, these 300 field records and more than five hundred vocabulary checklists are a modification of the Linguistic Atlas format. Ten fieldworkers each transcribed his/her own interviews. All informants were native or near native speakers. Informants are classified into the three Atlas types with 270 residing in California and 30 in Nevada. Both male and female, rural and urban, white and black, with ages ranging from 28 to 91 were interviewed. All 602 Linguistic Atlas items were transcribed. Microfilms of the carbon copies (arranged by the page of worksheets) along with a guide are available from the Bancroft Library at the University of California, Berkeley, California 94720. Questions can be directed to the Director of the collection or to the Bancroft Library.

20. Linguistic Atlas of the Pacific Northwest. Director: Carroll E. Reed, 190 Shays St., Amherst, MA 01002. Collected from 1953 to 1963, this Atlas style project followed the Linguistic Atlas of New England questionnaire with some modifications by David Reed and David Decamp as needed for Oregon, Washington, and Idaho. The materials include direct phonetic transcription supplemented by soundscriber discs with fourteen informants and reel-to-reel tapes for nineteen informants. In addition to the forty-nine records, there are nearly 300 postal check sheets with vocabulary items that were collected and tabulated. For use of the materials contact the director.

21. Linguistic Atlas of Pennsylvania German. Director Professor Wolfgang Moelleken, German Department, State University of New York at Albany, Albany, New York 12222. Collected from 1940

through 1950 by Carroll E. Reed, L. W. Seifert, and Moelleken, these tapes were transcribed by Reed and Seifert. The eighty-five informants and approximately 800 items are in the Linguistic Atlas format designed by Hans Kurath and classify informants according to Atlas type. In addition there are ten short questionnaire records on sound recordings. Questions should be sent to the director.

22. Linguistic Atlas of the Upper Midwest (LAUM). Director: The late Harold B. Allen. This collection is now housed at the Newberry Library, 60 W. Walton, Chicago, Illinois 60606. Interviewed between 1949 and 1962, the 208 informants are divided into the three types of Atlas informants and include both males and females from Minnesota, Iowa, North and South Dakota, and Nebraska with a few from Manitoba, Ontario, and Saskatchewan. About half of the interviews are supplemented by twenty or so minutes of recordings on reel to reel tapes which have been rerecorded from earlier wire recordings. The tapes have not been transcribed. The approximately 800 items of the Atlas work sheets were recorded in phonetic transcription for all 208 informants. These transcriptions were made while the interview was being conducted by the fieldworkers. In addition there are 1,064 mail checklists for 136 items. The questionnaire and results are described in the *Linguistic Atlas of the Upper Midwest*, by Harold B. Allen, 3 vols, Minneapolis: University of Minnesota Press, 1973-1976. Write to the Newberry Library for further details.

23. Lorenzo Turner Archives. The material that Lorenzo Turner collected for his *Africanisims in the Gullah dialect*, Chicago: University of Chicago Press, 1949. Speakers were recorded from seven communities in the coastal area and the sea islands of South Carolina and Georgia. When possible, three informants were selected, two being over sixty and one between forty and sixty at the time of recording. Both males and females are represented. Informants were natives of the community and were interviewed with worksheets based upon the Linguistic Atlas format, but with revisions to make them suitable for use with Gullah. In addition to voice recordings, there are a variety of other materials such as autobiographical sketches, prayers, narratives,

proverbs and folktales. The material may be used on site and under supervision. For details, write to the Director, Africana Collection, Northwestern University Library, 1935 Sheridan St., Evanston, Illinois 60208-2300.

24. Memorial University of Newfoundland Folklore and Language Archives (MUNFLA). An ongoing collection begun in 1968 which includes some 3,000 separate collections and over 5,000 original tape recordings, several thousand photographs and slides, and a small collection of video tapes. There are approximately 6,000 informants. Approximately one-quarter of the tapes have been transcribed into standard English. A guide to the collections is available to scholars. While the collections are primarily concerned with folklore, much of the material is suitable for dialect research. The geographical areas included in these collections are the Canadian Provinces of Labrador and Newfoundland along with some of the surrounding Maritime Provinces. Serious scholars may use the collections. They should write to the director of the collection at the Folklore Department, Memorial University of Newfoundland, St John's, Newfoundland, Canada A1C 587.

25. Nevada Language Survey. Director: Thomas L. Clark, English Department, University of Nevada -- Las Vegas, Las Vegas, Nevada 89154. Using a combination of a Labovian and a *Dictionary of American Regional English* questionnaire, the Director and six additional fieldworkers recorded approximately 110 informants on ninety minute cassettes and sixty checksheets from 1976-79. Sixty percent of those interviewed were native Nevadans and included the three types of Atlas informants. Forty counties of Nevada were included with an attempt made to collect representative informants from stable rural counties, the slowly growing Reno-Carson City area, and the rapid growth area around Las Vegas. For details of the survey see either Clark's 'Antecedents of the linguistic and onomastic survey of Nevada,' *The Nevada Historical Society Quarterly* 19,4 (1976), 251-260 or 'Language in Nevada: A prospectus,' *Halcyon: A Journal of the Humanities* 2, (1979) 103-117. Copies of the tapes and checksheets are available.

For details write the director.

26. Postal Survey of the English Spoken in British Columbia. Director: R. J. Gregg, Department of Linguistics, University of British Columbia, Vancouver, British Columbia, Canada V6T 1W5. Six hundred postal questionnaires with 110 items were returned from residents of British Columbia from 1963 through 1973. Copies are available to serious scholars. For information write to the director.

27. Recordings of Standard Regional English. Director: Mackie J. V. Blanton, English Department, University of New Orleans, New Orleans, Louisiana 70148. Begun by Al Davis in 1965, this tape collection of a 1200 item questionnaire was designed primarily for pronunciation. It records free conversation, minimal pairs, and a reading of 'Grip the Rat.' These approximately two-hour long tapes include speakers from the United States, England, and Canada. Its goal is to include representative tapes of English speakers wherever English is spoken as a native language. Inquiries should be addressed to the director.

28. Saskatchewan Folklore Collection. Director: Michael Taft, Diefenbaker Centre, University of Saskatchewan, Saskatoon, Saskatchewan, Canada S7N 0W0. An ongoing project begun in 1978, this collection has concentrated on Saskatchewan although some recordings have been made in other western Canadian provinces. There are over 300 cassette tapes, several manuscript collections, as well as slides and photographs. Since this is primarily a folklore collection, the tapes were not collected for the purpose of phonetic transcription, but should provide some phonetic material. The tapes were collected as free conversation. For information, write to the director.

29. Scotch-Irish Dialects in Ulster. Director: R. J. Gregg, Linguistics Department, University of British Columbia, Vancouver, British Columbia, Canada V6T 1W5. One hundred and twenty-five informants of the oldest generation available from 1960 to 1963 were interviewed with a questionnaire containing 665 items to establish each speaker's phonological system and to trace the reflexes of Middle

English sounds to establish dialect boundaries. Divergent lexical and grammatical features were also investigated to help establish the Scotch-Irish versus Hiberno-English dialects in the nine counties of the historical province of Ulster. Each interview lasted for three hours as responses were recorded in phonetic script during the interview. Copies are available at cost to serious scholars from the director. The results of the survey are reported in R. J. Gregg, The Scotch-Irish boundaries in Ulster, in M. F. Wakelin (ed.), *Patterns in the folk speech of the British Isles*, London: Athlone Press, 1972.

30. Sociolinguistic Survey of the Central Savannah River Area. Director: Michael I. Miller, English Department, Chicago State University, Chicago, Illinois 60628. This collection centers in and around Augusta, Georgia, and North-Augusta, South Carolina. The data were collected between 1975 and 1978 and concentrate on inflectional morphology. The thirty-seven native speakers are distributed in six social groups: old family upper class, new upper class, upper middle class, lower middle class, working class, and 'folk.' At the time of collection, the ages varied from fifteen to over sixty-five. There were seventeen black and twenty white informants. The corpus is composed of fifty-three reels of magnetic tape and field notes which include broad phonetic transcriptions of most elicited and some casual responses. The interview was based upon the Linguistic Atlas of the Gulf States questionnaire which was modified for the urban environment. Contact Miller to arrange for copies of materials or write to William Kretzschmar, Jr. at the Linguistic Atlas Project, English Department, University of Georgia, Athens, Georgia 30602.

31. Sociolinguistic Survey of Ottawa English. Director: R. J. Gregg, Linguistics Department, University of British Columbia, Vancouver, British Columbia, Canada V6T 1W5. During 1978 and 1979, one hundred male and female Atlas type informants were interviewed in Ottawa using a 752 item, Atlas type questionnaire. All 100 cassettes have been transcribed, coded, and computerized. Copies of tapes and other material are available to serious scholars. For information write to the director.

32. Sociolinguistic Survey of Vancouver English (SVEN). Director: R. J. Gregg, Linguistics Department, University of British Columbia, Vancouver, British Columbia, Canada V6T 1W5. From 1978 through 1983, three hundred male and female Atlas type informants from Vancouver and sixty-eight other British Columbians were interviewed with a 1058 item Atlas type questionnaire. Three hundred cassettes have been transcribed, coded, and computerized. Copies of tapes and other material are available to serious scholars. For information write to the director.

33. Speech in East Central Wisconsin. Director: Donald W. Larmouth, Communication Processes, University of Wisconsin-Green Bay, Green Bay, WI 55401. Collected by Larmouth and undergraduate students in linguistics, this collection represents Green Bay and the surrounding area. Collected between 1972 and 1983, these sixty cassette tapes include various ethnic groups such as Bohemian, German, Polish, Belgian, Norwegian, and French-Canadian that reside in the area. The interview, with some modification to elicit local forms, is in A. L. Davis, *Standard English in the U. S. and Canada.* The tapes are catalogued by community. Arrangements can be made with the director to obtain copies.

34. Speech of the Hudson Valley. Director: Jane Daddow Hawkins. Between 1938 and 1940, thirty-four lifetime residents of the counties along the Hudson River from Albany to Bergen on the west bank and from Putnam to Rensselar on the east bank were interviewed using the short work sheets of the Linguistic Atlas as revised by Kurath in 1937. Each record contains about 75 pages of questionnaire responses in addition to information about the community, informant, and informant's family. There are no electronic recordings, but the phonetic transcriptions follow the linguistic alphabet as described in chapter V of Hans Kurath's *Handbook of the linguistic geography of New England*, New York: American Council of Learned Societies, 1939. The original field books and the list manuscripts from which the Atlas was published are housed with the Linguistic Atlas Project, University of Georgia Special Collections, Department of English, University of

Georgia, Athens, Georgia 30602 under the supervision of William Kretzschmar, Jr.

35. Survey of Prince Edward Island English. Director: Terry K. Pratt, University of Prince Edward Island, Charlottetown, Prince Edward Island, Canada C1A 4P3. Approximately four hundred Prince Edward Island informants with varying backgrounds were interviewed between 1979 and 1983. For copies and further information contact the director.

36. U. S. A. Dialect Tape Center. Director: Joseph C. Mele, The University of South Alabama Library, U. S. A. Dialect Tape Center, C/O Instructional Media Center, Mobile, Alabama 36688. Collected from 1975 to 1980 by various professors from the same region as the informants, the Center has tapes of representative informants from thirty-one states in the Eastern and Southern United States with some from the Central States. In addition there are samples of English from non-native speakers from twenty-three foreign countries. The four hundred and twenty-one cassettes contain free conversation of personal experiences and a set of forty-four uniform sentences designed to illustrate dialect differences. Tapes are filed by reference to the informants' state of residence, year of birth, race, and gender and to the year recorded. Tapes can be used in the Media Center during regular business hours. Cassette copies are available, as is a catalogue. There are no transcriptions of the tapes. Questions should be directed to the director.

Index of Dialects by Archive Number

Index